Contents

Java for Students

Java

for Students

DOUGLAS BELL
MIKE PARR

Fourth edition

PEARSON
Prentice
Hall

Harlow, England • London • New York • Boston • San Francisco • Toronto • Sydney • Singapore • Hong Kong
Tokyo • Seoul • Taipei • New Delhi • Cape Town • Madrid • Mexico City • Amsterdam • Munich • Paris • Milan

Pearson Education Limited
Edinburgh Gate
Harlow
Essex CM20 2JE
England

and Associated Companies throughout the world

Visit us on the World Wide Web at:
www.pearsoned.co.uk

First published 1998
Fourth edition published 2005

ISBN 0131 246186

British Library Cataloguing-in-Publication Data
A catalogue record for this book is available from the British Library

Library of Congress Cataloging-in-Publication Data
Bell, Doug, 1994-
    Java for students/Douglas Bell, Mike Parr. – 4th ed.
        p.   cm.
    Includes bibliographical references and index.
    ISBN 0-13-124618-6 (pbk.)
      1. Java (Computer program language)   I. Parr, Mike, 1949-   II. Title.

    QA76.73.J38B45 2005
    005.2′762–dc22

                                                                2004053367

10   9   8   7   6   5   4   3   2   1
08   07   06   05

Typeset in 9.75/12pt Galliard by 35
Printed in Great Britain by Henry Ling Ltd at the Dorset Press, Dorchester, Dorset

The publisher's policy is to use paper manufactured from sustainable forests.

Detailed contents

Introduction

What this book will tell you

This book explains how to write Java programs that run either as independent applications or as applets (part of a web page).

This book is for novices

If you have never done any programming before – if you are a complete novice – this book is for you. This book assumes no prior knowledge of programming. It starts from scratch. It is written in a simple, direct style for maximum clarity. It is aimed primarily at first-year undergraduates at universities and colleges, but it is also suitable for novices studying alone.

Why Java?

Java is probably one of the best programming languages to learn and use because of the following features.

Java is small and beautiful

The designers of Java have deliberately left out all the superfluous features of programming languages; they cut the design to the bone. The result is a language that has all the necessary features, combined in an elegant and logical way. The design is lean and mean. It is easy to learn, but powerful.

Java is object oriented

Object-oriented languages are the latest and most successful approach to programming. Object-oriented programming is the most popular approach to programming. Java is completely object oriented from the ground up. It is not a language that has had object-orientedness grafted onto it as an afterthought.

Java supports the Internet

A major motivation for Java is to enable people to develop programs that use the Internet and the World-Wide Web. Java applets can easily be invoked from web browsers such as Internet Explorer to provide valuable and spectacular facilities. In addition, Java programs can be easily transmitted around the Internet and run on any computer.

Java is general purpose

Java is a truly general-purpose language. Anything that C++, Visual Basic, etc., can do, so can Java.

Java is platform independent

Java programs will run on almost all computers and with nearly all operating systems – unchanged! Try that with any other programming language. (You almost certainly can't!) This is summed up in the slogan 'write once – run anywhere'.

Java is robust

The Java compiler carries out many stringent checks as it prepares a program for execution. Once a program has been corrected and compiles without errors, it often performs correctly. However, if a Java program goes wrong (and programs do have that tendency), it won't create mayhem, damage and uncertainty.

Java has libraries

Because Java is a small language, most of its functionality is provided by pieces of program held in libraries. A whole host of library software is available to do graphics, access the Internet, provide graphical user interfaces (GUIs) and many other things.

● You will need

To learn to program you need a computer and some software. A typical system is a PC (personal computer) with the Java Software Development Kit (SDK). This is also available for Unix, GNU/Linux and Apple systems. This kit allows you to prepare and run Java programs. There are also more convenient development environments. We provide the SDK and additional software on the accompanying CD-ROM.

● Exercises are good for you

If you were to read this book time and again until you could recite it backwards, you still wouldn't be able to write programs. The practical work of writing programs and program fragments is vital to becoming fluent and confident at programming.

There are exercises for the reader at the end of each chapter. Please do some of them to enhance your ability to program.

There are also short self-test questions throughout the text with answers at the end of the chapter, so that you can check you have understood things properly.

● What's included?

This book explains the fundamentals of programming:

- variables;
- assignment;
- input and output;
- calculation;
- graphics and windows programming;
- selection using `if`;
- repetition using `while`.

It also covers integer numbers, floating-point numbers and character strings. Arrays are also described. All these are topics that are fundamental, whatever kind of programming you go on to do.

This book also thoroughly addresses the object-oriented aspects of programming:

- using library classes;
- writing classes;
- using objects;
- using methods.

We also look at some of the more sophisticated aspects of object-oriented programming, like:

- inheritance;
- polymorphism;
- interfaces.

● What's not included

This book describes the essentials of Java. It does not explain the bits and pieces, the bells and whistles. Thus the reader is freed from unnecessary detail and can concentrate on mastering Java and programming in general.

Applications or applets?

There are two distinct types of Java program:

■ a distinct free-standing program (this is called an application);
■ a program invoked from a web browser (this is called an applet).

In this book we concentrate on applications, because we believe that this is the main way in which Java is being used. (We explain how to run applets in an appendix.)

Graphics or text?

Throughout the text we have emphasized programs that use graphical images rather than text input and output. We think they are more fun, more interesting and clearly demonstrate all the important principles of programming. We haven't ignored programs that input and output text – they are included, but they come second best.

Graphical user interfaces (GUIs)

The programs we present use many of the features of a GUI, such as windows, buttons, scrollbars and using the mouse in lots of different ways.

AWT or Swing?

There are two Java mechanisms for creating and using GUIs – AWT and Swing. The Swing set of user-interface components is more complete and powerful than the AWT set. This book uses the Swing approach because it is being used more widely.

The sequence of material

Programming involves many challenging ideas, and one of the problems of writing a book about programming is deciding how and when to introduce new ideas. We introduce simple ideas early and more sophisticated ideas later on. We use objects from an early stage. Then later we see how to write new objects. Our approach is to start with ideas like variables and assignment, then introduce selection and looping, and then go on to objects and classes (the object-oriented features). We also wanted to make sure that the fun element of programming is paramount, so we use graphics right from the start.

Bit by bit

In this book we introduce new ideas carefully one at a time, rather than all at once. So there is a single chapter on writing methods, for example.

Computer applications

Computers are used in many different applications and this book uses examples from all these areas:

- information processing;
- games;
- scientific calculations.

The reader can choose to concentrate on those application areas of interest and spend less time on the other areas.

Different kinds of programming

There are many different kinds of programming – examples are procedural, logic, functional, spreadsheet, visual and object-oriented programming. This book is about the dominant type of programming – object-oriented programming (OOP) – as practised in languages like Visual Basic, C++, C#, Eiffel and Smalltalk.

Which version of Java?

Java is evolving, but slowly. From time to time Sun releases a new version of the Java Software Development Kit (SDK). A new version usually means additional items in the libraries – and a new version number. All versions from 1.2 have the generic name of Java 2. You can use this book with any version from version 1.2 onwards.

Have fun

Programming is creative and interesting, particularly in Java. Please have fun!

Visit our web site

All the programs presented in this book are available on our web site, which can be reached via: **www.booksites.net/bell**.

Changes to this edition

If you have used earlier editions of this book, you might like to know what is different about this edition.

In making changes we have tried to keep to the spirit of the original and at the same time simplify things where possible. We have also tried to follow the main trends in using Java. So while the older editions used applets and the AWT for GUIs, this edition uses applications and Swing. The older editions used the method **paint** extensively and everyone found it difficult to understand. So we have eliminated **paint** to give major simplifications.

We have also made minor changes, such as using the term 'call' rather than the long-winded term 'invoke'. We have also used **double** variables instead of **float** because declaring literals is easier.

There used to be a chapter on applet architecture, but we were never sure that it worked. With the elimination of method **paint** and the simpler structure of applications, we don't think this chapter is needed anymore. There was also a chapter on GUI components, which seemed out of place. So this chapter has been removed and incorporated within an improved appendix on the Java library, which presents sample programs.

The topic of abstract classes has been moved into the chapter on inheritance, where it rightly belongs. We have created a new chapter on array lists, which serves as an introduction to data structures.

We hope you like the changes.

● Any comments on this book?

If you want to email the authors, we are at D.H.Bell@shu.ac.uk and M.Parr@shu.ac.uk. We look forward to hearing from you.

A guided tour

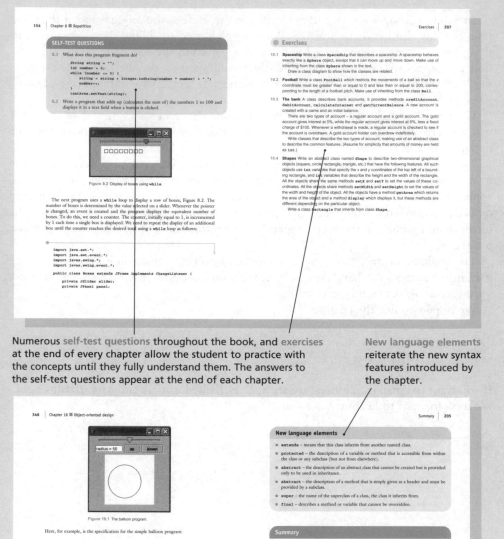

Numerous self-test questions throughout the book, and exercises at the end of every chapter allow the student to practice with the concepts until they fully understand them. The answers to the self-test questions appear at the end of each chapter.

New language elements reiterate the new syntax features introduced by the chapter.

Programs that use graphical images (particularly GUIs) rather than text input-output programs are used throughout. This demonstrates the creative and exciting side of programming which helps the student learn concepts faster.

Summaries offer a concise round-up of the key concepts covered by each chapter. They tie in with the objectives listed at the beginning of the chapter and are a great reference and revision aid.

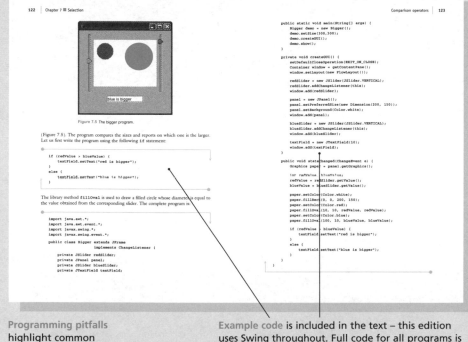

Programming pitfalls highlight common programming mistakes and how to avoid them.

Example code is included in the text – this edition uses Swing throughout. Full code for all programs is available on the accompanying CD-ROM.

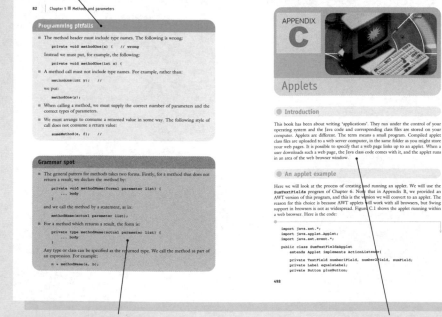

Grammar spot identifies the correct way to write code, reinforcing the student's understanding of Java syntax.

Appendices broaden the student's understanding of Java programming.

CHAPTER 1

The background to Java

This chapter explains:

- how and why Java came into being;
- the main features of Java;
- the introductory concepts of programming.

The history of Java

A computer program is a series of instructions that are obeyed by a computer. The point of the instructions is to carry out a task, e.g. play a game, send an email, etc. The instructions are written in a particular style: they must conform to the rules of the programming language we choose. There are hundreds of programming languages, but only a few have made an impact and become widely used. The history of programming languages is a form of evolution, and here we will look at the roots of Java. The names of the older languages are not important, but we provide them for completeness.

Around 1960, a programming language named Algol 60 was created. ('Algol' from the term 'algorithm' – a series of steps that can be performed to solve a problem.) This was popular in academic circles, but its ideas persisted longer than its use. At this time, other languages were more popular: COBOL for data processing, and Fortran for scientific work. In the UK, an extended version of Algol 60 was created (CPL – Combined Programming Language), which was soon simplified into basic CPL, or BCPL.

We then move to Bell Laboratories USA, where Dennis Ritchie and others transformed BCPL into a language named B, which was then enhanced to become C, around 1970. C was tremendously popular. It was used to write the Unix operating system, and much later, Linus Torvalds used it to write a major part of Unix – named Linux – for PCs.

The next step came when C++ ('C plus plus') was created around 1980 by Bjarne Stroustrup, also at Bell Labs. This made possible the creation and reuse of separate sections of code, in a style known as 'object-oriented programming'. (In C, you could use ++ to add one to an item – hence C++ is one up from C.) C++ is still popular, but hard to use – it takes a lot of study.

Now we move to Sun Microsystems in the USA. In the early 1990s, James Gosling was designing a new language named Oak, intended to be used in consumer electronics products. This project never came to fruition, but the Oak language became renamed Java (after the coffee).

In parallel, the Internet was becoming more popular, and a small company called Netscape had created a web browser. This went on to become the most popular browser, before Microsoft issued its Internet Explorer with every PC.

After discussions with Microsoft, Netscape agreed to provide support for Java in its web browser, with the result that Java programs could be downloaded alongside web pages. This provided a programming capability to enhance static pages. These programs were known as 'applets'. Netscape decided to allow users to download its browser for free, and this also spread the word about Java.

● The main features of Java

When James Gosling designed Java, he didn't create something from nothing. Rather, he took existing concepts, and integrated them to form a new language. Here are its main features:

- Java programs look similar to C++ programs. This meant that the C++ community would take it seriously, and also meant that C++ programmers can be productive quickly.

- Java was designed with the Internet in mind. As well as creating conventional programs, applets can be created which run 'inside' a web page. Java also had facilities for transferring data over the Internet in a variety of ways.

- Java programs are portable: they can run on any type of computer. In order for this to happen, a Java 'run-time system' has to be written for every type of computer, and this has been done for virtually all types of computer in use today. Java is also available for cellphones, so, in a sense, the abandoned Oak project has come to fruition.

- Java applets are secure. Computer viruses are widespread, and downloading and running programs over the Internet can be risky. However, the design of Java applets means that they are secure, and will not infect your computer with a virus.

- Though not a technical issue, Sun's marketing of Java is worthy of note. All the software needed to create and run Java programs was made available free, as an Internet download. This meant that Java became popular quickly. In addition, the Netscape web browser supported Java from its early days, and Microsoft provided similar facilities in its Internet Explorer web browser.

Java was very well received in industry because of its portability and Internet features. It was also well received in education, as it provides full object-oriented facilities in a simpler way than in C++.

Although Java is relatively new, it was influential in the design of Microsoft's C# (C Sharp) language. From an educational point of view, familiarity with Java will enable you to move to C# relatively easily.

● What is a program?

In this section we try to give the reader some impression of what a program is. One way to understand is by using analogies with recipes, musical scores and knitting patterns. Even the instructions on a bottle of hair shampoo are a simple program:

```
wet hair
apply shampoo
massage shampoo into hair
rinse
```

This program is a list of instructions for a human being, but it does demonstrate one important aspect of a computer program – a program is a sequence of instructions that is obeyed, starting at the first instruction and going on from one to the next until the sequence is complete. A recipe, musical score and a knitting pattern are similar – they constitute a list of instructions that are obeyed in sequence. In the case of a knitting pattern, knitting machines exist which are fed with a program of instructions, which they then carry out (or 'execute'). This is what a computer is – it is a machine that automatically obeys a sequence of instructions, a program. (In fact, if we make an error in the instructions, the computer is likely to do the wrong task.) The set of instructions that are available for a computer to obey typically includes:

- input a number;
- input some characters (letters and digits);
- output some characters;
- do a calculation;
- output a number;
- output some graphical image to the screen;
- respond to a button on the screen being clicked by the mouse.

The job of programming is one of selecting from this list those instructions that will carry out the required task. These instructions are written in a specialized language called a programming language. Java is one of many such languages. Learning to program means learning about the facilities of the programming language and how to combine them so as to do something you want. The example of musical scores illustrates another aspect of programs. It is common in music to repeat sections, e.g. a chorus section. Musical notation saves the composer from duplicating those parts of the score that are repeated and, instead, provides a notation specifying that a section of music is repeated. The same is true in a program; it is often the case that some action has to be repeated: for example, in a word-processing program, searching through a passage of text for the occurrence of a word. Repetition (or iteration) is common in programs, and Java has special instructions to accomplish this.

Recipes sometimes say something like: 'if you haven't got fresh peas, use frozen'. This illustrates another aspect of programs – they often carry out a test and then do one of two things depending on the result of the test. This is called selection, and, as with repetition, Java has special facilities to accomplish it.

If you have ever used a recipe to prepare a meal, you may well have got to a particular step in the recipe only to find that you have to refer to another recipe. For example, you might have to turn to another page to find out how to cook rice, before combining it with the rest of the meal: the rice preparation has been separated out as a sub-task. This way of writing instructions has an important analogue in programming, called methods in Java and other object-oriented languages. Methods are used in all programming languages, but sometimes go under other names, such as functions, procedures, subroutines or sub-programs.

Methods are sub-tasks, and are so called because they are a method for doing something. Using methods promotes simplicity where there might otherwise be complexity.

Now consider cooking a curry. A few years ago, the recipe would suggest that you buy fresh spices, grind them and fry them. Nowadays, though, you can buy ready-made sauces. Our task has become simpler. The analogy with programming is that the task becomes easier if we can select from a set of ready-made 'objects' such as buttons, scrollbars and databases. Java comes with a large set of objects that we can incorporate in our program, rather than creating the whole thing from scratch.

To sum up, a program is a list of instructions that can be obeyed automatically by a computer. A program consists of combinations of:

■ sequences;
■ repetitions;
■ selections;
■ methods;
■ ready-made objects;
■ objects you write yourself.

All modern programming languages share these features.

SELF-TEST QUESTIONS

1.1   Here are some instructions for calculating an employee's pay:

```
obtain the number of hours worked
calculate pay
print pay slip
subtract deductions for illness
```

Is there a major error?

1.2   Take the instruction:

```
massage shampoo into hair
```

and express it in a more detailed way, incorporating the concept of repetition.

1.3   Here are some instructions displayed on a roller-coaster ride:

```
Only take the ride if you are over 8 or younger than 70!
```

Is there a problem with the notice? How would you rewrite it to improve it?

Programming principles

- Programs consist of instructions combined with the concepts of sequence, selection, repetition and sub-tasks.

- The programming task becomes simpler if we can make use of ready-made components.

Programming pitfalls

Human error can creep into programs – such as placing instructions in the wrong order.

Summary

- Java is an object-oriented language, derived from C++.

- Java programs are portable: they can run on most types of computer.

- Java is integrated with web browsers. Applet programs can be executed by web browsers.

- A program is a list of instructions that are obeyed automatically by a computer.

- Currently the main trend in programming practice is the object-oriented programming (OOP) approach, and Java fully supports it.

● Exercises

1.1 This question concerns the steps that a student goes through to wake up and get to college. Here is a suggestion for the first few steps:

```
wake up
dress
eat breakfast
brush teeth
...
```

(a) Complete the steps. Note that there is no ideal answer – the steps will vary between individuals.

(b) The 'brush teeth' step contains repetition – we do it again and again. Identify another step that contains repetition.

(c) Identify a step that contains a selection.

(d) Take one of the steps, and break it down into smaller steps.

1.2 You are provided with a huge pile of paper containing 10000 numbers, in no particular order. Write down the process that you would go through to find the largest number. Ensure that your process is clear and unambiguous. Identify any selection and repetition in your process.

1.3 For the game of Tic Tac Toe (noughts and crosses), try to write down a set of precise instructions which enables a player to win. If this is not possible, try to ensure that a player does not lose.

Answers to self-test questions

1.1 The major error is that the deductions part comes too late. It should precede the printing.

1.2 We might say:

```
keep massaging your hair until it is washed.
```

or:

```
As long as your hair is not washed, keep massaging.
```

1.3 The problem is with the word 'or'. Someone who is 73 is also over 8, and could therefore ride.

We could replace 'or' by 'and' to make it technically correct, but the notice might still be misunderstood. We might also put:

```
only take this ride if you are between 8 and 70
```

but be prepared to modify the notice again when hordes of 8 and 70 year olds ask if they can ride!

CHAPTER 2

First programs

This chapter explains:

- how to create, compile and run Java programs;
- the use of an integrated development environment;
- the ideas of classes, objects and methods;
- how to display a message dialog;
- how to place text in a text field.

● Introduction

To learn how to program in Java you will need access to a computer with Java facilities, but fortunately the Java language has been designed to run on any operating system. Currently, the most widely used operating systems are Microsoft's Windows systems on PCs, but other operating systems in use are GNU/Linux on PCs and OS X on Apple Mac. Java can run on any of these systems. This is a major benefit, but it means that the detailed instructions for using Java will vary. Here we provide general information only. Appendix I explains how to use the Java system we provide on CD-ROM.

When Java has been installed, there are three stages involved:

- creating the program with an editor;
- compiling the program;
- running the program.

● Integrated development environments

There are two main ways to create and run your programs. Firstly, you might choose an integrated development environment (IDE). This is a software package designed to help with the complete process of creating and running a Java program. If you use an IDE, it is still a good idea to understand the ideas of files, editing, compilation and running, as described below.

Alternatively, you can use a text editor (rather like a simple word processor) to create your programs, and you can initiate compiling and running by typing in commands. We show this approach below, because it is similar on most operating systems.

It might appear that an IDE is by far the best solution. This can be the case, but some of them can be rather complex for beginners.

● Files and folders

The programs that are automatically loaded and run when the computer is switched on are collectively called the operating system. One major part of an operating system is concerned with storing files, and here we provide a brief introduction.

Information stored on a computer disk is stored in files, just as information stored in filing cabinets in an office is stored in files.

Normally you set up a file to contain related information. For example:

- a letter to your mother;
- a list of students on a particular course;
- a list of friends, with names, addresses and telephone numbers.

Each file has its own name, chosen by the person who created it. It is usual, as you might expect, to choose a name that clearly describes what is in the file. A file name has an *extension* – a part on the end – that describes the type of information that is held in the file. For example, a file called **letter1** that holds a letter and is normally edited with a word processor might have the extension **.doc** (short for document) so that its full name is **letter1.doc**. A file that holds a Java program has the extension **.java**, so that a typical file name might be **Game.java**.

On most computers, a group of related files is collected together into a folder (sometimes called a directory). So, in a particular folder you might hold all letters sent to the bank. In another folder you might store all the sales figures for one year. Certainly you will keep all the files that are used in a single Java program in the same folder. You give each folder a name – usually a meaningful name – that helps you to find it.

Normally folders are themselves grouped together in a folder. So you might have a folder called **Toms** within which are the folders **myprogs**, **letters**.

You might think that this will go on for ever, and indeed you can set up folders of folders *ad infinitum*. Your computer system will typically have hundreds of folders and thousands of files. Some of these will be yours (you can set them up and alter them) and some of them will belong to the operating system (leave them alone!).

So, a file is a collection of information with a name. Related files are collected together into a folder, which also has a name.

To actually see lists of folders and the files they contain, we make use of a program known as *Windows Explorer* on Microsoft Windows systems. Clicking on a folder reveals the files it contains. GNU/Linux and Apple Macs have similar facilities.

SELF-TEST QUESTION

2.1 (a) What is the difference between a folder and a directory?

(b) What is a folder?

(c) Is it possible to create two folders with the same name?

● Using an editor

The editor is a program that helps you to create and change files. Typically it provides facilities to:

■ create a new file;

■ retrieve (open) an existing file;

■ save a changed file;

■ delete, insert and change text in a file;

■ cut, copy and paste text from another file, or within the same file;

■ search for some text and (optionally) replace it by new text.

There are many text editors. For example, on Microsoft systems, the *Notepad* editor is usually provided. If you are using an IDE, your editor may be built in. Again, this book doesn't explain how to use an editor because there are so many of them. You will need to become fluent at using your editor, because you will often need to modify programs.

SELF-TEST QUESTION

2.2 (a) Find out how to start and use your editor.

(b) In your editor, enter some text containing the word **"he"** several times. Find out how your editor can be used to replace every occurrence of **"he"** by **"she"** with a single command.

● Creating a first Java program

You have already run (executed) programs that others have written (e.g. an editor, a game or a word processor). Now you will write your own program in Java, which displays two pop-up messages. No computer can directly understand Java, so you have to make use of several programs that help. The programs are, in order:

1. editor;
2. compiler;
3. Java Virtual Machine (JVM).

We will now look at each of these to see what they do.

Editor

Using the editor, key in your first small Java program, shown below. Do not worry about what it means at this stage. You will see that the program contains certain unusual characters and three different kinds of bracket. You might have to search for them on your keyboard. The text that you have entered is known as the Java *code*.

```java
import java.awt.*;
import java.awt.event.*;
import javax.swing.*;

public class Hello extends JFrame {

    public static void main(String[] args) {
        JOptionPane.showMessageDialog(null, "Hello World!");
        JOptionPane.showMessageDialog(null, "Goodbye");
        System.exit(0);
    }
}
```

Undoubtedly you will make mistakes when you key in this program. You can use the editor to correct the program. When it looks correct, save the program in a file, giving the file the name:

```
Hello.java
```

A file that holds a Java program must have the extension **java**. The first part of the name must match the name that follows the words **public class** in the Java code. This name can be chosen by the programmer. Any folder will do, though it is a good idea to create one specifically for your Java work. The first step is now complete.

Compiler

A compiler is a program that converts a program written in a language like Java into the language that the computer understands. So a compiler is like an automatic translator, able to translate one (computer) language into another. Java programs are converted into byte code. Byte code is not exactly the same as the language that a computer understands (machine code). Instead, it is an idealized machine language that means that your Java program will run on any type of computer. When your program is run, the byte code is interpreted by a program called the Java Virtual Machine. Appendix I provides more information on this stage.

If you have a Java IDE, click on a button or menu option to invoke the compilation process.

As it compiles your program, the compiler checks that the program obeys the rules of programming in Java and, if something is wrong, displays appropriate error messages. It also checks that the programs in any libraries that you are using are being employed correctly. It is rare (even for experienced programmers) to have a program compile correctly first time, so don't be disappointed if you get some error messages. Here is an example of an error message:

```
Hello.java:9: ';' expected
```

This message provides the name of the file, the line number of the error (**9** in this case) and a description of the error. The line in question is then shown.

One of the standing jokes of programming is that error messages from compilers are often cryptic and unhelpful. The compiler will indicate (note: not pinpoint) the position of the errors. Study what you have keyed in and try to see what is wrong. Common errors are:

■ semicolons missing or in the wrong place;

■ brackets missing;

■ single quotes (') rather than double quotes (").

Identify your error, edit the program and recompile. This is when your patience is on test! Repeat until you have eradicated the errors.

SELF-TEST QUESTION

2.3 Make an intentional error in your code, by omitting a semicolon. Observe the error message that the compiler produces. Finally, put the semicolon back.

Running your program – the JVM

After editing and compiling, we can run (or execute) the program. The compiler creates a file on disk with the extension **class**. The first part of the name matches the Java program name – so in this example, the file name is:

```
Hello.class
```

Figure 2.1 Screenshot of `Hello.java`.

With an IDE, a button-click will run the program. If you are working from the command line, consult Appendix I.

The program now runs. Firstly, it displays the message:

```
Hello World!
```

Click **OK** to close the message and to display the next message:

```
Goodbye
```

Click **OK** again. The program terminates. Figure 2.1 shows a screenshot of the first message.

● The libraries

As we saw, the output from the compiler is a `.class` file, which we execute with the JVM. However, the class file does not contain the complete program. In fact, every Java program needs some help from one or more pieces of program that are held in libraries. In computer terms, a library is a collection of already-written useful pieces of program, kept in files. Your small sample program needs to make use of such a piece of program to display information on the screen. In order to accomplish this, the requisite piece of program has to be linked to your program when it is run.

The libraries are collections of useful parts. Suppose you were going to design a new motor car. You would probably want to design the body shape and the interior layout. But you would probably want to make use of an engine that someone else had designed and built. Similarly, you might well use the wheels that some other manufacturer had produced. So, some elements of the car would be new, and some would be off the shelf. The off-the-shelf components are like the pieces of program in the Java library. For example, our example program makes use of a pop-up message dialog from a library.

Things can go wrong when the compiler checks the links to library software and you may get a cryptic error message. Common errors are:

- the library is missing;
- you have misspelled the name of something in the library.

The libraries are incorporated into your program when it runs.

SELF-TEST QUESTION

2.4 (a) Find two errors in this code:

```
JOptionpane.showMessageDialog(null, "Hello wirld");
```

(b) Which error will prevent the program from running?

● Demystifying the program

We will now provide an overview of the Java program. Even though it is quite small, you can see that the program has quite a lot to it. This is because Java is a real industrial-strength language, and even the smallest program needs some major ingredients. Note that at this early stage, we do not cover every detail. This comes in the following chapters.

We show the code of the program here again, in Figure 2.2. This time it has line numbers to help with the explanation. (Line numbers must not be part of a real program.) Lines 8 and 9 are the most important pieces of this program. They instruct the computer to display some text in a pop-up rectangle known as a message dialog, from the `JOptionPane` class. Line 8 displays the text `Hello World!`, which must be enclosed in double quotes. Text in quotes like this is called a string. The line ends with a semicolon, as do many lines in Java. Similarly, line 9 displays `"Goodbye"`. In Java, the letter `J` (standing for Java, of course) precedes many names (such as `JOptionPane`).

Figure 2.1 shows the effect of line 8. When OK is clicked, the program proceeds to line 9. This time the string `"Goodbye"` is displayed. Note that the message dialogs are displayed in sequence, working down the program.

```
1      import java.awt.*;
2      import java.awt.event.*;
3      import javax.swing.*;
4
5      public class Hello extends JFrame {
6
7          public static void main(String[] args) {
8              JOptionPane.showMessageDialog(null, "Hello World!");
9              JOptionPane.showMessageDialog(null, "Goodbye");
10             System.exit(0);
11         }
12     }
```

Figure 2.2 The `Hello` program.

2.5 Alter the program so that it displays a third message dialog, showing the string `"Finishing now"`.

At the top, lines 1, 2 and 3 specify information about the library programs that the program uses. The word **import** is followed by the name of a library that is to be used by the program. This program uses the AWT (Abstract Window Toolkit) and the Swing library in order to display a message dialog.

Line 4 is a blank line. We can use blank lines anywhere, to make a program more readable.

Line 5 is a heading which announces that this code is a program named **Hello**.

The program itself is enclosed within the curly brackets. The opening { in line 5 goes with (matches) the closing } on line 12. Within these lines, there are more curly brackets. The { at line 7 goes with the } at line 11.

Line 10 causes the program to stop running.

Later, we will present a longer program which displays text on the screen in a different way. Before we do, let us look at the use of 'objects' in Java.

● Objects, methods: an introduction

One of the reasons for Java's popularity is that it is *object oriented*. This is the book's main theme, and we cover it at length in future chapters. But here we will introduce the concept of objects via an analogy.

Firstly, consider a home with a CD player in the kitchen, and an identical one in the bedroom. In the Java jargon, we regard them as 'objects'. Next, we consider what facilities each CD player provides for us. In other words, what buttons does a CD player provide? In the Java jargon, each facility is termed a 'method'. (For example, we might have a start and a stop method, and a method for skipping to a track via its number.)

The term 'method' is rather strange, and it comes from the history of programming languages. Imagine it as meaning 'function' or 'facility', as in 'This CD player has a start and a stop method.'

Now consider the task of identifying each button on each player. It is not enough to state:

```
stop
```

because there are two players. Which player do we mean? Instead, we must identify the player as well. Moving slightly closer to Java, we use:

```
kitchenCD.stop
```

Note the use of the dot. It is used in a similar way in all object-oriented languages. We have two items:

■ the name of an object; this usually corresponds to a noun.

■ a method which the object provides; this is often a verb.

Note that you can imagine that the dot means 's in English, as in:

```
kitchenCD's stop button
```

Later, when we discuss methods in more detail, you will see that the exact Java version of the above is:

```
kitchenCD.stop();
```

Observe the semicolon, and the brackets with nothing between them. For some other methods, we might have to supply additional information for the method to work on, such as selecting a numbered track:

```
bedroomCD.select(4);
```

The item in brackets is known as a 'parameter'. (Again a traditional programming term rather than an instantly meaningful one.)

In general terms, the way we use methods is:

```
object.method(parameters);
```

If the particular method does not need parameters, we must still use the brackets. We cover parameters and methods in Chapter 5.

SELF-TEST QUESTION

2.6 Assume that our kitchen and bedroom CD players have facilities (methods) for stopping, starting and selecting a numbered track. Here is an example of using one method:

```
kitchenCD.select(6);
```

Give examples of using the other five methods.

● Classes: an analogy

The concept of a class is extremely important in object-oriented programming. Recall our analogy: we have two identical CD player objects in our house. In object-oriented jargon, we have two 'instances' of the CD player 'class'. A class is rather like a production line which can manufacture new CD players.

Let us distinguish between a class and instances of a class. The house has two instances of the CD player class, which really exist: we can actually use them. A class is a more abstract concept. Though the CD player production line possesses the design (in some form or another) of a CD player, an actual instance does not exist until the machine actually manufactures one. In Java, we use the word 'new' to instruct a class to manufacture a new instance. To summarize:

- objects are instances of a class;
- a class can produce as many instances as we require.

It is worth repeating that these concepts are the main ones of this book, and we cover them later in much more detail. We do not expect you to be able to write Java programs with objects and classes in this chapter.

Using a text field

The first program we saw used a message dialog. The second program we will introduce is rather longer, but it forms the basis for many of the programs in this book. It uses a *text field* to display a single line of text – the string `"Hello!"` in this case. Figure 2.3 shows a screenshot, and Figure 2.4 shows the code with line numbers.

At this stage, we need to remind you again that the details of Java really begin in the next chapter. For now, we are showing you some programs, and providing a general explanation of what they do. We do not (yet) expect you to be able to look at a line of code, and say precisely what it does.

As before, we provide line numbers to assist in our explanations, but the numbers should not be typed in. The name following the `public class` words is `Greeting`, so the program must be saved in a file named:

```
Greeting.java
```

Compile and run the program. To stop the program, click the cross at the top right of the window, or click the Java icon at the top left, then select **Close** from the menu.

We will now look at some of the uses of instances, methods and parameters.

Recall our analogies. We mentioned the use of the 'dot' notation for objects and their associated methods. Locate line 11:

```
frame.setSize(300, 200);
```

Figure 2.3 Screenshot of `Greetings.java`.

```
1      import java.awt.*;
2      import java.awt.event.*;
3      import javax.swing.*;
4
5      public class Greeting extends JFrame {
6
7          private JTextField textField;
8
9          public static void main (String[] args) {
10             Greeting frame = new Greeting();
11             frame.setSize(300, 200);
12             frame.createGUI();
13             frame.show();
14         }
15
16         private void createGUI() {
17             setDefaultCloseOperation(EXIT_ON_CLOSE);
18             Container window = getContentPane();
19             window.setLayout(new FlowLayout() );
20             textField = new JTextField("Hello!");
21             window.add(textField);
22         }
23     }
```

Figure 2.4 The **Greeting** program.

This uses the same notation – object, dot, method, parameters.

Imagine the frame object as the outer edge of the screenshot of Figure 2.3. The **setSize** method takes two parameters – the required width and height of the frame in units known as pixels. Here, we have used an object-oriented approach to setting the size of the frame.

SELF-TEST QUESTION

2.7   Modify the **Greeting** program so that the frame is half as wide.

Here is another use of objects. Locate the following lines in the program:

```
textField = new JTextField("Hello!");
window.add(textField);
```

First, a text field is being created, using the word **new**. At this stage, we can choose the text that will appear in the text field, though this can also be overtyped by the user when the program runs. Next, the window object has the text field added to it. When the program runs, the text field is displayed, and is centered automatically.

Finally, a general point about our second program. Most of the instructions are concerned with stating which libraries are needed, and setting up the visual appearance of the screen, i.e. the 'graphical user interface' or GUI.

Imagine the GUI of your favourite word processor. Across the top of its window, you will see a large number of menus and buttons. When you run the word processor, they all appear instantly, so it might surprise you to learn that behind the scenes, it starts with a totally blank window, and laboriously adds each menu and button to the window, one by one. Because of the speed of the computer, this process seems instantaneous.

When you write larger programs, the initial setup of the screen still has to be done, but that part of the code becomes less dominant in proportion to the code concerned with making the program carry out a task when a button or menu item is clicked.

Programming principles

- A major feature of Java is the widespread use of classes.
- The 'dot' notation for using objects is:

    `object.method(parameters)`

- Instructions are obeyed in sequence, from the top of the program to the bottom.

Programming pitfalls

- When you are editing a program, save it every 10 minutes or so to guard against losing your work should the computer fail.
- Make sure that when you key in a program, you copy the characters exactly, with capitals as shown.
- Make sure that the name of the file matches the name of the class in the file. For example:

    `public class Hello extends JFrame {`

    Here, the name following **class** is **Hello**. The file must be saved in **Hello.java**. The capital letter of the class is important.
- You will almost certainly make a mistake when you key in a program. The compiler will tell you what the errors are. Try not to get too frustrated by the errors.

Grammar spot

Java programs contain a number of opening and closing brackets. There must be the same number of closing brackets as opening brackets.

New language elements

A message dialog can display a text string along with an **OK** button, as in:

```
JOptionPane.showMessageDialog(null, "Hello World!");
```

Summary

- Java programs can be created and executed on most types of computer.

- An editor is used to create and modify your Java source code.

- A Java program must be compiled prior to running.

- Compilation errors must be corrected before a program can run.

- The compiler produces a file with the same name as the original Java file, but with the extension **class**. This file contains byte-code instructions.

- The JVM (Java Virtual Machine) is used to run (execute) programs.

- An IDE can be used to create and run programs. Alternatively, the command line can be used.

- Much of the power of Java comes from its libraries, which are linked in as the program runs.

- Java is object oriented. It uses the concepts of classes, instances and methods.

- The 'dot' notation occurs throughout Java programs. Here is an example:

```
frame.setSize(300, 200);
```

- Methods (such as **setSize**) cause tasks to be performed on the specified object (such as **frame**).

- Things can go wrong at any stage, and part of the programmer's job is identifying and correcting the errors. Don't forget: it is rare for everything to work smoothly first time. Be careful, be relaxed.

● Exercises

2.1 Ensure that you know how to compile and run Java programs on your computer. Compile and run the two programs from this chapter.

2.2 In the **Hello** program, add a message dialog to display your name.

2.3 In the **Greeting** program, make the text field display your name.

Answers to self-test questions

2.1 (a) No difference. The terms mean the same thing.

(b) A folder contains a number of files and/or other folders.

(c) Yes. As long as the two identically named folders are not within the same folder. (For example, the folders **Work** and **Home** might each contain a **letters** folder.)

2.2 (a) This depends on the editors available on your computer. If you use an IDE, the editor is contained within it.

(b) This depends on your editor. Many editors have a **Find...Replace** facility, which scans all of the text.

2.3 The error message will vary, depending on which semicolon you omitted.

2.4 (a) There is an incorrect 'p'. It should be 'P' as in **JOptionPane**. There is a misspelling of **wirld**.

(b) The 'p' error will prevent the program from compiling, hence it cannot run. The 'wirld' error will not prevent the program running, but the result will not be as you intended.

2.5 Insert the following line immediately below line 9, which displays **"Goodbye"**:

```
JOptionPane.showMessageDialog(null, "Finishing now");
```

Compile and run the modified program.

2.6
```
kitchenCD.start();
kitchenCD.stop();
bedroomCD.start();
bedroomCD.stop();
bedroomCD.select(3);
```

2.7 Replace **300** by **150** in line 11, then recompile and run the program.

2.8 Replace **"Hello!"** in line 20 by:

```
"Some text in a text field"
```

Compile and run the program.

2.9 It remains centred near the top of the frame.

CHAPTER 3

Using graphics methods

This chapter explains:

- the nature of events;
- how to draw shapes with graphics methods;
- the use of parameters;
- how to comment programs;
- how to use colours;
- the sequence concept.

Introduction

The term 'computer graphics' conjures up a variety of possibilities. We could be discussing a computer-generated Hollywood movie, a static photo, or a more simple image made up of lines. In this chapter we restrict ourselves to still images built from simple shapes, and focus on the use of library methods to create them. Our programs also introduce the use of a button to allow user interaction.

Events

Many programs are built in such a way to allow user interaction via a GUI. Such programs provide buttons, text fields, scrollbars, etc. In Java terms, the user manipulates the mouse and keyboard, creating 'events' which the program responds to. Typical events are:

- a mouse-click;
- a key press;
- using a scrollbar to move through some text.

The Java system regards events as falling into several categories. For example, scrolling through a page is regarded as a 'change' event, whereas clicking on a button is regarded as an 'action' event.

When you write a Java program, you must ensure that the program will detect the events – otherwise nothing will happen. The transmission of an event (such as a mouse-click) to a program does not happen automatically. Instead, the program has to be set up to 'listen' for types of event. Fortunately, the coding for this is standard, and you will reuse it from program to program rather than creating it anew for every program.

Responding to an event is known as 'handling' the event.

Here is a program which provides a button. Figure 3.1 shows the screenshot.

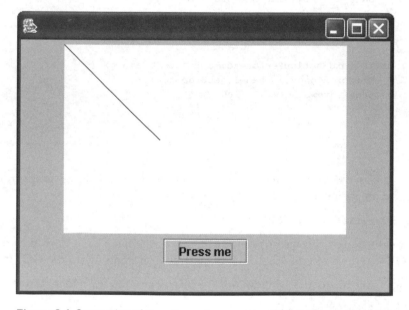

Figure 3.1 Screenshot of **DrawExample** program, after clicking on the button.

```java
import java.awt.*;
import java.awt.event.*;
import javax.swing.*;

public class DrawExample extends JFrame
    implements ActionListener {

    private JButton button;
    private JPanel panel;
```

```
public static void main(String[] args) {
    DrawExample frame = new DrawExample();
    frame.setSize(400, 300);
    frame.createGUI();
    frame.show();
}

private void createGUI() {
    setDefaultCloseOperation(EXIT_ON_CLOSE);
    Container window = getContentPane();
    window.setLayout(new FlowLayout() );

    panel = new JPanel();
    panel.setPreferredSize(new Dimension(300, 200));
    panel.setBackground(Color.white);
    window.add(panel);

    button = new JButton("Press me");
    window.add(button);
    button.addActionListener(this);
}

public void actionPerformed(ActionEvent event) {
    Graphics paper = panel.getGraphics();
    paper.drawLine(0, 0, 100, 100);
}
}
```

The user clicks the button, and a diagonal line is drawn. For the purpose of this chapter, we are mainly interested in this instruction:

```
paper.drawLine(0, 0, 100, 100);
```

As you might expect, this instruction actually draws the line. The rest of the code sets up the GUI, and we will discuss it only in general terms. Setting up the GUI involves:

- adding a button to the window, in a similar way that we added a text field in Chapter 2;
- adding a 'panel' to be used for drawing;
- stating that the program will listen for mouse-clicks (categorized as action events).

The following point is very important: in later chapters, we cover the creation of user interfaces. For now, treat the above GUI code as standard.

● The button-click event

The main event in this program is created when the user clicks the **"Press me"** button. A button-click causes the program to execute this section of program:

```
public void actionPerformed(ActionEvent event) {
    Graphics paper = panel.getGraphics();
    paper.drawLine(0, 0, 100, 100);
}
```

This section of program is a *method*, named `actionPerformed`. When the button is clicked, the Java system calls up (invokes) the method, and the instructions between the opening { and the closing } are executed in sequence. This is where we place our drawing instructions. We will now look at the details of drawing shapes.

The graphics coordinate system

Java graphics are based on pixels. A pixel is a small dot on the screen which can be set to a particular colour. Each pixel is identified by a pair of numbers (its coordinates), starting from zero:

- the horizontal position, often referred to as x in mathematics (and in the Java documentation) – this value increases from left to right;
- the vertical position, often referred to as y – this value increases downwards. Note that this differs from the convention in mathematics.

We use this system when we request Java to draw shapes. Figure 3.2 shows the approach. The top left of the drawing area is $(0, 0)$, and we draw relative to this point.

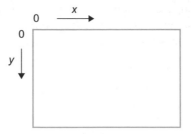

Figure 3.2 The pixel coordinate system.

Explanation of the program

The only section we are concerned with is the small part which does the drawing:

```
1  public void actionPerformed(ActionEvent event) {
2      Graphics paper = panel.getGraphics();
3      paper.drawLine(0, 0, 100, 100);
4  }
```

Line 1 introduces the section of program which is executed when the button is clicked. It is a method. Any instructions we place between the { of line 1 and the } of line 4 are executed in sequence, down the page.

Line 2 provides a graphics area for drawing shapes – we have chosen to name it **paper**. Recall Chapter 2, where we stated that Java is object oriented. Objects provide facilities for us. We considered a CD player, which provides a range of facilities, such as:

```
kitchenCD.select(4);
```

In fact, our drawing area is not just a blank sheet of paper – it is more like a drawing kit which comes with paper together with a set of tools, such as a ruler and protractor.

In line 3, the paper uses its **drawLine** method to draw a line on itself. The four numbers in brackets specify the position of the line.

The **drawLine** method is one of the many methods provided by the Java system in a library. Line 3 is a call (also known as an invocation) of the method, asking it to carry out the task of displaying a line.

When we make use of the **drawLine** method, we supply it with some values for the start and finish points of the line, and we need to get these in the correct order, which is:

1. the horizontal value (x) of the start of the line;
2. the vertical value (y) of the start of the line;
3. the horizontal value of the end of the line;
4. the vertical value of the end of the line.

The items are known as parameters in Java – they are inputs to the **drawLine** method. Parameters must be enclosed in brackets and separated by commas. (You may encounter the term 'argument', which is an alternative name for a parameter.) This particular method requires four parameters, and they must be integers (whole numbers). If we attempt to use the wrong number of parameters, or the wrong type, we get an error message from the compiler. We need to ensure that:

■ we supply the correct number of parameters;
■ we supply the correct type of parameters;
■ we arrange them in the right order.

Some methods do not require any parameters. In this case, we must still use the brackets, as in:

```
frame.show();
```

There are two kinds of method at work in our example:

■ Those that the programmer writes, such as **actionPerformed**. This is called up by the Java system when the button is clicked.
■ Those that are pre-written in the libraries, such as **drawLine**. Our program calls them.

A final point – note the semicolon ';' at the end of the **drawLine** parameters. In Java, a semicolon must appear at the end of every 'statement'. But what is a statement? The answer is not trivial! As you can see from the above program, a semicolon does not occur at the end of every line. Rather than provide intricate formal rules here, the advice is to base your initial programs on our examples. However, the use of a method followed by its parameters is in fact a statement, so a semicolon is required.

● Methods for drawing

As well as lines, the Java library provides us with facilities for drawing:

■ rectangles;
■ ovals (hence circles).

Here we list the parameters for each method, and provide an example program which uses them.

drawLine

■ the horizontal value of the start of the line;
■ the vertical value of the start of the line;
■ the horizontal value of the end of the line;
■ the vertical value of the end of the line.

drawRect

■ the horizontal value of the top left corner;
■ the vertical value of the top left corner;
■ the width of the rectangle;
■ the height of the rectangle.

drawOval

Imagine the oval squeezed inside a rectangle. We provide:

■ the horizontal value of the top left corner of the rectangle;
■ the vertical value of the top left corner of the rectangle;
■ the width of the rectangle;
■ the height of the rectangle.

The following shapes can also be drawn, but require additional Java knowledge. We will omit their parameter details, and won't use them in our programs.

■ arcs (sectors of a circle);
■ raised (three-dimensional) rectangles;
■ rectangles with rounded corners;
■ polygons.

Additionally, we can draw solid shapes with **fillRect** and **fillOval**. Their parameters are identical to those of the draw equivalents.

● Drawing with colours

It is possible to set the colour to be used for drawing. There are 13 standard colours:

```
black      blue     cyan        darkGray
gray       green    lightGray   magenta
orange     pink     red         white
yellow
```

(**cyan** is a deep green/blue, and **magenta** is a deep red/blue).

Take care with the spellings – note the use of capitals in the middle of the names. Here is how you might use the colours:

```
paper.setColor(Color.red);
paper.drawLine(0, 0, 100, 50);
paper.setColor(Color.green);
paper.drawOval(100, 100, 50, 50);
```

The above code draws a red line, then a green unfilled oval. If you don't set a colour, Java chooses black.

● Creating a new program

In the above **DrawExample** program, we concentrated on its **actionPerformed** method, which contained a call of the **drawLine** method. Our focus was to learn about calling and passing parameters to the drawing methods. But what about the other lines of code? They are concerned with such tasks as:

- creating the outer frame for the program;
- setting the size of the frame;
- adding the drawing area and button to the user interface.

These tasks are accomplished by calling methods. We explain the details in later chapters.

In fact, for every program in this chapter, the setting up of the user interface is identical. All the programs use a drawing area and a single button to initiate the drawing. However, we cannot use the identical code for each program, because the file name that we choose must match the name of the **public class** within the program. Look at the **DrawExample** program. It is stored in a file named **DrawExample.java**, and it contains the line:

```
public class DrawExample extends JFrame
```

The class name must start with a capital letter, and the name can only contain letters and digits. It cannot contain punctuation such as commas, full stops, hyphens, and cannot contain spaces. Choosing the class name fixes the file name we must use to contain the program.

There is an additional line:

```
DrawExample frame = new DrawExample();
```

This is contained within the **main** method of the program. When we run a Java program, the very first thing that happens is an automatic call of the **main** method. The first task of **main** is to create a new instance (an object) of the appropriate class (**DrawExample** here). In Chapter 6 we will examine the use of **new** to create new instances. For now, note that the **DrawExample** program contains three occurrences of the **DrawExample** name:

- one after the words **public class**;
- two in the **main** method.

When we create a new program, these three occurrences must be changed.

Here is an example. We assume that you are using a text editor, but will refer to IDE usage later. We will create a new program, named **DrawCircle**. The steps are:

1. Open the file **DrawExample.java** program in an editor.
2. Use the 'Save as' command, choosing the name **DrawCircle.java**.
3. Change the three occurrences of **DrawExample** into **DrawCircle**.
4. Save the file.

You can now focus on the main topic of this chapter, and place appropriate calls of the drawing methods within the **actionPerformed** method.

The approach with an IDE varies, depending on your particular system. Typically, you will create a new project with the name **DrawCircle**. Then remove any code that your IDE creates, and paste in the **DrawExample** code. Finally, alter the three occurrences of the class name, as before.

SELF-TEST QUESTION

3.1 Create a new program named **DrawCircle**. When the single button is clicked, it should draw a circle of **100** pixels diameter.

The sequence concept

When we have a number of statements in a program, they are performed from top to bottom, in sequence (unless we specify otherwise using the later concepts of selection and repetition). Here is a program which draws a variety of shapes. Figure 3.3 shows the resulting output. In the following listing we have omitted the code which creates the user interface, as this part is exactly the same as the previous program.

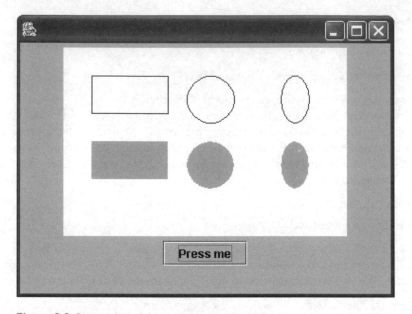

Figure 3.3 Screenshot of the **SomeShapes** program.

```
import java.awt.*;
import java.awt.event.*;
import javax.swing.*;

public class SomeShapes extends JFrame
    implements ActionListener {

//      GUI code omitted here...

    public void actionPerformed(ActionEvent event) {
        Graphics paper = panel.getGraphics();
        paper.drawRect(30, 30, 80, 40);
        paper.drawOval(130, 30, 50, 50);
        paper.drawOval(230, 30, 30, 50);
        paper.setColor(Color.lightGray);
        paper.fillRect(30, 100, 80, 40);
        paper.fillOval(130, 100, 50, 50);
        paper.fillOval(230, 100, 30, 50);
    }
}
```

The statements are obeyed (executed, performed, . . .) from top to bottom, down the page – though this is impossible to observe because of the speed of the computer. In future chapters, you will see that we can repeat a sequence of instructions over and over again.

3.2 Write and run a program which draws a large 'T' shape on the screen.

Adding meaning with comments

What does the following do?

```
paper.drawLine(20, 80, 70, 10);
paper.drawLine(70, 10, 120, 80);
paper.drawLine(20, 80, 120, 80);
```

The meaning is not instantly obvious, and you probably tried to figure it out with pencil and paper. The answer is that it draws a triangle with a horizontal base, but this is not apparent from the three statements. In Java, we can add comments (a kind of annotation) to the instructions, by preceding them by //. For example, we might put:

```
// draw a triangle
paper.drawLine(20, 80, 70, 10);
paper.drawLine(70, 10, 120, 80);
paper.drawLine(20, 80, 120, 80);
```

A comment can contain anything – there are no rules. It is up to you to use them to convey meaning.

Comments can also be placed at the end of a line, as in:

```
// draw a triangle
paper.drawLine(20, 80, 70, 10);
paper.drawLine(70, 10, 120, 80);
paper.drawLine(20, 80, 120, 80);    // draw base
```

Do not overuse comments. It is not normal to comment every line, as this often involves duplicating information. The following is a poor comment:

```
paper.drawRect(0, 0, 100, 100);    // draw a rectangle
```

Here, the statement says clearly what it does, without the need for a comment. Use comments to state the overall theme of a section of program, rather than restating the detail of each statement. In Chapter 19 you will learn about additional commenting styles which assist in program documentation.

Programming principles

- Java has a large set of library methods we can call.

- The parameters which we pass to methods have the effect of controlling the shapes that are drawn.

Programming pitfalls

■ Take care with the punctuation. Commas, semicolons and round and curly brackets must be exactly as in the examples.

■ Capitalization must be exact. For example, `drawline` is wrong, whereas `drawLine` is correct.

Grammar spot

The order and type of parameters must be correct for each method.

New language elements

■ `( )` to enclose a list of parameters separated by commas.

■ If no parameters are required, we follow the method name with `()`.

■ `//` to indicate comments.

Summary

■ Programs can listen for events.

■ Responding to an event is known as 'handling' the event.

■ Statements are obeyed in sequence, top to bottom (unless we request otherwise).

■ The Java library has a set of 'draw' methods which you can call up to display graphics.

■ Graphics positioning is based on pixel coordinates.

■ Parameter values can be passed into methods.

● Exercises

In the following, we recommend that you do rough sketches and calculations prior to writing the program. Choose a suitable name for each program, starting with a capital letter, and containing no spaces or punctuation. Base your program on the `DrawExample` code, inserting new instructions within the `actionPerformed` method.

3.1 (a) Draw a square of size **100** pixels, **10** pixels in from the drawing area top and left-hand edge. Use **drawRect**.

(b) Perform the same task, but call **drawLine** four times.

3.2 Draw a triangle, with one vertical side.

3.3 Draw an empty Tic Tac Toe (noughts and crosses) board.

3.4 Design a simple house, and draw it.

3.5 Draw a colour palette, consisting of 13 small squares, each one containing a different colour.

3.6 Here are rainfall figures for the country of Xanadu:

```
1994     150 cm
1995     175 cm
1996     120 cm
```

(a) Represent the data by a series of horizontal lines.

(b) Instead of lines, use filled rectangles with different colours.

3.7 Design an archery-style target with concentric circles. Then add different colours.

Answers to self-test questions

3.1 Open the existing **DrawExample** program with an editor. Save it under the name **DrawCircle.java**. Change the three occurrences of **DrawExample** into **DrawCircle**, ensuring that the capitalization is correct. Finally we call the **drawOval** method with appropriate parameters, in the **actionPerformed** method. Here is the complete program:

```java
import java.awt.*;
import java.awt.event.*;
import javax.swing.*;

public class DrawCircle extends JFrame
    implements ActionListener {

    private JButton button;
    private JPanel panel;

    public static void main(String[] args) {
        DrawCircle frame = new DrawCircle();
        frame.setSize(400, 300);
        frame.createGUI();
        frame.show();
    }
```

▶ *Answers to self-test questions continued*

```
private void createGUI() {
    setDefaultCloseOperation(EXIT_ON_CLOSE);
    Container window = getContentPane();
    window.setLayout(new FlowLayout() );

    panel = new JPanel();
    panel.setPreferredSize(new Dimension(300, 200));
    panel.setBackground(Color.white);
    window.add(panel);

    button = new JButton("Press me");
    window.add(button);
    button.addActionListener(this);
}

public void actionPerformed(ActionEvent event) {
    Graphics paper = panel.getGraphics();
    paper.drawOval(0, 0, 100, 100);
}
}
```

3.2
```
paper.drawLine(20, 20, 120, 20);
paper.drawLine(70, 20, 70, 120);
```

CHAPTER 4

Variables and calculations

This chapter explains:

- the types of numeric variables;
- how to declare variables and constants;
- the assignment statement;
- arithmetic operators;
- the use of message and input dialogs for input and output;
- the essentials of strings.

● Introduction

Numbers of one type or another occur in most programs: for example, drawing pictures using screen coordinates, controlling spaceflight trajectories, calculating salaries and tax deductions.

Here we will introduce the two basic types of number:

- whole numbers, known as integers in mathematics and as the **int** type in Java;
- 'decimal-point' numbers, known as 'real' in mathematics, and as **double** in Java. The general term for decimal-point numbers in computing is *floating-point numbers*.

Previously we used values to produce screen graphics, but for more sophisticated programs we need to introduce the concept of a variable – a kind of storage box used to remember values, so that these values can be used or altered later in the program.

There are undeniably some `int` situations:

- the number of students in a class;
- the number of pixels on a screen;
- the number of copies of this book sold so far.

And there are some undeniable `double` situations:

- my height in metres;
- the mass of an atom in grams;
- the average of the integers 3 and 4.

However, sometimes the type is not obvious; consider a variable for holding an exam mark – `double` or `int`? The answer is that you don't know yet – you must seek further clarification, e.g. by asking the marker if they mark to the nearest whole number, or if they ever use decimal places. Thus, the choice of `int` or `double` is determined by the problem.

The nature of `int`

When we use an `int` in Java, it can be a whole number in the range −2147483648 to +2147483647 or, approximately −2000000000 to +2000000000.

All `int` calculations are accurate, in the sense that all the information in the number is preserved exactly.

The nature of `double`

When we use a `double` number in Java, its value can be between -1.79×10^{308} and $+1.79 \times 10^{308}$.

In less mathematical terms, the largest value is 179 followed by 306 zeros – very large indeed! Numbers are held to an approximate accuracy of 15 digits.

The main point about `double` quantities is that they are stored approximately in many cases. Try this on a calculator:

```
7 / 3
```

Using seven digits (for example), the answer is 2.333333, whereas we know that a closer answer is:

```
2.33333333333333333
```

Even this is not the exact answer!

In short, because `double` quantities are stored in a limited number of digits, small errors can build up at the least significant end. For many calculations (e.g. exam marks) this is not important, but for calculations involving, say, the design of a space shuttle, it might be. However, **double** has such a large range and digits of precision that calculations involving everyday quantities will be accurate enough.

Writing very large (or very small) **double** values might require long sequences of zeros. To simplify this we can use 'scientific' or 'exponent' notation with **e** or **E**, as in:

```
double bigValue = 12.3E+23;
```

which stands for 12.3 multiplied by 10^{+23}. This feature is mainly used in mathematical or scientific programs.

Declaring variables

Once the type of our variables has been chosen, we need to name them. We can imagine them as storage boxes with a name on the outside and a number (value) inside. The value may change as the program works through its sequence of operations, but the name is fixed. The programmer is free to choose the names, and we recommend choosing meaningful ones rather than cryptic ones. But, as in most programming languages, there are certain rules that must be followed. In Java, names:

- must start with a letter (A to Z, a to z) or (unusually) an underscore '_';
- can contain any number of letters or digits (a digit is 0 to 9);
- can contain the underscore '_';
- can be up to 255 characters long.

Note that Java is case sensitive. The 'case' of a letter can be upper (capital) or lower. In Java, the case of a letter matters. For example, once you have declared **width**, you cannot refer to it as **Width** or **WIDTH**, because the case of the letters is different.

Those are the Java rules – and we have to obey the rules. But there is also a Java style – a way of using the rules which is followed when a variable consists of several words. The rules do not allow spaces in names, so rather than use short names or the underscore, the accepted style for variables is to capitalize the start of each word within a name.

There is another style guideline regarding whether or not the first letter of a name is capitalized. All variables should start with a lower-case letter, whereas class names (as we will see later) normally start with a capital letter. Thus, rather than:

```
Heightofbox
h
hob
height_of_box
```

we put:

```
heightOfBox
```

Here are some allowed names:

```
amount
x
pay2003
```

and here are some unallowable (illegal) names:

```
2001pay
%area
my age
```

Note that there are also some reserved names that Java uses and which can't be reused by the programmer. They are termed *keywords* in Java. You have seen some of them, such as:

```
private
new
int
```

A full list is provided in Appendix F.

SELF-TEST QUESTION

4.1 Which of the following variable names are allowed in Java, and which have the correct style?

```
volume
AREA
Length
3sides
side1
lenth
Mysalary
your salary
screenSize
```

Here is an example program, named **AreaCalculation**, which we will study in detail. It calculates the area of a rectangle. We have assumed that its sides are **int** quantities. The result is displayed in a message dialog.

```
import java.awt.*;
import java.awt.event.*;
import javax.swing.*;

public class AreaCalculation extends JFrame
    implements ActionListener {

    private JButton button;

    public static void main(String[] args) {
        AreaCalculation frame = new AreaCalculation();
        frame.setSize(400, 300);
        frame.createGUI();
        frame.show();
    }
```

```
private void createGUI() {
    setDefaultCloseOperation(EXIT_ON_CLOSE);
    Container window = getContentPane();
    window.setLayout(new FlowLayout() );

    button = new JButton("Press me");
    window.add(button);
    button.addActionListener(this);
}

public void actionPerformed(ActionEvent event) {
    int area;
    int length;
    int width;
    length = 20;
    width = 10;
    area = length * width;
    JOptionPane.showMessageDialog(null,"Area is: " + area);
}
}
```

Figure 4.1 shows the window, and the message dialog that pops up when the program runs.

Figure 4.1 Screenshot of **AreaCalculation** output, showing window and message dialog.

For our purposes here, the program falls into two parts. The first part is responsible for creating a window containing a single button. This will be standard for all the programs in this chapter. The part we will examine in detail is headed:

```
public void actionPerformed(ActionEvent event) {
```

This section will be executed whenever the user clicks the button. In fact, such a section is known as a *method*, and we must place our instructions between the opening and closing curly brackets – the 'braces' of the method.

In the program we have used three `int` variables, which eventually will hold our rectangle data. Recall that we can choose whatever names we like, but have opted for clear names rather than single-letter or funny names. (Funny names are only funny the first time you see them!)

Now that names are chosen, we must declare them to the Java system. Though this seems like tedious red tape at first, the point of introducing them is to enable the compiler to spot misspellings lower down the program. Here are the declarations:

```
int area;
int length;
int width;
```

We declare variables by preceding our chosen name by the type we require. (We used `int` above, so each variable will contain a whole number.)

Alternatively, we could have put:

```
int length, width, area;
```

using commas to separate each name. The style is up to you, but we have a preference for the first style, which enables you to comment each name if you need to. If you use the second style, only use it to group related names. For example, put:

```
int pictureHeight, pictureWidth;
int myAge;
```

rather than:

```
int pictureHeight, pictureWidth, myAge;
```

In the majority of programs we will use several types, and in Java we are free to intermingle the declarations, as in:

```
double personHeight;
int examMark;
double salary;
```

Additionally, we can choose to initialize the value of the variable as we declare it, as in:

```
double personHeight = 1.68;
int a = 3, b = 4;
int examMark = 65;
int betterMark = examMark + 10;
```

This is good style, but use it only when you really know the initial value. If you don't supply an initial value for variables declared within a method, Java views variables as being uninitialized and a compilation error will inform you about it if you try to use its value.

The assignment statement

Once we have declared our variables, we can place new values in them by means of the 'assignment statement', as in:

```
length = 20;
```

Pictorially, we can imagine the process as in Figure 4.2. We say: 'the value 20 has been assigned to the variable **length**' or '**length** becomes 20'.

Note:

- The movement of data is from the right of the = to the left.
- Whatever value was in **length** before is now 'overwritten' by 20. Variables have only one value – the current one. And just to give you a flavour of the speed: an assignment takes less than one-millionth of a second.

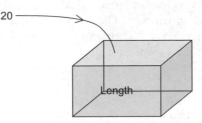

Figure 4.2 Assigning a value to a variable.

SELF-TEST QUESTION

4.2 Explain the problem with this fragment of code:

```
int a, b;
a = b;
b = 1;
```

Calculations and operators

Recall our rectangle program, which included the statement:

```
area = length * width;
```

The general form of the assignment statement is:

```
variable = expression;
```

An expression can take several forms: for example, a single number or a calculation. In our specific example, the sequence of events is:

1. `*` causes multiplication of the values stored in `length` and `width`, resulting in the value 200.

2. The equals symbol `=` causes the 200 to be assigned to (stored in) `area`.

The `*` is one of several 'operators' (so called because they operate on values) and, just as in mathematics, there are rules for their use.

An understanding of the movement of data is important, and enables us to understand the meaning of code such as:

```
int n = 10;
n = n + 1;
```

What happens is that the right-hand side of the `=` is calculated using the current value of `n`, resulting in `11`. This value is then stored in `n`, replacing the old value of `10`.

Years ago a large number of programs were studied, and statements of the form:

```
something = something + 1;
```

were found to be the most common instructions! In fact, Java has a shorthand version of this so-called *increment* instruction. The `++` and `--` operators perform incrementing and decrementing (subtracting 1). Their most frequent use is in loops (Chapter 8). Here is one way of using the `++` operator:

```
n = 3;
n++;       // n is now 4
```

The main point about `=` is that it does not mean 'is equal to' in the algebraic sense. You should imagine it as meaning 'becomes' or 'gets'.

● The arithmetic operators

Here we present a basic set of operators – the arithmetic ones, akin to the buttons on your calculator. By the way, in this context, we pronounce the adjective 'arithmetic' as 'arithMETic'.

Operator	Meaning
`*`	multiply
`/`	divide
`%`	modulo
`+`	add
`-`	subtract

Note that we have split the operators into groups, to indicate their 'precedence' – the order in which they are obeyed. Thus, `*`, `/` and `%` are carried out before `+` and `-`. We

can also use parentheses (brackets) to group calculations and force them to be calculated first. If a calculation involves operators of the same precedence, the calculation
is performed from left to right. Here are some examples:

```
int i;
int n = 3;
double d;
i = n + 3;              // set to 6
i = n * 4;              // set to 12
i = 7 + 2 * 4;          // set to 15
n = n * (n + 2) * 4;    // set to 60
d = 3.5 / 2;            // set to 1.75
n = 7 / 4;              // set to 1
```

Recall that the instructions form a sequence, executed from top to bottom of the page.
Wherever brackets are used, the items within them are calculated first. Multiply and
divide are performed before add and subtract. Thus:

```
3 + 2 * 4
```

is performed as if it had been written:

```
3 + (2 * 4)
```

We will explain the details of / and % below.

As a matter of style, note that we type a space before and after an operator. This is
not essential, in the sense that the program will still run if the spaces are omitted. We
use the spaces to make the program more readable to the programmer. Also, lines can
become too long for the screen. Here, we insert a new line at a convenient part (though
not in the middle of a name) and indent the second part of the line.

SELF-TEST QUESTION

4.3   In the following, what are the values of the variables after each statement?

```
int a, b, c, d;
d = -8;
a = 1 * 2 + 3;
b = 1 + 2 * 3;
c = (1 + 2) * 3;
c = a + b;
d = -d;
```

Now we know the rules. But there are still pitfalls for the beginner. Let us look
at some mathematical formulae, and their conversion into Java. We assume that all
variables have been declared as doubles, and initialized.

Mathematics version	Java version
1 $y = mx + c$	`y = m * x + c;`
2 $x = (a - b)(a + b)$	`x = (a - b) * (a + b);`
3 $y = 3[(a - b)(a + b)] - x$	`y = 3 * ((a - b)*( a + b)) - x;`
4 $y = 1 - \dfrac{2a}{3b}$	`y = 1 - (2 * a) / (3 * b);`

In example 1, we insert the multiply symbol. In Java, **mx** would be treated as one variable name.

In example 2, we need an explicit multiply between the brackets.

In example 3, we replace the mathematics square brackets by brackets.

In example 4, we might have gone for this incorrect version:

```
y = 1 - 2 * a / 3 * b
```

Recall the left-to-right rule for equal precedence operators. The problem is to do with ***** and **/**. The order of evaluation is as if we had put:

```
y = 1 - (2 * a / 3) * b
```

i.e. the **b** is now multiplying instead of dividing. The simplest way to handle potentially confusing calculations is to use extra brackets – there is no penalty in terms of program size or speed.

The use of **+**, **-** and ***** is reasonably intuitive, but division is slightly trickier, as we need to distinguish between **int** and **double** types. Here are the essential points:

■ When **/** works on two doubles, or a mixture of **double** and **int**, a double result is produced. Behind the scenes, any **int** values are regarded as **double** for the purposes of the calculation. This is how dividing works on a pocket calculator.

■ When **/** works on two integers, an integer result is produced. The result is truncated, meaning that any 'decimal point' digits are erased. This is **not** how a calculator works.

Here are some examples:

```
// double division
double d;
d = 7.61 / 2.1;      // set to 3.62
d = 10.6 / 2;        // set to 5.3
```

In the first case, the division takes place as you would expect. In the second case, the number **2** is treated as **2.0** (i.e. a **double**), and the division proceeds.

However, integer division is different:

```
/integer division
int i;
i = 10 / 5;          // set to 2
i = 13 / 5;          // set to 2
i = 33 / 44;         // set to 0
```

In the first case, the division with integers is as expected. The exact answer of 2 is produced. In the second case, the result is **2**, due to truncation. In the third case, the 'proper' answer of 0.75 is truncated, giving 0.

SELF-TEST QUESTIONS

4.4 My salary is $20000, and I agree to give you half using the following calculation:

```
int half = 20000 * (1 / 2);
```

How much do you get?

4.5 State the values that end up in **a**, **b**, **c** and **d**, after these calculations are performed:

```
int a, b, c, d;
a = 7 / 3;
b = a * 4;
c = (a + 1) / 2;
d = c / 3;
```

The % operator

Finally, we look at the **%** (modulo) operator. It is often used in conjunction with integer division, as it supplies the remainder part. Its name comes from the term 'modulo' used in a branch of mathematics known as modular arithmetic.

Earlier, we said that **double** values are stored approximately, and integers are stored exactly. So how can it be that 3/4 gives an integer result of 0? Surely losing the 0.75 means that the calculation is not accurate? The answer is that integers **do** operate exactly, but the exact answer is composed of two parts: the quotient (i.e. the main answer) and the remainder. Thus 4 divided by 3 gives an answer of 1, with remainder 1. This is more exact than 1.3333333 etc.

So, the **%** operator gives us the remainder, as if a division had taken place. Here are some examples:

```
int i;
double d;
i = 12 % 4;        // set to 0
i = 13 % 4;        // set to 1
i = 15 % 4;        // set to 3
d = 14.9 % 3.9;    // set to 3.2 (divides 3 times)
```

As a minor point of interest, note that **%** works with **double** as well, though by far the most frequent use of **%** is with **int** types. Here is a problem involving a remainder:

convert a whole number of cents into two quantities – the number of dollars and the number of cents remaining. The solution is:

```
int cents = 234;
int dollars, centsRemaining;
dollars = cents / 100;          // set to 2
centsRemaining = cents % 100;   // set to 34
```

SELF-TEST QUESTION

4.6   Complete the following, adding assignment statements to split `totalSeconds` into two variables: `minutes` and `seconds`.

```
int totalSeconds = 307;
```

● Joining strings with the + operator

So far we have looked at the use of numeric variables, but the processing of text data is also highly important. Java provides the `String` data type, and `String` variables can hold any characters. Here is an example of using strings:

```
String firstName = "Mike ";
String lastName, wholeName;
String greeting;
lastName = "Parr";
wholeName = firstName + lastName;
greeting = "Hi from " + wholeName;    // set to "Hi from Mike Parr"
```

In the above, we have declared some `String` variables, providing some initial values using double quotes. Note the capital `S` in `String`.

We then used assignment, in which the value of the string to the right of the = is stored in the variable used on the left of the =, in a similar manner to numeric assignment.

The next lines illustrate the use of the + operator, which (as well as adding numbers) works on strings by joining them end to end. This is known as 'concatenation'. After the statement:

```
wholeName = firstName + lastName;
```

the value of `wholeName` is `Mike Parr`.

In addition, there is a wide range of string methods which provide such operations as searching and modifying strings. We consider these in Chapter 15.

Earlier, we mentioned that the / operator regarded the items it is dividing as `double` items if one of them was a `double`. The + operator works in a similar way with strings. Here is an example:

```
int i = 7;
String name = "th Avenue";
String s = i + name;
```

Here, the **+** operator detects that **name** is a string, and converts **i** into a string prior to joining them. This is a convenient shorthand, avoiding the explicit conversion we cover below. But it can be misleading. Consider this code:

```
int i = 2, j = 3;
String s, note = "Answer is: ";
s = note + i + j;
```

What is the value of **s**? The two possibilities are:

- **Answer is: 23**, where both **+** operators work on strings.

- **Answer is: 5**, where the second **+** adds numbers.

In fact, the first case happens. Java works from left to right. The first **+** produces the string **"Answer is: 2"**. Then the second **+** joins **3** onto the end. However, if we put:

```
s = note + (i + j);
```

then **2 + 3** is calculated first, giving **5**. Finally, the string joining takes place.

However, most cases are simple, as in our area program:

```
JOptionPane.showMessageDialog(null,"Area is: " + area);
```

The message dialog (introduced in Chapter 2) can display a string. In the above, it is made up of a string in quotes joined to the string representing an integer. Alternatively, we can choose to make the conversion explicit, using a **toString** method shown below.

SELF-TEST QUESTION

4.7 Message dialogs can display a string. What do the following message dialogs display?

```
JOptionPane.showMessageDialog(null,
                       "5" + "5" + 5 + 5);
JOptionPane.showMessageDialog(null,
                       "5" + "5" + (5 + 5));
```

● Converting between strings and numbers

One crucial use of the **String** data type is in input and output, where we process data entered by a user, and display results on the screen. Many of Java's GUI classes work with strings of characters rather than numbers, so we need to know how to convert between numbers and strings.

To convert a numeric variable or calculation (in general an expression) into a string, we can use the **toString** methods of the **Integer** and **Double** classes. Here are some examples:

```
String s1, s2;
int num = 44;
double d = 1.234;
s1 = Integer.toString(num);    // s1 is "44"
s2 = Double.toString(d);       // s2 is "1.234"
```

Normally, a method name (such as **toString**) is preceded by an object for the method to work on, but here we supply a class name (**Integer** or **Double**). Methods which work in this way are termed **static**, and when we use them, we must identify the class they are contained in. The **Double** and **Integer** classes contain extra facilities for **double** and **int** types. Note that – as always – class names begin with a capital letter. Static methods are covered in Chapter 9.

To convert strings into numbers, we use the 'parse' methods of the **Double** and **Integer** classes. The term 'parse' is used in the sense of scanning along some text to examine it. Unlike the methods which we used in Chapter 2 (such as **drawLine**), these methods return a value when they are called, and we can store the returned value in a variable, or use it in some other way. Here are some examples showing how a string can be converted into an **int** or a **double**:

```
int i;
double d;
String s1 = "1234";
String s2 = "1.23";
i = Integer.parseInt(s1);
d = Double.parseDouble(s2);
```

The **parseInt** and **parseDouble** methods require one parameter, which must be of type **String**. We might provide a string in quotes, a string variable or a string expression.

As we will see later, the string may have been typed in by a user, and therefore could contain characters that are not allowed in numbers. The **parseInt** and **parseDouble** methods will detect such errors, and the program will terminate. In Chapter 16, we will see how a program can detect such errors ('exceptions') and can ask the user to re-enter a number. For now, we will assume that the user will always enter correct data.

SELF-TEST QUESTION

4.8   In the following code, what are the final values of **m**, **n** and **s**?

```
int m, n;
String s;
String v = "3";
m = Integer.parseInt(v + v + "4");
n = Integer.parseInt(v + v) + 4;
s = Integer.toString(Integer.parseInt(v)
    + Integer.parseInt(v)) + "4";
```

Message dialogs and input dialogs

Here we will look at dialogs in more detail. In our program which calculated the area of a rectangle, we made use of a message dialog to display the value of the area. This value must be in the form of a string. Rather than just displaying the number, we joined it to a message:

```
JOptionPane.showMessageDialog(null, "Area is: " + area);
```

Recall our previous discussion of + when applied to a string and a number: the number is automatically converted to a string, so we don't need to use **toString**. However, we could have converted it explicitly, as in:

```
int n = 33;
JOptionPane.showMessageDialog(null,
            "n is: " + Integer.toString(n));
```

Sometimes we might need to display the number without any accompanying text. Note that the following will not compile, because the **showMessageDialog** method expects a **String** as a parameter:

```
JOptionPane.showMessageDialog(null, area); // NO - will not compile!
```

Instead, you must put:

```
JOptionPane.showMessageDialog(null, Integer.toString(area));
```

Incidentally, the first parameter for a message dialog will always be **null** in our examples. This Java keyword causes the dialog to be positioned in the centre of the screen. Alternatively we can place the dialog over a particular window, but do not show this possibility here.

The **JOptionPane** class also provides an input dialog, which allows the user to type in a string. Here are some examples:

```
String firstName, lastName;
firstName = JOptionPane.showInputDialog(
                    "Enter your first name");
lastName = JOptionPane.showInputDialog(
                    "Enter your last name");
```

The single parameter of the **showInputDialog** method is a prompt, which is used to inform the user about the data that is required. When 'OK' is clicked, the string is returned to the program, where it can be assigned to a variable.

Let us return to our area program. In reality, it is unlikely that we will know the dimensions of the rectangle when we write the program. We will amend the program so that the program requests the dimensions as it runs. Here is the revised program, and the screenshot of the first input dialog is shown in Figure 4.3:

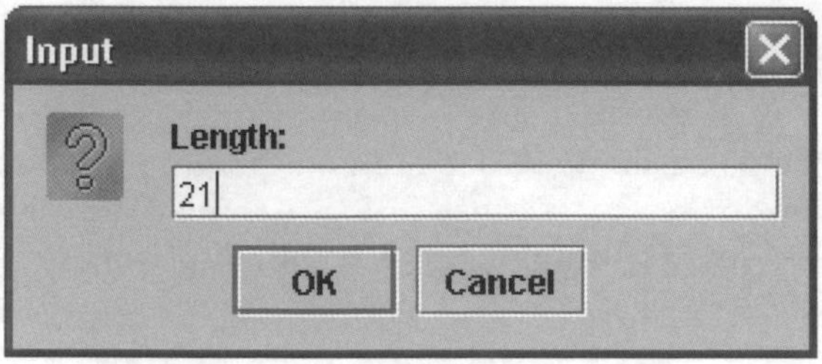

Figure 4.3 Screenshot of an input dialog from the **AreaDialogs** program.

```java
import java.awt.*;
import java.awt.event.*;
import javax.swing.*;
public class AreaDialogs extends JFrame
    implements ActionListener {

    private JButton button;

    public static void main(String[] args) {
        AreaDialogs frame = new AreaDialogs();
        frame.setSize(400, 300);
        frame.createGUI();
        frame.show();
    }

    private void createGUI() {
        setDefaultCloseOperation(EXIT_ON_CLOSE);
        Container window = getContentPane();
        window.setLayout(new FlowLayout() );

        button = new JButton("Press me");
        window.add(button);
        button.addActionListener(this);
    }

    public void actionPerformed(ActionEvent event) {
        int area;
        int length;
        int width;
        String lengthString;
        String widthString;
        lengthString = JOptionPane.showInputDialog("Length:");
        length = Integer.parseInt(lengthString);
        widthString = JOptionPane.showInputDialog("Width:");
        width = Integer.parseInt(widthString);
        area = length * width;
        JOptionPane.showMessageDialog(null, "Area is: " + area);
    }
}
```

Recall that input dialogs provide the program with strings, which must be converted to integers with the **parseInt** method.

● Formatting text in dialogs with \n

When displaying text, we often want to display it as several short lines, rather than one long line. To do this, we use a special pair of characters: the 'backslash' character, followed by an **n**. This combination, often referred to as a newline, breaks up the line. The **\n** should be used as part of the message, between quotes. Here is an example. The program is named **DollarsDialogs**, which displays the results from breaking up a number of cents into whole dollars and cents remaining. We only show the **actionPerformed** method. Note the output in Figure 4.4, and match it up to the use of **\n** in the message dialog.

```
public void actionPerformed(ActionEvent event) {
        int totalCents;
        int dollars;
        int centsRemaining;
        String totalCentsString;

        totalCentsString = JOptionPane.showInputDialog(
            "Enter your amount, in cents");
        totalCents = Integer.parseInt(totalCentsString);
        dollars = totalCents / 100;
        centsRemaining = totalCents % 100;
        JOptionPane.showMessageDialog(null,
            totalCentsString + " cents breaks down into:\n" +
            dollars + " dollars\n" +
            centsRemaining + " cents.");
    }
```

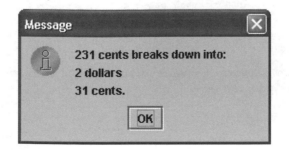

Figure 4.4 Output from the **DollarsDialogs** program.

● Converting between numbers

Sometimes, we need to convert numeric values from one type to another. The most common cases are converting an `int` to a `double`, and a `double` to an `int`.

Here is an example: we have nine apples, and we want to share them equally between four people. Clearly the values 9 and 4 are integers, but the answer is a `double` value. A knowledge of numeric conversion will help us to solve this problem.

Before we provide the answer, here are some examples of conversion:

```
int i = 33;
double d = 3.9;
double d1;
d1 = i;                 // set to 33.0
// or, explicitly:
d1 = (double)i;         // set to 33.0
i = (int)d;             // set to 3
```

The main points are:

■ Assigning an `int` to a `double` works without any additional programming. This is safe, as no information can be lost – there are no decimal places to worry about.

■ Assigning a `double` to an `int` may result in the loss of decimal places, which cannot fit into the integer. Because of this potential loss of information, Java requires that we explicitly acknowledge this by making use of *casting*. (We will also use this feature when discussing the more advanced features of object-oriented programming.)

■ To cast a `double` in the form of an `int`, we precede it with `(int)`. The value is truncated, removing any decimal places.

■ Note that we could use explicit casting when converting an `int` to a `double`, but this is not necessary.

Returning to our apple example, we can obtain a `double` answer by:

```
int apples = 9;    // or fetch value from a text box
int people = 4;    // or fetch value from a text box
JOptionPane.showMessageDialog(null, "A person gets: " +
    Double.toString((double)apples / (double)people));
```

Note that `(double)(apples / people)` would give the wrong answer, as an integer divide is performed prior to casting.

SELF-TEST QUESTION

4.9 What are the values of **a**, **b**, **c**, **i**, **j**, **k** after the following code is executed?

```
int i, j, k;
double a, b, c;
int n = 3;
double y = 2.7;
i = (int)y;
j = (int)(y + 0.6);
k = (int)((double)n + 0.2);
a = n;
b = (int)n;
c = (int)y;
```

● Constants: using `final`

So far, we have used variables, i.e. items whose value changes as the program runs. But sometimes we have values which never change. Here is an example:

```
double miles, km = 4.7;
miles = km * 0.6214;
```

The meaning of this line is not clear. What does **0.6214** stand for? In fact, it is the number of miles in a kilometre, and this value never changes.

Here is how we can rewrite the program, using the **final** keyword of Java:

```
final double milesPerKm = 0.6214;
double miles, km = 4.7;
miles = km * milesPerKm;
```

The word **final** states that the specified variable now has its final fixed value, which cannot change as the program runs. In other words, **milesPerKm** is a constant. Constants can be **double**, **int**, **String** or **boolean**.

Note that some programmers use capitals for constants (such as **MILESPERKM**) so that they can be clearly distinguished from variables.

If you write code (intentionally or accidentally) to alter the item, a compilation error occurs, as in:

```
milesPerKm = 2.1;    // compilation error
```

As well as declaring your own constants, the Java libraries also provide mathematical constants. For example, the **Math** class provides a value for *pi*, which can be used in this way:

```
double radius = 1.4, circumference;
circumference = 2 * Math.PI * radius;
```

The benefits of using constants are:

■ The program becomes more readable, with the use of names rather than numbers.

■ The use of constants minimizes typing errors, because repeated use of a long number in a program is error prone. For example, we might make a typing error and enter 0.6124 instead of 0.6214. Such errors are hard to spot. If we mis-type `milesPerKm` as `milesBerKm`, a compilation error is produced, and the spelling can be corrected.

SELF-TEST QUESTION

4.10   There are 2.54 cm in an inch. Declare a constant named `cmPerInch`, with the correct value. Show how it might be used in a calculation to convert inches to cm.

● The role of expressions

Though we have emphasized that expressions (calculations) can form the right-hand side of assignment statements, they can occur in other places. In fact, we can place an `int` expression anywhere we can place a single `int`. Recall our use of the `drawLine` method, which has four integers specifying the start and end of the line. We could (if it was useful) replace the numbers with variables, or with expressions:

```
int x = 100;
int y = 200;
paper.drawLine(100, 100, 110, 110);
paper.drawLine(x, y, x + 50, y + 50);
paper.drawLine(x * 2, y - 8, x * 30 - 1, y * 3 + 6);
```

The expressions are calculated, and the resulting values are passed into `drawLine` for it to make use of.

Here is another example. The `parseInt` method requires a string parameter, and the input dialog returns a string. We can combine these in one statement, as in:

```
int age;
age = Integer.parseInt(JOptionPane.showInputDialog(null,
                            "Enter age"));
```

In the above, we did not need to invent a temporary string variable to convey a string value from the input dialog to `parseInt`.

Programming principles

- A variable has a name, which the programmer chooses.

- A variable has a type, which the programmer chooses.

- A variable holds a value.

- The value of a variable can be changed with an assignment statement.

- Constants provide unchanging values. They can be given a meaningful name.

Programming pitfalls

- Take care with the spelling of variable names. For example, in:

  ```
  int circle;    // mis-spelling
  circle = 20;
  ```

  there is a misspelling of a variable, using a '1' (one) instead of a lower-case 'L'. The Java compiler will complain about the second spelling being undeclared. Another favourite error is using a zero instead of a capital 'O'.

- Compilation errors are tricky to spot at the beginning. Though the Java compiler gives an indication of where it thinks the error is, the actual error could be in a previous line.

- Brackets must balance – there must be the same number of '(' as ')'.

- When using numbers via message dialogs, remember to use the string conversion facilities, or to join the number to a string.

- When multiplying items, you must place * between them, whereas in mathematics it is omitted. When dividing items, remember that:

  - `int / int` gives an `int` answer.
  - `double / double` gives a `double` answer.
  - `int / double` and `double / int` give a `double` answer.

Grammar spot

- We declare variables by stating their type and their name, as in:

  ```
  int myVariable;
  String yourVariable = "Hello there!";
  ```

- The most useful types are `int`, `double` and `String`.

- The main arithmetic operators are `*`, `/`, `%`, `+`, `-`.

- The `+` operator is used to join strings.

- The `++` and `--` operators can be used for incrementing and decrementing.

- We can convert numbers to strings with the `Integer.toString` and the `Double.toString` methods.

- We can convert strings to numbers with the `Integer.parseInt` and the `Double.parseDouble` methods.

- Preceding a `double` item with the `(int)` cast converts it to an integer.

- Preceding an `int` item with the `(double)` cast converts it to a double value.

New language elements

- `int`, `double` and `String`;

- the operators `+`, `-`, `*`, `/`, `%`;

- `++` and `--` for increment and decrement;

- `=` for assignment;

- `final` for constants;

- type conversion: the `Integer` and `Double` classes, the `(double)` and `(int)` casts;

- the `JOptionPane` class, and its `showMessageDialog` and `showInputDialog` methods;

- the use of `\n` to represent a newline in a string.

Summary

- Variables are used to hold (store) values. They keep their value until explicitly changed (e.g. by another assignment statement).

- Operators operate on values.

- An expression is a calculation which produces a value. It can be used in a variety of situations, including the right-hand side of an assignment, and as a parameter of a method call.

Exercises

In these exercises, choose a new class name for each program, but base them all on the **AreaCalculation** program. Use message dialogs for output and input dialogs for input.

4.1 Write a program to compute the volume of a box, given its three dimensions.

4.2 Using the following value:

```
double radius = 7.5;
```

use assignment statements to calculate the circumference of a circle, the area of a circle and the volume of a sphere, based on the same radius. Display the results with message dialogs. The message should state what the result is, rather than merely displaying a number. Use **Math.PI**, as in:

```
volume = (4 * Math.PI / 3) * radius * radius * radius;
```

4.3 Write a program which inputs three integer exam marks, and which displays the mean (average) mark as a **double** value. Check your answer with a calculator.

4.4 Write a program which inputs three **double** exam marks, and which displays the mean (average) mark as a **double** value. Check your answer with a calculator.

4.5 Assume that individuals are taxed at 20% of their income. Obtain an income value via an input dialog, then calculate and display the initial amount, the amount after deductions and the deducted amount. Ensure that your output is easily understandable. Modify your program to use a **final** constant for the tax rate.

4.6 Using **int** types, write a program which converts a Fahrenheit temperature to its Celsius (centigrade) equivalent. The formula is:

```
c = (f - 32) * 5 / 9
```

4.7 Write a program which inputs a whole number of seconds, then converts this to hours, minutes and seconds. For example, 3669 seconds should result in a message dialog showing:

```
H:1 M:1 S:9
```

4.8 This problem is to do with electrical resistors, which 'resist' the flow of electrical current through them. An analogy is a hosepipe – a thin one has a high resistance and a thick one has a low resistance to water. We can imagine connecting two hosepipes in series, resulting in a higher resistance, or in parallel, reducing the resistance (effectively, a fatter pipe). Calculate and display the series resistance, given by:

$$series = r_1 + r_2$$

and the parallel resistance, given by:

$$parallel = \frac{r_1 \times r_2}{r_1 + r_2}$$

Input values for r_1 and r_2.

4.9 We require some software for installation in a European drink-dispensing machine. Here are the details: all items cost less than 1 euro (100 euro cents), and a 1 euro coin is the highest value that can be inserted. Given the amount inserted and the cost of the item, your program should give change, using the lowest number of coins. For example, if an item cost 45 cents and we paid with 100 cents, the result should be a series of message dialogs (one for each coin) of the form:

```
Number of 50 cent coins is 1
Number of 20 cent coins is 0
Number of 10 cent coins is 0
Number of 5 cent coins is 1
Number of 2 cent coins is 0
Number of 1 cent coins is 0
```

Hint: work in cents, and make extensive use of the **%** operator. The euro coins are:

100, 50, 20, 10, 5, 2, 1.

Answers to self-test questions

4.1 **volume** – allowed, correct style

AREA – allowed, but area preferred

Length – allowed, but lower-case 'l' preferred

3sides – not allowed, starts with a digit

side1 – allowed, correct style

lenth – allowed, even with incorrect spelling of length

Mysalary – allowed, but **mySalary** preferred

your salary – not allowed (no spaces allowed in middle of a name)

screenSize – allowed, correct style

4.2 At line 2, **b** is uninitialized. A compilation error will result because we are trying to store an uninitialized variable in **a**.

4.3 The final values of **a**, **b**, **c**, **d** are **5**, **7**, **12**, **8**.

4.4 Unfortunately, you get zero, as **(1 / 2)** is calculated first, resulting in 0. Multiply by 0.5 instead.

4.5 The final values of **a**, **b**, **c**, **d** are **2**, **8**, **1**, **0**.

4.6
```
int totalSeconds = 307;
int seconds, minutes;
minutes = totalSeconds / 60;
seconds = totalSeconds % 60;
```

4.7 The message dialogs display the strings **5555** and **5510** respectively.

In the first case, we proceed from left to right, joining strings. In the second case, the brackets are performed first, resulting in the integer **10**. Then the string-joining takes over.

4.8 The final values of **m**, **n** and **s** are **334**, **37** and **64**.

4.9 The values of the **int** variables **i**, **j**, **k** are **2**, **3**, **3**, and the values of the **double** variables **a**, **b**, **c** are **3.0**, **3.0**, **2.0**.

4.10
```
final double cmPerInch = 2.54;
double cm, inches = 23.6;
cm = inches * cmPerInch;
```

CHAPTER 5

Methods and parameters

This chapter explains:

- how to write methods;
- how formal and actual parameters are used;
- passing parameters to methods;
- using **return** in methods;
- method overloading.

● Introduction

Large programs can be complex, with the result that they can be difficult to understand and debug. The most significant technique for reducing complexity is to split a program into (relatively) isolated sections. This allows us to focus on an isolated section without the distractions of the complete program. Furthermore, if the section has a name, we can 'call' or 'invoke' it (cause it to be used) merely by using this name. In a way, it enables us to think at a higher level. In Java, such sections are known as methods. We made extensive use of pre-written graphics methods to draw shapes on the screen in Chapter 3.

Recall the **drawRect** method, which we call with four parameters in this manner:

```
paper.drawRect(10, 20, 60, 60);
```

Firstly, the use of parameters – the items in brackets – allows us to control the size and position of the rectangle. This ensures that **drawRect** is flexible enough for a variety of circumstances. The parameters modify its actions.

Secondly, note that if **drawRect** did not exist, we could still produce a rectangle by using four calls of **drawLine**. Bundling up the four **drawLine** instructions inside a method known as **drawRect** would be a sensible idea – it enables the programmer to think at a higher level.

Writing your own methods

Here, we will introduce the concept of creating our own methods. Initially, we will choose a toy example for simplicity, then move on to a more practical example.

The Worldwide Cardboard Box Corporation has a logo which consists of three squares within one another, as in Figure 5.1. The corporation wishes to use this logo in several positions on the screen, as in Figure 5.2. Here is the code to draw two identical logos at positions (10, 20) and (100, 100):

```
// draw logo at top left
paper.drawRect(10, 20, 60, 60);
paper.drawRect(10, 20, 40, 40);
paper.drawRect(10, 20, 20, 20);

// draw logo at bottom right
paper.drawRect(100, 100, 60, 60);
paper.drawRect(100, 100, 40, 40);
paper.drawRect(100, 100, 20, 20);
```

Note that the squares are of size 20, 40 and 60 pixels, with all their top left corners at the same point. Look at the code, and note that the three instructions to draw one logo are basically repeated, apart from the position of the top left of the logo. We will bundle up these three instructions as a method, so that a logo can be drawn with one instruction.

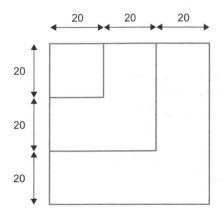

Figure 5.1 The company logo.

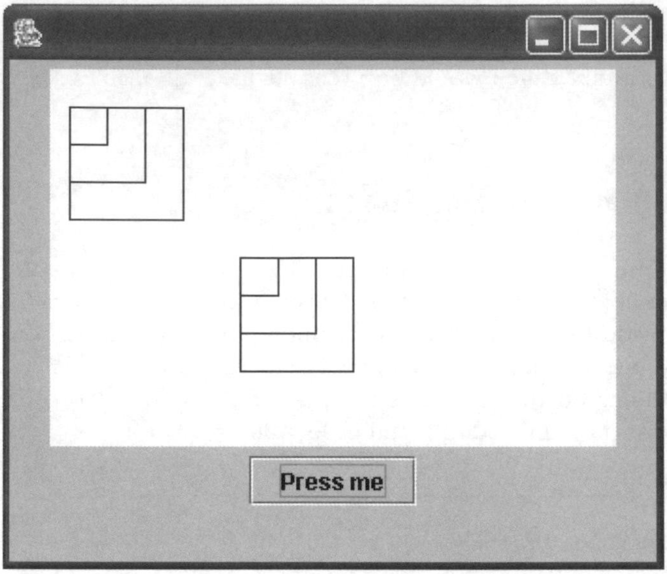

Figure 5.2 Screenshot of the `LogoMethod` program.

● A first method

Here is a complete program, named **LogoMethod**. It shows the creation and use of a method, which we chose to name as **drawLogo**. The Java style convention is to begin method names with a lower-case letter.

```java
import java.awt.*;
import java.awt.event.*;
import javax.swing.*;

public class LogoMethod extends JFrame
    implements ActionListener {

    private JButton button;
    private JPanel panel;

    public static void main(String[] args) {
        LogoMethod frame = new LogoMethod();
        frame.setSize(350, 300);
        frame.createGUI();
        frame.show();
    }
```

```
        private void createGUI() {
            setDefaultCloseOperation(EXIT_ON_CLOSE);
            Container window = getContentPane();
            window.setLayout(new FlowLayout() );

            panel = new JPanel();
            panel.setPreferredSize(new Dimension(300, 200));
            panel.setBackground(Color.white);
            window.add(panel);

            button = new JButton("Press me");
            window.add(button);
            button.addActionListener(this);
        }

        public void actionPerformed(ActionEvent event) {
            Graphics paper = panel.getGraphics();
            drawLogo(paper, 10, 20);
            drawLogo(paper, 100, 100);
        }

        private void drawLogo(Graphics drawingArea,
                              int xPos, int yPos) {
            drawingArea.drawRect(xPos, yPos, 60, 60);
            drawingArea.drawRect(xPos, yPos, 40, 40);
            drawingArea.drawRect(xPos, yPos, 20, 20);
        }
    }
```

The program has a panel for drawing, and a button. The user interface is identical to our drawing programs of Chapter 3. Clicking on the button causes two logos to be drawn, as in Figure 5.2.

The concept of methods and parameters is a major skill that all programmers need to master. We will now discuss the program in detail.

The overall form of the program is familiar – it has imports at the top, and a button which we click to initiate the drawing task. The **actionPerformed** part actually initiates the drawing. Look at the extract:

```
    private void drawLogo(Graphics drawingArea,
                          int xPos, int yPos) {
```

This declares (introduces) the method, and is known as the method header. It states the name of the method (which we had the freedom to choose) and the items that must be supplied to control its operation. Java uses the terms *actual parameters* and *formal parameters* in this area – we will examine them below. The rest of the method, enclosed in { }, is known as the *body*, and is where the work gets done. Often the header is a long line, and we may choose to split it up at suitable points (though not in the middle of a word).

A vital decision that the programmer must make is where can the method be called from. There are two main choices:

- The method can only be called from within the current program. In this case, we use the keyword `private`.

- The method can be called from another program. In this case, we use the keyword `public`. Methods such as `drawRect` are examples of methods which have been declared as `public` – they are intended for general use. (Creating public methods involves a deeper knowledge of object-oriented concepts, and we cover this in more detail in Chapter 9.)

Another decision for the programmer is:

- Will the method perform a task without the need to produce a result? In this case, we use the keyword `void` following `private`.

- Will the method calculate a result and return it to the section of code which called (invoked) it? In this case, we state the type of the result, instead of using `void`. This is covered later in the chapter.

In the `drawLogo` case, its task is to draw lines on the screen rather than supply an answer to a calculation. Here, we use `void`.

● Calling a method

In Java, we call a private method by stating its name, together with a list of parameters in brackets. In our program, the first call is:

```
drawLogo(paper, 10, 20);
```

This statement has two effects:

- The parameter values are automatically transferred into the method. We cover this in more detail below.

- The program jumps to the body of the method (the statements after the header), and executes the statements. When it runs out of statements and reaches the `}`, execution is continued back at the point where the method was called from.

The second call then takes place:

```
drawLogo(paper, 100, 100);
```

Figure 5.3 illustrates this. There are two calls, producing two logos.

● Passing parameters

It is essential to have an understanding of how parameters are transferred (i.e. passed) into methods. In our example, the concept is shown in the following lines:

```
drawLogo(paper, 10, 20);

private void drawLogo(Graphics drawingArea,
                      int xPos, int yPos) {
```

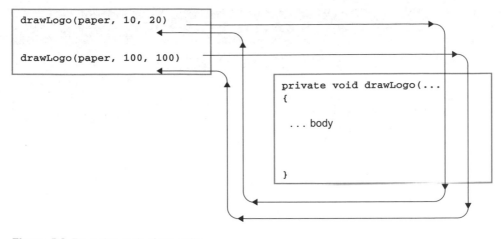

Figure 5.3 Execution path of two calls.

Figure 5.4 Transferring actual into formal parameters.

The area to focus on is the two lists of items in brackets. In a call, the items are termed *actual parameters*. In the header of the method, the items are termed *formal parameters*. To clarify the situation, we will extract the formal and actual parameters:

```
Actual parameters:  paper        10      20
Formal parameters:  drawingArea  xPos    yPos
```

Recall our likening of a variable to a box. Inside the method, a set of empty boxes (the parameters) awaits the transfer of parameter values. After the transfer, we have the situation shown in Figure 5.4. We don't have any numeric values to use for the passing of the drawing area, so focus on the passing of the coordinates.

The transfer takes place in a left-to-right order. The call must provide the correct number and type of parameters. If the caller (the user) accidentally gets parameters in the wrong order, the transfer process won't reorder them! When the **drawLogo** method executes, the above values control the drawing process. Though we have called the method with numbers, we can use expressions (i.e. involving variables and calculations), as in:

```
int x = 6;
drawLogo(paper, 20 + 3, 3 * 2 + 1); // 23 and 7
drawLogo(paper, x * 4, 20); // 24 and 20
```

SELF-TEST QUESTIONS

5.1 Whereabouts will the logos be drawn in the following code?

```
int a = 10;
int b = 20;
drawLogo(paper, a, b);
drawLogo(paper, b + a, b - a);
drawLogo(paper, b + a - 3, b + a - 4);
```

5.2 We could rewrite the **drawLogo** method so that it has a single parameter: the drawing area. The rewritten method could use input dialogs to obtain the drawing position from the user. What is the drawback of this approach?

● Formal and actual parameters

There are two bracketed lists that we are discussing, and it is important to be clear about the purpose of each list:

■ The writer of the method must choose which items the method will request via formal parameters. Thus, in **drawLogo**, the dimensions of the nested squares are always set to 20, 40 and 60, so the caller need not supply this data. However, the caller might wish to vary the position of the logo, so these items have been made into parameters.

■ The writer of the method must choose names for each formal parameter. If similar names are used in other methods, no problem arises – each method has its own copy of its parameters. In other words, the writer is free to choose any name.

■ The type of each formal parameter must be provided, preceding the parameter name. The types depend on the particular method. A comma is used to separate one parameter from another. Look at the **drawLogo** header to see the arrangement.

■ The caller must supply a list of actual parameters in brackets. The parameters must be in the correct order for the method, and must be of the correct type.

The two benefits of using a method for the logo drawing are that we remove the duplication of the three **drawRect** statements when several logos are needed, and giving the task a name enables us to think at a higher level.

Finally, we recognize that you might wish to transfer the programming skills that you learn here into other languages. The concepts are similar, but the terminology is different: in some languages, the term 'argument' is used, rather than 'parameter'. Other terminology involves the term 'invoke' rather than 'call'.

5.3   Explain what is wrong with these calls:

```
drawLogo(paper, 50, "10");
drawLogo(50, 10, paper);
drawLogo(paper, 10);
```

5.4   Here is the call of a method:

```
justDoIt("Oranges");
```

and here is the method itself:

```
private void justDoIt(String fruit) {
    JOptionPane.showMessageDialog(null, fruit);
}
```

What happens when the method is called?

A triangle method

In order to introduce more features of methods, we will create a more useful method, which we will name **drawTriangle**. Because *we* are writing the method (rather than making use of a pre-written one) we can choose what kind of triangle, and can choose the parameters that we want the caller to supply.

We will choose to draw a right-angled triangle, pointing to the right, as in Figure 5.5(a).

In choosing parameters, there are a number of possibilities – for example, we might demand that the caller gives us the coordinates of the three corners. However, we have chosen the parameters to be:

- the drawing area, as before;
- the coordinates of the top point of the triangle;
- the width of the triangle;
- the height of the triangle.

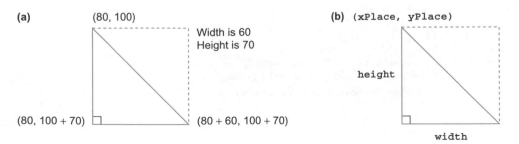

Figure 5.5 (a) Triangle coordinate calculations; (b) Formal parameters for **drawTriangle**.

Another way to regard these coordinates is that they specify the position of an enclosing rectangle for our right-angled triangle.

Figure 5.5(b) shows a triangle labelled with the parameters.

We can draw the lines in any order. Let us examine the drawing process with numbers at first. As an example, we will draw a triangle with the top corner at (80, 100) and with a width of 60 and a height of 70. Figure 5.5(a) shows the calculations. The process is:

1. Draw from (80, 100) down to (80, 100 + 70). Remember that the y coordinate increases as we move down.

2. Draw from (80, 100 + 70) across to (80 + 60, 100 + 70).

3. Draw from the top corner (80, 100) diagonally to (80 + 60, 100 + 70).

Ensure that you can follow the above – maybe sketch it out on paper.

Note that in our explanation, we did not simplify the calculations: we left 100 + 70 as it is, rather than as 170. When we come to the coding, the position of the triangle and the size of the triangle will be passed in as separate parameters.

Here is a complete program which is named **TriangleMethod**. It contains a **drawTriangle** method. It also contains the **drawLogo** method, to illustrate that a program can contain many methods.

```java
import java.awt.*;
import java.awt.event.*;
import javax.swing.*;

public class TriangleMethod extends JFrame
    implements ActionListener {

    private JButton button;
    private JPanel panel;

    public static void main(String[] args) {
        TriangleMethod frame = new TriangleMethod();
        frame.setSize(350, 300);
        frame.createGUI();
        frame.show();
    }

    private void createGUI() {
        setDefaultCloseOperation(EXIT_ON_CLOSE);
        Container window = getContentPane();
        window.setLayout(new FlowLayout() );

        panel = new JPanel();
        panel.setPreferredSize(new Dimension(300, 200));
        panel.setBackground(Color.white);
        window.add(panel);
```

```
        button = new JButton("Press me");
        window.add(button);
        button.addActionListener(this);
    }

    public void actionPerformed(ActionEvent event) {
        Graphics paper = panel.getGraphics();
        drawLogo(paper, 10, 20);
        drawLogo(paper, 100, 100);
        drawTriangle(paper, 100, 10, 40, 40);
        drawTriangle(paper, 10, 100, 20, 60);
    }

    private void drawLogo(Graphics drawingArea,
                          int xPos, int yPos) {
        drawingArea.drawRect(xPos, yPos, 60, 60);
        drawingArea.drawRect(xPos, yPos, 40, 40);
        drawingArea.drawRect(xPos, yPos, 20, 20);
    }

    private void drawTriangle(Graphics drawingArea,
                              int xPlace,
                              int yPlace,
                              int width,
                              int height) {
        drawingArea.drawLine(xPlace, yPlace,
            xPlace, yPlace + height);
        drawingArea.drawLine(xPlace, yPlace + height,
            xPlace + width, yPlace + height);
        drawingArea.drawLine(xPlace, yPlace,
            xPlace + width, yPlace + height);
    }
}
```

It has a button and a panel box. Click on the button to draw two logos and two triangles. Figure 5.6 shows the output.

Here are some points about the coding of the **drawTriangle** method:

■ We chose to name it **drawTriangle**, but it is up to us. We could have chosen **Triangle**, or even **drawThing**, but **drawTriangle** fits with the names of the library methods.

■ The names for the formal parameters **drawingArea**, **xPlace**, **yPlace**, **width** and **height** were our choice.

■ The order of the parameters was also under our control. We could recode the method to require the height before the width if we wanted to. (We put the width first because many of Java's library methods use this order.)

So – we have our triangle. We will use it to look at local variables, and also show how it can be a 'building brick' for more powerful methods.

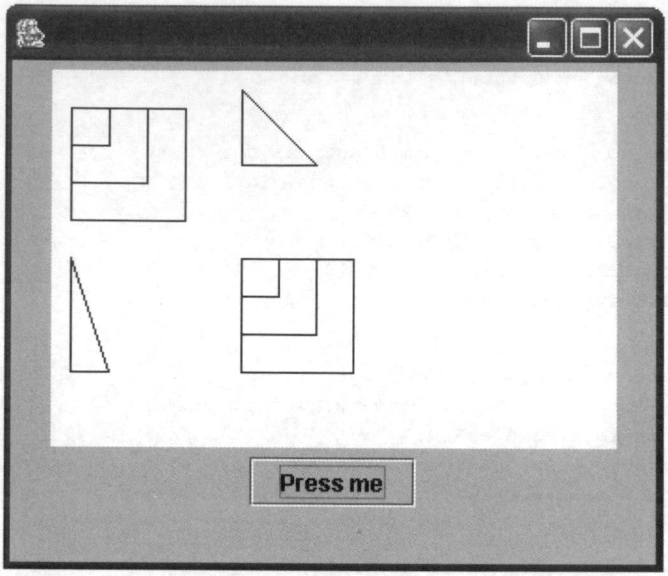

Figure 5.6 Screenshot of **TriangleMethod** program.

Local variables

Look at this modified version of **drawTriangle**, which we have named **drawTriangle2**:

```
private void drawTriangle2(Graphics drawingArea,
int xPlace,
int yPlace,
int width,
int height) {

    int rightCornerX, rightCornerY;
    rightCornerX = xPlace + width;
    rightCornerY = yPlace + height;

    drawingArea.drawLine(xPlace, yPlace,
        xPlace, rightCornerY);
    drawingArea.drawLine(xPlace, rightCornerY,
        rightCornerX, rightCornerY);
    drawingArea.drawLine(xPlace, yPlace,
        rightCornerX, rightCornerY);
}
```

It is called in just the same way as **drawTriangle**, but internally it uses two variables, named **rightCornerX** and **rightCornerY**, which have been introduced to simplify the calculations. Look at how they are used to refer to the rightmost point of the triangle. These variables exist only within **drawTriangle2**. They are local to the method (the terminology is that they have local *scope*). If variables of the same name exist within other methods, then there is no conflict, in that each method uses its own copy. Another way to look at this is that when programmers are creating methods they can invent local variables without cross-checking with other methods.

The role of local variables is to assist in the work of the method, whatever it is doing. The variables have a limited scope, restricted to their own method. Their existence is temporary – they are created when a method is called, and destroyed when it exits.

Name clashes

In Java, the creator of a method is free to choose appropriate names for local variables and parameters – but what happens if names are chosen which clash with other variables? We could have:

```java
private void methodOne(int x, int y) {
    int z = 0;
    // code...
}
private void methodTwo(int z, int x) {
    int w = 1;
    // code...
}
```

Let us assume that the methods have been written by two people. **methodOne** has **x** and **y** as parameters, and declares an integer **z**. These three items are all local to **methodOne**. In **methodTwo**, the programmer exercises the right of freedom to name local items, and opts for **z**, **x** and **w**. The name clash of **x** (and of **z**) does not give a problem, as Java treats the **x** of **methodOne** as different from the **x** of **methodTwo**.

SELF-TEST QUESTION

5.5 Here is the call of a method:

```java
int a = 3;
int b = 8;
doStuff(a, b);
JOptionPane.showMessageDialog(null, Integer.toString(a));
```

and here is the method itself:

```java
private void doStuff(int x, int y) {
    int a = 0;
    a = x + y;
}
```

What is shown by the message dialog?

Let us summarize the method facilities we have discussed so far. (Later we will include the **return** statement.)

■ The general form of a method declaration which does not produce a result and which has parameters passed by value is:

```
private void someName(formal parameter list) {
    body
}
```

The programmer chooses the method name.

■ The formal parameter list is a list of types and names. If a method doesn't need parameters, we use empty brackets for the parameter list when we declare it, and use empty brackets for the actual parameter list when we call it.

```
private void myMethod() {
    body
}
```

and the method call is:

```
myMethod();
```

■ A class can contain any number of methods, in any order. In this chapter, our programs only consist of one class. The essence of the layout is:

```
public class SomeClass... {
    public static void main(parameter list...) {
        body
    }
    private void someName(parameter list...) {
        body
    }
    private void anotherName(parameter list...) {
        body
    }
}
```

We will make use of the **public** and **class** keywords in Chapter 9. For now, merely note that a class can group together a series of methods.

● Event-handling methods and `main`

A class contains a set of methods. We write some of them ourselves (such as **drawLogo**) and we explicitly call them. However, there are other methods which we create but do not call, such as **main** and **actionPerformed**.

If a method were never to be called, it would have no effect. However, the above methods are called, but from the Java run-time system rather than explicitly from your program.

- When a program starts running, the **main** method is automatically called before anything else happens. Its main task is to call some methods which build the GUI by adding (for example) buttons to the window.

- The **actionPerformed** method will be called up by the Java run-time system whenever a button is clicked. This process is not quite automatic: the program has to state that it will 'listen' for button-clicks. We look at this in Chapter 6.

return and results

In our previous examples of formal and actual parameters, values were passed into methods, which the method made use of. However, often we need to code methods which perform a task and send a result back to the rest of the program, so that the result can be used later. In this case we can use the **return** statement. Let us look at a method which calculates the area of a rectangle, given its two sides as input parameters. Here is a complete program named **AreaMethod**, showing the method and a call:

```
import java.awt.*;
import java.awt.event.*;
import javax.swing.*;

public class AreaMethod extends JFrame
    implements ActionListener {

    private JButton button;
    private JPanel panel;

    public static void main(String[] args) {
        AreaMethod frame = new AreaMethod();
        frame.setSize(400, 300);
        frame.createGUI();
        frame.show();
    }

    private void createGUI() {
        setDefaultCloseOperation(EXIT_ON_CLOSE);
        Container window = getContentPane();
        window.setLayout(new FlowLayout() );

        panel = new JPanel();
        panel.setPreferredSize(new Dimension(300, 200));
        panel.setBackground(Color.white);
        window.add(panel);

        button = new JButton("Press me");
        window.add(button);
        button.addActionListener(this);
    }
```

```
public void actionPerformed(ActionEvent event) {
    int a;
    a = areaRectangle(10, 20);
    JOptionPane.showMessageDialog(null, "Area is: " + a);
}

private int areaRectangle(int length, int width) {
    int area;
    area = length * width;
    return area;
}
}
```

There are a number of new features in this example, which go hand in hand.

Examine the method header:

```
private int areaRectangle(int length, int width) {
```

Instead of **void**, we have specified the type of item that the method will return to the caller. In this case, because we are multiplying two **int** values, the type of the answer will also be an **int**.

The choice of this type depends on the problem. For example, it might be an integer or a string, but it could also be a more complicated object such as a button. The writer of the method chooses what type of value is returned.

To return a value from the method, we make use of the **return** statement. We put:

```
return expression;
```

The expression could be a number, a variable or a calculation (or even a method call), but it must be of the correct type, as specified in the declaration of the method, i.e. its header. Additionally, the **return** statement causes the current method to stop executing, and returns immediately to where it left off in the calling method. Now we will look at how a method which returns a result can be called.

Here is how **not** to call such a method. They should not be used as complete statements, as in:

```
areaRectangle(10, 20);    // no
```

Instead, the caller should arrange to 'consume' the returned value. Here is an approach to understanding the returning of values: imagine that the method call (the name and parameter list) is erased, and is replaced by the returned result. If the resulting code makes sense, then Java will allow you to make such a call. Look at this example:

```
answer = areaRectangle(30, 40);
```

The result is 1200, which we imagine as replacing the call, effectively giving:

```
answer = 1200;
```

This is valid Java. But if we put:

```
areaRectangle(30, 40);
```

the substitution would produce a Java statement consisting only of a number:

```
1200;
```

which is meaningless. (Though, strictly, the Java compiler will allow the previous call of **AreaRectangle** to run. However, disregarding the returned result from a method whose main purpose is to return such a result is not sensible.)

Here are some more ways that we might consume the result:

```
int n;
n = areaRectangle(10, 20);
JOptionPane.showMessageDialog(null, "area is " +
    areaRectangle(3, 4));
n = areaRectangle(10, 20) * areaRectangle(7, 8);
```

SELF-TEST QUESTION

5.6 Work through the above statements with pencil and paper, substituting results for calls.

To complete the discussion of **return**, note that it can be used with void methods. In this case, we must use **return** without specifying a result, as in:

```
private void demo(int n) {
    // do something
    return;
    // do something else
}
```

This can be used when we want the method to terminate at a statement other than the last one.

Let us look at an alternative way of coding our area example:

```
private int areaRectangle2(int length, int width) {
    return length * width;
}
```

Because we can use **return** with expressions, we have omitted the variable **area** in **areaRectangle2**.

Such reductions in program size are not always beneficial, because the reduction in meaningful names can reduce clarity, hence leading to more debugging and testing time.

SELF-TEST QUESTION

5.7 Here is a method named `twice`, which returns the doubled value of its `int` parameter:

```
private int twice(int n) {
    return 2 * n;
}
```

Here are some calls:

```
int n = 3;
int r;
r = twice(n);
r = twice(n + 1);
r = twice(n) + 1;
r = twice(3 + 2 * n);
r = twice(twice(n));
r = twice(twice(n + 1));
r = twice(twice(n) + 1);
r = twice(twice(twice(n)));
```

For each call, state the returned value.

● Building on methods: `drawHouse`

As an example of methods which make use of other methods, let us create a method which draws a primitive 'lean-to' house with a cross-section shown in Figure 5.7. The height of the roof is the same as the height of the walls, and the width of the walls is the same as the width of the roof. We will choose the `int` parameters to be:

- the horizontal position of the top right point of the roof;
- the vertical position of the top right point of the roof;

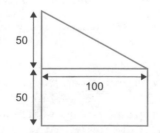

Figure 5.7 House with width of 100 and roof height of 50.

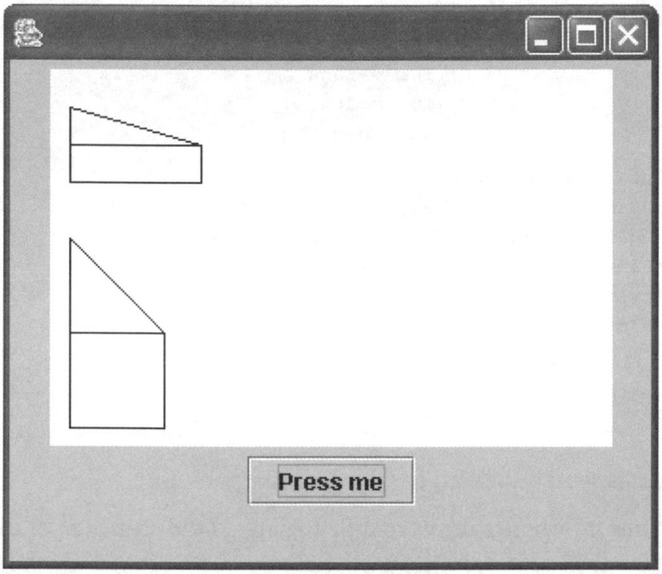

Figure 5.8 Screenshot of **HouseDemo** program

- the height of the roof (excluding the wall);
- the width of the house. The triangle for the roof and the rectangle for the walls have the same width.

We will use **drawRect** from the Java library, and use our own **drawTriangle**.

Here is the new code. The user-interface setup is identical to our previous program. The resulting image is shown in Figure 5.8.

```
public void actionPerformed(ActionEvent event) {
    Graphics paper = panel.getGraphics();
    drawHouse(paper, 10, 20, 70, 20);
    drawHouse(paper, 10, 90, 50, 50);
}

private void drawHouse(Graphics drawingArea,
    int topRoofX,
    int topRoofY,
    int width,
    int height) {

    drawTriangle(drawingArea, topRoofX, topRoofY, width, height);
    drawingArea.drawRect(topRoofX,
        topRoofY + height, width, height);
}
```

```
    private void drawTriangle(Graphics drawingArea,
                              int xPlace,
                              int yPlace,
                              int width,
                              int height) {
  drawingArea.drawLine(xPlace, yPlace,
      xPlace, yPlace + height);
  drawingArea.drawLine(xPlace, yPlace + height,
      xPlace + width, yPlace + height);
  drawingArea.drawLine(xPlace, yPlace,xPlace + width,
      yPlace + height);
}
```

The program is straightforward if you recall that:

- Methods return to where they were called from, so the sequence of calls is:
  - **actionPerformed** calls **drawHouse**;
  - **drawHouse** calls **drawRect**;
  - **drawHouse** calls **drawTriangle**;
  - **drawTriangle** calls **drawLine** (three times).
- Parameters can be expressions, so **yPlace + height** is evaluated, then passed into **drawLine**.
- The **width** and **height** of **drawHouse** and the **width** and **height** of **drawTriangle** are totally separate. Their values are stored in different places.

You will see that what might have been a longer program has been written as a short program, split into methods with meaningful names. This illustrates the power of using methods.

● Building on methods: areaHouse

Here we will look at a method which calculates and returns the cross-sectional area of our house. We will make use of our existing **areaRectangle** method, and will write an **areaTriangle** method, based on:

```
area = (base * height) / 2;
```

Here is a call of **areaHouse**:

```
int area = areaHouse(10, 10);
JOptionPane.showMessageDialog(null,
    "House area is " + area);
```

and here are the methods the call uses:

```
private int areaHouse(int width, int height) {
    return areaRectangle(width, height) +
        areaTriangle(width, height);
}

private int areaRectangle(int length, int width) {
    int area;
    area = length * width;
    return area;
}

private int areaTriangle(int base, int height) {
    return (base*height)/2;
}
```

Remember that in our simplified house, the roof part is as tall as the wall, so we only need to pass the width and the height. Here is how the methods work together:

- **areaHouse** calls **areaRectangle** and **areaTriangle**;
- **areaHouse** adds together the two returned results;
- **areaHouse** returns the final result.

Note that **areaTriangle** obtains its inputs via parameters, rather than requesting them from the user via input dialogs. This makes it flexible. For example, in this case, its parameter values are created in **areaHouse**.

Let us summarize our coverage of methods so far. We have seen:

- passing parameters to a method;
- passing a value out of a method with **return**.

this and objects

You are probably reading this book because Java is an object-oriented language, but you might be wondering why this chapter has not mentioned objects. The truth is that methods and objects are vitally connected. When you run small Java programs, you are running an instance of a class, i.e. an object. This object contains methods (e.g. **drawLogo**).

When an object calls a method which is declared within itself, we can simply put:

```
drawLogo(paper, 50, 10);
```

or we can use the full object notation, as in:

```
this.drawLogo(paper, 50, 10);
```

`this` is a Java keyword, and stands for the currently running object. So you have been doing object-oriented programming without realizing it. Here are some examples:

```
// works as expected
paper.drawLine(10, 10, 100, 100);

// compilation error
this.drawLine(10, 10, 100, 100);
```

In the above, an error is detected because we are asking Java to locate the `drawLine` method within the current object. In fact, `drawLine` exists outside the program in the `Graphics` class.

● Overloading

Our `areaTriangle` method is useful, in the sense that it can work with actual parameters of any name. The drawback is that they must be integers. But what if we wanted to work with two `double` variables? We might code *another* method:

```
private double areaTriangleDouble(double base, double height) {
    return 0.5 * (base * height);
}
```

However, it would be convenient to use the same name for both methods, and in Java we can. Here is how we code the method declarations:

```
private int areaTriangle(int base, int height) {
    return (base * height) / 2;
}

private double areaTriangle(double base, double height) {
    return (base * height) * 0.5;
}

private double areaTriangle(double side1, double side2,
                            double angle) {
    return 0.5 + side1 * side2 * Math.sin(angle);
}
```

Alongside the `int` and `double` versions, we have put an additional version, for those familiar with trigonometry. Here, the area is calculated based on the length of two sides and the sine of the angle between them, in radians. (`Math.sin` provides the sine function.) This version of `areaTriangle` has three `double` parameters. Here we call all three methods, and display the results in message dialogs:

```
public void actionPerformed(ActionEvent event) {
    double da = 9.5, db = 21.5;
    int ia = 10, ib = 20;
    double angle = 0.7;
    JOptionPane.showMessageDialog(null,
        "Area of triangle is "+areaTriangle(ia, ib));
    JOptionPane.showMessageDialog(null,
        "Area of triangle is "+areaTriangle(da, db));
    JOptionPane.showMessageDialog(null,
        "Area of triangle is "+areaTriangle(da, db, angle));
}
```

How does Java decide which method to use? There are three methods named **areaTriangle**, so Java additionally looks at the number of actual parameters in the call, and at their types. For example, if we call **areaTriangle** with two **double** parameters, it finds the appropriate declaration of **areaTriangle** with two (and only two) double parameters. The code contained by the methods can be different – it is the number of parameters and their types that determine which method is called. The combination of the number of parameters and their types is known as the *signature*.

If the method returns a result, the return type plays no part in determining which method is called, i.e. it is the parameter types of the method which must be different.

What we have done is termed *overloading*. The **areaTriangle** method has been overloaded with several possibilities.

So if you are writing methods which perform similar tasks, but differ in the number of parameters and/or types, it is sensible to make use of overloading by choosing the **same** name rather than invent an artificially different name.

SELF-TEST QUESTION

5.8 Write two methods, both named **addUp**. One should add two integers and return their sum. The other should add three integers and return the sum. Provide examples of calling your two methods.

Programming principles

- A method is a section of code which has a name. We call the method by using its name.
- We can code **void** methods, or ones which return a result.
- We can pass parameters to a method.
- If you can identify a well-defined task in your code, consider separating it out and writing it as a method.

Programming pitfalls

■ The method header must include type names. The following is wrong:

```
private void methodOne(x) {    // wrong
```

Instead we must put, for example, the following:

```
private void methodOne(int x) {
```

■ A method call must not include type names. For example, rather than:

```
methodOne(int y);    //
```

we put:

```
methodOne(y);
```

■ When calling a method, we must supply the correct number of parameters and the correct types of parameters.

■ We must arrange to consume a returned value in some way. The following style of call does not consume a return value:

```
someMethod(e, f);    //
```

Grammar spot

■ The general pattern for methods takes two forms. Firstly, for a method that does not return a result, we declare the method by:

```
private void methodName(formal parameter list) {
    ... body
}
```

and we call the method by a statement, as in:

```
methodName(actual parameter list);
```

■ For a method which returns a result, the form is:

```
private type methodName(actual parameter list) {
    ... body
}
```

Any type or class can be specified as the returned type. We call the method as part of an expression. For example:

```
n = methodName(a, b);
```

- The body of a method which returns a result must include a **return** statement featuring the correct type of value.

- When a method has no parameters, we use empty brackets **()** in both the declaration and the call.

- The formal parameter list is created by the writer of the method. Each parameter needs a name, a type.

- The actual parameter list is written by the caller of the method. It consists of a series of items in the correct (matching) order, and of the correct types. Unlike parameters within a method, the type names are not used.

New language elements

- The declaration of private methods.

- The call (or invocation) of a method, consisting of the method name and parameters.

- The use of **return** to exit and pass simultaneously a value back from a non-void method.

- The use of **return** to exit from a **void** method.

- The use of overloading.

- The use of **this** to stand for the current object.

Summary

- Methods contain sub-tasks of a program.

- We can pass parameters into methods.

- Using a method is termed calling (or invoking) the method.

- Non-void methods return a result.

Exercises

For the exercises which draw shapes, base your code on the **LogoMethod** program. For programs which only need message and input dialogs, base your code on the **AreaRectangle** program.

The first group of problems only involves **void** methods.

5.1 Write a method named **showName**, with one string parameter. It should display the supplied name in a message dialog. Test the program by inputting a name with an input dialog, and then calling **showName**.

5.2 Write a method named **showNames**, with two string parameters representing your first name and your last name. It should display your first name in a message dialog, and then display your last name in another message dialog.

5.3 Write a method named **displayEarnings**, with two integer parameters representing an employee's salary, and the number of years they have worked. The method should display their total earnings in a message dialog, assuming that they earned the same amount every year. The program should obtain values via input dialogs prior to calling **displayEarnings**.

5.4 Code a method which draws a circle, given the coordinates of the centre and the radius. Its header should be:

```
private void drawCircle(Graphics drawingArea,
                        int xCentre, int yCentre, int radius)
```

5.5 Code a method named **drawStreet**, which draws a street of houses, using the provided **drawHouse** method. For the purposes of this question, a street consists of four houses, and there should be a 20 pixel gap between each house. The parameters provide the location and size of the leftmost house, and are identical to **drawHouse**.

5.6 Code a method (to be known as **drawStreetInPerspective**), which has the same parameters as Exercise 5.5. However, each house is to be 20% smaller than the house to its left.

The following programs involve methods which return a result.

5.7 Write a method which returns the inch equivalent of its centimetre parameter. An example call is:

```
double inches = inchEquivalent(10.5);
```

Multiply centimetres by **0.394** to calculate inches.

5.8 Write a method which returns the volume of a cube, given the length of one side. A sample call is:

```
double vol = cubeVolume(1.2);
```

5.9 Write a method which returns the area of a circle, given its radius as a parameter. A sample call is:

```
double a = areaCircle(1.25);
```

The area of a circle is given by the formula **Math.PI * r * r**. Though we could use a number such as **3.14**, a more accurate value is provided by **Math.PI**.

5.10 Write a method named `secsIn`, which accepts three integers, representing a time in hours, minutes and seconds. It should return the total time in seconds. A sample call is:

```
int totalSecs = secsIn(1, 1, 2);    // returns 3662
```

5.11 Write a method which returns the area of a solid cylinder. Decide on its parameters. Your method should call `areaCircle` from above, to assist in calculating the area of the top and bottom. (The circumference of a circle is given by `2 * Math.PI * r`.)

5.12 Write a method called `increment`, which adds 1 to its integer parameter. An example of a call is:

```
int n = 3;
int a = increment(n);    // returns 4
```

5.13 Write a method named `fiveYearResult`, which has two parameters:

- a **double** amount initially invested;
- a **double** interest rate (e.g. **1.5** specifies 1.5% interest per year).

The method should return the amount after five years of compound interest.
　Hint: after one year, the new amount is:

```
amount = amount * (1 + interest / 100);
```

5.14 Write a method named `timeDifferenceInSecs`, with six parameters and a returned integer result. It takes in two times in hours, minutes and seconds, and returns the difference between them in seconds. Do this problem by calling the `secsIn` method (Exercise 5.10) from within your `timeDifferenceInSecs` method.

The following problems involve overloading:

5.15 Use any program which contains `secsIn`. Add an additional method also named `secsIn`, which has two parameters only, for minutes and seconds.

5.16 Recall the `drawCircle` method written in Exercise 5.4. Add another `drawCircle` method to your `drawCircle` program, with the following parameters:

- a drawing area;
- the **x** and **y** position of the centre.

A circle of radius **50** is to be drawn at the specified point.

Answers to self-test questions

5.1 At (10, 20), (30, 10), (27, 26).

5.2 The method is now more inflexible. The input dialogs would appear every time we called the method. In the original version of the method, the caller can obtain values for the position in a variety of ways before passing them as parameters.

5.3 In the first call, the quotes should not be used. They indicate a string, not an integer.
In the second call, the order should be:

```
paper, 50, 10
```

In the third call, a parameter is missing.

5.4 A message dialog displaying **Oranges** will appear.

5.5 The message dialog displays the original value of **a**, which is **3**. The **a** that is set to **0** inside the method is a local variable.

5.6 Here are the stages in replacing a call by its result. For:

```
n = areaRectangle(10, 20);
```

we have:

```
n = 200;
```

For the line:

```
JOptionPane.ShowMessageDialog(null, "area is " +
    areaRectangle(3, 4));
```

we have the stages:

```
JOptionPane.ShowMessageDialog(null, "area is " + 12);
JOptionPane.ShowMessageDialog(null, "area is 12");
```

For the line:

```
n = areaRectangle(10, 20) * areaRectangle(7, 8);
```

we have the stages:

```
n = 200 * 56;
n = 11200;
```

5.7 The values that **r** takes are:

```
6
8
7
18
12
16
14
24
```

5.8
```
private int addUp(int a, int b) {
    return a + b;
}

private int addUp(int a, int b, int c) {
    return a + b + c;
}
```

You might call the above by:

```
public void actionPerformed(ActionEvent event) {
    int sum2, sum3;
    int x = 22, y - 87, z = 42;
    sum2 = addUp(x,y);
    sum3 = addUp(x, y, z);
}
```

CHAPTER

6

Using objects

This chapter explains:

- the use of private instance variables;
- the use of library classes;
- the use of **new** and constructors;
- event handling;
- the **Random** class;
- the Swing label, text field, panel and button classes;
- the Swing slider and timer classes.

● Introduction

In this chapter, we will deepen our understanding of objects. In particular, we will look at the use of classes from the Java libraries. Note that, though there are many hundreds of these, the principles of using them are similar.

Here is an analogy: reading a book – whatever the book – involves opening it at the front, reading a page, then moving to the next page. We know what to do with a book. It is the same with objects. When you have used a few of them, you know what to look for when presented with a new one.

Instance variables

In order to tackle more advanced problems, we need to introduce a new place to declare variables. So far, we have used **int** and **double** to declare local variables within methods. But local variables alone are insufficient to tackle most problems.

Here we introduce a program (**CarCounter**, Figure 6.1) to assist in the running of a car park (or parking lot). It provides a single button, which the attendant clicks when a car enters. The program keeps a count of the number of cars in the park, and displays it in a message dialog.

In essence, we need to add **1** to a variable (which we will name **carCount**) in the **actionPerformed** method associated with the button-click. However, it is important to note that a local variable (declared within the **actionPerformed** method) will **not** work. Local variables are temporary – they are created when a method is entered, and destroyed when the method finishes. Any values they hold are not preserved.

Here is the correct code, with the user-interface parts removed for clarity:

```
public class CarCounter extends JFrame
    implements ActionListener {

    private int carCount = 0;

    public void actionPerformed(ActionEvent event) {
        carCount = carCount + 1;
        JOptionPane.showMessageDialog(null, "Cars:" + carCount);
    }
}
```

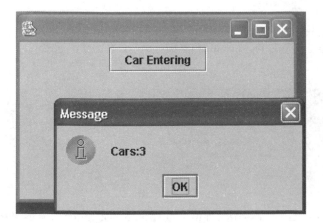

Figure 6.1 Screenshot of **CarCounter** program.

The point at issue here is the declaring of the **carCount** variable:

■ It is declared **outside** the method, but **inside** the class **CarCounter**. It can be used by **any** method of the class (though, here, we only use it in **actionPerformed**).

■ It has been declared as **private**, meaning that any other classes we might have cannot use it. The variable is *encapsulated* or sealed up inside **CarCounter**, i.e. it is for the use of the methods of **CarCounter** only.

■ **carCount** is an example of an *instance variable*. It belongs to an instance of a class, rather than to one method. Another term is 'class-level' variable.

■ **carCount** is said to have *class scope*. The scope of an item is the area of the program in which it can be used. The other type of scope we have seen is local scope used with local variables declared inside methods.

■ The preferred style for instance variables is to declare them as **private**.

■ The Java convention is not to capitalize the first letter of an instance variable.

Note that the programmer has free choice of names for instance variables. But what if a name coincides with a local variable name, as in the following?

```
public class SomeClass {

    private int n = 8;

    private void myMethod() {
        int n;
        n = 3;            // which n?
    }
    // other methods, omitted here

}
```

Although both variables are accessible (in scope) within **myMethod**, the rule is that the local variable is chosen. The instance variable (class-level) **n** remains set to **8**.

SELF-TEST QUESTION

6.1 In the above **SomeClass** class, what are the consequences of deleting the local declaration of **n**?

Instance variables are essential, but you should not ignore locals. For example, if a variable is used inside one method only, and need not keep its value between method calls, make it local.

Here is the complete **CarCounter** program, with the user-interface code as well:

```java
import java.awt.*;
import java.awt.event.*;
import javax.swing.*;

public class CarCounter extends JFrame
    implements ActionListener {

    private int carCount = 0;

    private JButton button;

    public static void main(String[] args) {
        CarCounter frame = new CarCounter();
        frame.setSize(300, 200);
        frame.createGUI();
        frame.show();
    }

    private void createGUI() {
        setDefaultCloseOperation(EXIT_ON_CLOSE);
        Container window = getContentPane();
        window.setLayout(new FlowLayout());

        button = new JButton("Car Entering");
        window.add(button);
        button.addActionListener(this);
    }

    public void actionPerformed(ActionEvent event) {
        carCount = carCount + 1;
        JOptionPane.showMessageDialog(null, "Cars:" + carCount);
    }
}
```

Do not be tempted to amend the user-interface code for now. It must be exactly as shown.

Now that we have introduced **private** scope, let us apply this to the user-interface coding. Items on a window – such as buttons – need to be there for the life of the program. In addition, they are often used by several methods. For these reasons, they are declared as instance variables, outside any methods. You can see this at work in the **CarCounter** class, where a button is declared by:

```java
private JButton button;
```

in the same area of code as the **carCount** variable. We shall return to the issue of user-interface classes later in this chapter.

SELF-TEST QUESTION

6.2 What does the following program do? (The creation of the GUI objects has been omitted intentionally, so you can focus on scopes.)

```
private int x = 0;

public void actionPerformed(ActionEvent event) {
    Graphics paper = panel.getGraphics();
    paper.drawLine(x, 0, x, 100);
    x = x + 10;
}
```

● Instantiation: using constructors with new

So far, you have written programs which used the **int** and **double** types. These are regarded as 'built-in' or 'primitive' types – they are **not** instances of classes (i.e. not objects). Recall that we can declare them and provide an initial value, as in:

```
int n = 3;
```

In effect we are saying 'make me a new integer named **n**, with an initial value of **3**'.

However, you have used other kinds of items (such as buttons and graphics drawing areas). They **are** instances of classes. We have to create them in a special way, using the word **new**. Creating an instance with **new** is known as *instantiation*.

To illustrate the use of **new**, we will study the library **Random** class.

● The Random class

Random numbers are very useful in simulations and in games; for example, we can give the game-player a different initial situation every time. Instances of the **Random** class provide us with a 'stream' of random numbers which we can obtain one at a time via the **nextInt** method. Here is a program (**RandomLines**) which draws a random line each time we click on the button. One end of the line is fixed at (0, 0), and the other end of the line has a random *x* and *y* position. Prior to drawing the line, we clear the drawing area by drawing a white rectangle which fills the drawing area (**100** by **100** here) and then we set the colour to black. Figure 6.2 shows two screenshots, and here is the code:

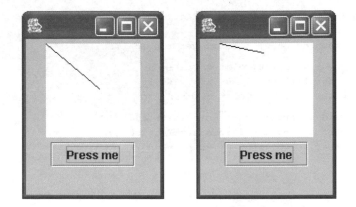

Figure 6.2 Two screenshots of the **RandomLines** program.

```java
import java.awt.*;
import java.awt.event.*;
import javax.swing.*;
import java.util.*;

public class RandomLines extends JFrame
    implements ActionListener {

    private Random randomPositions = new Random();
    private JButton button;
    private JPanel panel;

    public static void main(String[] args) {
        RandomLines frame = new RandomLines();
        frame.setSize(150, 200);
        frame.createGUI();
        frame.show();
    }

    private void createGUI() {
        setDefaultCloseOperation(EXIT_ON_CLOSE);
        Container window = getContentPane();
        window.setLayout(new FlowLayout() );

        panel = new JPanel();
        panel.setPreferredSize(new Dimension(100,100));
        panel.setBackground(Color.white);
        window.add(panel);

        button = new JButton("Press me");
        window.add(button);
        button.addActionListener(this);
    }
```

```
public void actionPerformed(ActionEvent event) {
    int xEnd, yEnd;
    Graphics paper = panel.getGraphics();

    paper.setColor(Color.white);
    paper.fillRect(0, 0, 100, 100);
    paper.setColor(Color.black);

    xEnd = randomPositions.nextInt(100);
    yEnd = randomPositions.nextInt(100);
    paper.drawLine(0, 0, xEnd, yEnd);
    }
}
```

To use **Random** in a convenient way, we need this import instruction:

```
import java.util.*;
```

If we omitted the import, we would have to refer to the class as:

```
java.util.Random
```

The use of **import** provides us with a shorthand.

We must then declare and initialize an instance of our class. This can be done in two ways. One approach is to use a single statement, as in:

```
private Random randomPositions = new Random();
```

Note that:

- We chose **private** scope, rather than local scope.
- Following **private**, we state the class of item we are declaring. Here, the item is an instance of the **Random** class.
- We chose the name **randomPositions** for our instance. Other suitable names for our instance might have been **randomNumbers**, **random**. Note the possibility of using **random** as the name of an instance. Java is case sensitive, and the convention is that all class names begin with a capital letter. Thus, **random** (with a lower-case letter) can be used for an instance name. In a program where we only create one instance from a class, it is common to use the same name as the class (but with a lower-case first letter). In this example, **randomPositions** conveys the meaning. We have used the plural because our instance can provide as many random numbers as we request.
- The word **new** precedes the use of the constructor, which is basically a method with the same name as the class: **Random**. The use of **new** creates a new instance of a class in RAM, which is assigned to **randomPositions**.
- Constructors may be overloaded, so you need to choose the most convenient constructor. **Random** has two constructors with differing parameters, and the one with no parameters is suitable here.
- You can consider the statement to be in two parts:

```
private Random randomPositions...
```

and:

```
... = new Random();
```

The first part declares **randomPositions** as a variable of class **Random**, but it does not yet have a concrete instance associated with it. The second part calls the constructor of the **Random** class to complete the task of declaring and initialization.

Another way to declare and initialize instances is with declaration and initialization in different areas of the program, as in:

```
public class RandomLines extends JFrame
    implements ActionListener {

    private Random randomPositions;

    ...

    private void someMethod() {
        randomPositions = new Random();
        ...

    }

}
```

Whichever approach we choose, there are a number of points:

- The declaration establishes the class of the instance. Here it is an instance of **Random**.
- The declaration establishes the scope of the instance. Here, **randomPositions** has class scope – it can be used by any method of the **RandomLines** class, rather than being local to a method.
- **randomPositions** is private. It cannot be used by other classes outside our **RandomLines** class. Normally we make all such instance variables private.
- The single-statement form of declaration is convenient, but is not always used. Sometimes we need to initialize an instance variable at a later stage, based on values calculated by the program. This must be done inside a method, even though the declaration is placed outside the methods. Examples of separating initialization from declaration are shown later in the chapter.

SELF-TEST QUESTION

6.3   What is wrong with this fragment of code?

```
public class SomeClass extends JFrame
    implements ActionListener {

    private Random r;
    r = new Random();
    ...
```

Let us return to the `RandomLines` program. So far, we have created an object, i.e. an instance of the `Random` class named `randomPositions`. We have yet to create any actual random numbers.

Once an object has been created with `new`, we can use its methods. The documentation tells us that there are several methods which provide us with a random number, and we chose to use the method which provides integers, and which lets us specify the range of the numbers. The method is named `nextInt` (in the sense of fetching the next random number from a sequence of numbers). In our program, we put:

```
xEnd = randomPositions.nextInt(100);
yEnd = randomPositions.nextInt(100);
```

The range of random numbers (`100` here) was chosen to be suitable for the size of the drawing area.

To summarize, we declare an instance of the appropriate class (`Random` here), and use `new` to create and initialize it. These two stages can be combined, or separated; it depends on the particular program you are working on. Then we use the `nextInt` method of the instance.

Let us broaden our discussion of the `Random` class. We will look at its constructors and its most useful methods.

Firstly, there are two constructors. Above, we used the one with no parameters. However, the constructor is overloaded: there is another version with a single parameter. Here are the two constructors in use:

```
private Random random = new Random();
private Random randomSame = new Random(1000);
```

The first version produces a different random sequence every time we run the program. The second version derives the random sequence from the number we supply – which can be any value. In this case the same random sequence occurs every time. We might use this second form if we wanted to perform many test runs with the same sequence.

Figure 6.3 shows the most useful methods.

Let us consider the `nextInt` method in more detail. In the `RandomLines` program, we put:

```
xEnd = randomPositions.nextInt(100);
yEnd = randomPositions.nextInt(100);
```

`nextInt(int n)`	Returns an `int` value `>= 0`, and `< n`
`nextDouble()`	This has no parameters. It returns a `double` value `>= 0.0`, and `< 1.0`

Figure 6.3 Methods of the `Random` class.

This will produce a random value in the range **0** to **99**. The value **100** will never occur. This is because the specification of **nextInt** states 'less than' rather than 'less than or equal to'. This is a common cause of programming errors, because most problems are stated with inclusive ranges, as in 'the throw of a die results in a number from **1** to **6**', or 'playing cards are numbered from **2** to **10**, excluding aces'. Similar warnings also apply to **nextDouble**, which will never produce a value of exactly **1.0**.

Here we will write a method which simplifies the use of random numbers. It has two parameters, letting us specify the minimum and maximum inclusive values of our numbers. Here is the code:

```
private int randomInRange(int min, int max) {
    return min+random.nextInt(max-min+1);
}
```

To simulate the throw of a die, we might put:

```
int lucky;
lucky = randomInRange(1, 6);
```

When you use a class, it is important to understand the facilities provided by its methods and constructors. Sometimes, the documentation that comes with Java systems is rather hard to understand, so in Appendix A we summarize all the classes that we use throughout the book.

SELF-TEST QUESTION

6.4 How would you call **randomInRange** to obtain a random age in the range **16** to **59** inclusive?

The **main** method and **new**

We have discussed the use of **new** in creating a new instance of a class, which we then use via its methods. However, if you step back from the detail of your programs, you will see that they are all classes, taking the form:

```
public class SomeName...{
    private declarations...
    a series of methods...
}
```

Informally, we have talked about 'writing a program' but in fact we should say 'writing a class'. But is the program a class, or an instance of a class?

Recall that the **main** method is called automatically by the Java system before anything else happens. Look at any of our **main** methods. Its first task is to use **new** to create an instance of the class which contains it.

We will continue to talk about programs, as this is more natural. To answer our question about programs and classes: a running program is an instance of a class. The **new** takes place in the **main** method.

● The Swing toolkit

When Java was created, it came with a set of classes containing user-interface components such as buttons, scrollbars, etc. The set of classes was known as the Abstract Window Toolkit (AWT). However, some of the components were rather low quality, and they also looked different on different platforms because they made use of the components provided by the operating system in use. We provide an overview of the AWT in Appendix B.

To improve the situation, a set of components was written in Java which provided more facilities, and which looked identical on any platform. The classes were referred to as the Swing toolkit. You have used the **JButton** class often – the **J** indicates that the class was written in Java.

Though Swing provides more power, we still need parts of the old AWT, as you will see from the **import** instructions we place at the top of our programs.

● Events

Above, we looked at **Random** and saw how to create new instances and manipulate these instances with their methods. We follow this approach for many classes. However, there are other classes – such as **JButton** – which are different, because they involve events. We will look at this class in detail, and then generalize the use of classes, to enable you to use any other classes you encounter.

We have used events in many of the programs you have seen. We provided a button, and code was placed in the **actionPerformed** method to respond to the event. Here we will cover events in more detail.

In Java, events are split into categories. For example, we have:

■ 'action' events, such as clicking on a button;
■ 'change' events, such as adjusting the position of a slider to change the volume of a computer loudspeaker.

Recall the **CarCounter** program, and locate the line:

```
public class CarCounter extends JFrame
    implements ActionListener {
```

The **extends** keyword expresses inheritance, which we cover in Chapter 10. The **implements** keyword can be used to provide event handling. Here is an analogy. Assume you have a SuperCredit card, and you see a sign outside a shop stating that SuperCredit cards are accepted. You assume that when you make a purchase, the shop will provide the facilities you need, such as a suitable machine to process your card. In other words, the shop implements the SuperCredit interface. We cover interfaces in Chapter 23.

When we use **implements ActionListener**, we are stating that our program implements the **ActionListener** interface. This requires that we provide a method named **actionPerformed**, which will be called when an action event happens – such as the click on a button.

In addition, we have to register the program as a 'listener' for types of event. This is covered below.

● Creating a `JButton`

Here we will look at the process of creating a button. Just like our use of **Random**, we must declare and initialize the object before using it. In addition, we must implement the **ActionListener** interface, and register as a listener for action events. Here again is the **CarCounter** program, which we will study:

```java
import java.awt.*;
import java.awt.event.*;
import javax.swing.*;

public class CarCounter extends JFrame
    implements ActionListener {

    private int carCount = 0;

    private JButton button;

    public static void main(String[] args) {
        CarCounter frame = new CarCounter();
        frame.setSize(300, 200);
        frame.createGUI();
        frame.show();
    }

    private void createGUI() {
        setDefaultCloseOperation(EXIT_ON_CLOSE);
        Container window = getContentPane();
        window.setLayout(new FlowLayout());

        button = new JButton("Car Entering");
        window.add(button);
        button.addActionListener(this);
    }

    public void actionPerformed(ActionEvent event) {
        carCount = carCount + 1;
        JOptionPane.showMessageDialog(null, "Cars:" + carCount);
    }
}
```

Here is the process:

■ Firstly, we state that our program implements the **ActionListener** interface:

```
public class CarCounter extends JFrame
    implements ActionListener {
```

This requires us to write a method named **actionPerformed**, as shown.

■ Then, we declare the button, as an instance variable:

```
private JButton button;
```

■ Then we create the button, providing the text that will appear on the button in its constructor. This could be done at the same time as the declaration, but we choose to group all the code concerned with initialization in a method, which we have named **createGUI**. The initialization is:

```
button = new JButton("Car Entering");
```

■ The next stage is to add the button to an instance of the **Container** class, which we have named **window**:

```
window.add(button);
```

Note that **add** is a method of **window**, not of **button**. The **add** method places the items on the screen in left-to-right order. Items in a row are centred. A new row of objects is automatically begun when a row is filled. (This layout scheme is known as 'flow layout'. There is another scheme known as 'border layout', which is discussed in Appendix A.)

■ We then register the program as a listener for action events from the button:

```
button.addActionListener(this);
```

■ Here is the event-handling method, where we place code to respond to the event:

```
public void actionPerformed(ActionEvent event) {
```

As you can see, the process is quite involved. The good news is that the process is almost identical each time we do it.

There are some arbitrary things we chose in the program. For example:

■ the name of the **JButton** instance – we chose **button**;

■ the text shown on the button – we chose **Car Entering**.

There are some essential unchangeable parts of the program:

■ the **import** instructions;

■ the **implements ActionListener**;

■ an **actionPerformed** method;

■ the use of **addActionListener** to register as a button listener;

■ the **main** method, and the parts of **createGUI** which set up the closing of the outer frame and the layout of the objects.

When we say unchangeable, we mean it. Don't invent your own names, such as `clickPerformed`.

Guidelines for using objects

We have seen how instances of the **Random** class and the **JButton** class can be incorporated into programs. Now we are in a position to step back and provide some general guidelines. Following these, we will apply them to the **JLabel**, **JTextField**, **JSlider**, **JPanel** and **Timer** classes.

Here is the approach.

1. Examine the documentation for the class in question. Determine the importing that is needed. Sometimes, additional classes will need importing, as well as the class in question (as in **JSlider** covered below).
2. Select a constructor, to be used with **new**.
3. If the class is a user-interface component, add it to the window.
4. Once the instance has been declared and created with **new**, use it via its methods.

Now we will examine other useful classes. There are no new facilities of Java required – we have seen how to incorporate classes and create instances. However, these classes are very useful, and appear in many of the following chapters.

The JLabel class

The **JLabel** lets us display non-changing text, such as user instructions or prompts. For text that will change – such as the result from a calculation – we would use a **JTextField**. The **SumTextFields** program (Figure 6.4) shows it in use, displaying the fixed = character. Let us examine its use.

- It is a Swing component, and our normal importing will suffice.
- Here is an example of its constructor, in which we supply the text to be displayed:

    ```
    equalsLabel = new JLabel(" = ");
    ```

Figure 6.4 Screenshot of the **SumTextFields** program.

- It is added to the window in a similar manner to a button.
- It produces no events, and it is unlikely that the program will manipulate it again, once it has been added to the window.

Here is the code of **SumTextFields**, which adds two values when the **+** button is clicked:

```java
import java.awt.*;
import java.awt.event.*;
import javax.swing.*;

public class SumTextFields extends JFrame
    implements ActionListener {

    private JTextField number1Field, number2Field, sumField;
    private JLabel equalsLabel;
    private JButton plusButton;

    public static void main(String[] args) {
        SumTextFields frame = new SumTextFields();
        frame.setSize(350, 100);
        frame.createGUI();
        frame.show();
    }

    private void createGUI() {
        setDefaultCloseOperation(EXIT_ON_CLOSE);
        Container window = getContentPane();
        window.setLayout(new FlowLayout());

        number1Field = new JTextField(7);
        window.add(number1Field);

        plusButton = new JButton("+");
        window.add(plusButton);
        plusButton.addActionListener(this);

        number2Field = new JTextField(7);
        window.add(number2Field);

        equalsLabel = new JLabel(" = ");
        window.add(equalsLabel);

        sumField = new JTextField(7);
        window.add(sumField);
    }

    public void actionPerformed(ActionEvent event) {
        int number1 = Integer.parseInt(number1Field.getText());
        int number2 = Integer.parseInt(number2Field.getText());
        sumField.setText(Integer.toString(number1 + number2));
    }
}
```

The JTextField class

The **JTextField** class provides a single-line area which can be used to display text or to input text. Let us examine its use:

- It is a Swing component, and our normal importing will suffice.

- When the user presses the 'enter' key in a text field, an action event is produced. If we wish to use this event, we must implement **ActionListener**, and provide an **actionPerformed** method. In our example, we will use a button-click rather than the 'enter' key to initiate the calculation.

- Here are examples of its constructors:

```
textField1 = new JTextField(15);
textField2 = new JTextField("Hello!", 15);
```

  The first one creates an empty text field with the specified width (in terms of characters), and the second one also lets us set up some initial text. Note that the default font of text fields is proportional, so **m** occupies more space than **1**. The width of a text field is based on the size of an **m**.

- It is added to the window in a similar manner to a button.

- Its contents can be manipulated by using the **setText** and **getText** methods, as in:

```
String s;
s = textField1.getText();
textField1.setText(s);
```

In the **SumTextFields** program, the user enters two integers into the text fields at the left. When the button is clicked, the sum is displayed in the third text field. Recall our use of input dialogs for inputting numbers in Chapter 4. Again, we need to convert the string entered in the text field into an integer, and we need to convert our integer result into a string in order to display it. We use **Integer.parseInt** and **Integer.toString**. Here is the code:

```
int number1 = Integer.parseInt(number1Field.getText());
int number2 = Integer.parseInt(number2Field.getText());
sumField.setText(Integer.toString(number1 + number2));
```

SELF-TEST QUESTION

6.5 Rewrite the **CarCounter** program so that the count is displayed in a text field rather than a message dialog.

The `JPanel` class

The panel can be used for drawing, or can be used to hold other objects such as buttons. When we create a drawing area, we often need to specify its size in pixels, rather than let Java treat it in the same way as it treats buttons.

Here is the standard code we use to create a panel with a specified size:

```
panel = new JPanel();
panel.setPreferredSize(new Dimension(200, 200));
panel.setBackground(Color.white);
window.add(panel);
```

To use the panel as a drawing area rather than a container for other objects, we use:

```
Graphics paper = panel.getGraphics();
```

The `Timer` class

The timer creates regularly spaced action events, which can be imagined as the tick of a clock. We can start and stop the timer, and can control its speed. Unlike a button, the timer has no on-screen representation. Here are the main timer facilities.

■ The timer creates ticks at regular intervals. Each tick is an event which is handled by the **actionPerformed** method.

■ Importing has to be done with care. There are two **Timer** classes in these libraries:

```
java.util
javax.swing
```

We require the one in the Swing library. If we import every class from each library and then try to declare an instance of class **Timer**, a compilation error occurs. Here is how we can resolve the conflict:

■ Most of our programs import every class from **javax.swing**. If the program doesn't need the **java.util** library, there is no problem. We declare a timer with:

```
private Timer timer;
```

■ If the program needs both libraries (as in the **Raindrops** program below) then we can declare a timer using:

```
private javax.swing.Timer timer;
```

We must use this long form every time we use the class name **Timer**.

■ The timer creates action events, so we specify **implements ActionListener** and provide an **actionPerformed** method.

- The constructor for the timer requires two parameters:
  - an integer specifying the number of milliseconds between events (ticks);
  - the program that is registered to detect the action events. As with buttons, we use **this**. Here is an example:

```
timer = new Timer(1000, this);
```

- We can start and stop the timer via **start** and **stop** methods.
- The time between events (in milliseconds) can be changed with **setDelay**, as in:

```
timer.setDelay(500);
```

Here is a program (**TimerExample**) which displays minutes and seconds on the screen. Figure 6.5 shows the screenshot, and here is the code.

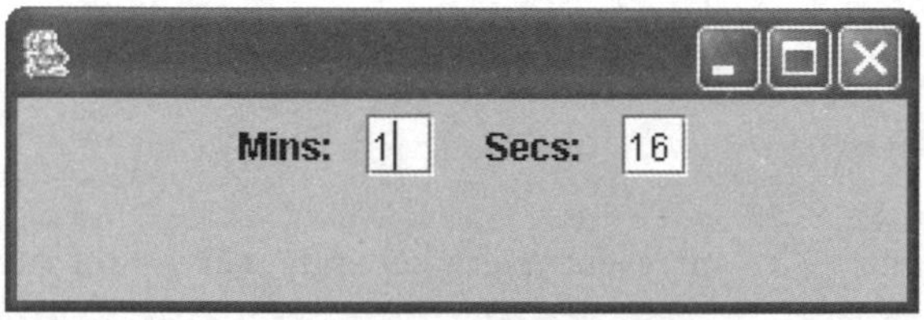

Figure 6.5 Screenshot of **TimerExample** program.

```
import java.awt.*;
import java.awt.event.*;
import javax.swing.*;

public class TimerExample extends JFrame
    implements ActionListener {

    private JTextField secsField, minsField;
    private JLabel secsLabel, minsLabel;
    private int ticks = 0;
    private Timer timer;

    public static void main (String[] args) {
        TimerExample frame = new TimerExample();
        frame.setSize(300,100);
        frame.createGUI();
        frame.show();
    }

    private void createGUI() {
        setDefaultCloseOperation(EXIT_ON_CLOSE);
        Container window = getContentPane();
        window.setLayout(new FlowLayout() );
```

```
            minsLabel = new JLabel("Mins: ");
            window.add(minsLabel);

            minsField = new JTextField(2);
            window.add(minsField);

            secsLabel = new JLabel(" Secs: ");
            window.add(secsLabel);

            secsField = new JTextField(2);
            window.add(secsField);
            timer = new Timer(1000, this);
            timer.start();
        }

    public void actionPerformed(ActionEvent event) {
            minsField.setText(Integer.toString(ticks / 60));
            secsField.setText(Integer.toString(ticks % 60));
            ticks = ticks + 1;
        }
    }
```

We create a timer with an event every second (**1000** milliseconds). The event handling involves:

- a private variable (**ticks**) to count the number of ticks;
- calculating minutes by dividing by **60**;
- using **%** to prevent the seconds display from exceeding **59**;
- updating the text fields;
- incrementing the counter.

SELF-TEST QUESTION

6.6 Explain why the **ticks** variable cannot be local.

● The JSlider class

Our final class is the slider. It provides a knob which can be dragged to select a value. You can see it at work in the **Raindrops** program in Figure 6.6. Here are the main points:

- We need to import the **javax.swing.event** library for event handling.
- It creates 'change' events. We need to use **implements ChangeListener**, and provide an event-handling **stateChanged** method.
- We create a slider by supplying four parameters for the constructor:
  - the orientation of the slider, specified by **JSlider.VERTICAL** or **JSlider. HORIZONTAL**;

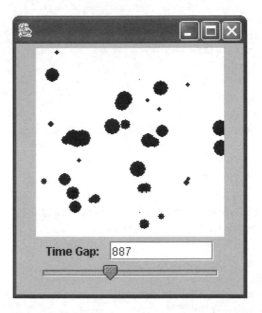

Figure 6.6 Screenshot of **Raindrops** program.

- the minimum value of the slider;
- the maximum value of the slider;
- the initial position of the knob.

- The current value is obtained by the **getValue** method.

- The **stateChanged** method is called when the user moves the knob. Several events will be created as the knob is dragged, but the final call will occur when the user settles on a value.

Here is the code of **Raindrops**. Figure 6.6 shows its screenshot.

```java
import java.awt.*;
import java.awt.event.*;
import javax.swing.*;
import javax.swing.event.*;
import java.util.*;

public class Raindrops extends JFrame implements
    ActionListener, ChangeListener {

    private JPanel panel;
    private Random random;
    private javax.swing.Timer timer;
    private JSlider slider;
    private JTextField gapField;
    private JLabel gapLabel;
```

```
public static void main (String[] args) {
    Raindrops frame = new Raindrops();
    frame.setSize(250, 300);
    frame.createGUI();
    frame.show();
}

private void createGUI() {
    setDefaultCloseOperation(EXIT_ON_CLOSE);
    Container window = getContentPane();
    window.setLayout(new FlowLayout() );
    random = new Random();

    panel = new JPanel();
    panel.setPreferredSize(new Dimension(200, 200));
    panel.setBackground(Color.white);
    window.add(panel);

    gapLabel = new JLabel("Time Gap:  ");
    window.add(gapLabel);
    gapField = new JTextField(10);
    window.add(gapField);

    slider = new JSlider(JSlider.HORIZONTAL, 200, 2000, 1000);
    window.add(slider);
    slider.addChangeListener(this);
    gapField.setText(Integer.toString(slider.getValue()));
    timer = new javax.swing.Timer(1000, this);
    timer.start();
}

public void actionPerformed(ActionEvent event) {
    int x, y, size;
    Graphics paper = panel.getGraphics();
    x=random.nextInt(200);
    y = random.nextInt(200);
    size = random.nextInt(20);
    paper.fillOval(x,y, size, size);
}

public void stateChanged(ChangeEvent e) {
    int timeGap = slider.getValue();
    gapField.setText(Integer.toString(timeGap));
    timer.setDelay(timeGap);
}
}
```

The program simulates raindrops of a random size falling on a sheet of paper. The user can alter the time between drops by dragging on the slider.

Every time a timer event happens, the program draws a randomly sized circle, at a random position. When the slider is moved, the current value of the slider is displayed in a text field, and the speed of the timer is altered. The slider range of **200** to **2000** was found by experimentation. The program uses most of the classes we have examined, but there are two new points:

- We declare the timer with the full form of its name, because the **util** library has been imported for **Random**.
- We exploit the interdependency of the components during the initialization phase. We set the initial value of the text field to the initial value of the slider.

SELF-TEST QUESTION

6.7 In the **Raindrops** example, the current position of the knob is displayed in a text field. What are the consequences of altering the initial position of the knob in the call of **JSlider** constructor?

Programming principles

For many years it has been the dream of programmers to be able to build programs in the same way that hi-fi systems are built, i.e. from off-the-shelf components such as speakers, amplifiers, volume controls, etc. The rise in object-oriented programming coupled with the extensive Java class libraries brings this dream closer.

Programming pitfalls

- If an instance is declared but its initialization with **new** is omitted, a run-time error is produced, of type **nullPointerException**. Run-time errors (i.e. bugs) are more problematic than compile-time errors; they are harder to find, and they are more serious, because the program's execution is halted.

- The Java GUI class names begin with **J**, such as **JButton**. There are similarly named classes in the AWT library, but without the **J** (such as **Button**). A run-time error results if you use these classes. Remember the **J**.

Grammar spot

- Instance variables are declared outside methods, using **private**, as in:

```
private int yourVariable;
private Random myVariable = new Random();
```

- Instance variables can be initialized at declaration time, or inside a method.

New language elements

- **private** instance variables.
- Using **new** for instantiation.
- **import** to allow easy use of libraries.
- The **JButton, JLabel, JTextField, Random** and **Timer** classes.

Summary

The Java system has a vast number of classes which you can (and ought to) use. Do not write your own code without investigating the libraries first.

Exercises

6.1 Write a program which calculates the area of a rectangle. The dimensions should be input from text fields, and the result should be displayed in a text field. Ensure that the input fields are clearly labelled.

6.2 Write a program which produces a random number between 200 and 400 each time a button is clicked. The program should display this number and the sum and average of all the numbers so far. As you click again and again, the average should converge on 300. If it doesn't, we would suspect the random number generator – just as we would be suspicious of a coin that came out heads 100 times in a row!

6.3 (a) Write a program which converts degrees Celsius to degrees Fahrenheit. The Celsius value should be entered in a text field – use integer values. Clicking on a button should cause the Fahrenheit value to be displayed in another text field. The conversion formula is:

```
f = (c * 9) / 5 + 32;
```

(b) Modify the program so that the Celsius value is entered via a slider, with its minimum set to 0, and its maximum set to 100.

(c) Represent both the temperatures as long thin rectangles, to be drawn on after every 'change' event. Remember to clear the drawing area and to reset the drawing colour each time.

6.4 Write a program which calculates the volume of a swimming pool, and which also displays its cross-section in a picture box. The width of the pool is fixed at 5 metres and the length is fixed at 20 metres. The program should have two sliders – one to adjust the depth of the

Length

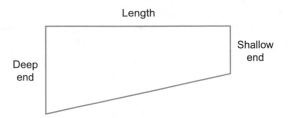

Shallow
end

Deep
end

Figure 6.7 Swimming pool cross-section.

deep end, and one to adjust the depth of the shallow end. The minimum depth of each end is 1 metre. Redraw the pool in the **stateChanged** method. Choose suitable values for the maximum and minimum slider values at design time. The volume formula is:

```
v = averageDepth * width * length;
```

Figure 6.7 shows the cross-section.

6.5 Write a program which displays changing minutes and seconds, representing them by two long rectangles: make the maximum width of the rectangles equal to 600 pixels to simplify the arithmetic (10 pixels for each minute and each second). Set the size of the frame to 700 pixels wide, and set the preferred width of the drawing panel to 700 pixels. Redraw the two rectangles every second. Figure 6.8 shows a representation of 30 minutes and 15 seconds.

600 pixels wide

Figure 6.8 Time display – for 30 minutes, 15 seconds.

The program should count up in seconds with a timer, and display the total seconds and the time in minutes and seconds. In order to speed up testing the program, you should reduce the timer interval from 1000 milliseconds to, say, 200.

6.6 This question guides you through the writing of a geometry game:

(a) Write a program with two sliders which control the horizontal and vertical position of a circle of 200 pixels diameter. Clear the screen and redraw the circle in the **stateChanged** method.

(b) Add a third slider to control the diameter of the circle.

(c) What follows is based on the mathematical fact that a circle can be drawn through any three points. The program should initially display three points (each is a small filled circle). Good initial positions are (100, 100), (200, 200), (200, 100), but you can add a small random number to them for variety. The player has to manipulate the circle until the circle goes through each point.

Answers to self-test questions

6.1 The program will still compile and run – but will probably produce the wrong results. It now modifies the value of a variable that can be used in other methods. Before, it modified a local variable.

6.2 Each button-click draws a vertical line, 100 pixels long. Each line is located 10 pixels to the right of the previous one.

6.3 The second instruction must be placed inside a method. Alternatively, the single-statement form could be used, as in:

```
private Random r = new Random();
```

6.4
```
int age = randomInRange(16, 59);
```

6.5 We add a text field to the window using the same coding as in the **SumTextFields** program. A suitable name is **countField**. Rather than displaying the answer in a message dialog, we put:

```
countField.setText(Integer.toString(carCount));
```

6.6 Local variables are created afresh when their method is entered, and their values are erased when a method finishes. If **ticks** were local, the count would not be maintained.

6.7 There are no consequences, because the value of the text field is initialized with the current value of the slider knob, irrespective of what the value is.

CHAPTER 7

Selection

This chapter explains:

- how to use **if** and **switch** statements to carry out tests;
- how to handle multiple events;
- how to use comparison operators such as **>**;
- how to use the logical operators **&&**, **||** and **!**;
- how to declare and use **boolean** data;
- how to compare strings.

● Introduction

We all make selections in daily life. We wear a coat if it is raining. We buy a CD if we have enough money. Selections are also used a lot in programs. The computer tests a value and, according to the result, takes one course of action or another. Whenever the program has a choice of actions and decides to take one action or the other, an **if** or a **switch** statement is used to describe the situation.

We have seen that a computer program is a series of instructions to a computer. The computer obeys the instructions one after another in sequence. But sometimes we want the computer to carry out a test on some data and then take one of a choice of actions depending on the result of the test. For example, we might want the computer to test someone's age and then tell them either that they may vote or that they are too young. This is called selection. It uses a statement (or instruction) called the **if** statement, the central subject of this chapter.

if statements are so important that they are used in every programming language that has ever been invented.

The *if* statement

Our first example is a program that simulates the digital lock on a safe. The screen is as shown in Figure 7.1. The safe is locked unless the user enters the correct code into a text field, initially empty. When the button is clicked, the program converts the entered text into a number and compares it with the correct code. If the code is correct, a message is displayed.

Figure 7.1 Screen for the safe program.

```java
import java.awt.*;
import java.awt.event.*;
import javax.swing.*;

public class Safe extends JFrame implements ActionListener {

    private JLabel greetingLabel;
    private JTextField codeField;
    private JButton button;
    private JTextField outcomeTextField;

    public static void main(String[] args) {
        Safe demo = new Safe();
        demo.setSize(100,150);
        demo.createGUI();
        demo.show();
    }

    private void createGUI() {
        setDefaultCloseOperation(EXIT_ON_CLOSE);
        Container window = getContentPane();
        window.setLayout(new FlowLayout());

        greetingLabel = new JLabel("enter code");
        window.add(greetingLabel);
```

```
        codeField = new JTextField(5);
        window.add(codeField);

        button = new JButton("unlock");
        window.add(button);
        button.addActionListener(this);

        outcomeTextField = new JTextField(5);
        window.add(outcomeTextField);
    }

    public void actionPerformed(ActionEvent event) {
        String codeString;
        int code;

        codeString = codeField.getText();
        code = Integer.parseInt(codeString);
        if (code == 123) {
            outcomeTextField.setText("unlocked");
        }
    }
}
```

The **if** statement tests the value of the number entered. If the number equals the value 123, the statement sandwiched between the curly brackets (braces) is carried out. Next, any statement after the closing brace is executed. On the other hand, if the number is not equal to 123, the sandwiched statement is ignored and any statement after the closing brace is executed.

Notice that the condition being tested is enclosed in brackets and this is a grammatical rule of Java.

Notice also that a test for equality uses the **==** operator (not the **=** operator, which is used for assignment).

One way of visualizing an **if** statement is as an activity diagram (Figure 7.2). This shows the above **if** statement in graphical form. To use this diagram, start at the blob

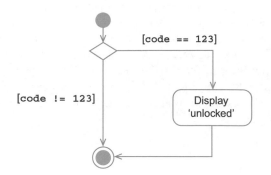

Figure 7.2 Activity diagram for an **if** statement.

at the top and follow the arrows. A decision is shown as a diamond, with the two possible conditions shown in square brackets. Actions are shown in rounded boxes and the end of the sequence is a specially shaped blob at the bottom of the diagram.

There are two parts to the **if** statement:

- the condition being tested;
- the statement or sequence of statements to be executed if the condition is true.

All programs consist of a sequence of actions, and the sequence evident here is:

1. A piece of text is input from the text field.
2. Next, a test is done.
3. If appropriate, a message is displayed to say that the safe is unlocked.

Very often we want not just one, but a complete sequence of actions carried out if the result of the test is true, and these are sandwiched between the braces.

Notice that a line is indented to reflect the structure of the **if** statement. Indentation means using spaces to push the text over to the right. Although indentation is not essential, it is highly desirable so that the (human) reader of a program can understand it easily. All good programs (whatever the language) have indentation and all good programmers use it.

SELF-TEST QUESTION

7.1 Enhance the **if** statement so that it clears a number with the correct code entered into the text field.

● `if...else`

Sometimes we want to specify two sequences of actions – those that are carried out if the condition is true and those that are carried out if the condition is false.

The user of the voting checker program enters their age into a text field and the program decides whether they can vote or not. The screen is shown in Figure 7.3. When the user clicks on the button, the program extracts the information that the user has entered into the text field, converts the string into an integer and places the number in the variable called **age**. Next, we want the program to take different actions depending on whether the value is:

- greater than 17, or
- less than or equal to 17.

This is achieved using the **if** statement:

Figure 7.3 The voting checking program screen.

```
if (age > 17) {
    decisionField.setText("you may vote");
    commentaryField.setText("congratulations");
}
else {
    decisionField.setText("you may not vote");
    commentaryField.setText("sorry");
}
```

The results of the test are displayed in a number of text fields. The complete program is as follows:

```
import java.awt.*;
import java.awt.event.*;
import javax.swing.*;

public class Voting extends JFrame implements ActionListener {

    private JLabel greetingLabel;
    private JTextField ageField;
    private JButton button;
    private JTextField decisionField;
    private JTextField commentaryField;
    private JTextField signOffField;

    public static void main(String[] args) {
        Voting demo = new Voting();
        demo.setSize(125,200);
        demo.createGUI();
        demo.show();
    }
```

```
        private void createGUI() {
            setDefaultCloseOperation(EXIT_ON_CLOSE);
            Container window = getContentPane();
            window.setLayout(new FlowLayout());

            greetingLabel = new JLabel("enter your age");
            window.add(greetingLabel);

            ageField = new JTextField(5);
            window.add(ageField);

            button = new JButton("check");
            window.add(button);
            button.addActionListener(this);

            decisionField = new JTextField(10);
            window.add(decisionField);

            commentaryField = new JTextField(10);
            window.add(commentaryField);

            signOffField = new JTextField(10);
            window.add(signOffField);
        }

        public void actionPerformed(ActionEvent event) {
            int age;

            age = Integer.parseInt(ageField.getText());
            if (age > 17)
            {
                decisionField.setText("you may vote");
                commentaryField.setText("congratulations");
            }
            else
            {
                decisionField.setText("you may not vote");
                commentaryField.setText("sorry");
            }
            signOffField.setText("Best Wishes");
        }
    }
```

There are three parts to the **if** statement in this program:

■ the condition being tested – in this case whether the age is greater than 17;

■ the statement or sequence of statements to be executed if the condition is true, enclosed in braces;

■ the statement or statements to be executed if the condition is false, enclosed in braces.

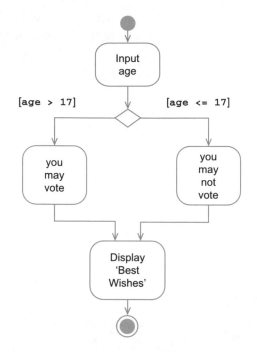

Figure 7.4 Activity diagram for an `if...else` statement.

The new element here is the word **`else`**, which introduces the second part of the **`if`** statement. Notice again how the indentation helps to emphasize the intention of the program.

We can visualize an **`if...else`** statement as an activity diagram, as shown in Figure 7.4. The diagram shows the condition being tested and the two separate actions.

● Comparison operators

The programs above used some of the comparison (sometimes called relational) operators. Here is a complete list:

Symbol	Meaning
>	greater than
<	less than
==	equals
!=	not equal to
<=	less than or equal to
>=	greater than or equal to

Notice again that Java uses two equals signs (`==`) to test whether two things are equal.

Choosing the appropriate operator often has to be done with great care. In the program to test whether someone can vote, the appropriate test should probably be:

```
if (age >= 18) {
    decisionField.setText("you can vote");
}
```

Note that it is always possible to write conditions in either of two ways. The following two program fragments achieve exactly the same result, but use different conditions:

```
if (age >= 18) {
    decisionField.setText("you may vote");
}
else {
    decisionField.setText("sorry");
}
```

achieves the same end as:

```
if (age < 18) {
    decisionField.setText("sorry");
}
else {
    decisionField.setText("you may vote");
}
```

Although these two fragments achieve the same end result, the first is probably better, because it spells out more clearly the condition for eligibility to vote.

SELF-TEST QUESTION

7.2 Do these two `if` statements achieve the same end or not?

```
if (age > 18) {
    decisionField.setText("you may vote");
}
if (age < 18) {
    decisionField.setText("you may not vote");
}
```

Humans sometimes have difficulty in judging the relative sizes of circles of different colours. The next program uses two sliders, and displays circles with equivalent sizes

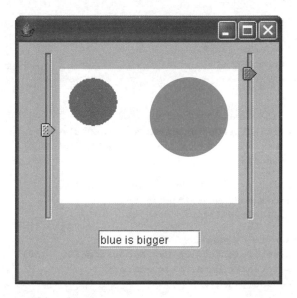

Figure 7.5 The bigger program.

(Figure 7.5). The program compares the sizes and reports on which one is the larger. Let us first write the program using the following **if** statement:

```
if (redValue > blueValue) {
    textField.setText("red is bigger");
}
else {
    textField.setText("blue is bigger");
}
```

The library method **fillOval** is used to draw a filled circle whose diameter is equal to the value obtained from the corresponding slider. The complete program is:

```
import java.awt.*;
import java.awt.event.*;
import javax.swing.*;
import javax.swing.event.*;

public class Bigger extends JFrame
                    implements ChangeListener {

    private JSlider redSlider;
    private JPanel panel;
    private JSlider blueSlider;
    private JTextField textField;
```

```java
public static void main(String[] args) {
    Bigger demo = new Bigger();
    demo.setSize(300,300);
    demo.createGUI();
    demo.show();
}

private void createGUI() {
    setDefaultCloseOperation(EXIT_ON_CLOSE);
    Container window = getContentPane();
    window.setLayout(new FlowLayout());

    redSlider = new JSlider(JSlider.VERTICAL);
    redSlider.addChangeListener(this);
    window.add(redSlider);

    panel = new JPanel();
    panel.setPreferredSize(new Dimension(200, 150));
    panel.setBackground(Color.white);
    window.add(panel);

    blueSlider = new JSlider(JSlider.VERTICAL);
    blueSlider.addChangeListener(this);
    window.add(blueSlider);

    textField = new JTextField(10);
    window.add(textField);
}

public void stateChanged(ChangeEvent e) {
    Graphics paper = panel.getGraphics();

    int redValue, blueValue;
    redValue = redSlider.getValue();
    blueValue = blueSlider.getValue();

    paper.setColor(Color.white);
    paper.fillRect(0, 0, 200, 150);
    paper.setColor(Color.red);
    paper.fillOval(10, 10, redValue, redValue);
    paper.setColor(Color.blue);
    paper.fillOval(100, 10, blueValue, blueValue);

    if (redValue > blueValue) {
        textField.setText("red is bigger");
    }
    else {
        textField.setText("blue is bigger");
    }
}
}
```

This program seems to work fine, but again illustrates the importance of care when you use **if** statements. In this program, what happens when the two values are equal? The answer is that the program finds that blue is bigger – which is clearly not the case. We could enhance the program to spell things out more clearly by changing the **if** statement to:

```
if (redValue > blueValue) {
    textField.setText("red is bigger");
}
if (blueValue > redValue) {
    textField.setText("blue is bigger");
}
if (redValue == blueValue) {
    textField.setText("They are equal");
}
```

This next example is a program that keeps track of the largest value achieved, as a number changes. This is a common exercise in programming. Some thermometers have a mechanism for recording the maximum temperature that has been reached. This program simulates such a thermometer using a slider. It displays the value of the maximum value that the slider is set to (see Figure 7.6).

The program uses a variable named **max**, a class-level variable that holds the value of the largest temperature achieved so far. **max** is declared like this:

```
private int max = 0;
```

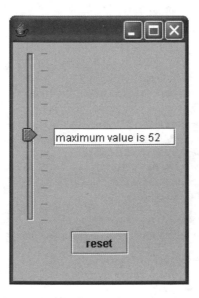

Figure 7.6 Screen for the thermometer.

An **if** statement compares the current value of the slider with the value of **max**, and alters **max** if necessary:

```
int temp;

temp = slider.getValue();
if (temp > max) {
    max = temp;
}
```

The complete program is:

```
import java.awt.*;
import java.awt.event.*;
import javax.swing.*;
import javax.swing.event.*;

public class Max extends JFrame implements ChangeListener,
                                           ActionListener {

    private JSlider slider;
    private JTextField textField;
    private JButton button;

    private int max = 0;

    public static void main(String[] args) {
        Max demo = new Max();
        demo.setSize(200,300);
        demo.createGUI();
        demo.show();
    }

    private void createGUI() {
        setDefaultCloseOperation(EXIT_ON_CLOSE);
        Container window = getContentPane();
        window.setLayout(new FlowLayout());
        slider = new JSlider(JSlider.VERTICAL, 0, 100, 0);
        slider.setMajorTickSpacing(10);
        slider.setPaintTicks(true);
        slider.addChangeListener(this);
        window.add(slider);

        textField = new JTextField(12);
        window.add(textField);

        button = new JButton("reset");
        button.addActionListener(this);
        window.add(button);
    }
```

```
public void stateChanged(ChangeEvent e) {
    int temp;
    temp = slider.getValue();
    if (temp > max) {
        max = temp;
    }
    display();
}

public void actionPerformed(ActionEvent event) {
    textField.setText("");
    max = 0;
}

private void display() {
    textField.setText("maximum value is " + max);
}
}
```

SELF-TEST QUESTION

7.3 Write a program that displays the numeric value of the minimum value that the slider is set to.

We now consider a program that simulates throwing two dice. The computer decides the die values randomly. We will create a button, with the caption 'throw'. When it is clicked, the program will obtain two random numbers and use them as the die values (Figure 7.7).

To get a random number, we use the method **nextInt** from the library class **Random**. We met this class back in Chapter 6. What we need for our purpose is an integer in the range 1 to 6. So we get numbers in the range 0 to 5 and simply add 1 to them.

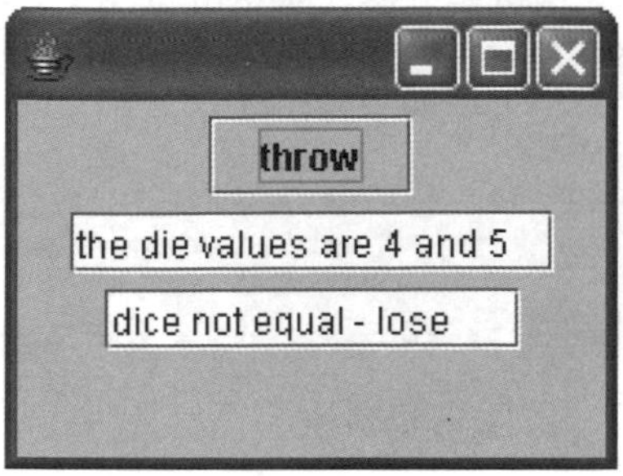

Figure 7.7 Gambling.

The program to throw two dice is given below:

```java
import java.awt.*;
import java.awt.event.*;
import javax.swing.*;
import java.util.*;
class Gambling extends JFrame implements ActionListener {
    private JButton button;
    private JTextField valuesTextField, resultTextField;
    private Random random;
    public static void main(String[] args) {
        Gambling demo = new Gambling();
        demo.setSize(200,150);
        demo.createGUI();
        demo.show();
    }
    private void createGUI() {
        setDefaultCloseOperation(EXIT_ON_CLOSE);
        Container window = getContentPane();
        window.setLayout(new FlowLayout());
        button = new JButton("throw");
        window.add(button);
        button.addActionListener(this);
        valuesTextField = new JTextField(14);
        window.add(valuesTextField);
        resultTextField = new JTextField(12);
        window.add(resultTextField);
        random = new Random();
    }
    public void actionPerformed(ActionEvent event) {
        int die1, die2;
        die1 = random.nextInt(6) + 1;
        die2 = random.nextInt(6) + 1;
        valuesTextField.setText("the die values are "
            + Integer.toString(die1) + " and "
            + Integer.toString(die2));
        if (die1 == die2) {
            resultTextField.setText("dice equal - a win");
        }
        else {
            resultTextField.setText("dice not equal - lose");
        }
    }
}
```

Multiple events

The **if** statement can fulfil an important role in handling multiple events. For example, a simple program has two buttons, with the captions 1 and 2, Figure 7.8. When a button is clicked, the program displays the number of the button. Whichever button-click event occurs, the same method, **actionPerformed**, is called. So how do we distinguish between them? An **if** statement is used to detect which button was clicked. Then the appropriate action can be taken.

When a button event occurs, the operating system calls method **actionPerformed**. This, central, part of the program is:

```java
public void actionPerformed(ActionEvent event) {
    Object source = event.getSource();
    if (source == button1) {
        textField.setText("button 1");
    }
    else {
        textField.setText("button 2");
    }
}
```

The parameter passed to **actionPerformed**, named **event** in the program, provides information about the nature of the event. Using method **getSource** on **event** returns the object that was responsible for the event. We place this in a variable named **source**, an object of the class **Object**. Then we use an **if** statement to compare this object with the possible candidates. Thus we are using the **==** operator to compare objects, not numbers or strings. (Note that it is not the = operator.)

Figure 7.8 Multiple buttons.

The full text of the program is:

```java
import java.awt.*;
import java.awt.event.*;
import javax.swing.*;

class Buttons extends JFrame implements ActionListener {
    private JButton button1, button2;
    private JTextField textField;

    public static void main(String[] args) {
        Buttons demo = new Buttons();
        demo.setSize(100,100);
        demo.createGUI();
        demo.show();
    }

    private void createGUI() {
        setDefaultCloseOperation(EXIT_ON_CLOSE);
        Container window = getContentPane();
        window.setLayout(new FlowLayout());

        button1 = new JButton("1");
        window.add(button1);
        button1.addActionListener(this);

        button2 = new JButton("2");
        window.add(button2);
        button2.addActionListener(this);

        textField = new JTextField(6);
        window.add(textField);
    }

    public void actionPerformed(ActionEvent event) {
        Object source = event.getSource();
        if (source == button1) {
            textField.setText("button 1");
        }
        else {
            textField.setText("button 2");
        }
    }
}
```

SELF-TEST QUESTION

7.4 Suppose there are three buttons, with captions 1, 2 and 3. Write the code to display the number of the button that is clicked.

● And, or, not

Often in programming we need to test two things at once. Suppose, for example, we want to test whether someone should pay a junior rate for a ticket:

```java
if (age >= 6 && age < 16) {
    textField.setText("junior rate");
}
```

The word `&&` is one of the Java logical operators and simply means 'and' as we would use it in English.

Additional brackets can be used to improve the readability of these more complex conditions. For example, we can rewrite the above statement as:

```java
if ((age >= 6) && (age < 16)) {
    textField.setText("junior rate");
}
```

Although the inner brackets are not essential, they serve to distinguish the two conditions being tested.

It might be very tempting to write:

```java
if (age >= 6 && < 16) // error!
```

but this is incorrect. Instead, the conditions have to be spelled out in full as follows:

```java
if (age >= 6 && age < 16) // OK
```

We would use the `||` operator, meaning or, in an `if` statement like this:

```java
if (age < 6 || age >= 60) {
    textField.setText("reduced rate");
}
```

in which the reduced rate is applicable for people who are younger than 6 or 60 plus.

The `!` operator means 'not' and gets a lot of use in programming, even though in English the use of a negative can suffer from lack of clarity. Here is an example of the use of not:

```java
if (! (age > 16)) {
    textField.setText("too young");
}
```

This means: test to see if the age is greater than 16. If this result is true, the `!` makes it false. If it is false, the `!` makes it true. Then, if the outcome is true, display the message. This can, of course, be written more simply without the `!` operator.

SELF-TEST QUESTION

7.5   Rewrite the above `if` statement without using the `!` operator.

Figure 7.9 The dice program.

The next program illustrates complex tests. Two dice are thrown in a betting game and the program has to decide what the result is. The program uses two sliders, each with a range of 1 to 6 to specify the values of each of the two dice (Figure 7.9). The outcome is displayed in two text fields. Initially, we make the rule that only a total score of 6 wins anything.

The program code is given below. Whenever either of the two sliders is moved, the program displays the total value and uses an **if** statement to see whether there is a win.

```java
import java.awt.*;
import java.awt.event.*;
import javax.swing.*;
import javax.swing.event.*;

public class Dice extends JFrame implements ChangeListener {
    private JSlider slider1, slider2;
    private JTextField totalTextField, commentTextField;
    public static void main(String[] args) {
        Dice demo = new Dice();
        demo.setSize(200,150);
        demo.createGUI();
        demo.show();
    }

    private void createGUI() {
        setDefaultCloseOperation(EXIT_ON_CLOSE);
        Container window = getContentPane();
        window.setLayout(new FlowLayout());

        slider1 = new JSlider(1, 6, 3);
        slider1.addChangeListener(this);
        window.add(slider1);

        slider2 = new JSlider(1, 6, 3);
        slider2.addChangeListener(this);
        window.add(slider2);

        totalTextField = new JTextField(10);
        window.add(totalTextField);
```

```
        commentTextField= new JTextField(10);
        window.add(commentTextField);
    }
    public void stateChanged(ChangeEvent e) {
        int die1, die2, total;
        die1 = slider1.getValue();
        die2 = slider2.getValue();
        total = die1 + die2;
        totalTextField.setText("total is " + total);
        if (total == 6) {
            commentTextField.setText("you have won");
        }
        else {
            commentTextField.setText("you have lost");
        }
    }
}
```

Now we will alter the rules and see how to rewrite the program. Suppose that any pair of identical values wins, i.e. two ones, two twos, etc. Then the **if** statement is:

```
if (die1 == die2) {
    commentTextField.setText("you have won");
}
```

Now let's suppose that you only win if you get a total of either 2 or 7:

```
if ((total == 2) || (total == 7)) {
    commentTextField.setText("you have won");
}
```

Notice again that we have enclosed each of the conditions within brackets. These brackets aren't strictly necessary in Java, but they help a lot to clarify the meaning of the condition to be tested.

The Java and, or and not operators are summarized in the following table:

Symbol	Meaning
&&	and
||	or
!	not

SELF-TEST QUESTIONS

7.6   Alter the dice program so that a win is a total value of 2, 5 or 7.

7.7   Write **if** statements to test whether someone is eligible for full-time employment. The rule is that you must be 16 or above and younger than 65.

● Nested `ifs`

Look at the following program fragment:

```
if (age < 6) {
    textField.setText("child rate");
}
else {
    if (age < 16) {
    textField.setText("junior rate");
    }
    else {
        textField.setText("adult rate");
    }
}
```

You will see that the second **if** statement is completely contained within the first. (The indentation helps to make this clear.) This is called nesting. Nesting is not the same as indentation – it is just that the indentation makes the nesting very apparent.

The effect of this piece of program is:

■ if the age is less than 6, the rate is the child rate;

■ otherwise, if the age is less than 16, the rate is the junior rate;

■ otherwise, if none of the above conditions are true, the rate is the adult rate.

It is common to see nesting in programs, but a program like this has a complexity which makes it slightly difficult to understand. This section of program can be rewritten, in a style of nested **if**s known as the **else if**, as follows:

```
if (age < 6) {
    textField.setText("child rate");
}
else if (age < 16) {
    textField.setText("junior rate");
}
else {
    textField.setText("adult rate");
}
```

This version is exactly the same as the above version above except that the indentation is different and some of the pairs of braces have been eliminated. This is because the rule is that when there is only a **single** statement to be executed, you can dispense with the braces. This is the only occasion when we recommend omitting the braces.

Here is a third version of this piece of program. Sometimes it is possible to write a program more simply using the logical operators. Here, for example, the same result as above is achieved without nesting:

```
if (age < 6) {
    textField.setText("child rate");
}
if ((age >= 6) && (age < 16)) {
    textField.setText("junior rate");
}
if (age >= 16) {
    textField.setText("adult rate");
}
```

We now have three pieces of program that achieve the same end result, two with nesting and one without. Some people argue that it is hard to understand nesting, such a program is prone to errors and that therefore nesting should be avoided. Nesting can often be avoided using the logical operators.

SELF-TEST QUESTIONS

7.8 Write a program to input a salary from a slider and determine how much tax someone should pay according to the following rules:

People pay no tax if they earn up to $10000. They pay tax at the rate of 20% on the amount they earn over $10000 but up to $50000. They pay tax at 90% on any money they earn over $50000. The slider should have a range from 0 to 100000.

7.9 Write a program that creates three sliders and displays the largest of the three values.

7.10 The Young and Beautiful vacation company restricts its clients to ages between 18 and 30. (Below 18 you have no money; after 30 you have too many wrinkles.) Write a program to test whether you are eligible to go on vacation with this company. The age is entered into a text field. The outcome is displayed in a second text field when a button is clicked.

switch

The **switch** statement is another way of doing a lot of **if** statements. You can always accomplish everything you need with the aid of **if** statements but **switch** can be neater in appropriate circumstances. For example, suppose we need a piece of program to display the day of the week as a string. Suppose that the program represents the day of the week as an **int** variable called **dayNumber**, which has one of the values 1 to 7, representing the days Monday to Sunday. We want to convert the integer version of the day into a string version called **dayName**. We could write the following series of **if** statements:

```
if (dayNumber == 1) {
    dayName = "Monday";
}
if (dayNumber == 2); {
    dayName = "Tuesday";
}
if (dayNumber == 3); {
    dayName = "Wednesday";
}
if (dayNumber == 4); {
    dayName = "Thursday";
}
if (dayNumber == 5) {
    dayName = "Friday";
}
if (dayNumber == 6) {
    dayName = "Saturday";
}
if (dayNumber == 7) {
    dayName = "Sunday";
}
```

Now although this piece of coding is clear and well structured, there is an alternative that has the same effect using the **switch** statement:

```
switch (dayNumber) {

    case 1:
        dayName = "Monday";
        break;

    case 2:
        dayName = "Tuesday";
        break;
```

```
case 3:
    dayName = "Wednesday";
    break;

case 4:
    dayName = "Thursday";
    break;

case 5:
    dayName = "Friday";
    break;

case 6:
    dayName = "Saturday";
    break;

case 7:
    dayName = "Sunday";
    break;
}
```

The word **case** precedes each of the possible values. The **break** statement transfers control to the very end of the **switch** statement, marked with a brace. This now exploits the symmetry of what needs to happen more clearly than the equivalent series of **if**s.

A **switch** statement like this can be visualized as an activity diagram in Figure 7.10.

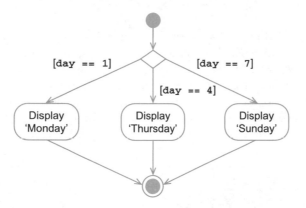

Figure 7.10 Activity diagram showing part of a **switch** statement.

SELF-TEST QUESTION

7.11 Write a method that converts the integers 1, 2, 3 and 4 into the words diamonds, hearts, clubs and spades respectively.

Several statements can follow one of the options in a **switch** statement. For example, one of the options could be:

```
case 6:
    JOptionPane.showMessageDialog(null, "hurray");
    dayName = "Saturday";
    break;
```

Another feature of the **switch** statement is grouping several options together, like this:

```
switch (dayNumber) {
    case 1:
    case 2:
    case 3:
    case 4:
    case 5:
        dayName = "weekday";
        break;

    case 6:
    case 7:
        dayName = "weekend";
        break;
}
```

Another, sometimes useful, part of the **switch** statement is the **default** option. Suppose in the above example that the value of the integer denoting the day of the week is input from a text field. Then there is the distinct possibility that the user will erroneously enter a number that is not in the range 1 to 7. Any decent program needs to take account of this, in order to prevent something odd happening or the program crashing. The **switch** statement is very good at dealing with this situation, because we can supply a 'catch-all' or default option that will be used if none of the others are valid:

```
switch (dayNumber) {
    case 1:
        dayName = "Monday";
        break;

    case 2:
        dayName = "Tuesday";
        break;

    case 3:
        dayName = "Wednesday";
        break;
```

```
        case 4:
            dayName = "Thursday";
            break;

        case 5:
            dayName = "Friday";
            break;

        case 6:
            dayName = "Saturday";
            break;

        case 7:
            dayName = "Sunday";
            break;

        default:
            dayName = "illegal day";
            break;
    }
```

If a **default** option is omitted from a **switch** statement and if none of the cases provided corresponds to the actual value of the variable, then all the options are ignored.

● Boolean variables

All of the types of variable that we have met so far are designed to hold numbers, strings or objects. Now we meet a new kind of variable called a **boolean**, which can only hold either the value **true** or the value **false**. The words **boolean**, **true** and **false** are reserved keywords in Java and cannot be used for any other purpose. This type of variable is named after the nineteenth-century British mathematician George Boole who made a large contribution towards the development of mathematical logic, in which the ideas of true and false play a central role.

This next program displays a shop sign (Figure 7.11). The sign says open or closed. A **boolean** variable, named **open**, is used to record whether the shop is open (**true**) or closed (**false**). Two buttons enable the shopkeeper to switch the sign to open or to closed. Another two buttons switch the sign on and off. The program displays large-font letters by using the **setFont** method.

The **boolean open** is a class-level variable, initially false, to denote that the shop is closed:

```
    private boolean open = false;
```

When the **Open** button is clicked:

```
    open = true;
```

Figure 7.11 The shop sign.

When the **Closed** button is clicked:

```
open = false;
```

When the **On** button is clicked, the value of **open** is tested with an **if** statement and the appropriate sign displayed:

```
if (open) {
    textField.setText("Open");
}
else {
    textField.setText("Closed");
}
```

The complete code is:

```
import java.awt.*;
import java.awt.event.*;
import javax.swing.*;
public class ShopSign extends JFrame implements ActionListener {
    private JButton onButton, offButton, openButton, closedButton;
    private JTextField textField;
    private boolean on = false, open = false;
    public static void main(String[] args) {
        ShopSign demo = new ShopSign();
        demo.setSize(250,200);
        demo.createGUI();
        demo.show();
    }
```

```java
private void createGUI() {
    setDefaultCloseOperation(EXIT_ON_CLOSE);
    Container window = getContentPane();
    window.setLayout(new FlowLayout());

    onButton = new JButton("On");
    window.add(onButton);
    onButton.addActionListener(this);

    offButton = new JButton("Off");
    window.add(offButton);
    offButton.addActionListener(this);

    textField = new JTextField(4);
    textField.setSize(5, 100);
    textField.setFont(new Font(null, Font.BOLD, 60));
    window.add(textField);

    openButton = new JButton("Open");
    window.add(openButton);
    openButton.addActionListener(this);

    closedButton = new JButton("Closed");
    window.add(closedButton);
    closedButton.addActionListener(this);
}
public void actionPerformed(ActionEvent event) {
    Object source = event.getSource();
    if (source == onButton) {
        handleOnButton();
    }
    else if (source == offButton) {
        handleOffButton();
    }
    else if (source == openButton) {
        handleOpenButton();
    }
    else handleClosedButton();
    drawSign();
}
private void handleOnButton() {
    on = true;
}
private void handleOffButton() {
    on = false;
}
private void handleOpenButton() {
    open = true;
}
private void handleClosedButton() {
    open = false;
}
```

```
    private void drawSign() {
        if (open) {
            textField.setText("Open");
        }
        else {
            textField.setText("Closed");
        }
        if (!on) {
            textField.setText("");
        }
    }
}
```

In the above program, one of the **if** statements is as follows, because the variable **open** is either true or false and can be tested directly:

```
if (open) {
```

This is the neater way of testing the value of a **boolean** variable. It can be rewritten less concisely as:

```
if (open == true) {
```

To summarize, **boolean** variables are used in programming to remember something, perhaps for a short time, perhaps for the whole time that the program is running.

SELF-TEST QUESTION

7.12 The shop owner needs an additional sign that says 'SALE'. Can we still use a **boolean** variable?

Methods can use **boolean** values as parameters and as return values. For example, here is a method that checks whether three numbers are in numerical order:

```
private boolean inOrder(int a, int b, int c) {
    if ((a <= b) && (b <= c)) {
        return true;
    }
    else {
        return false;
    }
}
```

● Comparing strings

Thus far, we have looked at programs that use the comparison operators (such as >) to compare numbers. However, many programs need to compare strings. The comparison operators are not appropriate and, instead, we use the **equals** method.

The safe program above required the user to enter a numeric code. Suppose instead that the code is alphabetic. In this case, the program needs to compare the string entered with the correct code (say 'Bill'). The appropriate **if** statement is:

```
String code;
code = codeField.getText();
if (code.equals("Bill")) {
    outcomeTextField.setText("unlocked");
}
```

The method **equals** is called. The parameter is the string 'Bill'. The method returns true or false. Then the **if** statement acts accordingly.

Programming principles

The computer normally obeys instructions one by one in a sequence. An **if** statement instructs the computer to test the value of some data and then take one of a choice of actions depending on the result of the test. This choice is sometimes called selection. The test of the data is called a condition. After an **if** statement is completed, the computer continues obeying the instructions in sequence.

Programming pitfalls

Brackets

The condition within an **if** statement must be enclosed in brackets. For example:

```
if (a > b)   etc.
```

Equals

If you want to test for equality, use the **==** operator (not a single equals sign, =). So this is correct:

```
if (a == b)   etc.
```

▶

▶ *Programming pitfalls continued*

Unfortunately, a program that uses a single = will compile correctly but work incorrectly.

Comparing strings

If you want to compare two strings, you must use the **equals** method, like this:

```
if (string1.equals(string2))  etc.
```

Braces

Next, we look at braces. This statement is entirely correct:

```
if (code == 123)
        outcomeTextField.setText("unlocked");
```

even though the braces that surround the statement are missing. The Java rule is that if there is only a **single** statement to be done, then the braces are not necessary. However, this can lead to nuisance programming problems, and the overwhelming advice is to insert the braces at all times. There is an exception to this suggestion when you use nested **if** statements in the **else if** style, explained above.

Compound conditions

You might find that you have written an **if** statement like this:

```
if (a > 18 && < 25)
```

which is wrong. Instead, the **&&** must link two complete conditions, preferably in brackets for clarity, like this:

```
if ((a > 18) && (a < 25))
```

switch

The **switch** statement is very useful, but unfortunately it is not as flexible as it could be. Suppose, for example, we want to write a piece of program to display two numbers, with the larger first, followed by the smaller. Using **if** statements, we would write:

```
if (a > b) {
    textField.setText(Integer.toString(a) + " is greater than "
                + Integer.toString(b));
}
```

```
if (b > a) {
    textField.setText(Integer.toString(b) + " is greater than "
                    + Integer.toString(a));
}
if (a == b) {
    textField.setText("they are equal");
}
```

We may be tempted to rewrite this using a **switch** statement as follows:

```
switch (?) { // beware! illegal Java
    case a > b:
        textField.setText(Integer.toString(a) + " is greater than"
                                    + Integer.toString(b));
        break;

    case b > a:
        textField.setText(Integer.toString(b) + " is greater than"
                                    + Integer.toString(a));
        break;

    case a == b:
        textField.setText("they are equal");
        break;
}
```

but this is not allowed because, as indicated by the question mark, **switch** only works with a single integer variable (or a **char** variable) as its subject and **case** cannot use the operators **>**, **==**, **<**, etc.

Grammar spot

The first type of **if** statement has the structure:

```
if (condition) {
    statements
}
```

The second type of **if** statement has the structure:

```
if (condition) {
    statements
}
else {
    statements
}
```

▶

> *Grammar spot continued*

The `switch` statement has the structure:

```
switch (variable) {
    case value1:
        statements
        break;
    case value2:
        statements
        break;
    default:
        statements
        break;
}
```

The default section is optional.

New language elements

■ Control structures for decisions:

```
if, else
switch, case, break, default
```

■ The comparison operators >, <, ==, !=, <= and >=.
■ The logical operators &&, || and !.
■ Variables declared as `boolean`, which can take either the value `true` or the value `false`.

Summary

`if` statements allow the programmer to control the sequence of actions by making the program carry out a test. Following the test, the computer carries out one of a choice of actions. There are two varieties of `if` statement:

■ `if`
■ `if...else`

The `if` statement can be used to identify the source of a GUI event. The method `getSource` returns the object that caused the event. This object is compared with each of the objects that could have caused the event, using the `==` comparison operator.

The `switch` statement provides a convenient way of carrying out a number of tests. However, the `switch` statement is restricted to tests on integers or on strings.

A `boolean` variable can be assigned the value `true` or the value `false`. A `boolean` variable can be tested with an `if` statement. A `boolean` variable is useful in situations when a variable has only two meaningful values.

Exercises

7.1 **Movie theatre (cinema) price** Write a program to work out how much a person pays to go to the cinema. The program should input an age from a slider or a text field and then decide on the following basis:

- under 5, free;
- aged 5 to 12, half price;
- aged 13 to 54, full price;
- aged 55, or over, free.

7.2 **The elevator** Write a program to simulate a very primitive elevator. The elevator is represented as a filled black square, displayed in a tall, thin, white panel. Provide two buttons – one to make it move 20 pixels up the panel and one to make it move down. Then enhance the program to make sure that the elevator does not go too high or too low.

7.3 **Sorting** Write a program to input numbers from three sliders, or three text fields, and display them in increasing numerical size.

7.4 **Betting** A group of people are betting on the outcome of three throws of a die. A person bets $1 on predicting the outcome of the three throws. Write a program that uses the random number method to simulate three throws of a die and displays the winnings according to the following rules:

- all three throws are sixes: win $20;
- all three throws are the same (but not sixes): win $10;
- any two of the three throws are the same: win $5.

7.5 **Digital combination safe** Write a program to act as the digital combination lock for a safe. Create three buttons, representing the numbers 1, 2 and 3. The user clicks on the buttons, attempting to enter the correct numbers (say 331121). The program remains unhelpfully quiet until the correct buttons are pressed. Then it congratulates the user with a suitable message. A button is provided to restart.

Enhance the program so that it has another button which allows the user to change the safe's combination, provided that the correct code has just been entered.

7.6 **Deal a card** Write a program with a single button on it which, when clicked, randomly selects a single playing card. First use the random number generator in the library to create a number in the range 1 to 4. Then convert the number to a suit (heart, diamond, club and spade). Next, use the random number generator to create a random number in the range 1 to 13. Convert the number to an ace, 2, 3, etc., and finally display the value of the chosen card.

Hint: use `switch` as appropriate.

7.7 **Rock, scissors, paper game** In its original form, each of the two players simultaneously chooses one of rock, scissors or paper. Rock beats scissors, paper beats rock and scissors beats paper. If both players choose the same, it is a draw. Write a program to play the game. The player selects one of three buttons, marked rock, scissors or paper. The

Figure 7.12 The calculator.

computer makes its choice randomly using the random number generator. The computer also decides and displays who has won.

7.8 **The calculator** Write a program which simulates a primitive desk calculator (Figure 7.12) that acts on integer numbers. It has one button for each of the 10 digits, 0 to 9. It has a button to add and a button to subtract. It has a **clear** button, to clear the display (a text field), and an equals (=) button to get the answer.

When the **clear** button is clicked the display is set to 0 and the (hidden) total is set to 0.

When a digit button is pressed, the digit is added to the right of those already in the display (if any).

When the + button is pressed, the number in the display is added to the total (and similarly for the - button).

When the = button is pressed, the value of the total is displayed.

7.9 **Nim** is a game played with matchsticks. It doesn't matter how many matches there are. The matches are put into three piles. Again, it doesn't matter how many matches there are in each pile. Each player goes in turn. A player can remove any number of matches from any one pile, but only one pile. A player must remove at least one match. The winner is the player who causes the other player to take the last match.

Write a program to play the game. Initially the computer deals three piles, with a random number (in the range 1 to 200) of matches in each pile. The three quantities are displayed in text fields. One player is the computer, which chooses a pile and an amount randomly. The other player is the human user, who specifies the pile number with a button and quantity using a text field.

There is also a 'new game' button.

7.10 **Turtle graphics** Turtle graphics is a way of making programming easy for young children. Imagine a pen fixed to the belly of a turtle. As the turtle crawls around a floor, the pen draws on the floor. The turtle faces north, south, east or west. The turtle can be issued with commands, with one button for each, as follows:

- pen up
- pen down
- turn left 90°
- turn right 90°
- go forward *n* pixels

Initially the turtle is at the top left of the panel and facing east.

So, for example, we can draw a rectangle using the sequence:

1. pen down
2. go forward 20 pixels
3. turn right 90°
4. go forward 20 pixels

5. turn right 90°
6. go forward 20 pixels
7. turn right 90°
8. go forward 20 pixels

The number of pixels, *n*, to be moved is input via a slider or a text field. The direction of the turtle (north, south, east, west) is displayed in a text field.

Answers to self-test questions

7.1
```
if (code == 123) {
    outcomeTextField.setText("unlocked");
    codeField.setText("");
}
```

7.2 No, because they treat the particular age of 18 differently.

7.3 The essential part of this program is:
```
if (temp < min) {
    min = temp;
}
textField.setText("Minimum value is " + min);
```

7.4
```
public void actionPerformed(ActionEvent event) {
    Object source;
    source = event.getSource();
    if (source == button1) {
        textField.setText("button 1");
    }
    if (source == button2) {
        textField.setText("button 2");
    }
    if (source == button3) {
        textField.setText("button 3");
    }
}
```

7.5
```
if (age <= 16) {
    textField.setText("too young");
}
```

7.6
```
if ((total == 2) || (total == 5) || (total == 7)) {
    textField.setText("you have won");
}
```

7.7
```
if ((age >= 16) && (age < 65)) {
    JOptionPane.showMessageDialog(null, "you are eligible");
}
```

7.8
```
int salary, tax;

salary = slider.getValue();

if ((salary > 10000) && (salary <= 50000)) {
    tax = (salary - 10000)/5;
}
if (salary > 50000) {
    tax = 8000 + ((salary - 50000) * 9 / 10);
}
if (salary <= 10000) {
    tax = 0;
}
```

7.9
```
public void stateChanged(ChangeEvent e) {
    int a, b, c;
    int largest;

    a = slider1.getValue();
    b = slider2.getValue();
    c = slider3.getValue();

    if ((a >= b) && (a >= c)) {
        largest = a;
    }
    else if ((b >= a) && (b >= c)) {
        largest = b;
    }
    else {
        largest = c;
    }
    JOptionPane.showMessageDialog(null,
            "largest value is " + largest);
}
```

7.10
```
int age;
age = Integer.parseInt(ageTextField.getText());
if ((age >= 18) && (age <= 30)) {
    outcomeTextField.setText("you are eligible");
}
```

7.11
```
private String convert(int s) {
    String suit;

    switch (s) {
        case 1:
            suit = "diamonds";
            break;
        case 2:
            suit = "hearts";
            break;
        case 3:
            suit = "clubs";
            break;
        case 4:
            suit = "spades";
            break;
        default:
            suit = "error";
        break;
    }
    return suit;
}
```

7.12 No, because now there are three possible values, not two.

CHAPTER

8

Repetition

This chapter explains:

- how to perform repetitions using **while** statements;
- how to perform repetitions using **for** statements;
- how to use the logical operators **&&**, **||** and **!** in loops;
- how to perform repetitions using the **do** statement.

● Introduction

We humans are used to doing things again and again – for example, eating, sleeping and working. Computers similarly perform repetition. Examples are:

- adding up a list of numbers;
- searching a file for some desired information;
- solving a mathematical equation iteratively, by repeatedly obtaining better and better approximations;
- making a graphical image move on the screen (animation).

We have already seen that a computer obeys a sequence of instructions. Now we shall see how to repeat a sequence of instructions a number of times. Part of the power of computers arises from their ability to perform repetitions extremely quickly. In the language of programming, a repetition is called a loop.

There are two main ways in which the Java programmer can instruct the computer to perform repetition – **while** and **for**. Either of these can be used to carry out repetition, but there are differences between them, as we shall see.

while

We begin by using a loop to display the integers 1 to 10 (Figure 8.1) in a text field using the following code:

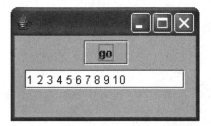

Figure 8.1 Display of the numbers 1 to 10.

```java
import java.awt.*;
import java.awt.event.*;
import javax.swing.*;

public class OneToTen extends JFrame implements ActionListener {

    private JButton button;
    private JTextField textField;

    public static void main(String[] args) {
        OneToTen demo = new OneToTen();
        demo.setSize(200, 120);
        demo.createGUI();
        demo.show();
    }

    private void createGUI() {
        setDefaultCloseOperation(EXIT_ON_CLOSE);
        Container window = getContentPane();
        window.setLayout(new FlowLayout());

        button = new JButton("go");
        window.add(button);
        button.addActionListener(this);

        textField = new JTextField(15);
        window.add(textField);
    }
```

```
public void actionPerformed(ActionEvent event) {
    int number;
    String oneToTen = "";

    number = 1;
    while (number <= 10) {
        oneToTen = oneToTen + Integer.toString(number) + " ";
        number++;
    }
    textField.setText(oneToTen);
}

}
```

The word **while** signifies that a repetition is required. The statements enclosed between the curly brackets (braces) are repeated and this is called the body of the loop. The condition in brackets immediately after the word **while** controls the loop. If the condition is true, the loop continues. If it is false, the loop ends and control is transferred to the statement after the closing brace. Thus in this case, the loop continues while every **number** is less than or equal to 10.

Before the loop starts, the value of **number** is made equal to 1. At the end of each loop, the value of **number** is incremented by 1, using the **++** operator that we met in an earlier chapter. So **number** takes the values 1, 2, 3, . . . up to and including 10.

The string **oneToTen** is initially empty. Each time the loop repeats, a number (and a space) are added to the string using the **+** string operator.

The above program fragment used the less than or equal to (**<=**) operator. This is one of a number of available comparison operators, which are the same as those used in **if** statements. Here, again, is the complete list of the comparison (sometimes called relational) operators:

Symbol	Meaning
>	greater than
<	less than
==	equals
!=	not equal to
<=	less than or equal to
>=	greater than or equal to

The indentation of the statements within the loop assists us in seeing the structure of the loop.

If your development system provides a debugger, it can be used to good effect to follow the execution of this loop.

SELF-TEST QUESTIONS

8.1   What does this program fragment do?

```
String string = "";
int number = 0;
while (number <= 5) {
    string = string + Integer.toString(number * number) + " ";
    number++;
}
textArea.setText(string);
```

8.2   Write a program that adds up (calculates the sum of) the numbers 1 to 100 and displays it in a text field when a button is clicked.

Figure 8.2 Display of boxes using `while`.

The next program uses a `while` loop to display a row of boxes, Figure 8.2. The number of boxes is determined by the value selected on a slider. Whenever the pointer is changed, an event is created and the program displays the equivalent number of boxes. To do this, we need a counter. The counter, initially equal to 1, is incremented by 1 each time a single box is displayed. We need to repeat the display of an additional box until the counter reaches the desired total using a `while` loop as follows:

```
import java.awt.*;
import java.awt.event.*;
import javax.swing.*;
import javax.swing.event.*;

public class Boxes extends JFrame implements ChangeListener {

    private JSlider slider;
    private JPanel panel;
```

```java
    public static void main(String[] args) {
        Boxes demo = new Boxes();
        demo.setSize(250,150);
        demo.createGUI();
        demo.show();
    }

    private void createGUI() {
        setDefaultCloseOperation(EXIT_ON_CLOSE);
        Container window = getContentPane();
        window.setLayout(new FlowLayout());

        slider = new JSlider(0, 10, 1);
        window.add(slider);
        slider.addChangeListener(this);

        panel = new JPanel();
        panel.setPreferredSize(new Dimension(180, 50));
        panel.setBackground(Color.white);
        window.add(panel);
    }

    public void stateChanged(ChangeEvent e) {
        Graphics paper = panel.getGraphics();
        int x, numberOfBoxes, counter;
        numberOfBoxes = slider.getValue();
        paper.setColor(Color.white);
        paper.fillRect(0, 0, 180, 50);
        x = 10;
        counter = 1;
        paper.setColor(Color.black);
        while (counter <= numberOfBoxes) {
            paper.drawRect(x, 10, 10, 10);
            x = x + 15;
            counter++;
        }
    }
}
```

This program will draw as many boxes as we like. Imagine how many instructions we would need to write in order to display 100 boxes, if we were not able to use a `while` statement. Notice also that this program will draw zero boxes if this is what the user selects with the slider. Thus the `while` statement is completely flexible – it will supply as many, or as few, repetitions as are required.

One way to visualize a `while` loop is using an activity diagram, as shown in Figure 8.3. The computer normally obeys instructions in sequence from top to bottom as shown by the arrows. A `while` loop means that the condition is tested before the loop is executed and again before any repetition of the loop. If the condition is true, the loop is executed. When, finally, the condition is false, the body of the loop ceases to be executed and the repetition ends.

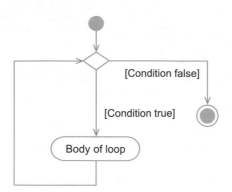

Figure 8.3 Activity diagram of the **while** loop.

It is wise to exercise great care when you write a **while** loop to make sure that the counting is done properly. A common error is to make the loop repeat one too many times or one too few times. This is sometimes known as an 'off by one' error. Sometimes a loop is written so as to start with a count of 0 and the test is to see whether it is less than the number required, as follows:

```
count = 0;
while (count < numberRequired) {
    // body
    count++;
}
```

Alternatively the loop is written to start with a count of 1 and the test is to see whether it is less than or equal to the number required, as follows:

```
count = 1;
while (count <= numberRequired) {
    // body
    count++;
}
```

Both of these styles are used in this book.

SELF-TEST QUESTIONS

8.3 **Prison bars** Write a program to draw five vertical parallel lines.

8.4 **Chessboard** Write a program to draw a chessboard with nine vertical lines, 10 pixels apart, and nine horizontal lines, 10 pixels apart.

8.5 **Squaring numbers** Write a program to display the numbers 1 to 5 and their squares, one number (and its square) per line in a text area. Use the string **"\n"** to move to the start of a new line.

● for

In the **for** loop, many of the ingredients of a **while** loop are bundled up together in the header of the statement itself. For example, here is the program given above to display the numbers 1 to 10, rewritten using **for**:

```
oneToTen.setText("");
for (int number = 1; number <= 10; number++) {
    oneToTen = oneToTen + Integer.toString(number) + " ";
}
```

Within the brackets of the **for** statement there are three ingredients, separated by semicolons:

■ An initial statement. This is carried out once only, before the loop starts.

Example: `int number = 1`

■ A condition. This is tested before any execution of the loop.

Example: `number <= 10`

■ A final statement. This is carried out at the end of each loop, just prior to the end of each loop.

Example: `number++`

The condition determines whether the **for** loop is executed or completed as follows:

■ if the condition is true, the body of the loop is executed;

■ if the condition is false, the loop ends and the statements after the closing brace are executed.

Notice that you can write a complete variable declaration within the header of a **for** statement, together with its initialization, and this is a common thing to do. This variable can be used throughout the body of the **for** statement.

Here is another example program that uses a **for** loop to display 20 small circles at random coordinates in a black panel, like the night sky (Figure 8.4).

```
public void actionPerformed(ActionEvent event) {
    Graphics paper = panel.getGraphics();
    paper.setColor(Color.black);
    paper.fillRect(0, 0, 200, 200);
    paper.setColor(Color.white);
    for (int count = 0; count < 20; count++) {
        int x, y, radius;
        x = random.nextInt(200);
        y = random.nextInt(200);
        radius = 5;
        paper.fillOval(x, y, radius, radius);
    }
}
```

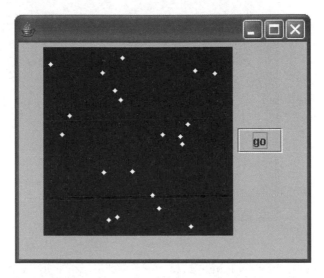

Figure 8.4 The stars program.

It is always possible to rewrite a **for** loop as a **while** loop and vice versa. But usually one or the other will be clearer. The **for** loop is generally used when you are counting by adding or subtracting a fixed value at each step.

Also it is considered poor style to terminate the loop before completing the pattern described in the heading of a **for** loop.

SELF-TEST QUESTION

8.6   Rewrite the stars program using **while** instead of **for**.

● And, or, not

On occasions, the condition that controls a loop is more complex and we need the logical operators and, or and not. You would use these in everyday life if you wanted to say 'I'm going for a walk until it starts raining or it is 5 o'clock.' We've already met these operators in Chapter 7 on decisions using the **if** statement. They are:

Symbol	Meaning
&&	and
||	or
!	not

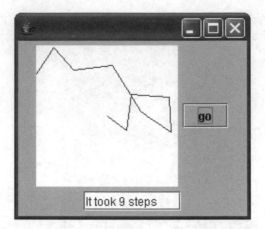

Figure 8.5 Random walk.

If we wanted to describe how long we are going walking for using a **while** statement, we would say 'While it is not raining and it is not 5 o'clock, I am going walking.' Notice that each of the two conditions (raining, 5 o'clock) is preceded by a 'not' and that the two conditions are linked by an 'and'. This is what tends to happen when you write a loop with a **while** statement – and you have to be very careful to write the condition very clearly.

The next program uses these operators. A drunken person attempts to reach any one of the walls of a room (represented as a panel). Initially the person is at the centre of the panel. The person makes random-sized steps in random directions until a wall is reached (Figure 8.5).

The person's position at any time is specified by *x* and *y* coordinates. The loop continues until one of the four sides of the panel is reached. Thus the **for** statement involves four conditions, linked by **&&** operators. As you will see, this is a moderately complex combination of conditions. A combination such as this can be hard to write and hard to comprehend.

```
public void actionPerformed(ActionEvent event) {
    Graphics paper = panel.getGraphics();
    int x, y, xStep, yStep, xNew, yNew, steps;
    paper.setColor(Color.white);
    paper.fillRect(0, 0, paperWidth, paperHeight);
    x = paperWidth / 2;
    y = paperHeight / 2;
    for (steps = 0;
        x < paperWidth && x > 0
        &&
        y < paperHeight && y > 0;
        steps++) {
        xStep = random.nextInt(100) - 50;
        yStep = random.nextInt(100) - 50;
```

```
        xNew = x + xStep;
        yNew = y + yStep;
        paper.setColor(Color.black);
        paper.drawLine(x, y, xNew, yNew);

        x = xNew;
        y = yNew;
    }
    textField.setText("It took " + steps + " steps");
}
```

SELF-TEST QUESTION

8.7   What is displayed when the following code is executed?

```
int n, m;
n = 10;
m = 5;
while ((n > 0) || (m > 0) {
    n = n - 1;
    m = m - 1;
}
JOptionPane.showMessageDialog(null,
            ("n = " + Integer.toString(n) +
            " m = " + Integer.toString(m));
```

do...while

If you use **while** or **for**, the test is always carried out at the beginning of the repetition. The **do** loop is an alternative structure in which the test is carried out at the end of each repetition. This means that the loop is always repeated at least once. We illustrate the **do** loop by writing pieces of program to display the numbers 0 to 9 in a text field using all three available loop structures. The text is accumulated in a string.

Using **while**:

```
int count;
String string = "";
count = 0;
while (count <= 9) {
    string = string + Integer.toString(count) + " ";
    count++;
}
```

Using `for`:

```
String string = "";
for (int count = 0; count <= 9; count++) {
    string = string + Integer.toString(count) + " ";
}
```

Using `do` (with the test at the end of the loop):

```
int count;
String string = "";
count = 0;
do {
    string = string + Integer.toString(count) + " ";
    count++;
}
while (count < 10)
```

Next is an example in which a loop needs to be carried out at least once. In a lottery, numbers are selected at random, but two numbers cannot be the same. We consider a very small lottery in which only two numbers are selected. Initially we obtain the first random number. Then we need a second, but it must not be equal to the first. So we repeatedly choose a second number, until it is not equal to the first. Hence the program:

```
int number1, number2;
Random random = new Random();

number1 = random.nextInt(10) + 1;
do {
    number2 = random.nextInt(10) + 1;
}
while (number1 == number2);

textField.setText("the numbers are "
    + number1 + " and " + number2);
```

● Nested loops

A nested loop is a loop within a loop. Suppose, for example, we want to display the output shown in Figure 8.6, which is a crudely drawn block of apartments. The size of the building is determined by the position of the sliders. Suppose that there are four floors, each with five apartments, shown as rectangles. The loop that draws an individual floor has this structure:

```
for (int apartment = 1; apartment <= 5; apartment++) {
    // code to draw one apartment
}
```

and the loop that draws a number of floors has this structure:

```
for (int floor = 1; floor <= 3; floor++) {
    // code to draw one floor
}
```

What we need is to enclose the first loop within the second loop so that the loops are nested. We make the number of apartments per floor and the number of floors both set by sliders. Whenever either slider is changed, an event is caused and we will execute this code:

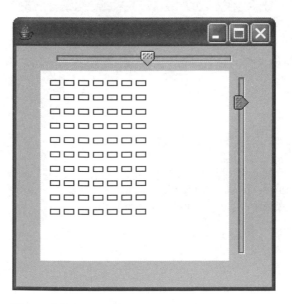

Figure 8.6 Display of apartment block.

```
int floors, apartments;
int x, y;
y = 10;
paper.setColor(Color.white);
paper.fillRect(0, 0, 200, 200);

apartments = slider1.getValue();
floors = slider2.getValue();
for (int floor = 0; floor <= floors; floor++) {
    x = 10;
    for (int count = 0; count <= apartments; count++) {
        paper.setColor(Color.black);
        paper.drawRect(x, y, 10, 5);
        x = x + 15;
    }
    y = y + 15;
}
```

You will see that the indentation helps considerably in understanding the program. It is always possible to rewrite nested loops using methods, and this is sometimes clearer. We explore this further in Chapter 19 on style.

SELF-TEST QUESTION

8.8 A music score is written on paper printed with staves. Each stave consists of five horizontal lines across the page, approximately 2 mm (1/10 inch) apart. Each page holds eight of these staves. Write a program to draw a page of musical score.

● Combining control structures

In the previous chapter we looked at selection using the **if** and **switch** statements and in this chapter we have looked at repetition using **while**, **for** and **do**. Most programs consist of combinations of these control structures. In fact most programs consist of:

■ sequences;

■ loops;

■ selections;

■ calls of library methods;

■ calls of methods that the programmer writes.

Programming principles

Repetitions are used widely in programming. There are three varieties of looping statement available in Java – `while`, `for` and `do`. So which one do you choose to use?

`while` and `for` are similar. But `for` tends to be used when there is a counter associated with the loop. Thus the prototype `for` loop has this structure:

```
for (int count = 0; count <= finalValue; count++) {
    // body of the loop
}
```

The counter `count` has an initial value, a final value and is incremented each time the loop is repeated.

The `while` loop is used when the number of repetitions cannot be calculated in advance – the loop continues until something becomes true. An example is the random walk program given above, in which the repetition continues until the person reaches the wall. The prototype `while` loop has the structure:

```
while (condition) {
    // body of the loop
}
```

Use the `do` loop when the test for the end of the repetition needs to be made at the end of the loop, remembering that a `do` loop is always carried out at least once.

Loops come into their own in programs that process collections of data. We will meet various collections later in this book, including array lists, strings, files and arrays.

Programming pitfalls

Always be very careful when writing the condition in a loop. It is a very common error to make a loop finish one repetition too early or else repeat one too many times. This is sometimes called an 'off by one' error.

Be careful with complex conditions in loops. For example, do you need || or do you need &&?

If the body of a loop is only a single statement, it need not be surrounded by braces. But it is generally safer to use them, and this is the approach we have used throughout this book.

Grammar spot

The `while` loop has the structure:

```
while (condition) {
    statement(s)
}
```

where the condition is tested before any repetition of the loop. If it is true the loop continues. If it is false, the loop ends.

The `for` loop has the structure:

```
for (initial action; condition; action) {
    statement(s)
}
```

where:

- `initial action` is carried out once, before the loop is executed.
- `condition` is tested before each repetition: if it is true the loop is repeated; if it is false the loop ends.
- `action` is carried out at the end of each repetition.

The `do` loop has the structure:

```
do {
    statement(s)
}
while (condition)
```

The test is performed after each repetition.

New language elements

The control structures for repetition:

- `while`
- `for`
- `do`

Summary

- A repetition in programming is called a loop.

- There are three ways in Java of instructing the computer to loop – `while`, `for` and `do`.

- Use `for` when you want to describe the main features of the loop inside the loop statement itself.

- `do` is used when a condition needs to be tested at the end of a loop and/or when a loop has to be performed at least once.

● Exercises

8.1 **Cubes** Write a program that uses a loop to display the integer numbers 1 to 10 together with the cubes of each of their values.

8.2 **Random numbers** Write a program to display 10 random numbers using a loop. Use the library class `Random` to obtain integer random numbers in the range 0 to 9. Display the numbers in a text field.

8.3 **The milky way** Write a program that draws 100 circles in a panel at random positions and with random diameters up to 10 pixels.

8.4 **Steps** Write a program to draw a set of steps made from bricks, as shown in Figure 8.7. Use the library method `drawRect` to draw each brick.

Figure 8.7 Steps.

8.5 **Sum of the integers** Write a program that adds up the numbers 0 to 39 using a loop. Check that it has obtained the right answer by using the formula for the sum of the numbers 0 to n:

$$\text{sum} = n \times (n + 1)/2$$

8.6 **Saw-tooth pattern** Write a program to display a saw-tooth pattern in a text area, as shown in Figure 8.8. The program will need to display the string **"\n"** to obtain a new line.

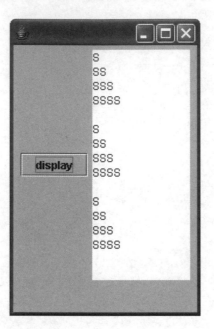

Figure 8.8 Saw-tooth pattern.

8.7 **Multiplication table** Write a program to display a multiplication table, such as young children use. For example, the table for numbers up to 5 is shown in Figure 8.9. In addition to using string **"\n"** to obtain a new line, the program should use the string **"\t"** to tab to the next tab position, so that the information is displayed neatly in columns.

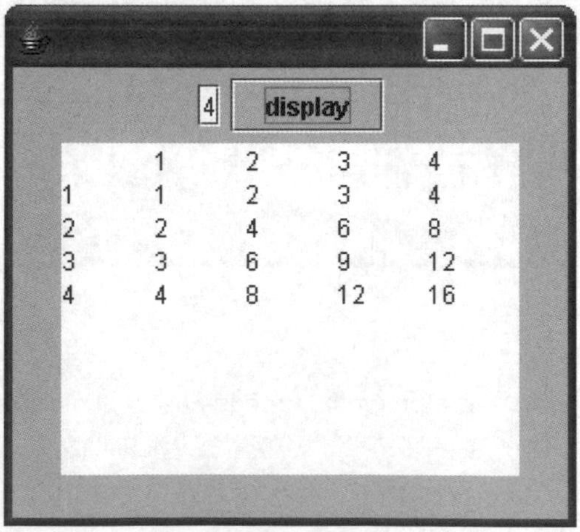

Figure 8.9 Multiplication table.

The program should be capable of displaying a table of any size, specified by an integer entered into a text field. Use the method **setTabSize** to control the layout. A typical call is:

```
textArea.setTabSize(4);
```

8.8 **Sum of series** Write a program to calculate and display the sum of the series:

$1 - 1/2 + 1/3 - 1/4 + \ldots$

until a term is reached that is less than 0.0001. (The answer is approximately 0.6936.)

8.9 **Nursery rhyme** Write a program to display all the verses of a nursery rhyme in a text area with a vertical scrollbar. The first verse is:

10 green bottles, hanging on a wall,
10 green bottles, hanging on a wall,
If 1 green bottle were to accidentally fall
There'd be 9 green bottles, hanging on the wall.

In successive verses there are reduced numbers of bottles, as they fall off the wall.

Answers to self-test questions

8.1 It displays the numbers 0 1 4 9 16 25.

8.2 The central part of the program is:

```
int number;
int sum;

sum = 0;
number = 1;
while (number <= 100) {
    sum = sum + number;
    number++;
}
textField.setText(The sum is " + Integer.toString(sum));
```

This program makes use of a common programming technique – a running total. The value of the variable **sum** is initially equal to 0. Each time the loop is repeated, the value of **number** is added to the value of **sum** and the result placed back in **sum**.

8.3
```
int x, counter, numberOfBars;
numberOfBars = 5;
x = 10;
counter = 1;
while (counter <= numberOfBars) {
    paper.drawLine(x, 10, x, 100);
    x = x + 15;
    counter++;
}
```

Answers to self-test questions continued

8.4
```
int x, y, counter;
x = 10;
counter = 1;
while (counter <= 9) {
    paper.drawLine(x, 10, x, 90);
    x = x + 10;
    counter++;
}

y = 10;
counter = 1;
while (counter <= 9) {
    paper.drawLine(10, y, 90, y);
    y = y + 10;
    counter++;
}
```

8.5
```
int number = 1;
while (number <= 5) {
    textArea.append(Integer.toString(number) + " "
            + Integer.toString(number * number) + "\n");
    number++;
}
```

8.6 The essence of the loop is:

```
int count = 0;
while (count < 20) {
    // body of loop
    count++;
}
```

8.7 $n = 0$ and $m = -5$.

8.8
```
int y;
paper.setColor(Color.white);
paper.fillRect(0, 0, 150, 100);

y = 10;
for (int staves = 1; staves <= 8; staves++) {
    for (int lines = 1; lines <= 5; lines++) {
        paper.setColor(Color.black);
        paper.drawLine(10, y, 90, y);
        y = y + 2;
    }
    y = y + 5;
}
```

CHAPTER
9

Writing classes

This chapter explains:

- how to write a class;
- how to write **public** methods;
- how to use **private** variables within a class;
- how to write constructor methods.

Introduction

In earlier chapters we have seen how to make use of library classes. In this chapter we see how to write our own classes. A class describes any number of similar objects that can be manufactured from it using the keyword **new**.

We will see that a class typically consists of:

- **private** data (variables) that hold information about the object.
- **public** methods that can be called by the user of the object to carry out useful functions.
- Optionally, one or more constructor methods, used when an object is created. They are used to carry out any initialization, e.g. assigning initial values to the variables within the object.
- **private** methods that are used purely within the object and are inaccessible from outside the object.

Designing a class

When a programmer is thinking about a new program, they may see the need for an object that is not already available in the Java library of classes. As our first illustration we will use a program to display and manipulate a simplified balloon and we will represent the balloon as an object. The program simply displays a balloon as a circle in a panel, as shown in Figure 9.1. Buttons are provided to change the position and size of the balloon.

Figure 9.1 The balloon program.

We will construct this program from two objects and therefore two classes:

■ Class **Balloon** represents the balloon. It provides methods named **move** and **changeSize** – with obvious meanings.

■ Class **UseBalloon** provides the GUI for the program. It uses class **Balloon** as necessary.

These classes are shown in the UML class diagram, Figure 9.2. Each class is represented as a rectangle. A relationship between classes is shown as a line joining the two. In this case the relationship is shown as an annotation above the line: class **UseBalloon** uses class **Balloon**.

Figure 9.2 Class diagram showing the two classes in the balloon program.

We will first complete class **UseBalloon** and then we will write class **Balloon**. The complete code for **UseBalloon** is:

```
import java.awt.*;
import java.awt.event.*;
import javax.swing.*;
```

```
public class UseBalloon extends Jframe
           implements ActionListener {

    private JButton growButton, moveButton;
    private JPanel panel;

    private Balloon balloon;

    public static void main(String[] args) {
        UseBalloon demo = new UseBalloon();
        demo.setSize(200,220);
        demo.createGUI();
        demo.show();
    }

    private void createGUI() {
        setDefaultCloseOperation(EXIT_ON_CLOSE);
        Container window = getContentPane();
        window.setLayout(new FlowLayout());

        panel = new JPanel();
        panel.setPreferredSize(new Dimension(150, 150));
        panel.setBackground(Color.white);
        window.add(panel);

        moveButton = new JButton("move");
        window.add(moveButton);
        moveButton.addActionListener(this);

        growButton = new JButton("grow");
        window.add(growButton);
        growButton.addActionListener(this);

        balloon = new Balloon();
    }

    public void actionPerformed(ActionEvent event) {
        Graphics paper = panel.getGraphics();
        if (event.getSource() == moveButton) {
            balloon.moveRight(20);
        }
        else {
            balloon.changeSize(20);

        }
        paper.setColor(Color.white);
        paper.fillRect(0, 0, 150, 150);
        balloon.display(paper);
    }
}
```

At the head of the class **UseBalloon**, we declare instance variables as usual, including a variable named **balloon**:

```
private Balloon balloon;
```

Within the class **UseBalloon**, we perform any necessary initialization, including creating a new instance of the class **Balloon**. This is the crucial step where we create an object from our own class.

```
balloon = new Balloon();
```

Next, the code to respond to button-clicks. If the **move** button is clicked, then the method **moveRight** is called. Otherwise **changeSize** is called.

```
public void actionPerformed(ActionEvent event) {
    Graphics paper = panel.getGraphics();
    if (event.getSource() == moveButton) {
        balloon.moveRight(20);
    }
    else {
        balloon.changeSize(20);
    }
    paper.setColor(Color.white);
    paper.fillRect(0, 0, 150, 150);
    balloon.display(paper);
}
```

This concludes the coding for the class **UseBalloon**. Writing this code helps us to clarify how a balloon object will be used, enabling us to see what methods need to be provided by class **Balloon**, as well as the nature of any parameters. This leads us to write the code for class **Balloon**:

```
public class Balloon {

    private int x = 50;
    private int y = 50;
    private int diameter = 20;

    public void moveRight(int xStep) {
        x = x + xStep;
    }

    public void changeSize(int change) {
        diameter = diameter + change;
    }

    public void display(Graphics paper) {
        paper.setColor(Color.black);
        paper.drawOval(x, y, diameter, diameter);
    }
}
```

The heading of a class starts with the keyword **class**, and gives the class name, followed by a curly bracket (brace). The complete class is terminated with a brace. A class is labelled as **public** so that it can be used widely. The Java convention (and in most OO languages) is that the name of a class starts with a capital letter. The body of a class consists of declarations of variables and methods. Note how the readability of the class is enhanced using blank lines and indentation. In the next few sections of this chapter we will look in detail at each of the ingredients in the above class for balloons.

In summary, the overall structure of a class is:

```
public class Balloon {

    // instance variables
    // methods
}
```

Now that we have written class **Balloon**, we can create any number of instances of it. We have already created one object by doing this:

```
balloon = new Balloon();
```

but we can in addition do the following:

```
Balloon balloon2 = new Balloon();
```

Classes and files

When a program consists of just a single class, we have already seen that the Java source code must be placed in a file which has the same name as the class, but with the extension **.java**. Thus, for example, a class named **Game** goes in a file named **Game.java** and the header for the class is:

```
public class Game etc.
```

The **import** statements must precede this header. The compiler translates the Java code to byte code, which it places in a file named **Game.class**.

When a program consists of two or more classes, there are two different approaches to placing classes in files:

1. Place all the classes in a single file.
2. Place each class in its own file.

Now the details of using each of these approaches will depend on which development system you are using. But here are some typical scenarios.

Single file

To adopt this approach:

1. Place all the classes in one file.
2. Declare as **public** the class containing method **main**.

3. Declare all other classes as not **public**, i.e. with no access description.

4. Make the file name equal to the name of the **public** class.

5. Put the **import** statements at the start of the file. They apply to all the classes in the file.

For example, the file **UseBalloon.java** contains both classes:

```
import java.awt.*;
import java.awt.event.*;
import javax.swing.*;

public class UseBalloon extends JFrame
            implements ActionListener {
    // body of class UseBalloon
}

class Balloon {
    // body of class Balloon
}
```

This approach has the advantage that all the classes are in one place. Moreover, the **import** statements are only needed once.

Separate files

To adopt this approach:

1. Place each class in a file by itself.

2. Declare every class as **public**.

3. Make each file name equal to the name of the class it contains.

4. Place the appropriate **import** statements at the start of each class.

5. Place all the files in the same folder.

For example, the file **UseBalloon.java** contains:

```
import java.awt.*;
import java.awt.event.*;
import javax.swing.*;

public class UseBalloon extends JFrame
            implements ActionListener {

    // body of class UseBalloon
}
```

A second file, **Balloon.java**, consists of:

```
import java.awt.*;

public class Balloon {

    // body of class Balloon
}
```

This approach has the advantage that the classes are in different files and therefore can be reused more easily.

It is vital to compile the files in dependency order. Class **UseBalloon** uses a **Balloon** object and therefore the **Balloon** class must be compiled first.

private variables

A balloon has data associated with it – its size (diameter) and its position (as x and y coordinates). A balloon object must remember these values. This data is held in variables that are described like this:

```
private int x = 50;
private int y = 50;
private int diameter = 20;
```

The variables **diameter**, **x** and **y** are declared at the top of the class. They can be accessed by any of the statements in the class. They are called *class-level variables* or *instance variables*.

The word used to introduce variables – **int**, for example – has been augmented with the word **private**. Class-level variables are almost always declared as **private**. This means that they are accessible from anywhere within the class, but inaccessible from outside.

Although we **could** describe these variables as **public**, it would be bad practice. It is best to keep variables hidden from outside. So we keep them as **private**, and use methods to access their values from outside the class. We will shortly see how to do this.

SELF-TEST QUESTION

9.1 Extend the balloon object so that it has a variable that describes the colour of the balloon.

---

public methods

Some features of an object need to be publicly available to other pieces of program. These are those methods which, after all, have been designed for the use of others. As we have seen, a balloon has actions associated with it – for example, to change its size. These actions are written as methods. Changing the size is accomplished by:

```
public void changeSize(int change) {
    diameter = diameter + change;
}
```

To signify that a method is publicly available, by users of the class, we precede the method header with the Java word **public**. Next, we write the method to move a balloon:

```
public void moveRight(int xStep) {
    x = x + xStep;
}
```

To complete the class we provide a method for a balloon to display itself when requested to do so:

```
public void display(Graphics paper) {
    paper.setColor(Color.black);
    paper.drawOval(x, y, diameter, diameter);
}
```

We have now distinguished clearly between those items that we are making publicly available and those that are private. This is an important ingredient of the philosophy of OOP. Data (variables) and actions (methods) are bundled up together, but in such a way as to hide some of the information from the outside world. Normally it is the data that is hidden away from the rest of the world. This is termed *encapsulation* or *information hiding*.

So a class normally consists of:

- **public** methods, and
- **private** variables.

SELF-TEST QUESTIONS

9.2 Write a method that moves a balloon upwards by an amount given as the parameter. Name the method **moveUp**.

9.3 Write a method that an enables the colour of a balloon to be changed.

9.4 Rewrite method **display** so that it displays a coloured balloon.

A class (or object) has the general structure shown in Figure 9.3. This is the view as seen by the programmer who writes the class – it consists of variables and methods. The view of an object as seen by its users is shown in Figure 9.4. The view to its users, to whom it is providing a service, is very different. Only the **public** items (usually methods) are visible – everything else is hidden within an impenetrable box.

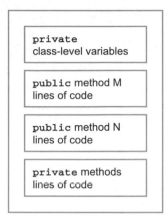

Figure 9.3 Structure of an object or class as seen by the programmer who writes it.

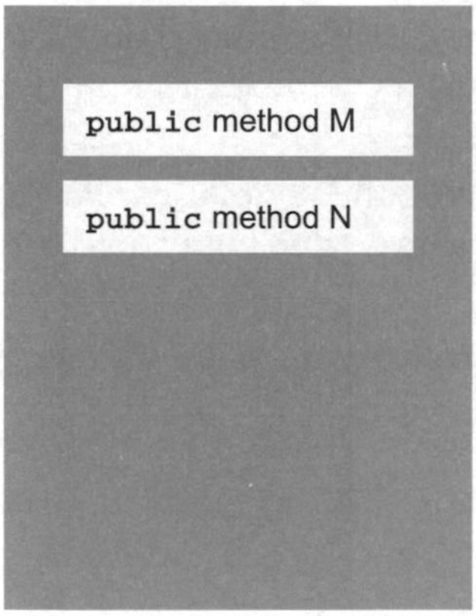

Figure 9.4 Structure of an object or class as seen by its users.

● The get and set methods

It is very bad practice to allow external access to the variables within an object. For example, suppose that a class needs to know the x coordinate of a balloon. It is very appealing simply to declare the value `x` as `public`. Then the user of the object could simply refer to the value as `balloon.x`. This is feasible, but it is poor design. Instead, access to variables is controlled by providing methods that access them. So we provide a method named `getX`, part of the class `Balloon`. A user can use it like this:

```
int position = balloon.getX();
```

The coding for method **getX** is as follows:

```
public int getX() {
    return x;
}
```

Users need either to read the value of a variable or to change it – or both. So we need a method to supply the value, conventionally named a *get* method and a method to change it, conventionally named a *set* method. The words 'get' and 'set' are not Java keywords.

The methods **getText** and **setText** of the **JTextField** class are typical widely used examples of get and set methods within the Java libraries.

There are several reasons why using methods to control access to variables are preferable:

■ The class can hide the internal representation of the data from the users, while still maintaining the external interface. For example, the author of the balloon class might choose to hold the coordinates of the centre point of a balloon, but provide users with the coordinates of the top left of an enclosing square.

■ The author of the class can decide to restrict access to data. For example, the class could restrict the value of the x coordinate to read-only (get) access, while disallowing write (set) access.

■ The class can validate or check the values used. For example, the class could ignore an attempt to provide a negative value for a coordinate.

SELF-TEST QUESTION

9.5   Write a method to allow a user only get access to the y coordinate of a balloon.

● Constructors

When a balloon object is created, the position and size of the balloon need to be given some values. This is called initializing the variables. There are two ways to do the initialization of variables. One way is to do the initialization as part of the declaration of the class-level variables. For example:

```
private int x = 50;
private int y = 50;
private int diameter = 20;
```

Another way to initialize an object is to write a special method to do the initialization. This method is named a *constructor method* or simply a *constructor* (because it is involved in the construction of the object). This method always has the same name as the class. It has no return value, but it will usually have parameters. Here is a constructor method for the **Balloon** class:

```
public Balloon(int initialX, int initialY,
                     int initialDiameter) {
    x = initialX;
    y = initialY;
    diameter = initialDiameter;
}
```

This method assigns the values of the parameters (the size and position) to the appropriate variables within the object. A constructor method such as this is written at the top of the class, after the declarations of the class-level variables. Constructors are labelled as **public**, because they must be accessed from outside their class. Notice that the constructor has no return type, or even **void**.

The above constructor method would be used as shown by this example:

```
Balloon balloon = new Balloon(10, 10, 50);
```

If a variable is not explicitly initialized by the programmer, the Java system gives every variable a default value. This is zero for any numbers, **false** for a **boolean**, **""** (an empty string) for a **String** and the value **null** for any object.

It is regarded as bad practice to rely on this method of initialization of variables. Instead, it is better to do it explicitly, either when the information is declared or by statements within a constructor.

Other actions that a constructor method might take include creating any other objects that the object needs to use or opening a file that the object uses.

If a class does not have an explicit constructor, then it is assumed to have a single constructor with zero parameters. This is known as the default constructor or zero-arg constructor.

Multiple constructors

A class can have none, one or several constructor methods. If a class has one or more constructors, they will normally involve parameters and must be called with the appropriate parameters. For example, in the **Balloon** class, we can write the two constructors:

```
public Balloon(int initialX, int initialY,
                     int initialDiameter) {
    x = initialX;
    y = initialY;
    diameter = initialDiameter;
}
```

```
public Balloon(int initialX, int initialY) {
    x = initialX;
    y = initialY;
    diameter = 20;
}
```

which would allow us to create balloon objects in either of the following ways:

```
Balloon balloon1 = new Balloon(10, 10, 50);
Balloon balloon2 = new Balloon(10, 10);
```

but not allow:

```
Balloon balloon3 = new Balloon();
```

So if you write several constructors, but you still need a constructor with zero parameters, you must write it explicitly. For example:

```
public Balloon() {
    x = 50;
    y = 50;
    diameter = 20;
}
```

We have now written three constructors for the class **Balloon**, and here is how they might be used to create three different objects from the same class:

```
Balloon balloon1 = new Balloon(10, 10, 50);
Balloon balloon2 = new Balloon(10, 10);
Balloon balloon3 = new Balloon();
```

SELF-TEST QUESTION

9.6   Write a constructor method to create a new balloon, specifying only the diameter.

● `private` methods

The whole purpose of writing a class is to allow the creation of objects that present useful facilities to other objects. These facilities are the **public** methods that the object offers. But often a class has methods that do not need to be made **public** and, indeed, all the methods in the programs given earlier in this book are **private**.

Here is a class **Ball** that represents a ball that can be animated, bouncing around a panel. It uses **private** methods, as well as a **public** method and a constructor. It uses the **private** methods as a way of clarifying what might otherwise be a complex piece of program. The **public** method **animate** is called at frequent regular intervals in order to redraw an image. It calls **private** methods **move**, **bounce**, **delete** and **draw**.

We have created **private** methods that act in support of the **public** methods in the class. In this example, the **private** methods do not use parameters, but, in general, **private** methods have parameters.

```
class Ball {

    private JPanel panel;
    private int x = 7, xChange = 7;
    private int y = 0, yChange = 2;
    private int diameter = 10;
    private int width = 100, height = 100;

    public Ball(JPanel thePanel) {
        panel = thePanel;
    }

    public void animate() {
        delete();
        move();
        bounce();
        draw();
    }

    private void move() {
        x = x + xChange;
        y = y + yChange;
    }

    private void bounce() {
        if (x <= 0 || x >= width)
            xChange = -xChange;

        if (y <= 0 || y >= height)
            yChange = -yChange;
    }

    private void draw() {
        Graphics paper = panel.getGraphics();
        paper.setColor(Color.red);
        paper.fillOval(x, y, diameter, diameter);
    }

    private void delete() {
        Graphics paper = panel.getGraphics();
        paper.setColor(Color.white);
        paper.fillOval (x, y, diameter, diameter);
    }
}
```

To call a method from within the object, you do it like this:

```
move();
```

giving the name of the method and any parameters as usual. If we really want to emphasize which object is being used, we could write the following equivalent code:

```
this.move();
```

using the keyword **this**, which means the current object.

Depending on its size and complexity, a class might have a number of **private** methods. Their purpose is to clarify and simplify the class.

● Scope rules

In programming, the term *accessibility* (sometimes called *scope rules* or *visibility*) means the rules for accessing variables and methods. For humans, accessibility rules are like the rule that in Australia you must drive on the left, or the rule that you should only enter someone's home via the front door. In a program, rules like these are rigidly enforced by the compiler, to prevent deliberate or erroneous access to protected information. Accessibility rules constrain the programmer, but help the programmer to organize a program in a clear and logical manner. The accessibility rules associated with classes and methods allow the programmer to encapsulate variables and methods in a convenient manner.

The programmer can describe each variable and method as either **public** or **private**. Within a class, any instruction anywhere in the class can call any method, **public** or **private**. Also any instruction can refer to any instance variable. The exception is that local variables, those declared within a method, are only accessible by instructions within the method.

When one class refers to another, only those methods and variables labelled as **public** are accessible from outside a class. All others are inaccessible. It is good design practice to minimize the number of methods that are **public**, restricting them so as to offer only the services of the class. It is also good practice never (or very rarely) to make variables **public**. If a variable needs to be inspected or changed, methods should be provided to do the job.

In summary, a variable or method within a class can be described as either:

1. **public** – accessible from anywhere (from within the class or from any other class); or
2. **private** – accessible only from within the class.

In addition, local variables, which are variables declared within a method, are accessible only within the method.

Classes are labelled **public** so that they can be used as widely as possible. Constructors are labelled as **public** because they need to be called from outside the class.

We will revisit scope rules when we study the topic of inheritance in Chapter 10.

● Operations on objects

Many of the objects that are used in Java programs must be declared as instances of classes, but some do not. Variables declared as `int`, `boolean` and `double` are called *primitive* types. They come ready-made as part of the Java language. Whereas class names usually start with a capital letter, the names of these primitive types start with lower case. When you declare one of these variables, it is immediately usable. For example:

```
int number;
```

both declares the variable `number` and creates it. By contrast, the creation of any other objects has to be done explicitly using `new`. For example:

```
Balloon balloon = new Balloon(10, 20, 50);
```

So variables in Java are either:

1. primitive types such as `int`, `boolean` and `double`; or
2. objects explicitly created from classes, by using `new`.

Variables which are declared to be of a primitive type come ready-made with a whole collection of things you can do with them. For example, with variables of type `int` you can:

- declare variables;
- assign values using =;
- carry out arithmetic;
- compare using ==, <, etc.;
- use as a parameter or as a return value.

You cannot necessarily do all these things with objects. Many things that a Java program uses are objects but, as we have seen, not everything is an object. And it is tempting to assume that it is possible to use all these operations with any object – but this is not so. What can you do with an object? The answer is that when you write a class, you define the set of operations that can be performed on objects of that type. With the `Balloon` class, for example, we have defined the operations `changeSize`, `move` and `display`. You should not assume that you can do anything else to a balloon. However, you can confidently assume that for every object you can:

- create it using `new`;
- use it as a parameter and as a return value;
- assign it to a variable of the same class using =;
- use the methods that are provided as part of its class.

9.7 Suggest a list of operations that are possible with an object of the class **Balloon** and give examples of using them.

● Object destruction

We have seen how objects are created, using the powerful word **new**. How do they die? One obvious and certain situation is when the program ceases to run. They can also die when they cease to be used by the program. For example, if we do this to create a new object:

```
Balloon balloon;
balloon = new Balloon(20, 100, 100);
```

and then:

```
balloon = new Balloon(40, 200, 200);
```

what happens is that the first object created with **new** lived a brief life. It died when the program no longer had any knowledge of it and its value was usurped by the newer object.

When an object is destroyed, the memory that was used to store the values of its variables and any other resources is reclaimed for other uses by the run-time system. This is termed *garbage collection*. In Java, garbage collection is automatic. (In some other languages, notably C++, it is not automatic and the programmer has to keep track of objects that are no longer needed.)

Finally, we can destroy an object by assigning the value **null** to it. For example:

```
balloon = null;
```

The word **null** is a Java keyword that describes a non-existent (uninstantiated) object.

● static **methods**

Some methods do not need an object to work on. An example is the mathematical square root function. Mathematical methods such as square root, **sqrt**, and sine of an angle, **sin**, are provided within a library class named **Math**. In a program to use them, we write statements such as:

```
double x, y;
x = Math.sqrt(y);
```

In this statement there are two **double** variables, **x** and **y**, but no objects. Note that **Math** is the name of a class, not an object. The square root method **sqrt** acts on its parameter **y**. The question is: if **sqrt** is not a method of some object, what is it? The answer is that methods like this are part of a class, but they are described as **static**.

When you use one of these methods, its name must be preceded with the name of its class (instead of the name of an object).

The class **Math** has the following structure (the code shown is incomplete). The methods are labelled as **static**:

```
public class Math {

    public static double sqrt(double x) {
        // body of sqrt
    }

    public static double sin(double x) {
        // body of sin
    }
}
```

Another example of a **static** method is **parseInt** within class **Integer**. The method **main** that appears at the head of every Java application is also a **static** method.

What is the point of **static** methods? In OOP, everything is written as a part of a class; nothing exists other than within classes. If we think about the **Balloon** class, it contains **private** variables such as **x** and **y** that record the state of an object. But some methods, such as **sqrt**, do not involve a state. However, free-standing methods such as **sqrt** which are not obviously part of some class have to obey the central rule of OOP – they have to be a part of some class. Hence the reason for **static** methods. It is common for programmers to make use of the library **static** methods but it is rare for novice programmers to write them.

static methods are also termed class methods because they belong to the class rather than to any object created from the class.

SELF-TEST QUESTION

9.8   The **static** method **max** within the class **Math** finds the maximum of its two **int** parameters. Write a sample call on **max**.

static **variables**

A variable declared at the head of a class can be described as **static**. This means that it belongs to the class and not to any individual objects that are created as instances of the class.

As an example, the class **Math** contains a static variable, the mathematical constant pi. This variable is referred to as **Math.PI**, again preceding the variable name by the class name. Making data values public like this is very unusual in OOP, because normally variables are labelled **private** in the spirit of information hiding. Access to the mathematical constants is an exception to this general rule. The variable **PI** is declared as follows within the class **Math**:

```
public class Math {

    public final static double PI = 3.142;

    // remainder of class Math
}
```

(Except that the value of pi is given to a greater precision.)

Another example of **static** variables is in the class **Color**, which provides variables that are referred to as **Color.black**, **Color.white**, etc.

The description **static** does not mean that a **static** variable cannot be changed. It means that, unlike non-static variables, a copy of the variable is not created when an object is created from the class. The description **static** implies uniqueness, i.e. there is only one copy of this variable for the whole class, rather than one copy for each instance of the class.

static variables are sometimes known as class variables, but they are not the same as class-level variables.

Programming principles

OOP is about constructing programs from objects. An *object* is a combination of some data (variables) and some actions (methods) that performs some useful role in a program. The programmer designs an object so that the data and the actions are closely related, rather than being randomly collected together.

In Java, as in most OOP languages, it is not possible to write instructions that describe an object directly. Instead the language makes the programmer define all objects of the same class. For example, if we need a button object, we create an instance of the **JButton** class. If we need a second button, we create a second instance of this same class. The description of the structure of all possible buttons is called a *class*. A class is the template or the master plan to make any number of them; a class is a generalization of an object.

The idea of classes is a common idea in most design activity. It is usual before actually constructing anything to create a design for the object. This is true in automobile design, architecture, construction – even in fine art. Some kind of a plan is drafted, often on paper, sometimes on a computer. Sometimes it is called a blueprint. Such a design specifies the desired object completely, so that if the designer gets run over by a bus, someone else can carry out the construction of the object. Once designed, any number of identical objects can be constructed – think of cars, books or computers. So the design specifies the composition of one or any number of objects. The same is true in OOP – a class is the plan for any number of identical objects. Once we have specified a class, we can construct any number of objects with the same behaviour.

Considering the **JButton** library class again, what we have is the description of what each and every button object will look like. Buttons only differ in their individual properties, such as their positions on the form. So in OOP, a class is the specification for any number of objects that are the same. Once a class has been written, a particular object is constructed by creating an *instance* of the class. It's a bit like saying we have had an instance of flu in the home. Or, this Model T Ford is an instance of the Model T Ford design. Your own bank account is an instance of the bank account class.

An object is a logical bundling together of variables and methods. It forms a self-contained module that can be easily used and understood. The principle of information hiding or encapsulation means that users of an object have a restricted view of an object. An object provides a set of services as `public` methods that others can use. The remainder of the object, its variables and the instructions that implement the methods are hidden from view. This enhances abstraction and modularity.

In computer science a class is sometimes called an *abstract data type* (ADT). A data type is a kind of variable, like an `int`, a `double` or a `boolean`. These primitive types are types built into the Java language and are immediately available for use. Associated with each of these types is a set of operations. For example, with an `int` we can do assignment, addition, subtraction and so on. The `Balloon` class above is an example of an ADT. It defines some data (variables), together with a collection of operations (methods) that can carry out operations on the data. The class presents an abstraction of a balloon; the concrete details of the implementation are hidden.

We can now fully understand the overall structure of a program. Every Java program has a heading similar to this (but with the appropriate class name):

```
public class UseBalloon
```

This is a description of a class named `UseBalloon`, because like everything else in Java, a program is a class. When a program starts, the `static` method `main` is called.

Programming pitfalls

Novices sometimes want to code an object straight away. You can't – instead you have to declare a class and then create an instance of the class.

Do not forget to initialize instance variables. Explicitly initialize them by means of a constructor method or as a part of the declaration itself and do not rely on Java's default initialization.

If you declare:

```
Balloon balloon;
```

and then perform:

```
balloon.display(paper);
```

your program will terminate with an error message that says there is a `null` pointer exception. This is because you have declared an object but not created it (with `new`). The object `balloon` does not exist. More accurately, it has the value `null` – which amounts to the same thing. In most elementary programming you do not make use of `null` – except if you inadvertently forget to use `new`.

Grammar spot

■ A class has the structure:

```
public class ClassName {
    // declarations of instance variables
    // declarations of methods
}
```

■ Variables and methods can be described as either **public** or **private**.

■ One or more of the methods in a class can have the same name as the class. Any one of these constructor methods may be called (with appropriate parameters) to initialize the object when it is created.

■ The declaration of a **public** method has the structure:

```
public void methodName(parameters) {
    // body
}
```

■ A **static** method is prefixed by the word **static** in its header.

■ To call a **static** method of a class:

```
ClassName.methodName(parameters);
```

New language elements

■ **class** – appears in the heading of a class;

■ **public** – the description of a variable or method that is accessible from anywhere;

■ **private** – the description of a variable or method that is only accessible from within the class;

■ **new** – used to create a new instance of a class (a new object);

■ **this** – the name of the current object;

■ **null** – the name of an object that does not exist;

■ **static** – the description attached to a variable or method that belongs to a class as a whole, not to any instance created as an object from the class.

Summary

- An object is a collection of data and the associated actions, methods, that can act upon the data. Java programs are constructed as a number of objects.

- A class is the description of any number of objects.

- Items in a class can be declared to be **private** or **public**. A **private** item can be referred to only from within the class. A **public** item can be referred to by anything (inside or outside the class). In designing a Java program, **public** variables are avoided so as to enhance information hiding.

- Methods that have the same name as the class carry out the initialization of a newly created object. These are termed constructor methods.

- The description **static** means that the variable or method belongs to the class and not to particular objects. A **static** method can be called directly, without any need for instantiating an instance of the class with **new**. A **static** method is useful when a method does not need to be associated with a particular object, or for carrying out actions for the class as a whole. **static** variables are typically used as constants within library classes such as class **Math**.

Exercises

9.1 **Balloons** Add to the class **Balloon** some additional data: a **String** that holds the name of the balloon and a **Color** variable that describes its colour. Add code to initialize these values using a constructor method. Add the code to display the coloured balloon and its name.
   Enhance the balloon program with buttons that move the balloon left, right, up and down.

9.2 **Thermometer** Some thermometers record the maximum and minimum temperatures that have been reached.
   Write a program that simulates a thermometer using a slider and displays in text fields the values of the maximum and minimum values that the slider has been set to. Write the piece of program that remembers the largest and smallest values and compares new values as a separate class. This class has methods **setNewValue**, **getLowestValue** and **getHighestValue**.

9.3 **Bank account** Write a program that simulates a bank account. A button allows a deposit to be made into the account. The amount is entered into a text field. A second button allows a withdrawal to be made. The amount (the balance) and the state of the account is continually displayed – it is either OK or overdrawn. Create a class named **Account** to represent bank accounts. It has methods **deposit**, **withdraw**, **getCurrentBalance** and **setCurrentbalance**.

9.4 **Scorekeeper** Design and write a class that acts as a scorekeeper for a computer game. It maintains a single integer, the score. It provides a method to initialize the score to zero, a method to increase the score, a method to decrease the score, and a method to return the score. Write a program to create a single object and use it. The current score is always on display in a text field. Buttons are provided to increase, decrease and initialize the score by an amount entered into a text field.

9.5 **Dice** Design and write a class that acts as a die, which may be thrown to give a value 1 to 6. Initially write it so that it always gives the value 6. Write a program that creates a die object and uses it. The screen displays a button, which when pressed causes the die to be thrown and its value displayed.

Then alter the die class so that it gives the value one higher than when it was last thrown, e.g. 4 when it was 3. When the last value was 6, the new value is 1.

Then alter it so that it uses the library random number generator.

Some games such as backgammon need two dice. Write Java statements to create two instances of the die class, throw the dice and display the outcomes.

9.6 **Random number generator** Write your own integer random number generator as a class that uses a formula to obtain the next pseudo-random number from the previous one. A random number program works by starting with some 'seed' value. Thereafter the current random number is used as a basis for the next by performing some calculation on it which makes it into some other (apparently random) number. A good formula to use for integers is:

```
nextR = ((oldR * 25173) + 13849) % 65536;
```

which produces numbers in the range 0 to 65535. The particular numbers in this formula have been shown to give good, random-like, results.

Initially, make the seed value equal to 1. Then, in a more sophisticated program, obtain the milliseconds part of the time using library class **Calendar** (see Appendix A) to act as the seed.

9.7 **Parking Lot (Car Park).** A program provides two buttons. The parking attendant clicks on one button when a car enters the lot and the other button when a car leaves. If a car attempts to enter when the lot is already full, a warning is displayed in an option pane.

Implement the count of cars and its operations as a class. It provides a method named **enter**, which increments the count and a method named **leave**, which decrements the count. A third method (named **full**) returns a **boolean** specifying whether the lot is full or not.

9.8 **Complex numbers** Write a class called **Complex** to represent complex numbers (together with their operations). A complex number consists of two parts – a real part (a **double**) and an imaginary part (a **double**). The constructor method should create a new complex number, using the **double** values provided as parameters, like this:

```
Complex c = new Complex(1.0, 2.0);
```

Write methods **getReal** and **getImaginary** to get the real part and the imaginary part of a complex number and which is used like this:

```
double x = c.getReal();
```

Write a method **sum** to add two complex numbers and return their sum. The real part is the sum of the two real parts. The imaginary part is the sum of the two imaginary parts. A call of the method looks like:

```
Complex c = c1.sum(c2);
```

Enter values for **c1** via two text fields and do the same for **c2**. Display the values of **c** also in two text fields.

Write a method **prod** to calculate the product of two complex numbers. If one number has components x_1 and y_1 and the second number has components x_2 and y_2:

the real part of the product $= x_1 \times x_2 - y_1 \times y_2$
the imaginary part of the product $= x_1 \times y_2 + x_2 \times y_1$

Answers to self-test questions

9.1
```
private Color color;
```

9.2
```
public void moveUp(int amount) {
    yCoord = yCoord - amount;
}
```

9.3
```
public void changeColor(Color newColor) {
    color = newColor;
}
```

9.4
```
public void display(Graphics paper) {
    paper.setColor(color);
    paper.drawOval(x, y, diameter, diameter);
}
```

9.5
```
public int getY() {
    return y;
}
```

9.6
```
public Balloon(int initialDiameter) {
    diameter = initialDiameter;
}
```

9.7 Methods are: `changeColor`, `moveLeft`, `moveRight`, `changeSize`, `display`, `getX`, `getY`.
Examples are:

```
balloon.changeColor(Color.red);
balloon.moveLeft(20);
balloon.moveRight(50);
balloon.changeSize(10);
balloon.display(paper);
int x = balloon.getX();
int y = balloon.getY();
```

9.8
```
int x;
x = Math.max(7, 8);
```

CHAPTER

10

Inheritance

This chapter explains:

- how to create a new class from an existing class using inheritance;
- when and how to declare variables and methods as **protected**;
- when and how to use overriding;
- how to draw a class diagram that describes inheritance;
- how to use the **super** keyword;
- how to write constructors for subclasses;
- the meaning of **final**;
- how to use abstract classes and **abstract**.

● Introduction

Programs are built from objects, which are instances of classes. Some classes are in the Java library and some classes the programmer writes. When you start to write a new program you look for useful classes in the library and you look at any classes you have written in the past. This OO approach to programming means that instead of starting programs from scratch, you build on earlier work. It's not uncommon to find a class that looks useful, and does nearly what you want, but not exactly what you want. Inheritance is a way of resolving this problem. With inheritance, you use an existing class as the basis for creating a modified class.

Here is an analogy. Suppose you want to buy a new car and you go to a showroom and see a range of mass-produced cars. You like one in particular – but it doesn't have that special feature that you want. Like the description of a class, the car has been manufactured from plans that describe many identical cars. If inheritance was available, you could specify a car that had all the features of the mass-produced car, but with the added extras or changes that you require.

● Using inheritance

We start with a class similar to one used already in this book. It is a class to represent a sphere. A sphere has a radius and a position in space. When we display a sphere on the screen, it will be shown as a circle. (The method to display a sphere simply calls the library method **drawOval**.) The diameter of the sphere is fixed at 20 pixels. We have only modelled the *x* and *y* coordinates of a sphere (and not the *z* coordinate) because we are displaying a two-dimensional representation on the screen.

Here is the description for class **Sphere**:

```
public class Sphere {

    protected int x = 100, y = 100;

    public void setX(int newX) {
        x = newX;
    }

    public void setY(int newY) {
        y = newY;
    }

    public void display(Graphics paper) {
        paper.drawOval(x, y, 20, 20);
    }

}
```

You will notice that there are a number of new elements to this program, including the word **protected**. This is because the class has been written in such a way that it can be used for inheritance. We will see during the course of this chapter what these new elements mean.

Let us suppose that someone has written and tested this class, and made it available for use. But now we come to write a new program and find that we need a class very much like this, but one that describes bubbles. This new class, called **Bubble**, will allow us to do additional things – for example, to change the size of a bubble and move it vertically. The limitation of class **Sphere** is that it describes objects that do not move and whose size cannot change. Firstly, we need an additional method that will allow us to set a new value for the radius of the bubble. We can do this without altering the existing class, instead writing a different class that uses the code that is already in **Sphere**. We say that the new class inherits variables and methods from the old class. The new class is a subclass of the old. The old class is called the superclass of the new class. This is how we write the new class:

```
public class Bubble extends Sphere {

    protected int radius = 10;

    public void setSize(int size) {
            radius = size;
        }

    public void display(Graphics paper) {
        paper.drawOval(x, y, 2 * radius, 2 * radius);
    }
}
```

This new class has the name **Bubble**. The keyword **extends** and the mention of class **Sphere** mean that **Bubble** inherits from class **Sphere** or we say that **Bubble** is a subclass of **Sphere**. This means that **Bubble** inherits all the items not described as **private** within class **Sphere**. We will explore the other features of this class in the following sections.

● protected

When you use inheritance, **private** is just too private and **public** is just too public. If a class needs to give its subclasses access to particular variables or methods, but prevent access from any other classes, it can label them as **protected**. In the family analogy, a mother allows her descendants to use her car keys but not anyone else.

Looking at the class **Sphere**, we need variables to describe the coordinates. We **could** write:

```
private int x, y;
```

This is a sound decision, but there may be a better idea. It might be that someone later writes a class that inherits this class and provides an additional method to move a sphere. This method will need access to the variables **x** and **y** – which are unfortunately inaccessible because they have been labelled **private**. So to anticipate this possible future use, we might instead decide to label them as **protected**:

```
protected int x, y;
```

This declaration now protects these variables against possible misuse by any arbitrary classes, but permits access by certain privileged classes – the subclasses. The same principle applies to methods.

Suppose we had declared **x** and **y** as **private**, as originally planned. The consequence is that it would have been impossible to reuse the class by employing inheritance. The only option would be to edit the class, replacing the description **private** by **protected** for these particular items. But this violates one of the principles of OOP, which is never to alter an existing class that is tried and tested. So when we write a class we strive to think ahead about possible future users of the class. The programmer who writes a class always writes it in the hope that someone will reuse the class by extending it. Careful use of **protected** instead of **public** or **private** can help make a class more attractive for inheritance. This is another of the principles of OOP.

● Scope rules

In summary, the four levels of accessibility (scope rules) of a variable or method in a class are:

1. **public** – accessible from anywhere. As a rule, any methods offering a service to users of a class should be labelled as **public**.
2. **protected** – accessible from this class and from any subclass.
3. **private** – accessible only from this class. Generally, instance variables should be declared as **private** but sometimes as **protected**.
4. Local variables (variables declared within a method) are never accessible from outside the particular method.

So a class can have good, but controlled, access to its immediate superclass and the superclasses above it in the class hierarchy, just as if the classes are part of the class itself. If we make the family analogy, it is like being able freely to spend your mother's money or that of any of her ancestors – provided that they have put their money in an account labelled **public** or **protected**. People outside the family can only access **public** money.

● Additional items

An important way of constructing a new class from another is to include additional variables and methods.

You can see that the class **Bubble** given above declares an additional variable and an additional method:

```
protected int radius = 10;

public void setSize(int size) {
    radius = size;
}
```

The new variable is **radius**, which is additional to the existing variables (**x** and **y**) in **Sphere**. The number of variables is thereby extended.

The new class also has the method **setSize** in addition to those in **Sphere**.

SELF-TEST QUESTION

10.1 A ball object is like a **Sphere** object, but it has the additional features of being able to move left and move right. Write a class called **Ball** which inherits the class **Sphere** but provides additional methods **moveLeft** and **moveRight**.

● Overriding

Another feature of the new class **Bubble** is a new version of the method **display**:

```
public void display(Graphics paper) {
    paper.drawOval(x, y, 2 * radius, 2 * radius);
}
```

This is needed because the new class has a radius that can be changed, whereas in class **Sphere**, the radius was fixed. This new version of **display** in **Bubble** supersedes the version in the class **Sphere**. We say that the new version *overrides* the old version.

Do not confuse overriding with overloading, which we met in Chapter 5 on methods:

■ Overloading means writing a method (in the same class) that has the same name, but a different list of parameters.

■ Overriding means writing a method in a subclass that has the same name and parameters.

In summary, in the inheriting class we have:

■ created an additional variable;

■ created an additional method;

■ overridden a method (provided a method which is to be used instead of the method that is already provided).

Let us sum up what we have accomplished. We had an existing class called **Sphere**. We had a requirement for a new class, **Bubble**, that was similar to **Sphere**, but needed additional facilities. So we created the new class by extending the facilities of the old class. We have made maximum use of the commonality between the two classes, and we have avoided rewriting pieces of program that already exist. Both of the classes we have written, **Sphere** and **Bubble**, are of course available to use.

Making an analogy with human families, inheritance means you can spend your own money and also that of your mother.

It is technically possible to override variables – to declare variables in a subclass that override variables in the superclass. We will not discuss this further for two good reasons: one, there is never any need to do this, and two, it is very bad practice. When you subclass a class (inherit from it) you only ever:

■ add additional methods;

■ add additional variables;

■ override methods.

● Class diagrams

A good way to visualize inheritance is by using a class diagram, and an example is shown in Figure 10.1. This shows that **Bubble** is a subclass of **Sphere**, which is in turn a sub-class of **Object**. Each class is shown as a rectangle. A line between classes shows an inheritance relationship. The arrow points from the subclass to the superclass.

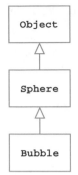

Figure 10.1 Class diagram for classes **Sphere** and **Bubble**.

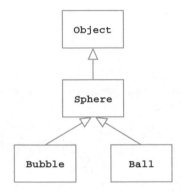

Figure 10.2 Class diagram showing a tree structure.

Every class in the library or written by the programmer fits within a class hierarchy. If you write a class beginning with the heading:

```
public class Sphere
```

which has no explicit superclass, it is implicitly a subclass of the class **Object**. Every class is therefore either implicitly or explicitly a subclass of **Object**.

Figure 10.2 shows another class diagram in which another class, called **Ball**, is also a subclass of **Sphere**. The diagram is now a tree structure, with the root of the tree, **Object**, at the top. In general a class diagram is a tree, like a family tree, except that it only shows one parent.

● Inheritance at work

As the class **Bubble** shows, a class often has a superclass, which in turn has a superclass, and so on up the inheritance tree. It is not only the **public** and **protected** items in the immediate superclass that are inherited, but all the **public** and **protected** variables and methods in all of the superclasses up the inheritance tree. So you inherit from your mother, your grandmother and so on.

Suppose we create an object **bubble** from the class **Bubble**:

```
Bubble bubble = new Bubble();
```

What happens if we use the method **setX** as follows?

```
bubble.setX(200);
```

Now **bubble** is an object of the class **Bubble** but **setX** is not a method of **Bubble**. It is a method of a different class **Sphere**. This is OK because all the methods labelled **public** (and **protected**) within the immediate superclass (and all the superclasses in the class hierarchy) are available to a subclass. And since **Bubble** is a subclass of **Sphere**, **setX** is available to objects of class **Bubble**.

The rule is that when a method is used, the Java system first looks in the class of the object to find the method. If it cannot find it there, it looks in the class of the immediate superclass. If it cannot find it there, it looks at the class for the superclass of the superclass, and so on up the class hierarchy until it finds a method with the required name. In the family analogy, you implicitly inherit from your grandmother, your great-grandmother and so on.

The Java language allows a class to inherit from only one immediate superclass. This is called single inheritance. In the family analogy it means that you can inherit from your mother but not from your father.

super

A class will sometimes need to call a method in its immediate superclass or one of the classes up the tree. There is no problem with this – the methods in all the classes up the inheritance tree are freely available, provided that they are labelled as **public** or **protected**. The only problem that can arise is when the desired method in the superclass has the same name as a method in the current class (because overriding has been used). To fix this problem, prefix the method name with the keyword **super**. For example, to call the method **display** in a superclass use:

```
super.display(paper);
```

Generally this is neater and shorter than duplicating instructions and can help make a program more concise by making the maximum use of existing methods.

Constructors

Constructors were explained in Chapter 9 on writing classes. They allow us to pass parameters to an object when we create it using **new**. A constructor is a method with the same name as the class. Remember that:

■ if you write a class without constructors, Java assumes that there is a single constructor (with zero parameters);

- if you write a class with one or more constructors with parameters, and a zero-parameter constructor is also needed, you must explicitly write it.

As far as inheritance and constructors are concerned, there are two principles:

- constructors are not inherited;
- a subclass must call a constructor in the superclass.

We will look at each of these rules in turn.

Constructor methods are not inherited. This is a reasonable rule; it says that a constructor is associated with initializing a particular class, not any subclasses. But it means that if you need one or more constructors – as you often will – in a subclass, you need to write them explicitly.

A subclass constructor must call a constructor in the superclass. Further, this must be carried out as the first action of the constructor. This, again, is only reasonable: the superclass must be properly initialized, and it must be initialized before any new items are created and initialized in the subclass. If the first instruction in a constructor is not a call on a constructor in the superclass, then Java automatically calls the zero-parameter constructor in the superclass. Thus Java forces the programmer to call a constructor in the superclass.

We will now look at how this works in practice. Suppose, for example, we have an existing class, with two constructors:

```java
public class Balloon {

    protected int x, y, radius;

    public Balloon() {
        x = 10;
        y = 10;
        radius = 20;
    }

    public Balloon(int initialX, int initialY,
                       int initialRadius) {
        x = initialX;
        y = initialY;
        radius = initialRadius;
    }

    // remainder of class
}
```

If we now write a new class named **DifferentBalloon** that inherits from class **Balloon**, the options are:

1. Do not write a constructor in the subclass. Java assumes that there is a zero-parameter constructor.

2. Write one or more constructors.

3. Write one or more constructors that call an appropriate constructor in the super-class, using **super**.

For novice programmers (and maybe experts too) it is probably wise to make things clear and therefore to write explicitly a call to a superclass constructor. We do this in the following examples.

Here is a subclass of **Balloon** with a constructor that calls the zero-parameter constructor in the superclass, using **super**:

```
public class DifferentBalloon extends Balloon {

    public DifferentBalloon(int initialX, int initialY) {
        super();
        x = initialX;
        y = initialY;
        radius = 20;
    }

    // remainder of class

}
```

and here is a subclass with a constructor that explicitly calls the second constructor in the superclass, again using **super**:

```
public class ModifiedBalloon extends Balloon {

    public ModifiedBalloon(int initialX, int initialY,
                           int initialRadius) {
        super(initialX, initialY, initialRadius);
    }

    // remainder of class

}
```

SELF-TEST QUESTIONS

10.2 A coloured sphere is like a sphere, but with some colour. Write a new class named **ColoredSphere** that extends **Sphere** to provide a colour that can be set when the balloon is created. This is accomplished using a constructor method, so that your class should enable the following to be written:

```
ColoredSphere coloredSphere =
    new ColoredSphere(Color.red);
```

SELF-TEST QUESTIONS

10.3   What is wrong with the subclass in the following?

```
public class BankAccount {

    protected int deposit;

    public BankAccount(int initialDeposit) {
        // remainder of constructor
    }

// remainder of class
}

public class BetterAccount extends BankAccount {

    public BetterAccount() {
        deposit = 1000;
    }

// remainder of class

}
```

● final

Inheriting and overriding is all about changing the behaviour of classes and objects. Inheritance is very powerful, but sometimes it is reassuring to have some things fixed and unchanging. For example, it is good to know precisely what **sqrt** does, what **drawLine** does and so on. In OOP there is always a danger that someone will extend the classes that these belong to and thereby change what they do. This could be by error or in a misplaced attempt to be helpful. To prevent this, the programmer can describe a method as **final**. This means that it cannot be overridden. Most of the library methods are described as **final**. This means that whenever you use them you can be completely confident of what they do.

As we have seen from an early stage in this book, variables can also be declared as **final**. This means also that their values cannot be changed. They are constants. For example:

```
final double cmPerInch = 2.54;
```

declares a variable whose value cannot be altered. Thus the prefix **final** has the same meaning whether it is attached to a variable or to a method.

A whole class can be described as **final**, which means that it cannot be subclassed. In addition, all of its methods are implicitly **final**.

Making a class or a method **final** is a serious decision because it prevents inheritance – one of the power tools of OOP.

● Abstract classes

Consider a program that maintains graphical shapes of all types and sizes – circles, rectangles, squares, triangles, etc. These different shapes, similar to the classes we have already met in this chapter, have information in common – their position, colour and size. So we will declare a superclass, named **Shape**, which describes this common data. Each individual class inherits this common information. Here is the way to describe this common superclass:

```
public abstract class Shape {
    protected int x, y ;
    protected int size;
    public void moveRight() {
        x = x + 10;
    }

    public abstract void display(Graphics paper);
}
```

The class to describe circles inherits from the class **Shape** as follows:

```
public class Circle extends Shape {
    public void display(Graphics paper) {
        paper.drawOval(x, y, size, size);
    }
}
```

Thus in writing class **Circle**, we have exploited the facilities provided by class **Shape**.

It is fruitless to try to create an object from the class **Shape** – because it is incomplete. This is why the keyword **abstract** is attached to the header of **Shape**, and the compiler will prevent any attempt to create an instance of this class. The method **moveRight** is provided and is complete, and is inherited by any subclass. But the method **display** is simply a header (without a body). It is described with the keyword **abstract** to say that any subclass must provide an implementation of **display**. The class **Shape** is termed an abstract class because it does not exist as a full class but is provided simply to be used for inheritance.

There is a reasonable rule that if a class contains any methods that are **abstract**, the class itself must be labelled as **abstract**.

Abstract classes enable us to exploit the common features of classes. Declaring a class as **abstract** forces the programmer who is using the class (by inheritance) to provide the missing methods. This is a way, therefore, by which the designer of a class can encourage a particular design.

The term abstract is used because as we look higher and higher up a class hierarchy, the classes become more and more general or abstract. In the example above, the class **Shape** is more abstract and less concrete than a **Circle**. The superclass abstracts features, such as the position and size in this example, that are common between its subclasses. It is common in large OO programs to find that the top few levels of the class hierarchies consist of abstract methods. Similarly in biology, abstraction is used with classes like mammals, which do not exist (in themselves), but serve as abstract superclasses to a diverse set of subclasses. Thus we have never seen a mammal object, but we have seen a cow, which is an instance of a subclass of mammal.

SELF-TEST QUESTION

10.4   Write a class **Square** that uses the abstract class **Shape** given above.

Programming principles

Writing programs as a collection of classes means that programs are modular. Another bonus is that the parts of a program can be reused in other programs. Inheritance is another way in which OOP provides potential for reusability. Sometimes programmers are tempted to reinvent the wheel – they want to write new software when they could simply make use of existing software. One of the reasons for writing new software is that it is fun. But software is increasingly becoming more complex, so there simply is not enough time to write it from scratch. Imagine having to write the software to create the GUI components provided by the Java libraries. Imagine having to write a mathematical function like **sqrt** every time you needed it. It would just take too long. So a good reason for reusing software is to save time. It is not just the time to write the software that you save, it is the time to test it thoroughly – and this can take even longer than actually writing the software. So reusing classes makes sense.

One reason why programmers sometimes don't reuse software is that the existing software doesn't do exactly what they need it to do. Maybe it does 90% of what they want, but some crucial bits are missing or some bits do things differently. One approach would be to modify the existing software to match the new needs. This, however, is a dangerous strategy because modifying software is a minefield. Software is not so much soft as brittle – when you try to change it, it breaks. When you change software it is very easy to introduce new and subtle bugs into it, which necessitate extensive debugging and correction. This is a common experience, so much so that programmers are very reluctant to modify software.

This is where OOP comes to the rescue. In an OO program, you can inherit the behaviour of those parts of some software that you need, override those (few) methods that you want to behave differently, and add new methods to do additional things. Often you can inherit most of a class, making only the few changes that are needed using inheritance. You only have to test the new bits, sure in the knowledge that all the rest has been tested before. So the problem of reuse is solved. You can make use of existing software in a safe way. Meanwhile, the original class remains intact, reliable and usable.

Inheritance is like going to buy a car. You see the car you like, and it is almost perfect, but you would like some minor change, such as a different colour or the inclusion

> ►   *Programming principles continued*

of satellite navigation. With inheritance, you can inherit the standard car but change the parts as required.

OOP means building on the work of others. The OO programmer proceeds in steps:

1. Clarify the requirements of the program.
2. Browse the library for classes that perform the required functions and use them to achieve the desired results.
3. Review the classes within other programs you have written and use them as appropriate.
4. Extend library classes or your own classes using inheritance when useful.
5. Write your own new classes.

This is why OO programs are often very short – they simply use the library classes or they create new classes that inherit from library classes. This approach requires an investment in time – the programmer needs a very good knowledge of the libraries. This idea of reusing OO software is so powerful that some people think of OOP entirely in this way. In this view, OOP is the process of extending the library classes so as to meet the requirements of a particular application.

Nearly every program in this book uses inheritance. Every program starts with lines very similar to the following:

```
public class Safe extends JFrame
```

This says that the class **Safe** inherits features from the library class **JFrame**. The features in **JFrame** include methods for creating a GUI window, with the usual icons to resize and close the window. Extending the class **JFrame** is the main way in which the programs in this book extend the library classes.

Beware: sometimes inheritance is not the appropriate technique. Instead, composition – using existing classes unchanged – is very often better. This issue is discussed in Chapter 18 on design.

Programming pitfalls

Novice programmers use inheritance of a library class, the class **JFrame**, from their very first program. But learning to use inheritance within your own classes takes time and experience. It usually only becomes worthwhile in larger programs. Don't worry if you don't use inheritance for quite some time.

It is common to confuse overloading and overriding:

- *Overloading* means writing two or more methods in the same class with the same name (but a different list of parameters).
- *Overriding* means writing a method in a subclass to be used instead of the method in the superclass (or one of the superclasses above it in the inheritance tree).

New language elements

- **extends** – means that this class inherits from another named class.

- **protected** – the description of a variable or method that is accessible from within the class or any subclass (but not from elsewhere).

- **abstract** – the description of an abstract class that cannot be created but is provided only to be used in inheritance.

- **abstract** – the description of a method that is simply given as a header and must be provided by a subclass.

- **super** – the name of the superclass of a class, the class it inherits from.

- **final** – describes a method or variable that cannot be overridden.

Summary

Extending (inheriting) the facilities of a class is a good way to make use of existing parts of programs (classes).

A subclass inherits the facilities of its immediate superclass and all the superclasses above it in the inheritance tree.

A class has only one immediate superclass. (It can only inherit from one class.) This is called *single inheritance* in the jargon of OOP.

A class can extend the facilities of an existing class by providing one or more of:

- additional methods;
- additional variables;
- methods that override (act instead of) methods in the superclass.

A variable or method can be described as having one of three types of access:

- **public** – accessible from any class.
- **private** – accessible only from within this class.
- **protected** – accessible only from within this class and any subclass.

A class diagram is a tree showing the inheritance relationships.

The name of the superclass of a class is referred to by the word **super**.

An abstract class is described as **abstract**. It cannot be instantiated to give an object, because it is incomplete. An abstract class provides useful variables and methods for inheritance by subclasses.

● Exercises

10.1 **Spaceship** Write a class `SpaceShip` that describes a spaceship. A spaceship behaves exactly like a `Sphere` object, except that it can move up and move down. Make use of inheriting from the class `Sphere` shown in the text.

Draw a class diagram to show how the classes are related.

10.2 **Football** Write a class `FootBall` which restricts the movements of a ball so that the *x* coordinate must be greater than or equal to 0 and less than or equal to 200, corresponding to the length of a football pitch. Make use of inheriting from the class `Ball`.

10.3 **The bank** A class describes bank accounts. It provides methods `creditAccount`, `debitAccount`, `calculateInterest` and `getCurrentBalance`. A new account is created with a name and an initial balance.

There are two types of account – a regular account and a gold account. The gold account gives interest at 5%, while the regular account gives interest at 6%, less a fixed charge of $100. Whenever a withdrawal is made, a regular account is checked to see if the account is overdrawn. A gold account holder can overdraw indefinitely.

Write classes that describe the two types of account, making use of an abstract class to describe the common features. (Assume for simplicity that amounts of money are held as `int`.)

10.4 **Shapes** Write an abstract class named `Shape` to describe two-dimensional graphical objects (square, circle, rectangle, triangle, etc.) that have the following features. All such objects use `int` variables that specify the *x* and *y* coordinates of the top left of a bounding rectangle, and `int` variables that describe the height and the width of the rectangle. All the objects share the same methods `setX` and `setY` to set the values of these coordinates. All the objects share methods `setWidth` and `setHeight` to set the values of the width and height of the object. All the objects have a method `getArea` which returns the area of the object and a method `display` which displays it, but these methods are different depending on the particular object.

Write a class `Rectangle` that inherits from class `Shape`.

Answers to self-test questions

10.1
```java
public class Ball extends Sphere {

    public void moveLeft(int amount) {
        x = x - amount;
    }

    public void moveRight(int amount) {
        x = x + amount;
    }
}
```

10.2
```java
public class ColoredSphere extends Sphere {

    private Color color;

    public ColoredSphere(Color initialColor) {
        color = initialColor;
    }
}
```

10.3 The compiler will find fault with the subclass. There is no explicit call to a constructor of the superclass, so Java will try to call a zero-parameter constructor in the superclass and no such constructor has been written.

10.4
```java
public class Square extends Shape {

    public void display(Graphics paper) {

        paper.drawRect(x, y, size, size);
    }

}
```

CHAPTER 11

Calculations

This chapter explains:

- how to use the mathematical library functions;
- how to format numbers so that they can be displayed conveniently;
- how to carry out both business and scientific calculations.

Introduction

We have already seen in Chapter 4 how to carry out simple calculations. This chapter is about more serious calculations. It enhances the earlier explanation and brings together all the information needed to write programs that carry out calculations. If you are not interested in programs that do numerical calculations, skip this chapter.

Calculations arise in many programs – not only programs that carry out mathematical, scientific or engineering calculations, but also information systems, accountancy and forecasting. In graphics, calculations are necessary to scale and move images on the screen.

Chapter 4 explained several important ideas about numbers and calculations. The reader might like to review that chapter before continuing. The ideas were:

- declaring variables as either **int** or **double**;
- input and output using text fields;
- conversion between the string representations of numbers and their internal representations;
- precedence rules in expressions;
- conversions in expressions that mix **int** and **double** data.

● Library mathematical functions and constants

It is common in mathematical, scientific or engineering programs to use functions like sine, cosine and log. In Java, these are provided in one of the libraries – the **Math** library. To use one of the functions, you can write, for example:

```
x = Math.sqrt(y);
```

Some of the more widely used functions in the **Math** library are given in alphabetical order below. Where the parameter is an angle, it must be expressed in radians.

`cos(x)`	cosine of the angle x, where x is expressed in radians
`sin(x)`	sine of the angle x, expressed in radians
`tan(x)`	tangent of the angle x, expressed in radians
`abs(x)`	the absolute value of x, sometimes written $\lvert x \rvert$ in mathematics
`min(x, y)`	the smaller of x and y
`max(x, y)`	the larger of x and y
`log(x)`	natural logarithm of x (to the base e)
`random()`	provide a pseudo-random number in the range 0.0 to 0.999 . . .
`sqrt(x)`	the positive square root of x
`pow(x, y)`	x raised to the power of y, or x^y
`exp(x)`	e^x

When you use these methods, you sometimes have to be careful about the type of the variables or literals used as parameters. For example, the method **abs** can be passed any numeric value but the method **cos** can only be passed a **double** number.

The mathematical constants π and e are also available as constants within the **Math** library, so that we can write, for example:

```
double x, y;
x = Math.PI;
y = Math.E;
```

● Formatting numbers

Formatting is about displaying numbers in a readable way. For example, we don't always need the detail of unnecessary decimal places. If the value **33.124765** represents the area of a room in square metres, then all the decimal places are probably not necessary, and we might typically only need to display the number as **33.12**.

Java has a range of facilities for formatting values, but here we restrict ourselves to the most common cases of formatting **int** and **double** values. The steps are:

1. Create an instance of library class `DecimalFormat`, supplying a pattern as a parameter.

2. Call method `format`, supplying the number to be formatted as a parameter, returning the formatted value as a string.

We will start out with `int` values. Suppose we have an integer value:

```
int i = 123;
```

We have already widely used the `toString` method to convert a number. For example:

```
textField.setText(Integer.toString(i));
```

which gives the string:

```
123
```

Now instead we use the formatting method `format` to achieve the same result:

```
int i = 123;
DecimalFormat formatter = new DecimalFormat("###");
textField.setText(formatter.format(i));
```

This causes the text field to be given the same value:

```
123
```

The `#` character within a pattern means insert a digit. In this case, if there are less than three digits, no character is created.

When we know that an integer may be up to, say, five digits long, and we want to align the numbers in tabular form, we can use this:

```
int i = 123;
DecimalFormat formatter = new DecimalFormat("00000");
textField.setText(formatter.format(i));
```

which produces:

```
00123
```

This formats the number using five digits, right aligned and padded with zeros on the left as necessary.

For large numbers, commas can make the number more readable. This is illustrated by the following code:

```
int i = 123456;
DecimalFormat formatter = new DecimalFormat("###,###");
textField.setText(formatter.format(i));
```

Here the `,` character denotes that a comma character is to be placed at this position. This gives the string:

```
123,456
```

Formatting tends to be more useful when **double** values are to be displayed. In this example:

```
double d = 12.34;
DecimalFormat formatter = new DecimalFormat("###.##");
textField.setText(formatter.format(d));
```

the text field is given the value:

```
12.34
```

The two **#** characters specify two digits after the decimal point. On the left of the decimal point, digits are displayed as needed to present all of the number. But at least one digit is displayed. On the right of the decimal point, the number is rounded, if necessary, in order to fit into the two digits specified.

The facility is also provided to display **double** numbers in scientific notation, using the letter **E** within the formatting information:

```
double number = 12300000;
DecimalFormat formatter = new DecimalFormat("0.###E0");
textField.setText(formatter.format(number));
```

gives:

```
1.23E7
```

Finally, money values can be displayed using the letter **$** within the pattern. For example:

```
double money = 12.34;
DecimalFormat formatter = new DecimalFormat("$###.##");
textField.setText(formatter.format(money));
```

gives:

```
$12.34
```

where the currency symbol (**$** in this case) is determined by the local specification. Here the number is displayed with two digits after the decimal point (rounded if necessary).

The following table gives a summary of using some typical patterns.

Type of data	Sample value	Pattern	Formatted string
integer	123	###	123
integer with leading zeros	123	00000	00123
floating-point	12.34	##.##	12.34
scientific notation	12300000	0.###E0	1.23E7
money	12.34	$###.##	$12.34

And the following table summarizes the formatting characters that can be used to make up patterns:

Character	Meaning
#	insert a digit if there is one
0	always insert a digit
,	insert a comma
.	insert a decimal point
E	insert E followed by the power of 10
$	insert a dollar sign

The class `DecimalFormat` is within the package `java.text.DecimalFormat` and so the following `import` statement is needed at the head of a program that uses it:

```
import java.text.DecimalFormat;
```

SELF-TEST QUESTION

11.1 We know that the result of a calculation will be a floating-point number in the range 0 to 99, with two digits to be displayed after the decimal point. Choose a suitable formatting.

● Case study – money

We will now trace the development of a program to carry out calculations with money. In most countries, money comes in two parts – for example, dollars and cents, euros and cents, pounds and pence. We have a choice – we can represent an amount of money either as a `double` quantity (like 20.25 dollars) or as an `int` (2025 cents). If we use cents, we will need to convert amounts into dollars and cents and vice versa. We will opt to use `double` variables to represent values.

We will construct a program that calculates compound interest. An amount is invested at a particular annual interest rate and accumulates in value. The user enters the initial amount (as a whole number) and an interest rate (a number that may have a decimal point) into text fields. The user then clicks on a button to see the amount accumulated each year, as shown in Figure 11.1.

When the button is clicked to move on to the next year, the program must calculate:

```
newAmount = oldAmount + (oldAmount * rate / 100);
```

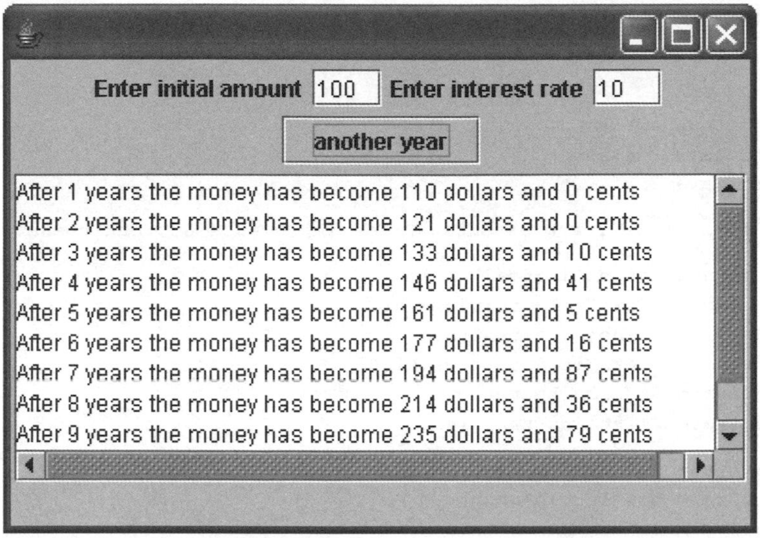

Figure 11.1 Interest calculation.

When we display an amount of money, we need to display a whole number of dollars and a whole number of cents, so that if the value is 127.2341 dollars, for example, we need to display it as 127 dollars and 23 cents.

First the dollar part. Simple use of the cast operator **(int)** converts the double number to an **int**, truncating the fractional part:

```
dollars = (int) newAmount;
```

Next, the cents part. We need to eliminate the dollars part of the number. We can do this by subtracting the whole number of dollars so that a number like 127.2341 will become 0.2341. Now we multiply by 100 to convert to cents, so that 0.2341 becomes 23.41. Next we use **Math.round** to convert to the nearest whole number (23.0). Then finally we convert the double value to an **int** value using **(int)**:

```
cents = (int) Math.round(100 * (newAmount - dollars));
```

We can now display the values properly converted. Finally the program does this:

```
oldAmount = newAmount;
```

which is what investment is all about.

At the class level, the instance declarations are:

```
private int year = 1;
private double oldAmount;
```

The complete program is:

```java
import java.awt.*;
import java.awt.event.*;
import javax.swing.*;

public class Interest extends JFrame implements ActionListener {
    private JLabel initialLabel;
    private JTextField initialField;
    private JLabel interestLabel;
    private JTextField interestField;
    private JButton button;
    private JTextArea textArea;

    private int year = 1;
    private double oldAmount;

    public static void main(String [] args) {
        Interest frame = new Interest();
        frame.setSize(400,300);
        frame.createGUI();
        frame.show();
    }

    private void createGUI() {
        setDefaultCloseOperation(EXIT_ON_CLOSE);
        Container window = getContentPane();
        window.setLayout(new FlowLayout());

        initialLabel = new JLabel("Enter initial amount");
        window.add(initialLabel);

        initialField = new JTextField(3);
        window.add(initialField);

        interestLabel = new JLabel("Enter interest rate");
        window.add(interestLabel);

        interestField = new JTextField(3);
        window.add(interestField);

        button = new JButton("another year");
        window.add(button);
        button.addActionListener(this);

        textArea = new JTextArea(10, 35);
        window.add(textArea);

        JScrollPane scrollPane = new JScrollPane(textArea);
        window.add(scrollPane);
    }
```

```
    public void actionPerformed(ActionEvent event) {
        oneYear();
    }

    private void oneYear() {
        String newLine = "\n";
        double rate, newAmount;
        int dollars, cents;

        if (year == 1) {
            oldAmount = Double.parseDouble(initialField.getText());
        }

        rate = Double.parseDouble(interestField.getText());

        newAmount = oldAmount + (oldAmount * rate / 100);

        dollars = (int) newAmount;
        cents = (int) Math.round(100 * (newAmount - dollars));
        textArea.append("After " + Integer.toString(year) + " years "
            + "the money has become "
            + Integer.toString(dollars) + " dollars and "
            + Integer.toString(cents) + " cents" + newLine);

        oldAmount = newAmount;
        year++;
    }
}
```

You will see that we have added a scroll pane so that the text area has a scrollbar.

● Case study – iteration

It is quite common in numerical programming to write iterations – loops that continue searching for a solution to an equation until the solution is found to sufficient accuracy.

As an example of using iteration, here is a formula for the sine of an angle:

$$\sin(x) = x - x^3/3! + x^5/5! - x^7/7! + \ldots$$

(Note that if we need the sine of an angle in a program, we don't need to use this formula, because it is available as a library function.)

We can see that each term is derived from the previous term by multiplying by:

$$-x^2/(n + 1) \times (n + 2)$$

so we can construct a loop that iterates until the new term is less than some acceptable figure, say 0.0001:

```
private double sin(double x) {
    double term, result;

    result = 0.0;
    term = x;
    for (int n = 1; Math.abs(term) >= 0.0001; n = n + 2) {
        result = result + term;
        term = - term * x * x / ((n + 1) * (n + 2));
    }
    return result;
}
```

in which the library method **abs** calculates the absolute value of its parameter.

● Graphs

It is common to present mathematical, engineering and financial information graphically. We will now look at a program to draw mathematical functions. Suppose we want to draw the function:

$$y = ax^3 + bx^2 + cx + d$$

with values for a, b, c and d input via sliders as in Figure 11.2.

We must resolve several design issues. First we want to see the graph with the y coordinate going up the screen, whereas y pixel coordinates measure downwards. We will distinguish between **x** and its equivalent pixel coordinate **xPixel**, and between **y** and **yPixel**.

Next we have to ensure that the graph will fit conveniently within the panel, that it is not too small to see or too big to fit. Solving this problem is called scaling. We will assume that the available area in a panel is 200 pixels in the x direction and 200 pixels in the y direction. We will design the program to display x and y values in the range −5.0 to +5.0. So 1 unit of x (or y) is 20 pixels.

Finally, since we will be using **drawLine** to draw the graph, we will draw a curved shape as a large number of small lines. We will move along the x direction, one pixel at a time, drawing a line from the equivalent y coordinate to the next. For each x pixel, the program:

1. calculates the x value from the x pixel value,
2. calculates the y value, the value of the function,
3. calculates the y pixel value from the y value,

using the following statements:

```
x = scaleX(xPixel);
y = theFunction(x);
yPixel = scaleY(y);
```

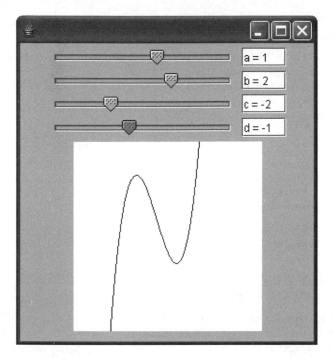

Figure 11.2 Graph drawer.

The program then goes on to the next *x* pixel:

```
nextXPixel = xPixel + 1;
```

Finally the small section of the curve is drawn:

```
paper.drawLine(xPixel, yPixel, nextXPixel, nextYPixel);
```

You will see that the program uses several private methods to help simplify the logic. Also, just one method is used to handle the events from all the four sliders. Here is the complete code for this graph-drawing program.

```
import java.awt.*;
import java.awt.event.*;
import javax.swing.*;
import javax.swing.event.*;

public class Graph extends JFrame implements ChangeListener {

    int a, b, c, d;

    private JSlider aSlider, bSlider, cSlider, dSlider;
    private JTextField aText, bText, cText, dText;
```

```java
    private JPanel panel;
    private int height = 200, width = 200;

    public static void main (String[] args) {
        Graph frame = new Graph();
        frame.setSize(320,350);
        frame.createGUI();
        frame.show();
    }

    private void createGUI() {

        setDefaultCloseOperation(EXIT_ON_CLOSE);
        Container window = getContentPane();
        window.setLayout(new FlowLayout());

        aSlider = new JSlider(-5, 5);
        aSlider.addChangeListener(this);
        window.add(aSlider);

        aText = new JTextField(4);
        window.add(aText);

        bSlider = new JSlider(-5, 5);
        bSlider.addChangeListener(this);
        window.add(bSlider);

        bText = new JTextField(4);
        window.add(bText);

        cSlider = new JSlider(-5, 5);
        cSlider.addChangeListener(this);
        window.add(cSlider);

        cText = new JTextField(4);
        window.add(cText);

        dSlider = new JSlider(-5, 5);
        dSlider.addChangeListener(this);
        window.add(dSlider);

        dText = new JTextField(4);
        window.add(dText);

        panel = new JPanel();
        panel.setPreferredSize(new Dimension(width, height));
        panel.setBackground(Color.lightGray);
        window.add(panel);
    }

    public void stateChanged(ChangeEvent e) {
        a = aSlider.getValue();
        b = bSlider.getValue();
        c = cSlider.getValue();
        d = dSlider.getValue();
```

```
        aText.setText("a = " + Integer.toString(a));
        bText.setText("b = " + Integer.toString(b));
        cText.setText("c = " + Integer.toString(c));
        dText.setText("d = " + Integer.toString(d));
        draw();
    }

    private void draw() {
        Graphics paper = panel.getGraphics();
        paper.setColor(Color.white);
        paper.fillRect(0, 0, width, height);
        double x, y, nextX, nextY;
        int xPixel, yPixel, nextXPixel, nextYPixel;
        paper.setColor(Color.black);
        for (xPixel = 0; xPixel <= width; xPixel++ ) {
            x = scaleX(xPixel);
            y = theFunction(x);
            yPixel = scaleY(y);
            nextXPixel = xPixel + 1;
            nextX = scaleX(nextXPixel);
            nextY = theFunction(nextX);
            nextYPixel = scaleY(nextY);
            paper.drawLine(xPixel, yPixel, nextXPixel, nextYPixel);
        }
    }

    private double theFunction(double x) {
        return a * x * x * x + b * x * x + c * x + d;
    }

    private double scaleX(int xPixel) {
        double xStart = -5, xEnd = 5;
        double xScale = width / (xEnd - xStart);
        return (xPixel - (width / 2)) / xScale;
    }

    private int scaleY(double y) {
        double yStart = -5, yEnd = 5;
        int pixelCoord;
        double yScale = height / (yEnd - yStart);
        pixelCoord = (int) (-y * yScale) +
            (int) (height / 2);
        return pixelCoord;
    }
}
```

If you run this program you can alter the slider values to see the effect of changing the parameters. You can also draw quadratics (by making the value of coefficient *a* equal to 0) and straight lines, of course.

● Exceptions

If you are reading this chapter for the first time, you should probably skip this section, because it deals with things that don't happen very often.

When you write a program that does calculations you have to watch out that you don't exceed the size of numbers that are allowed. It is not like doing a calculation on a piece of paper, where numbers can get as big as you like – it is more like using a calculator, which has a definite upper limit on the size of numbers that it will hold.

So, for example, if you declare an `int`:

```
int number;
```

you must be aware that the biggest number that can be held in an `int` is large, but limited to 2147483647. So if you write this:

```
number = 2147483647;
number = number + 2147483647;
```

the result of the addition cannot be accommodated as an `int` value. The program terminates and an error message is displayed. This is called overflow and is one of a number of possible exceptions that can arise as a program executes.

Overflow can happen more subtly than this, particularly when a user enters data into a text field and its size is therefore unpredictable. For example, here is a simple program to calculate the area of a room, in which overflow could occur:

```
int length, area;
length = Integer.parseInt(inputTextField.getText());
area = length * length;
```

Situations that can lead to overflow are:

■ adding two large numbers;

■ subtracting a large positive number from a large negative number;

■ dividing by a very small number;

■ multiplying two large numbers.

You can see that even with a simple calculation that looks harmless, vigilance is required. There are several ways to deal with an exception:

1. Ignore it, hope it will not happen, and be prepared for the program to crash and/or give strange results when it does. This is OK for novice programs, but may be less than ideal for real programs designed to be robust.

2. Allow the exception to arise but handle the exception by writing an exception handler as described later in Chapter 16.

3. Avoid it by writing in checks to ensure that such a situation is prevented. For example, in a program to calculate the area of a room, avoid overflow by checking the size of the data:

```
if (length > 10000) {
    answerTextField.setText("value too large");
}
```

We have seen how overflow can happen when a program uses **int** values. We might expect the same thing to happen if **double** values get too large – but it doesn't. Instead, if a value gets too large, the program keeps on going, and the value takes one of the special values – **NaN** (Not a Number), **PositiveInfinity** or **NegativeInfinity** as appropriate.

Programming principles

- Many programs in science, engineering, mathematics and statistics employ lots of calculations. But even small programs that might not obviously need to do computations often use some arithmetic.

- The first and key step is deciding what types of variable to use to represent the data. The main choice is between **int** and **double**.

- The library of mathematical functions is invaluable in programs of this type.

- Numbers can be formatted for display.

- It is common to use iteration in numerical computation as the solution converges towards the answer. This involves a loop.

- Exceptional situations, like overflow, can arise during calculations and should be anticipated if the program is to work robustly in all circumstances.

Programming pitfalls

- Exceptional situations such as trying to divide by zero can lead to strange results or else the program terminating. Make your programs robust.

Summary

- The main ways of representing numbers are as either **int** or **double**. These provide different ranges and precision.

- Library functions provide the common mathematical functions, e.g. the sine of an angle.

- The method **format** of the library class **DecimalFormat** can be used to format numbers for display.

- The programmer should be aware of exceptions that might arise during calculations.

● Exercises

11.1   **Cost of phone call** A phone call costs 10 cents per minute. Write a program that inputs via text fields the duration of a phone call, expressed in hours, minutes and seconds, and displays the cost of the phone call in cents, accurate to the nearest cent.

11.2   **Measurement conversion** Write a program to input a measurement expressed in feet and inches via two text fields. When a button is clicked, convert the measurement to centimetres and display it in a text field, correct to 2 decimal places. There are 12 inches in a foot; 1 inch is 2.54 centimetres.

11.3   **Mouse-click** Write a program that displays a panel. When the user clicks the mouse within the panel, an option pane displays the distance of the mouse from the top left corner of the panel. Refer to Appendix A to see how to obtain the mouse-click coordinates.

11.4   **Cash register** Write a program that represents a cash register. Amounts of money can be entered into a text field and are added to the running total when a button is clicked. The running total is displayed in another text field. Another button allows the sum to be cleared (made zero).

11.5   **Sum of integers** The sum of the integers from 1 to n is given by the formula:

$$\text{sum} = n(n + 1)/2$$

Write a program that inputs a value for n from a text field and calculates the sum two ways – firstly by using the formula and secondly by adding up the numbers using a loop.

11.6   **Interest calculation** The program given in the text calculates interest year by year. An alternative is to use a formula for calculating interest. If an amount p is invested at interest rate r for n years, the accumulated value v is:

$$v = p(1 + r)^n$$

Write a program that accepts values for p (in dollars), r (as a percentage) and n from text fields and displays the accumulated value in a text field.

11.7   **Random numbers** Random numbers are often used in computational and simulation programs, called Monte Carlo methods. We have already met the library class **Random** that enables us to create a random number generator as follows:

```
Random random = new Random();
```

Then we call **nextInt** to obtain an integer random number in the range 0 to 1 as follows:

```
int number = random.nextInt(2);
```

Write a program to check out the random number generator. Provide a button that creates a set of 100 random numbers that have the value either 0 or 1. Count the number of values equal to 0 and the number equal to 1. (They should be approximately equal.)

11.8   **Series for e** The value of e^x can be calculated by summing the series:

$$e^x = 1 + x + x^2/2! + x^3/3! + \ldots$$

Write a program to input a value of x from a text field and calculate e^x to a desired degree of accuracy. Check the value against the value obtained by using method **exp** in the **Math** library.

11.9 **Tax calculation** Write a program that carries out a tax calculation. The tax is zero on the first $10000, but is 33% on any amount over that amount. Write the program to input a salary in dollars from a text field and calculate the tax payable. Watch out for errors when you perform the calculation – the answer needs to be accurate to the nearest cent!

11.10 **Area of triangle** The area of a triangle with sides of length a, b, c is:

$$\text{area} = \sqrt{s(s-a)(s-b)(s-c)}$$

where:

$$s = (a+b+c)/2$$

Write a program that inputs the three values for the sides of a triangle from text fields and uses this formula to calculate the area. Your program should first check that the three lengths specified do indeed form a triangle. So, for example, $a + b$ must be greater than c.

11.11 **Square root** The square root of a number can be calculated iteratively as shown below. Write a program to do this for a number input using a text field.
The first approximation to the square root of x is $x/2$.
Then successive approximations are given by the formula:

$$\text{nextApproximation} = (\text{lastApproximation}^2 - x)/2 + \text{lastApproximation}$$

Check the value against that obtained by using the library method **sqrt**.

11.12 **Mathematical calculator** Write a program that acts as a mathematical calculator. It provides buttons with which to enter numbers, which are displayed like the display on a desk calculator. Buttons are also provided to carry out standard mathematical calculations like sine, cosine, natural logarithm and square root.

11.13 **Interest calculator** Rewrite the calculation part of the program given above in the text so as to use an **int** number (instead of a **double**) to represent an amount of money (expressed in cents).

11.14 **Graph drawer** Enhance the graph-drawing program in the text so that it:

- draws the x and y axes;
- inputs the coefficients from text fields instead of sliders (to provide precision);
- inputs a horizontal and a vertical scaling (zoom) factor from sliders;
- draws a second graph of the same function, but with different coefficients;
- draws the graphs of some other functions. One way to do this would be to rewrite the method **theFunction**.

11.15 **Numerical integration** Write a program that calculates the integral of a function y using the 'trapezium rule'. The area under the graph of the function is divided into n equal strips of width d. Then the area under the curve (the integral) is approximately the sum of all the (small) trapeziums:

$$\text{area} \cong \tfrac{1}{2}d(y_0 + 2y_1 + 2y_2 + \ldots + 2y_{n-1} + y_n)$$

or:

area = (half the width of the strip) × (first + last + twice the sum of the others)

Use a function for which you know the answer, and experiment by using smaller and smaller values of d.

11.16 **Mandelbrot set** The Mandelbrot set (Figure 11.3) is a famous and striking image produced by repeatedly evaluating a formula at each point in a two-dimensional space. Take a point, with coordinates x_{start} and y_{start}. Then repeatedly calculate new values of x and y from the old values using the formulae:

$$x_{new} = x_{old}^2 - y_{old}^2 - x_{start}$$

$$y_{new} = 2x_{old}y_{old} - y_{start}$$

The first values of x_{old} and y_{old} are x_{start} and y_{start}. For each iteration, calculate $r = \sqrt{x_{new}^2 + y_{new}^2}$. Repeat until $r > 10000$ or 100 iterations, whichever comes first. If r is greater than 10000 colour the pixel corresponding to this coordinate white, otherwise black.

Repeat for all points with x between −1.0 and +2.0 and y in the range −2.0 to +2.0.

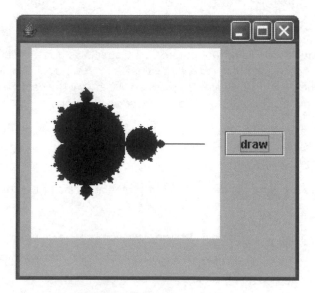

Figure 11.3 The Mandelbrot set.

As the iteration proceeds, starting from particular values of x_{start} and y_{start}, the value of r sometimes remains reasonably small (around 1.0). For other values of x_{start} and y_{start}, the value of r quickly becomes very large and tends to shoot off to infinity.

Incidentally, you sometimes see images of the Mandelbrot set that are the mirror image of the one shown in Figure 11.3. These are generated by the slightly different formulae:

$$x_{new} = x_{old}^2 - y_{old}^2 + x_{start}$$

$$y_{new} = 2x_{old}y_{old} + y_{start}$$

Answer to self-test question

11.1
```
double answer;
DecimalFormat formatter = new DecimalFormat("##.##");
textField.setText(formatter.format(answer));
```

CHAPTER 12

Array lists

This chapter explains:

- the idea of an array list;
- how to display an array list;
- how to add and remove items from an array list;
- how to obtain the size of an array list;
- the idea of an index;
- how to carry out typical operations on an array list, such as lookup, arithmetic and searching.

● Introduction

An array list is a collection of data such as a shopping list, a list of people's names or a set of rainfall figures. Java provides facilities to create a new array list, to add items and to delete items. Like other variables, an array list is held in main memory (RAM) and is therefore invisible unless we display the information in, for example, a text area.

An array list has a name as a whole. But we can refer to individual items within an array list by referring to their position in the array list. This position is known as the index. Index values are integers and start at 0.

We will use as an example a shopping list, building it up by adding items one by one. After several items have been added to the list, the information in it can be displayed as shown in Figure 12.1.

Array lists provide a good introduction to using data structures because they are convenient to use. This chapter explores using array lists as data structures and it can be read and studied independently of the chapters on arrays.

Figure 12.1 An array list displayed in a text area.

Creating an array list

The **ArrayList** class is provided within the Java **util** package and therefore the following **import** statement is necessary at the head of any program that uses an array list:

```
import java.util.*;
```

An array list is created just like any other object. We give the array list a convenient name and we use the keyword **new**:

```
ArrayList list = new ArrayList();
```

This creates an empty array list. We shall see shortly how to add items.

Adding items to a list

One way of placing items in an array list is to do it when the array list is initialized, using the library method **add**. For example:

```
list.add("eggs");
```

In this example the name of the array list is **list**. The method **add** adds the item to the end of the existing array list. Its parameter is the value to be added to the array list, in this case the string 'eggs'.

Another way of placing information in an array list is to obtain data from the user. The example program shown in Figure 12.2 allows the user to add items to an array list.

This program responds to a button-click, calling the method **add** to place an item of shopping at the end of the array list:

```
private void addAnItem(ArrayList list) {
    list.add(textField.getText());
}
```

Figure 12.2 Adding items to a shopping list.

An array list expands as necessary to accommodate however much data is added. It is as if an array list is made of elastic.

The length of a list

We can find out how long an array list is by using the library method **size**. For example:

```
int numberOfItems = list.size();
```

Here is a method that displays an option pane containing the number of items currently in the array list:

```
private void displayLength(ArrayList list) {
    JOptionPane.showMessageDialog(null, Integer.toString(list.size()));
}
```

Indices

A program refers to individual items in an array list by an *index*. An index is an integer that says which item is being referred to. The first item has index value 0, the second 1, etc. We can visualize the shopping array list as a table as shown in Figure 12.3, with the index values alongside. These index values are not actually stored with the data.

0	bread
1	milk
2	coffee

Figure 12.3 Diagram of an array list showing the indexes.

Displaying an array list

An array list is held in main memory (RAM), so normally it is invisible. We now look at a method that displays the contents of an array list (the shopping list named **list**) in a text area. This method produces the display shown in Figure 12.4.

Figure 12.4 Displaying an array list.

The program makes use of the **size** method that tells us how long the list is. We use a **for** statement, because we know that a repetition is needed. The method **get** is used to obtain the values from the array list. The parameter for **get** specifies the index value of the required item. **get** simply obtains the value (makes a copy of it) without disturbing the list.

```
private void display(ArrayList list) {
    String newLine = "\n";
    textArea.setText("");
    for (int index = 0; index < list.size(); index ++) {
        textArea.append(list.get(index) + newLine);
    }
}
```

Sometimes a text area will be too small to display all of an array list. To solve this problem we can attach (horizontal and vertical) scrollbars to the text area, see for example Figure 12.5. These appear only if they are needed – when the data is too big to be displayed as a whole. The additional code to provide scrollbars is simply:

```
JScrollPane scrollPane = new JScrollPane(textArea);
window.add(scrollPane);
```

where **textArea** is the name of the text area.

Figure 12.5 Scrollbars.

Using index values

We have already seen how to display an array list. We can also display the values alongside their index values, Figure 12.6. The code is:

```
private void displayWithIndices(ArrayList list) {
    String newLine = "\n";
    String tab = "\t";
    textArea.setTabSize(3);
    textArea.setText("");
    for (int index = 0; index < list.size(); index ++) {
        textArea.append(Integer.toString(index)
                        + tab
                        + list.get(index) + newLine);
    }
}
```

Figure 12.6 Display of an array list together with the index values.

Figure 12.7 Displaying an item from an array list.

Figure 12.7 shows a program that allows the user to display the value at a particular index value. The code to display the item is:

```
private void displayItem(ArrayList list) {

    int index;

    index = Integer.parseInt(indexTextField.getText());
    value.setText((String)list.get(index));
}
```

This program obtains an index value from a text field and converts it from its string representation into an **int** using **Integer.parseInt**, placing in it the variable **index**. Next the index value is used to access the corresponding element in the list. The method **get** is used to obtain the value from the array list.

Finally the value of an item from the array list must be converted into a string, using **(String)**, before it can be displayed in a text field. This is because, when items are added to an array list, they are automatically converted into items of type **Object**. Thus when an object is removed from an array list, it must be converted back to its former type using a casting operator – in this case **(String)**.

SELF-TEST QUESTION

12.1 In Figure 12.7, what item is at index value 1?

● Removing items from an array list

We have seen how to add items to an array list. Now we consider removing information. The method **remove** of the class **ArrayList** removes the item at a particular index value. So if we have an array list **list**, we can remove the item at index value 3 by:

```
list.remove(3);
```

When this happens, the gap created is closed up. The array list shrinks to the reduced size necessary.

An array list can be completely emptied of data using the **clear** method, as in:

```
list.clear();
```

12.2 What is the size of an array list after the **clear** method has been used on it?

● Inserting items within an array list

We have seen how to add items to the end of a list using the method **add**. It is also easy to insert items within the body of a list, also using method **add**. Given an existing list, we can, for example, do this:

```
list.add(5, "tea");
```

The item formerly at index value 5 is moved down the list, along with any subsequent items. The array list expands to accommodate the new item.

● Lookup

A table such as an array list is conveniently used for lookup. For example, we can construct an array list (as indicated in Figure 12.8) that contains the names of the months January to December. When someone gives us a month expressed as a number (1 to 12) we can use the table to convert the number to the equivalent text.

Figure 12.9 shows how the program looks to its user. We create an array list:

```
ArrayList months = new ArrayList();
```

and then place the string values in it:

```
months.add("January");
months.add("February");
months.add("March");
etc.
```

0	January
1	February
2	March
3	etc.

Figure 12.8 Diagram of an array list for converting integers to month names.

Figure 12.9 The month conversion program.

The user enters a number into a text field and clicks on the button. The program responds to the event as follows:

```
public void actionPerformed(ActionEvent event) {

    int monthNumber;
    String monthName;

    monthNumber = Integer.parseInt(monthNumberTextField.getText());
    monthName = (String) months.get(monthNumber - 1);
    monthNameTextField.setText(monthName);
}
```

The numbers representing a month run from 1 to 12, whereas index values start at 0. Therefore we need to subtract 1 from the month number, as shown, to convert it into an appropriate index. Then we use the method get to obtain the month name.

Using a lookup table as above is an alternative to writing a series of if statements to carry out the conversion. The equivalent if statements begin:

```
if (monthNumber == 1) {
    monthName = "January";
}
else {
    if (monthNumber == 2) {
        monthName = "February";
    }
}
```

Yet another alternative would be to use a switch statement. Employing if statements or a switch statement makes use of actions to carry out the conversion. In contrast, using a table (such as an array list) embodies the conversion information more neatly within the table.

● Arithmetic on an array list

We now look at an array list, named **numbers**, that contains integer numbers and we will carry out arithmetic on the numbers. (An array list can accommodate any kind of data.) Figure 12.10 shows a program that allows its user to enter numbers into an array list. Then one button causes the sum of the numbers to be displayed and another button causes the largest number to be displayed.

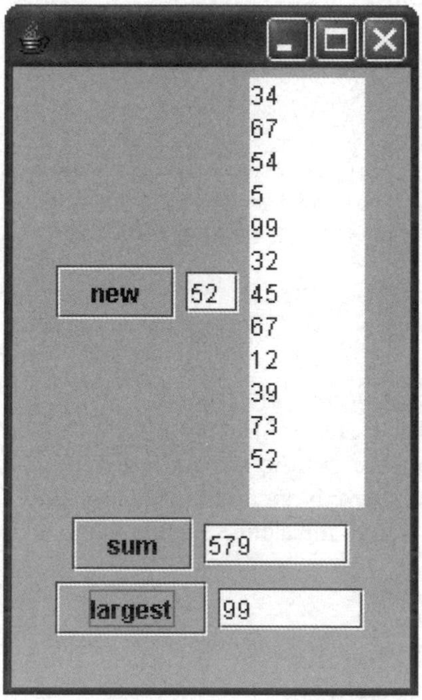

Figure 12.10 Arithmetic on an array list.

Here is the method to add together all the numbers in a list. Because we are processing all the numbers in the array list, we use a **for** statement to carry out a loop. Each value in the list is extracted using the **get** method. Next, because items placed in an array list are automatically converted into objects, we need to convert each one back into a string, using the casting operator **(String)** as shown. Next, the string is converted into an **int** using **Integer.parseInt**. Finally, the integer is added to a running total, called **sum**, which is initially made equal to 0. After the loop, the value of the **sum** is placed in a text field.

```
private void getSum(ArrayList numbers) {

    int sum = 0;

    for (int index = 0; index < numbers.size(); index ++) {
        int number = Integer.parseInt((String) (numbers.get(index)));
        sum = sum + number;
    }
    sumField.setText(Integer.toString(sum));
}
```

Next we study a method to find the largest item in a list of numbers. A variable called **largest** is used to keep track of the largest value. Initially, **largest** is made equal to the value at index 0 in the array list (the first element in the list). This is copied from the list, but before it can be used it first must be converted into a string using **(String)**, and then into an **int** using **Integer.parseInt**.

A **for** statement is used to process the numbers in the list. Each element in the list is compared with **largest**, and if it is larger, the value of **largest** is updated. So when we get to the end of the list, **largest** holds the largest value.

```
private void getLargest(ArrayList numbers) {
    int largest;

    largest = Integer.parseInt((String) (numbers.get(0)));
    for (int index = 0; index < numbers.size(); index++) {
        int number = Integer.parseInt((String) (numbers.get(index)));
        if (number > largest) {
            largest = number;
        }
    }
    largestField.setText(Integer.toString(largest));
}
```

SELF-TEST QUESTION

12.3   Modify this method very simply so as to find the smallest item in the list.

These two sections of program illustrate a common feature of programs that manipulate lists: whenever you need to process every item in a list, a **for** statement is probably more appropriate than a **while** statement.

● Searching

This next program carries out a search. It assumes that a list (e.g. the shopping list) is already set up and that we want to search the list for some item. The user enters the desired item (e.g. sugar) into a text field and clicks on a button as shown in Figure 12.11.

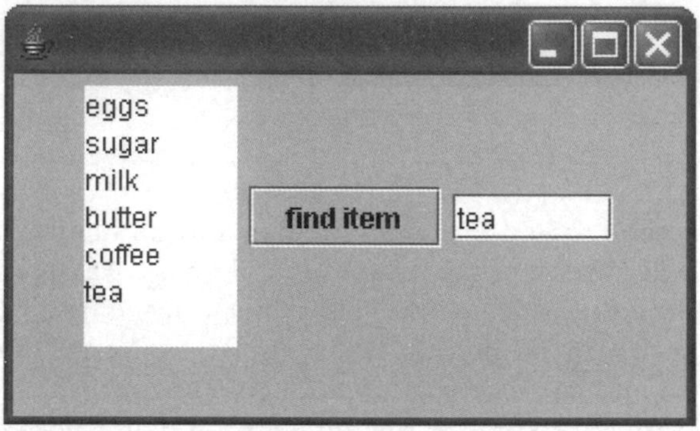

Figure 12.11 Searching an array list.

The program starts from the first item in the list and continues down the list, one item at a time, trying to find the desired item. If it is not found, the index value becomes equal to the length of the list, **size**, and the loop ends. If the item is found, the **boolean** variable **found** is set to **true** and the loop terminates.

```
private void search(ArrayList list) {
    int length;
    int index;
    boolean found;
    String itemWanted;

    length = list.size();

    itemWanted = textField.getText();

    found = false;
    index = 0;
    while ((found == false) && (index < length)) {
        if (((String)list.get(index)).equals(itemWanted)) {
            found = true;
            JOptionPane.showMessageDialog(null, "Item found");
        }
        else {
            index++;
        }
    }
}
```

This is a classical serial search method.

Programming principles

Array lists are perhaps the simplest kind of data structure provided by Java. They enable a list of objects to be assembled, displayed and manipulated. A data structure is a group of data items that can be processed in a uniform manner. A data structure such as an array list is set up in the main memory of the computer (not on backing storage) so that it exists only as long as the program runs. When the program terminates, the data structure is destroyed.

Lists are one of the classic structures in computing. One of the oldest and most venerated languages, LISP (short for LIST Processing), uses nothing but lists. A list is a sequence of items that can grow and shrink in length. Items can be added to the end of a list and removed from anywhere within the list. Also the values of items within a list can be changed. Thus a list is a flexible structure for representing a collection of items that are related in some way.

Another major type of data structure is the array (explained in Chapter 13). An array is a collection of similar data items, each distinguished by an index. Items can be inserted and removed from within the body of an array list, but arrays do not support these facilities. An array list expands and contracts to accommodate the required data, but an array, once created, has a fixed size. Accessing an array list does not use any special syntax, whereas arrays use square brackets.

When it is added to an array list, an item is converted into an object of the type `Object`. So, when it is removed, it must be converted back into its true identity, using a casting operator such as `(String)`.

The method to find the largest item in a list of numbers is a classic problem in programming. This is also true of the search method.

Programming pitfalls

A common error is to think that index values start at 1. (They start at 0.)

Summary

An array list is one example of a data structure. An array list can accommodate any number of objects, growing and shrinking as necessary to accommodate items as they are added and removed.

An array list as a whole is given a name. Individual items within an array list are identified using a unique index value – an integer. The index values start at 0 and go up to whatever size is necessary to identify all the items in the array list. Index values are not stored in the array list.

▶ *Summary continued*

A program can add items to the end of an array list, remove an item, change an item or insert an item anywhere within an array list. The available methods are:

- **add** – add an item either to the end or in the middle of an array list;
- **get** – extract an item;
- **remove** – remove an item;
- **set** – replace an item;
- **clear** – remove all the items;
- **size** – returns the length of the list.

● Exercises

12.1 Write a program in which an item in an array list is deleted. Provide a 'delete' button to delete the item that is specified as an index in a text field.

12.2 Add a button to the program in Exercise 12.1 that causes the array list to be emptied, using the method **clear**.

12.3 Alter the program in Exercise 12.1 so that an item in the array list can be replaced by some other text. For example, 'milk' is replaced by 'sugar'. Provide a button marked 'replace' that carries out this action. The position (index value) of the item to be replaced is entered in a text field. The new text is also entered into a text field.

12.4 Write a program that allows items to be inserted into or removed from any position within an array list, using suitable buttons.

12.5 Improve the search method so that it displays a message whether or not the required item is found in the array list.

12.6 Use an array list to implement a queue (line in the USA). A line is formed when you queue at a supermarket checkout or a self-service café. Implement the following:

- Placing a person's name at the end of the queue using a button and a text field.
- Removing a name from the head of the queue using a button.
- Displaying the whole queue in a text area.

Hint: the head of the queue is the first item in the list – the item with index 0.

12.7 Implement a stack using an array list. In some card games, e.g. solitaire, you deal the cards face down onto a pile. Later you pick them up from the top of the pile. So you add cards and remove cards from the same end – the top. Implement the following:

■ Placing a card on the pile, using a button and a text field.

■ Removing a card from the pile, using a button.

■ Displaying the pile in a text area.

Hint: the top of the pile is the first item in the array list – the item with index 0.

Answers to self-test questions

12.1 Milk.

12.2 The size becomes zero.

12.3 Change the greater than sign to a less than sign.

CHAPTER 13

Arrays

This chapter explains:

- how to declare an array;
- how to use an index;
- how to obtain the size of an array;
- how to pass arrays as parameters;
- how to initialize an array;
- how to carry out typical operations such as lookup and searching;
- how to create arrays of objects.

● Introduction

So far in this book, with the exception of array lists, we have described data items (variables) that are individual and isolated. For example:

```
int count, sum;
String name;
```

These live on their own, performing useful roles in programs as counters, sums or whatever. We can think of these variables as places in memory that have individual names attached to them.

In contrast, we very often in life deal with data that is not isolated, but grouped together into a collection of information. Sometimes the information is in tables. Examples are a train timetable, a telephone directory or a bank statement. In programming, these things are called data structures. The information in a table is related in some way to the other information within the table. One of the simplest types of data structure in programming is an array. An array can be regarded simply as a table, with a single row of information. (Alternatively, you can visualize a table as a single column of information.) This could be a table of numbers, a table of strings or a table of anything.

In this chapter we will look at arrays of numbers, arrays of strings and arrays of other objects, such as graphical objects.

Figure 13.1 shows an array of numbers.

23	54	96	13	7	32

Figure 13.1 An array of numbers.

This array might represent the ages of a group of people at a party. Figure 13.2 shows a table of words, which holds the names of the members of a band.

John	Paul	George	Ringo

Figure 13.2 An array of strings.

In Java, a table like this is called an array. In programming, an item in an array is known as an *element* and we refer to an element by its position in the array, called the *index*. (In the world of programming, the term *component* is sometimes used instead of element, and the term *subscript* instead of index.) To us humans, the name `John` is in the first position in this table, but in Java the first position in an array is called the zeroth position. Positions in an array are the zeroth, first, second, third, etc. Thus the string `Ringo` is in the third position in the above array. We can therefore picture an array, together with its indices, as shown in Figure 13.3.

Array:

John	Paul	George	Ringo

Indices: 0   1   2   3

Figure 13.3 An array of strings and its indices.

Remember that the indices are not held in the computer's memory – only the data. The indices are the way that we locate information in an array.

The other array, containing numbers, is shown in Figure 13.4. The indices for the array are also shown.

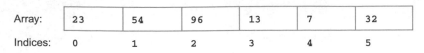

Array:

23	54	96	13	7	32

Indices: 0   1   2   3   4   5

Figure 13.4 An array of numbers with its indices.

In a program (as in real life) we typically have to carry out the following operations on arrays:

■ Create the array – say how long it is and what sort of things it will contain.

■ Put some values in the array (e.g. enter some numbers into a personal telephone directory).

■ Display the contents of the array on the screen (an array is held in the computer memory and it is therefore invisible).

■ Search the array to find some value (e.g. searching the train timetable to find a train at a convenient time).

■ Add up the contents of the array (e.g. working out how much a customer spent at the supermarket).

During this chapter we shall see how to carry out these actions one by one and build up to doing all these things in a complete program. We will start by looking at arrays of numbers. Our plan, during the course of this chapter, is to develop a program with the screen layout shown in Figure 13.5 below. The program uses an array that holds the data on the rainfall for the seven days in a week (Monday to Sunday). The user of the program can change the value of any individual data item in the array. The largest of the numbers in the array is to be displayed.

● Creating an array

In Java, an array is declared just like any other object using **new**, usually either at the top of a class or at the top of a method. The programmer gives the array a name, like this:

```
int[] ages = new int[6];
String[] band = new String[4];
```

The variable named **ages** is now ready to hold an array of integers. As with any other variable, it is usual (and a good idea) to choose a name for the array that describes clearly what it is going to be used for. The name is the name for the complete array – the complete collection of data. The rules for choosing the name of an array are the same as for choosing any other variable name in Java. The number in square brackets after the array name is the size of the array.

The array called **ages** is big enough to contain six numbers, with indices going from 0 to 5. The array called **band** is big enough to contain four strings. The indices go from 0 to 3.

SELF-TEST QUESTION

13.1 Declare an array to hold data for the rainfall for each of the seven days of the week.

Indices

The way that a program refers to an individual item in an array is to specify an index value (sometimes called a subscript). Thus in the above example `ages[3]` refers to the element in the array with index 3 – the value 13 in this case. Similarly, `band[2]` contains the string `George`. Remember that indices start at 0, so an array of length 4 has indices that go from 0 to 3. Therefore a reference to `band[4]` is an error. The program will stop and an error message will be displayed.

In summary, index values:

- start at zero;
- are integer;
- go up to one less than the size of the array (the value specified when the array is declared).

Sometimes, as we will see, it is useful to use a variable value as an index. In such cases, we use `int` variables as indices.

We can input a value for an element of an array using a text field:

```
ages[2] = Integer.parseInt(textField.getText());
band[3] = textField.getText();
```

and similarly output values:

```
textField.setText("the first age is " + Integer.toString(ages[0]));
textField.setText("the 4th band member is " + band[3]);
```

This second example confirms how careful you have to be with array indices.

You can change the values of individual elements of an array with assignment statements, like this:

```
ages[3] = 99;
band[2] = "Mike";
```

In all these program fragments, we are referring to individual elements in an array by specifying the value of an index.

SELF-TEST QUESTION

13.2   Given the declaration:

```
int[] table = new int[3];
```

how long is the array and what is the valid range of indices?

Very often we want to refer to the *n*th element in an array, where *n* is a variable. This is how the power of arrays really comes into its own. Suppose, for example, we want to add up all the numbers in an array of numbers. Let us suppose that we have an array with seven elements that hold the number of computers sold in a shop during each day in a week:

```
int[] sale = new int[7];
```

We will insert values into the array with assignment statements. Suppose that on Monday (day 0), 13 computers are sold:

```
sale[0] = 13;
```

and so on for the other days:

```
sale[1] = 8;
sale[2] = 22;
sale[3] = 17;
sale[4] = 24;
sale[5] = 15;
sale[6] = 23;
```

Next we want to find the total sales for the week. The clumsy way to add up the sales would be to write:

```
sum = sale[0] + sale[1] + sale[2] + sale[3]
        + sale[4] + sale[5] + sale[6];
```

which is quite correct, but does not exploit the regularity of an array. The alternative is to use a **for** loop. A variable called, say, **dayNumber** is used to hold the value of the index representing the day of the week. The index is made initially equal to 0 and then incremented each time the loop is repeated:

```
int sum = 0;
for (int dayNumber = 0; dayNumber <= 6; dayNumber++) {
    sum = sum + sale[dayNumber];
}
```

Each time the loop is repeated, the next value in the array is added to the total. This program fragment is actually no shorter than what it replaces. But it would be considerably shorter if the array had 1000 items to add up! The other advantage is that the **for** loop explicitly shows that it is performing a systematic operation on an array.

Indices are the one place in programming where it is permissible (sometimes) to use a name that is a little cryptic. In the above program fragment, however, using the name **dayNumber** as the index is clear and relates strongly to the problem being solved.

SELF-TEST QUESTION

13.3 What does the following program fragment do?

```
int[] table = new int[10];

for (int index = 0; index <= 10; index++) {
    table[index] = index;
}
```

The length of an array

A running program can always find out how long an array is. For example, if we have an array declared like this:

```
int[] table = new int[10];
```

we can access its length by making use of the property **length** like this:

```
int size;
size = table.length;
```

size has the value 10 in this case.

The property **length** is a special feature of Java. It is very much like a **public** variable within the class **Array**, which allows us to access the value of the size of an array. We can obtain the value but we are not allowed to change the value of **length**. Note that the word **length** is not followed by brackets, (), as it would be if **length** was a method.

It may seem odd to want to know the length of an array – after all we specify the length when we declare an array. But we shall see that this facility is very useful.

Once you have created an array, its length is fixed. Arrays are not made of elastic – an array will not expand as necessary to hold information – so it is vital to create an array that is sufficiently large for the needs of the particular program. But you can reuse an array variable, creating a new array of some different size, using **new**. However, the data in the original array is lost.

When you design a new program, you need to consider how big any array should be. This is sometimes obvious from the nature of the problem. For example, if the data relates to the days of the week, then you know that the array needs seven elements. However, there are other types of data structure (such as an array list) that expand and contract piecemeal as needed.

Passing arrays as parameters

As we have seen in earlier chapters of this book, methods are very important in programming. An important aspect of using methods is passing information as parameters and returning a value. We now explain how to pass and return arrays.

Suppose we want to write a method whose job it is to calculate the sum of the elements in an array of integers. Being perceptive programmers, we want the method to be general purpose, so that it will cope with arrays of any length. But that is OK because the method can easily find out the length of the array. So the parameter to be passed to the method is simply the array and the result to be returned to the user of the method is a number, the sum of the values.

A sample call of the method looks like this:

```
int[] table = new int[24];
int total;

total = sum(table);
```

The method itself is:

```
private int sum(int[] array) {
    int total = 0;
    for (int index = 0; index < array.length; index++) {
        total = total + array[index];
    }
    return total;
}
```

Notice that in the header for the method the parameter is declared as an array, with square brackets. But there is no parameter that spells out how long the array actually is. The method finds out the size using the property **length**, explained above. Because it will accept an array of any length, this method is general purpose and potentially very useful. This is highly preferable to a special-purpose method that will only work when the array is, say, eight elements long.

SELF-TEST QUESTION

13.4 Write a method that displays an array of integers, one per line, in a text area. The single parameter to the method is the array.

● Using constants

In a program with several arrays, there are declarations of the arrays and almost certainly a number of **for** loops. The arrays, together with their lengths, will be passed around the program as parameters. There is plenty of scope for confusion, particularly if two different arrays have the same length.

Suppose, for example, we are writing a program to analyze marks that students obtain in assignments. Suppose there are 10 students. We want one array to hold the average mark for each student:

```
int[] studentMark = new int[10];
```

By coincidence, there are also 10 courses. We also want a second array to hold the average mark for each course:

```
int[] courseMark = new int[10];
```

The problem is that, wherever we see the number 10 in the program, we do not know whether it is the number of students or the number of courses. As things stand, of course, it doesn't matter – because they are the same! But suppose we needed to alter the program so that it deals with 20 students. We would very much like to change every occurrence of the number 10 to the number 20 using the 'replace' function within a text editor. But because the arrays are the same length, this would cause great damage to the program.

One way to clarify such a program is to declare the lengths of the arrays as constants, and then to use the constants in **for** loops like this:

```
final int students = 20;
final int courses = 24;
```

Then we can use the constants as follows:

```
int[] studentMark = new int[students];
int[] courseMark = new int[courses];

for (int index = 0; index < students; index++) {
    // body of loop
}
```

We can now make changes to the program with confidence, simply by changing a single number in the constant declaration.

SELF-TEST QUESTION

13.5 Write the code to place zeros in every element of the array **courseMark**.

● Initializing an array

Initializing means giving a variable an initial or starting value. If you write this:

```
int[] table = new int[10];
```

then an array is set up in memory and the array contains zeros. When the programmer does not explicitly give initial values, the compiler inserts default values. These are zeros for numbers, **""** for strings and **null** for objects.

A common way of explicitly initializing an array is to do it when the array is declared. The required initial values are enclosed in curly brackets and separated by commas. But the size of the array must **not** be given in its usual place. For example:

```
int[] ages = {23, 54, 96, 13, 7, 32};
```

in which the length of the array is not given explicitly, is equivalent to:

```
int[] ages = new int[6];
ages[0] = 23;
ages[1] = 54;
ages[2] = 96;
ages[3] = 13;
ages[4] = 7;
ages[5] = 32;
```

Here is another example, initializing an array of strings:

```
String[] band = {"John", "Paul", "George", "Ringo"};
```

Another way to initialize an array is to use a loop as we saw earlier, like this:

```
int[] table = new int[25];
for (int index = 0; index < table.length; index++) {
    table[index] = 0;
}
```

If the program needs periodically to reset the array back to its initial values, then the way to do it is by using the **for** loop as shown above.

SELF-TEST QUESTION

13.6 Declare an array called **numbers** of five integers and fill it with the numbers 1 to 5 as part of the declaration.

● A sample program

Now we will combine all the things we have explained into a program to input some numbers, put them in an array and display them. The screen is shown in Figure 13.5. The data displayed represents the rainfall for the seven days in a week (Monday to Sunday). The user of the program enters a day number into one text field and a rainfall value into another text field. The largest of the rainfall values is displayed.

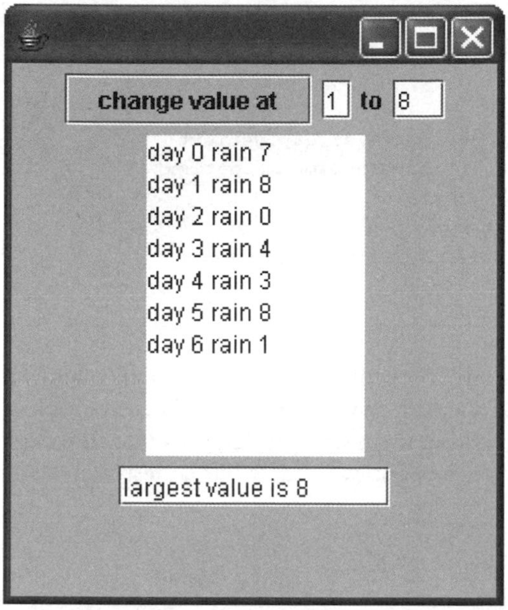

Figure 13.5 The rainfall program.

Firstly, the array is declared at the top of the class, so that it can be accessed by all of the methods. It has its values initialized to a selection of values.

```
private int[] rain = {7, 8, 0, 4, 3, 8, 1};
```

Next, the code to display the array values in a text area:

```
private void display() {
    data.setText("");
    for (int dayNumber = 0; dayNumber <= 6; dayNumber++) {
        data.append("day " + Integer.toString(dayNumber)
            + " rain " + Integer.toString(rain[dayNumber])
            + "\n");
    }
}
```

Then we look at the code to place a new value in an element of the array. The index value is in one text field; the actual value of the data is in another. Finally the method **display** is called to display the updated array, and **largest** is called to display the largest value:

```
private void newValue() {
    int index;
    int data;
    index = Integer.parseInt(day.getText());
    data = Integer.parseInt(amount.getText());
    rain[index] = data;
    display();
    largest();
}
```

We now look at the code to calculate the largest rainfall value. The approach used is to start by assuming that the first item is the largest. Then we look at the remainder of the elements in turn, comparing them with this largest value. If we find a value that is larger than the one we have already got, we update our largest value. This is a classic approach.

```
private void largest() {
    int highest;

    highest = rain[0];
    for (int index = 0; index <= 6; index++) {
        if (highest < rain[index]) {
            highest = rain[index];
        }
    }
    stats.setText("largest value is " + Integer.toString(highest));
}
```

You will see that it is very common to use the **for** statement in conjunction with arrays. They go together like a horse and carriage, love and marriage. It is, of course, because a **for** loop makes the maximum use of the uniformity of arrays.

SELF-TEST QUESTION

13.7   Write a method to calculate and display the total rainfall for the week.

● Lookup

Part of the power of arrays is that you can look up something very easily and quickly. In the rainfall program, we can extract the value of Tuesday's rainfall simply by referring to **rain[1]**. The same is true of any information that can be referred to by an integer index. For example, if we have a table showing the average height of people according to age, we can index the table using an age (25 in this example):

```
double[] height = new double[100];

double myHeight;
myHeight = height[25];
```

Similarly, if we have numbered the days of the week as 0 to 6, we can convert a number to a text string like this:

```
int dayNumber;
String dayName;
String[] name = {"Monday", "Tuesday", "Wednesday", "Thursday",
                 "Friday", "Saturday", "Sunday"};

dayName = name[dayNumber];
```

This could be accomplished in another way, using a **switch** statement, which is slightly longer and probably more cumbersome.

Using an array to look up something is extremely useful, simple and exploits the power of arrays.

SELF-TEST QUESTION

13.8   Rewrite the above conversion using a **switch** statement.

● Searching

Another way of accessing information in an array is to search for it. This is what humans do in a telephone directory or a dictionary. The example we will consider is a telephone directory (Figure 13.6).

We will set up two arrays, one to hold names and one to hold the equivalent telephone numbers:

```
private String[] names = new String[20];
private String[] numbers = new String[20];
```

Figure 13.6 The telephone directory.

Now that the arrays have been created, we can place some data in them:

```
names[0] = "Alex";
numbers[0] = "2720774";

names[1] = "Megan";
numbers[1] = "5678554";

names[2] = "END";
```

A simple and effective way to search the directory is to start at the beginning and go from one entry to the next until we find the name that we are looking for. However, the name we seek might not be in the directory, and we must cater for that situation arising. So the search continues until either we find what we are looking for or we get to the end of the entries. We could check that we have got to the end of the array, but a more convenient approach is to put a special entry into the array to signify the end of the useful data. This end marker will consist of an entry with the name **END**.

Now we can write the loop to search for a desired telephone number:

```
private void find() {
    int index;
    String wanted;

    wanted = name.getText();
    index = 0;
    for (index = 0;
        !(names[index].equals(wanted)) &&
        !(names[index].equals("END"));
        index++) {
    }

    if (names[index].equals(wanted)) {
        number.setText("number is " + numbers[index]);
    }
    else {
        number.setText("name not found");
    }
}
```

This is called a *serial* search. It starts at the beginning of the array, with the index 0, and continues searching item by item, adding 1 to the index. The search continues until either the wanted item is found or the special name **END** is reached.

This type of search makes no assumptions about the order of the items in the table – they can be in any order. Other search techniques exploit the ordering of items in the table, such as alphabetical ordering. These techniques are beyond the scope of this book.

Information like telephone numbers is normally stored in a file, rather than an array, because data held in a file is more permanent. Usually the file is searched for the required information rather than an array. Alternatively, the file is input into memory, held in an array and searched as shown above.

● Arrays of objects

Arrays can hold anything – integers, floating-point numbers, strings, buttons, sliders, any object in the library, or any object that the programmer constructs. The only constraint is that all the objects in an array must be of the same type. We will create and display an array of balloon objects (Figure 13.7). We introduced the balloon object earlier in this book.

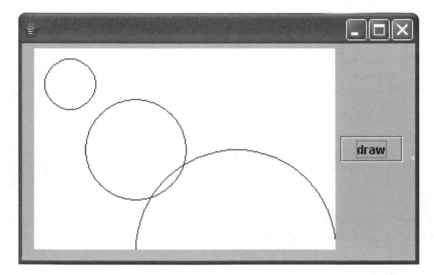

Figure 13.7 Displaying an array of balloons.

A balloon object (really just a circle) has a size and a position on the screen. Methods are provided as part of the object to move it, change its size and display it. Here is the class:

```java
public class Balloon {

    private int x;
    private int y;
    private int diameter;

    public Balloon(int initialX, int initialY,
                   int initialDiameter) {
        x = initialX;
        y = initialY;
        diameter = initialDiameter;
    }
```

```
    public void changeSize(int change) {
        diameter = diameter + change;
    }

    public void display(Graphics paper) {
        paper.drawOval(x, y, diameter, diameter);
    }

}
```

We can now create an array of balloons:

```
    private Balloon[] party = new Balloon[10];
```

But this only creates the array, ready to hold balloons. We now need to create some balloons as follows:

```
    party[0] = new Balloon(10, 10, 50);
    party[1] = new Balloon(50, 50, 100);
    party[2] = new Balloon(100, 100, 200);
```

and display all the balloons:

```
    private void displayBalloons(Graphics paper) {
        for (int b = 0; b <= 2; b++) {
            party[b].display(paper);
        }
    }
```

The advantage of storing the balloon objects in an array is that we can do something with them all in a convenient way. For example, we can change the size of all the balloons at once:

```
    private void changeSize() {
        for (int b = 0; b <= 2; b++) {
            party[b].changeSize(20);
        }
    }
```

Finally, we have said that all the elements in an array must be of the same type. There is an exception: if you declare an array of objects of the class **Object**, then you can place different types of objects in the array. This is because **Object** is the superclass of every other class.

Programming principles

An array is a collection of data items with a single name. All the items in an array are of the same type. Individual elements in an array are identified by means of an index, an integer. So if, for example, an array is named **table**, an individual element is referred to as **table[2]**, where 2 is the index. You can similarly refer to an element of an array using a integer variable as an index, e.g. `table[index]`. It is this facility that makes arrays powerful.

Once created, an array has a length and this length stays fixed.

Arrays can hold data of any type – for example, `int`, `double`, `bool`, `JButton`, `JTextField`. (But in any one array the data must all be of the same type.)

The array is the oldest and most widely used data structure. Arrays are compact and are accessed very quickly using support from the computer's hardware instructions.

It is common to use the `for` loop in conjunction with arrays.

An understanding of arrays helps complete a picture of the programs presented in this book. Most of the programs include the statement:

```
public static void main(String[] args)
```

This is the header of the method that is called when an application is initiated. It must have the name **main**. The method has a single parameter, named **args** by convention. As can be seen, this parameter is an array of strings. The size of this array depends on the role of the program. Often, as is the case with most of the programs in this book, the array is of zero length. When **main** is called, it is supplied with an array of strings. This allows a program to be initiated, usually from a command line, with appropriate information to direct its behaviour. See Chapter 17 for more detail.

Programming pitfalls

A common error in Java is to confuse the length of an array with the range of valid indices. For example, the array:

```
int[] table = new int[10];
```

has 10 elements. The valid range of indices for this array is 0 to 9. Reference to `table[10]` is a reference to an element of the array that simply does not exist. Luckily the Java system checks for violations like this as the program is running and will issue an error message.

Here is a common example of how to do things wrongly:

```
int[] table = new int[10];

for (int index = 0; index <= 10; index++) { // warning, erroneous
    table[index] = 0;
}
```

This will place a zero in all of the elements of the array **table**, but then go on to try to place a zero in whatever data item happens to be immediately after the array in the computer memory. The program then fails with an **ArrayIndexOutOfBoundsException** message. It is always worthwhile carefully checking the condition for terminating a **for** loop used with an array.

Students sometimes have difficulty in visualizing where an array is. An array is held in main memory; it is invisible; it only has a life while the program is running.

Grammar spot

An array with 20 elements is declared like this:

```
double[] table = new double[20];
```

To refer to an element of an array, the index is written in square brackets, as in:

```
table[3] = 12.34;
```

Summary

An array is a collection of data. It is given a name by the programmer. All the items in an array must be of the same type (e.g. all int).

An array is declared, along with other variables, like this:

```
int[] harry = new int[25];
```

This array has 25 elements. The value of the largest index is 24.

An individual element in an array is referred to by an integer index. For example:

```
harry[12] = 45;
```

Indices have values that start from zero and go up to the largest index value.

● Exercises

Games

13.1 **Nim** A human plays against the computer. At the start of the game there are three piles of matches. In each pile there is a random number of matches in the range 1 to 20. The three piles are displayed throughout the game. A random choice determines who goes first. Players take it in turns to remove as many matches as they like from any one pile, but only from one pile. A player must remove at least one match. The winner is the player who makes the other player take the last match. Make the computer play randomly: that is, it chooses a pile randomly and then a number of matches randomly from those available.

13.2 **Safe combination** Set up an array to contain the six digits that open a safe. Ask the user to input six digits one by one from buttons labelled with the digits 0 to 9, and check whether they are correct. When a digit is entered, tell the user whether it is correct or not and give them three tries before making them start from the beginning again.

13.3 **Blackjack** (sometimes called Twenty-One, *vingt-et-un* or Pontoon) Write a program to play this card game. The computer acts as the dealer. The dealer first deals you two playing cards. These are random cards. (In the real game, the dealer has an enormous hand of cards, comprising several shuffled packs.) Your aim is to get a score higher than the dealer's, without going beyond 21. Ace counts as either 1 or 11. At any time, you can say 'twist', which means that you want another card, or 'stick', which means you are content with what you have. You may also have gone 'bust', which means you have more than 21. When you finally stick or bust, it is the dealer's turn to deal cards for itself. The dealer's aim is to get a bigger score than you, without going bust. But the dealer does not know your score and so gambles on what you might have.

Provide buttons to start a new game, twist and stick. At the end of the game, display both sets of cards that were dealt.

Basic operations on arrays

13.4 **Rain data** Complete the program to handle rainfall data by including the following operations:

- Add up the values and display the total.
- Find the smallest value and display it.
- Find the index of the largest value.

13.5 **String array** Write a program that uses an array of 10 strings. Write methods that carry out each of the following operations:

- Input words from the keyboard via a text field.
- Display all the words. (You can now observe that they have been entered correctly into your array.)
- Input a word from a text field and search to see whether it is present in the array. Display a message to say whether it is present in the array or not.

13.6 **Bar chart** Bar charts are useful for displaying data like rainfall. Write a method that displays a bar chart of the data that is passed to it as an array. The array holds a number of values, such as the rainfall on each of the seven days of the week. The library method `fillRect` can be used to draw individual bars.

13.7 **Pie chart** Pie charts show the proportions of quantities and are therefore useful for data like personal budgets or company budgets. Write a method that displays a pie chart of the data that is passed to it as an array. The array holds the amounts spent on, for example, travel, food, housing, etc. Investigate the `fillArc` method in the Java library class `Graphics` that is useful in this program.

13.8 **Graph drawer** Write a method to draw a graph of data given as an array of *x* coordinates and an array of corresponding *y* coordinates. It has the heading:

```
private void drawGraph(double[] x, double[] y)
```

The method draws straight lines from one point to the next. It also draws the axes.

Statistics

13.9 **Sum and mean** Write a program that inputs a series of integers into an array. The numbers are in the range 0 to 100.

Calculate and display:

- the largest number;
- the smallest number;
- the sum of the numbers;
- the mean of the numbers.

Display a histogram (bar chart) that shows how many numbers are in the ranges 0 to 9, 10 to 19, etc.

Random numbers

13.10 **Check out the random number generator** Check to see that the random number generator class (Chapter 6) works correctly. Set it up to provide random numbers in the range 1 to 100. Then call the method 100 times, placing the frequencies in an array as in the previous exercise. Finally display the frequency histogram, again as in the previous exercise. Random numbers should be random, so the histogram should have bars of approximately equal height.

Words

13.11 **Word perm** Write a program that inputs four words and then displays all possible permutations of the words. So, for example, if the words mad, dog, bites and man are entered, then the following are output:

```
man bites mad dog
mad man bites dog
mad bites man dog
etc.
```

(Not all of the sentences will make sense!)

Information processing – searching

13.12 **Dictionary** Set up two arrays to contain pairs of equivalent English and Spanish words. Then input an English word, look up its Spanish equivalent and display it. Make sure you check to see whether the word is actually in the dictionary. Then add the facility to translate in the opposite direction, using the same data.

13.13 **Library** Each member of a library has a unique user code, an integer. When someone wants to borrow a book, a check is made that the user code is valid.

Write a program that searches a table of user codes to find a particular code. The program should display a message saying that the code is either valid or invalid.

13.14 **Telephone directory** Enhance the telephone directory program given above within the chapter so that new names and numbers can be added to the directory. Then add the facility to remove a name and number.

Information processing – sorting

13.15 **Sorting** Write a program that inputs a series of numbers, sorts them into ascending numerical order and displays them.

This program is not the easiest to write. There are very many approaches to sorting – in fact there are whole books on the subject. One approach is as follows.

Find the smallest number in the array. Swap it with the first item in the array. Now the first item in the array is in the right place. Leave this first item alone and repeat the operation on the remainder of the array (everything except the first item). Repeat, carrying out this operation on a smaller and smaller array until the complete array is in order.

Arrays of objects

13.16 **Balloons** Extend the program that maintains an array of balloons. Add functionality to:

- blow up all the balloons by a random factor;
- move all the balloons by the same amount.

13.17 **Telephone directory** Write a program to create and maintain a telephone directory. Each element in the array is an object of the class **Entry**:

```
public class Entry {

    private String theName;
    private String theNumber;

    // methods to access the name and the number

}
```

Complete the class **Entry**. Then create the array:

```
private Entry[] directory = new Entry[1000];
```

and place data into it like this, using the methods:

```
directory[0].setName("Douglas Bell");
directory[0].setNumber("01 0114 255 3103");
```

Provide a GUI to enter data into the directory. Provide a search facility so that if a name is entered into a text field, the corresponding telephone number is displayed.

13.18 **Playing cards** This is an example that might be part of a game using playing cards. Each card is described by the class:

```
public class Card {

    private int rank;
    private String suit;

    // methods to access the rank and the suit

}
```

Complete the class **Card**. Then create an array that holds a complete deck of cards:

```
private Card[] deck = new Card[52];
```

Initialize the deck using a **for** loop to run through the four suits and a nested **for** loop to run through the different card ranks.

Answers to self-test questions

13.1
```
int[] rainfall = new int[7];
```

13.2 The array is three elements long. Valid indices are 0 to 2.

13.3 The program fragment places the numbers 0 to 10 in the array. But it attempts to access a non-existent element with index value 10. So the program will fail.

13.4
```java
private void display(int[] array) {
    textArea.setText("");
    for (int index = 0; index < array.length; index++) {
        textArea.append(Integer.toString(array[index]) + "\n");
    }
}
```

13.5
```java
for (int index = 0; index < courses; index++) {
    courseMark[index] = 0;
}
```

13.6
```java
int[] numbers = {1, 2, 3, 4, 5};
```

13.7
```java
private void weekTotal() {
    int total = 0;
    for (int index = 0; index <= 6; index++) {
        total = total + rain[index];
    }
    stats.setText("total is " + Integer.toString(total));
}
```

13.8
```java
switch (dayNumber) {
    case 0:
        dayName = "Monday";
        break;
    case 1:
        dayName = "Tuesday";
        break;
    case 2:
        dayName = "Wednesday";
        break;
    case 3:
        dayName = "Thursday";
        break;
    case 4:
        dayName = "Friday";
        break;
    case 5:
        dayName = "Saturday";
        break;
    case 6:
        dayName = "Sunday";
        break;
}
```

CHAPTER
14

Arrays – two dimensional

This chapter explains:

- how to declare a two-dimensional array;
- how indices are used with two-dimensional arrays;
- how to obtain the size of a two-dimensional array;
- how to pass two-dimensional arrays as parameters;
- how to initialize a two-dimensional array.

● Introduction

Two-dimensional arrays, or tables, are very common in everyday life:

- a chessboard;
- a train timetable;
- a spreadsheet.

In the previous chapter, we looked at one-dimensional arrays. Java provides a natural extension of one-dimensional arrays to two dimensions. So, for example, the declaration:

```
int[][] sales = new int[4][7];
```

declares a two-dimensional array of integers. It holds figures for the sales of computers at each of four shops on each of the seven days in a week (Figure 14.1). The array is called **sales**. We can think of it as having four rows and seven columns. Each row represents a week at a particular shop. Each column represents a single day at each of the four shops. The indices for the rows go from 0 to 3. The indices for the columns go from 0 to 6. Column 0 is Monday, column 1 is Tuesday, etc.

Column numbers (days)

Row numbers (shops)

	0	1	2	3	4	5	6
0	22	49	4	93	0	12	32
1	3	8	67	51	5	3	63
2	14	8	23	14	5	23	16
3	54	0	76	31	4	3	99

Figure 14.1 A two-dimensional array.

SELF-TEST QUESTION

14.1 Which column represents Saturday? How many computers were sold on Thursday at shop 3? Which row and column number is this?

Declaring an array

An array is declared along with other variables and objects using **`new`**, either at the top of the class or at the top of a method. The programmer gives the array a name, like this:

```
int[][] sales = new int[4][7];

double[][] temps = new double[10][24];
```

When you declare an array, you say how many rows it has and how many columns there are. The array called **`sales`** has four rows – one for each of four shops. It has seven columns – one for each day in the week. The array contains sales figures for each of four shops for each day of the week. The array called **`temps`** holds information about the temperatures in each of 10 ovens, each hour during a 24-hour period.

As with any other variable, it is usual (and a good idea) to choose a name for the array that describes clearly what it is to be used for. The name is the name for the complete array – the complete collection of data.

SELF-TEST QUESTION

14.2 Declare an array to represent an 8 × 8 chessboard. Each position in the array is to hold a string.

Indices

A program refers to an individual item in a two-dimensional array by specifying the values of two integer indices (sometimes called subscripts). Thus `sales[3][2]` refers to the element in the array with row 3 and column 2, meaning shop number 3 and the day number 2 (Wednesday). Similarly, `chessBoard[2][7]` might contain the string 'pawn'.

We can input a value for an element of an array like this:

```
sales[2][3] = Integer.parseInt(textField.getText());

chessBoard[3][4] = textField.getText();
```

and similarly display the values of the elements of an array using text fields.

We can change the values with assignment statements, like this:

```
sales[3][2] = 99;
chessBoard[2][7] = "knight"; // place a knight on a square
```

In all these program fragments, we are referring to individual elements in an array by specifying the values of the indices that identify the particular element that we are interested in.

Often we want to refer to an element in an array by specifying *variables* for each of the two indices. This is the way in which the power of arrays can be exploited. Suppose, for example, we want to add up all the numbers in the array of numbers that holds data on sales of computers in four shops over a period of seven days:

```
int[][] sales= new int[4][7];
```

The clumsy way to add up the sales would be to write:

```
sum =
        sales[0][0] + sales[0][1] + sales[0][2] + sales[0][3]
            + sales[0][4] + sales[0][5] + sales[0][6]
    + sales[1][0] + sales[1][1] + sales[1][2]
            + sales[1][3] + sales[1][4] + sales[1][5] + sales[1][6]
    + etc.
```

which is longwinded, difficult to understand, prone to error – but correct. But it does not exploit the regularity of an array. The alternative is to use a `for` loop. Variables are used to hold the values of the indices. Each index is made initially equal to 0 and then incremented each time the loop is repeated:

```
int[][] sales = new int[4][7];
int sum;

sum = 0;
for (int shop = 0; shop <= 3; shop++) {
    for (int dayNumber = 0; dayNumber <= 6; dayNumber++) {
        sum = sum + sales[shop][dayNumber];
    }
}
```

which is considerably shorter and much neater than if we had written out all the sums in explicit detail.

SELF-TEST QUESTION

14.3 Write statements to place the text 'empty' on each square of the chessboard.

● The size of an array

Once created like this:

```
double[][] info = new double[20][40];
```

an array has a fixed size that cannot be changed unless the complete array is re-created using **new**.

The size of an array can always be obtained using the property **length**. For the above array:

```
int rowSize = info.length;
```

has the value 20 and

```
int columnSize = info[0].length;
```

has the value 40. This gives the length of the zeroth row of the array, but since all the rows are the same size, this is OK.

Note that the property **length** is *not* followed by brackets, ().

SELF-TEST QUESTION

14.4 What is the value of **chessBoard.length**?

Passing arrays as parameters

Suppose we want to write a method whose job it is to calculate the sum of the elements in an array of integers. We want the method to be general purpose, able to deal with arrays of any size. So we will pass the name of the array to the method as the parameter and the result to be returned to the user of the method is a number – the sum of the values.

A call of the method looks like this:

```
int[][] sales = new int[24][12];
int total;
total = sum(sales);
```

The method itself is:

```
private int sum(int[][] array) {
    int total = 0;
    for (int row = 0; row < array.length; row++) {
        for (int col = 0; col < array[0].length; col++) {
            total = total + array[row][col];
        }
    }
    return total;
}
```

Constants

Using constants can avoid confusion, particularly if two different arrays have the same length. For example, in the program to analyze the sales figures of computers at a number of shops over a number of days, we used a two-dimensional array to hold the figures. Each column represents a day. The rows are the data for each shop. Now suppose that, by coincidence, there are seven shops. The array is:

```
int[][] sales = new int[7][7];
```

The problem is that, wherever we see the number 7 in the program, we do not know whether it is the number of shops or the number of days. As things stand, of course, it doesn't matter – because they are the same! But suppose we needed to alter the program so that it deals with eight shops. We would very much like to change every occurrence of the number 7 to the number 8 using the editor. This is impossibly dangerous because the lengths are the same.

An excellent way to clarify such a program is to declare the maximum values of the index values as constants, like this:

```
final int days = 7;
final int shops = 7;
```

and then declare the array as:

```
int[][] sales = new int[shops][days];
```

Now if the number of shops changes, we can make the corresponding change to the program with confidence, simply by changing one number in the constant declaration. We can also write **for** loops that make use of the constants:

```
for (int index = 0; index < shops; index++) {
    // body of loop
}
```

● Initializing an array

Initializing means giving a variable an initial or starting value. If you write this:

```
int[][] table= new int[10][10];
```

then space for the array is set up in memory and the array contains zeros. The compiler assigns initial values to arrays that are not explicitly initialized. If the array consists of numbers, it assigns zeros. If the array consists of strings it assigns the value `""`. If the array consists of objects, it assigns the value **null** to all the elements of the array.

One way to initialize an array explicitly is to use nested loops, like this:

```
for (int row = 0; row <= 9; row++) {
    for (int col = 0; col <= 9; col++) {
        table[row][col] = 99;
    }
}
```

Another way of initializing an array is to declare it like this:

```
int[][] array =
                {{1, 0, 1},
                 {0, 1, 0}};
```

Note the use of curly brackets (braces) and commas. This both creates an array with two rows and three columns and gives it initial values. When this form of initialization is used, the size of the array must **not** appear in the brackets. Note also that the initialization is carried out once, when the array is created. If the program changes the value of an element in the array, the value will not change back to its original value – not until the program is run again.

If the program needs periodically to reset the array back to its initial values, then the way to do it is with **for** loops as shown above.

SELF-TEST QUESTION

14.5   Write the declaration of a 3 × 3 array of strings in such a way that the array is filled with the words one, two, three, etc.

A sample program

This program maintains a two-dimensional array of integers. These represent the rainfall over seven days at each of three locations. The screen is shown in Figure 14.2. The array is displayed in a text area with an initial assortment of values. The user can change a value in the array by specifying its index values and the new value of the data.

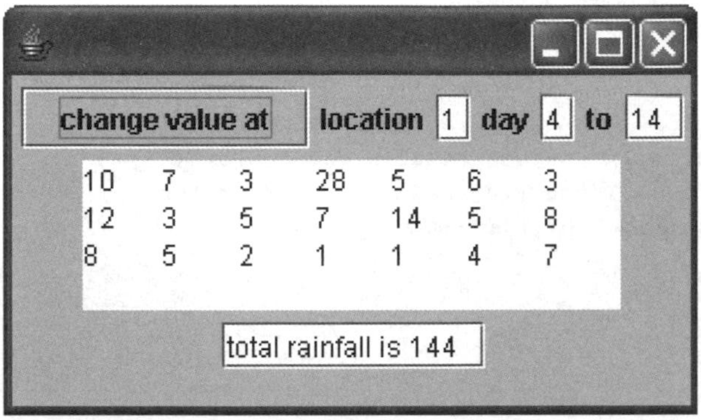

Figure 14.2 Two-dimensional array of rainfall data.

Firstly we declare the array:

```
private int[][] rainData =
    {{10, 7, 3, 28, 5, 6, 3},
     {12, 3, 5, 7, 12, 5, 8},
     { 8, 5, 2, 1, 1, 4, 7}};
```

To display all the data:

```
private void display() {
    data.setText("");
    data.setTabSize(3);
    String newLine = "\n";
    String tab = "\t";

    for (int location = 0; location <= 2; location++) {

        for (int dayNumber = 0; dayNumber <= 6; dayNumber++) {
            data.append(Integer.toString
                (rainData[location][dayNumber])
                + tab);
        }
        data.append(newLine);
    }
}
```

The inner **for** loop deals with the different days, while the outer **for** loop deals with the different locations. We have set the tab size to a convenient value using method **setTabSize**.

To change an element in the array, the day number, location number and new data value are extracted from their text fields:

```
private void changeValue() {
    int dataValue;
    int dayNumber;
    int location;

    dayNumber = Integer.parseInt(day.getText());
    location = Integer.parseInt(place.getText());
    dataValue = Integer.parseInt(newData.getText());
    rainData[location][dayNumber] = dataValue;

    display();
    calculateTotal();
}
```

To calculate the total rainfall across all the locations:

```
private void calculateTotal() {
    int total = 0;

    for (int location = 0; location <= 2; location++) {
        for (int dayNumber = 0; dayNumber <= 6; dayNumber++) {
            total = total + rainData[location][dayNumber];
        }
    }
    stats.setText("total rainfall is " + Integer.toString(total));
}
```

When you run this program, be careful to enter row numbers in the range 0 to 2, and column numbers in the range 0 to 6.

You will see again that it is very common to see nested **for** statements used with two-dimensional arrays, because they make the maximum use of the uniformity of arrays.

Programming principles

A two-dimensional array is a collection of data, with a single name (e.g. **rainData**). An array can be visualized as a two-dimensional table, with rows and columns. Suppose we want to represent the rainfall data for each of seven days at each of three places. We declare an array:

```
int[][] rainData = new int[7][3];
```

Elements in such an array are distinguished by specifying two indices, which are integers, e.g. `rainData[4][2]`. We can think of the first index as describing the row number and the second as describing the column number. When the array is created the sizes of the two dimensions of the array are specified – seven and three in this example. This array has seven rows and three columns. Indices always start at 0. In this example the row indices go from 0 to 6, and the column indices from 0 to 2.

The elements of an array can be any type – **int**, **double**, **String**, or any other object. But all the elements in an array must be of the same type – **int** in this example. The exception is when an array is declared to consist of **Object**. In this case such an array can accommodate any mix of objects.

It is common to use nested **for** loops in conjunction with two-dimensional arrays.

In this book we have explored both one-dimensional and two-dimensional arrays. Java provides for arrays with up to 60 dimensions, but dimensions above 3 are rarely used in practice.

Programming pitfalls

A common error in Java is to confuse the length of an array with the range of valid indices. For example, the array:

```
int[][] table = new int[11][6];
```

has 11 rows and 6 columns. The valid range of indices for the rows is 0 to 10. The valid range of indices for the columns is 0 to 5. Reference to `table[11][6]` will make the program stop and an error message will be displayed.

Summary

- A two-dimensional array is a collection of data in a table, with rows and columns. An array is given a name by the programmer.

- An array is declared, along with other variables, like this:

```
int[][] alice = new int[25][30];
```

in which 25 is the number of rows and 30 is the number of columns.

- An individual element of an array is referred to by integer indices. For example:

```
alice[12][3] = 45;
```

● **Exercises**

Basic operations on two-dimensional arrays

14.1 **Data handler** Write a program that uses a 4 × 7 array of numbers similar to the rainfall program (with output as shown in Figure 14.2). Extend the program to carry out the following operations:

■ When a button is pressed marked 'sums', add up the values for each of the seven columns and add up all the values of each of the four rows and display them.

■ When a button marked 'largest' is pressed, find the largest value in each row, the largest in each column and the largest value in the complete array.

■ When a button marked 'scale' is pressed, multiply every number in the array by a number entered into a text field. (This could be used to convert from centimetres to inches.)

Statistical measures

14.2 Extend the rainfall program so that it provides a button to calculate the average rainfall per day for each location. So, for example, the average rainfall per day in location 2 might be 23.

Extend it further to provide a button to calculate the mean and standard deviation of the daily rainfall in any location. So for illustration, the mean rainfall in any location could be 19, with a standard deviation of 6.4.

Bar charts and pie charts

14.3 Extend the rainfall program so that the user can specify a row (a location). The information is then displayed as a bar chart.

Extend the program to display the information in a single row or a single column as a pie chart. To do this, make use of the library method **fillArc** in the class **Graphics**.

Mathematical operations

14.4 **Transpose** The transpose of an array is the technical term used to describe swapping the elements in an array across one of the diagonals. The numbers on the diagonal do not change. So if an array is as shown in Figure 14.3 then its transpose is as shown in Figure 14.4.

1	2	3	4
6	7	8	9
10	11	12	13
14	15	16	17

Figure 14.3 Array before transposition.

1	6	10	14
2	7	11	15
3	8	12	16
4	9	13	17

Figure 14.4 Transposed array.

Write a program to input the elements of an array in the same manner as the rainfall program. It transposes the array when a button is clicked, and displays it.

Games

14.5 **Tic Tac Toe** Tic Tac Toe (or noughts and crosses) is played on a 3 × 3 grid, which is initially empty. Each of two players goes in turn. One places a cross in a blank square. Then the other places a nought in a blank square.

The winner is the person who gets a line of three noughts or three crosses. Thus Figure 14.5 represents a win for noughts.

```
o | x | o
--+---+--
x | o |
--+---+--
x |   | o
```

Figure 14.5 Tic Tac Toe.

Games can end in a draw, where neither side has obtained a line.

Write a program to play the game. A button is provided to start a new game. The program shows the noughts and crosses graphically, each in its own panel. The human player specifies a move by clicking with the mouse on the panel where the cross is to be placed. The other player is the computer, which plays as noughts and decides where to play on a random basis.

Artificial life

14.6 **Cellular life** An organism consists of single cells that are on (alive) or off (dead). Each generation of life consists of a single row of cells. Each generation of life (each row) of the organism depends on the previous one (just like real life). Time moves downwards, from top to bottom. Each row represents a generation. The lives look like Figure 14.6.

In the beginning, there is just one cell alive. Whether a cell is alive or dead depends on a combination of factors – whether or not it was alive in the last generation and whether or not its immediate neighbours were alive in the last generation. You can see that, even after only five generations, a pattern is emerging. These patterns are very subtle and mimic the patterns found in real living organisms. The rules are as follows.

<table>
<tr><td></td><td></td><td></td><td></td><td>*</td><td></td><td></td><td></td><td></td><td></td></tr>
<tr><td></td><td></td><td></td><td>*</td><td>*</td><td>*</td><td></td><td></td><td></td><td></td></tr>
<tr><td></td><td></td><td>*</td><td>*</td><td></td><td></td><td>*</td><td></td><td></td><td></td></tr>
<tr><td></td><td></td><td>*</td><td>*</td><td></td><td>*</td><td>*</td><td>*</td><td>*</td><td></td></tr>
<tr><td></td><td>*</td><td>*</td><td></td><td></td><td>*</td><td></td><td></td><td></td><td>*</td></tr>
<tr><td>*</td><td>*</td><td></td><td>*</td><td>*</td><td>*</td><td>*</td><td></td><td>*</td><td>*</td></tr>
</table>

Figure 14.6 Cellular life.

A cell lives only if:

■ it was dead, but only its left neighbour was alive;

■ it was dead, but only its right neighbour was alive;

■ it was alive, but its immediate neighbours were dead;

■ it was alive, and only its right neighbour was alive.

So, for example, given the generation shown in Figure 14.7:

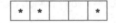

Figure 14.7 Before a cycle.

■ The first cell lives, because even though it was dead, its immediate right neighbour was alive.

■ The second cell lives because only its immediate right neighbour was alive.

■ The third living cell dies (through overcrowding, we surmise!).

■ The fourth cell dies.

■ The fifth cell lives because, although it was dead, its immediate left neighbour was alive.

So the new generation is as shown in Figure 14.8.

Figure 14.8 After one cycle.

Write a program that uses a two-dimensional array to chart the progress of the life form. Display the development on the screen as asterisks, as above. Provide a button that allows the user to go on to the next generation.

14.7 **Conway's Game of Life** In this life form, again, an organism consists of single cells that are on (alive) or off (dead). The organisms exist in a two-dimensional grid world, as in Figure 14.9.

The rules governing this organism are:

1. If a live cell has two or three neighbours, it will survive. Otherwise it will die of isolation or overcrowding.

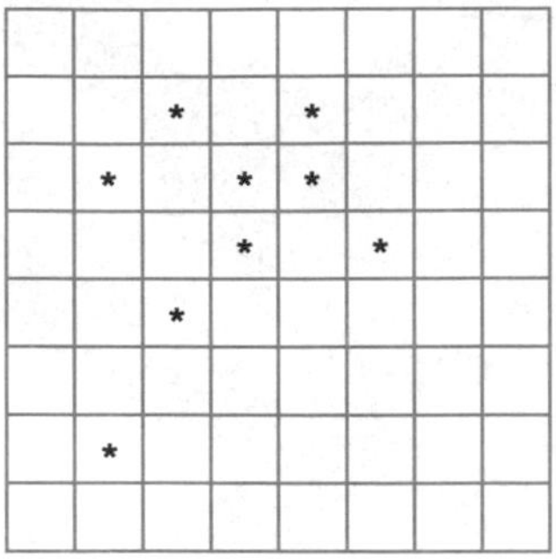

Figure 14.9 Game of Life.

2. If an empty cell is surrounded by exactly three cells, then a new live cell will be born to fill the space.

3. All births and deaths take place simultaneously.

Write a program to simulate this kind of life. The program should initially allow the user to click on the cells that are to be alive. Provide a button that allows the user to go on to the next generation and display it.

The program needs two arrays – one to represent the current state of life and another to represent the next generation. After each new generation is created, the roles of the two arrays are swapped.

Answers to self-test questions

14.1 Column 5 is Saturday. 31 computers were sold at shop 3 on Thursday. This is row 3 and column 3.

14.2
```
String[][] chessBoard = new String[8][8];
```

14.3
```
String[][] chessBoard = new String[8][8];
for (int row = 0; row <= 7; row++) {
    for (int col = 0; col <= 7; col++) {
        chessBoard[row][col] = "empty";
    }
}
```

14.4 The value is 8

14.5
```
String[][] numbers =
            {
                    {"one", "two", "three"},
                    {"four", "five", "six"},
                    {"seven", "eight", "nine"}
            };
```

String manipulation

This chapter explains:

- the string facilities you have seen so far;
- the main methods of the **String** class.

● Introduction

Strings of characters are very important in software. All programming languages have facilities for primitive character manipulation, but Java has a particularly useful collection of methods. In this chapter, we will bring together the string features we have made use of up to now, and extend this by studying the set of string-processing methods.

Here are some situations in which strings are used:

- To display messages on the screen, which might involve placing text on labels.
- To input text from the user. Often, we use a text field.
- To store data in files. When we examine files in Chapter 17 we will see that the content of many types of file can be regarded as sequences of strings. Additionally, file names and folder names are strings.
- For searching web pages.
- To hold text in memory for word processors and editors.

Using strings – a recap

Here, we bring together the string facilities that have been shown so far.

We can declare variables and provide an initial value, as in:

```
String x, y;
String myCity;
String myName = "Parr";
String myCountry = new String("Japan");
```

In the final line above, we have shown the full way of providing an initial value, because it illustrates that, behind the scenes, the use of **new** is always involved to allocate space for the string value. However, there is no advantage in using this form – a **new** is performed whether you explicitly request it or not.

We can assign one string to another, as in:

```
x = "England";
x = "France";
y = x;
x = "";           // a zero-length string
```

This illustrates that the length of a string can vary. Strictly, the old string is destroyed and is replaced with a totally new value. The space that was occupied by the old value will be made available for other data via garbage collection.

We can use the + operator to concatenate strings, as in the familiar:

```
int number = 123;
textField.setText("value is "+ number);
```

Take care when using several + operators, as in:

```
textField.setText("value is "+22+33);
```

The Java rule is that when one item is a string, the others are converted to strings, so the above displays:

```
value is 2233
```

We can force the numeric addition to be performed first by putting:

```
textField.setText("value is "+(22+33));
```

which displays:

```
value is 55
```

A common feature of string processing is to begin with an initially empty string, and to join items onto it as the program runs. We might put:

```
x = x + "something";
```

which adds to the end of **x**. This is known as 'appending'.

We can compare strings, as in:

```
if (x.equals(y))...
```

We can create arrays of strings (with subscripts starting from 0), as in:

```
String[] cities = new String[10]; // 10 elements, 0 to 9
```

and manipulate elements, as in:

```
cities[1] = "Los Angeles";
```

We can convert strings to **int** and **double**. This is useful when we are presented with strings from a text field (or from a file, as we shall see later). For example, we may put:

```
int intValue = Integer.parseInt(dataString);
```

If the input string does not contain a valid number, this method produces an error indication – an exception. We will study data input in more detail later in the chapter, and in Chapter 16 we will see how errors can be detected and controlled.

This much we have seen. Now we will look at the detail of strings and the available methods.

● The characters within strings

String values are placed between double-quote characters – but what if we need to display a double quote on the screen? We could try the following:

```
textField.setText("A "tricky" problem!");  // wrong
```

This won't compile, as the second " is taken as the end of the complete string. Instead, we can make use of the 'backslash' character \, which instructs Java to treat its following character as an ordinary character, rather than one with a special meaning. The jargon for \ is the 'escape' character. So, the solution to our quoting problem is:

```
textField.setText("A \"tricky\" problem!");
```

which displays:

```
A "tricky" problem!
```

The sequences \n and \t also have a special meaning in Java:

- \n stands for the newline character.
- \t stands for the tab character. This can be useful for aligning columns of data, as we did with arrays in Chapter 13.

● A note on the `char` type

In this book we are stressing program clarity rather than execution speed. However, sometimes we encounter situations in which we might wish to avoid the extra time penalty of using strings. As an example, consider the case when our strings only hold one character. Java has an additional primitive type called **char**, which stores each item as a 16 bit Unicode character, and a result of this is that **char** comparison can be done as swiftly as **int** comparison, whereas the comparison of strings takes longer. Here, we provide examples of its use.

We can declare variables and provide an initial value:

```
char initial = 'M';
char marker = '\n';
char letter;
```

Note the use of the single-quote characters. They can only enclose a single character. The **\n**, though it looks like two characters, is replaced at compile-time by the single newline (or 'enter') character.

We can assign values, as in:

```
initial = 'P';
letter = initial;
```

We can compare, as in:

```
if (initial == 's')...
```

and we can make use of the behind-the-scenes number representation of the characters: the digit characters **0** to **9** have successive integer values, so we can use **<** to mean 'before', and **>** to mean 'after', as in:

```
if ((initial >= '0') && (initial <= '9')) //test if digit
```

The characters **A** to **Z** and **a** to **z** also have the same property, so we can put:

```
if ((initial <= 'A') && (initial <= 'Z')) //test if upper-case letter
```

The **char** type is used rarely, but it is efficient in terms of run-time speed. It is vital to note that, along with **int**, **boolean**, **double**, it is a primitive type. We can compare **char** values with **==**. On the contrary, items of class **String** are proper objects, not primitive types, and we must use the **equals** method of the **String** class, as in:

```
String s;
if(s.equals("fred"))...
```

● The `String` class

As you know from previous examples, we can create strings and arrays of strings. We can also concatenate (join) them, display them and input them from a text field. What we have not seen up to now is the detailed use of library methods in the class **String**. We have been discussing 'strings' in general here, with a lower-case 's', and we will continue to use the term – but to be precise, we mean instances of the class **String**.

● The `String` class methods

Firstly, some general points. Each character in a string has an index (or position number). The first character is numbered `0`. Furthermore, many of the `String` methods require you to provide index values, and if you accidentally provide a negative index or one that is too large, a message containing the exception name `StringIndexOutOfBoundsException` will be produced.

Here we will look at the most useful methods of `String`. Because you might want to run programs to confirm your understanding of each method, we will provide a basic program with two text field inputs, a 'do it' button, and a text field output. When the button is clicked, your choice of string operation will be performed. Figure 15.1 shows a screenshot.

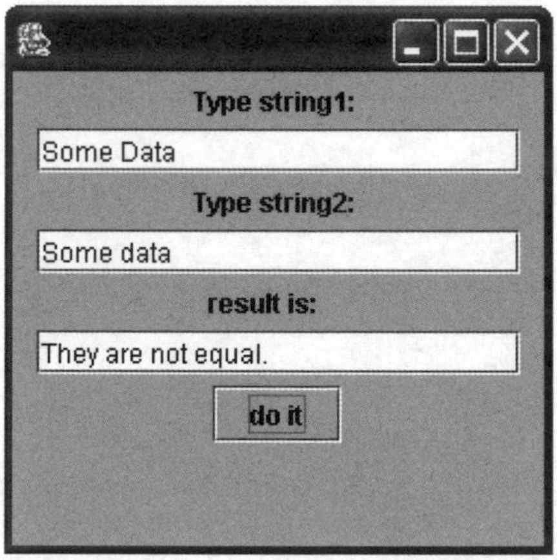

Figure 15.1 The `StringTemplate` program, showing the `equals` method.

To display the results, we have used a text field which can display text via the `setText` method.

The program is suitable for use with those methods below which provide an explicit example. Look at the coding below to see where your statements should be inserted. Here is the program:

```
import java.awt.*;
import java.awt.event.*;
import javax.swing.*;

public class StringTemplate extends JFrame
    implements ActionListener {

    private JTextField string1Field, string2Field, resultField;
    private JLabel string1Label, string2Label, resultLabel;
    private JButton goButton;
```

```java
public static void main(String[] args) {
    StringTemplate frame = new StringTemplate();
    frame.setSize(250, 250);
    frame.createGUI();
    frame.show();
}

private void createGUI() {
    setDefaultCloseOperation(EXIT_ON_CLOSE);
    Container window = getContentPane();
    window.setLayout(new FlowLayout());

    string1Label = new JLabel("Type string1: ");
    window.add(string1Label);

    string1Field = new JTextField(20);
    window.add(string1Field);

    string2Label = new JLabel("Type string2: ");
    window.add(string2Label);

    string2Field = new JTextField(20);
    window.add(string2Field);

    resultLabel = new JLabel("result is: ");
    window.add(resultLabel);

    resultField = new JTextField(20);
    window.add(resultField);

    goButton = new JButton("do it");
    window.add(goButton);
    goButton.addActionListener(this);
}

public void actionPerformed(ActionEvent event) {
    String result ="";
    if (event.getSource() == goButton) {
        String string1 = string1Field.getText();
        String string2 = string2Field.getText();
        // string example - equals
        //.... insert your code here
        if(string1.equals(string2))
            result="They are equal.";
        else
            result="They are not equal.";
        // end of example

        resultField.setText(result);
    }
}
}
```

● Comparing strings

The most important methods in this area are `equals`, `equalsIgnoreCase` and `compareTo`.

equals

This is used to compare values; we should not use `==` to do this. Here is an example, which can be inserted in the demonstration program:

```
// String example - equals
if (string1.equals(string2))
    result = "They are equal.";
else
    result = "They are not equal.";
// end of example
```

equalsIgnoreCase

This provides a similar facility to `equals`, except the case (upper or lower) of each character is ignored. `"This String"` will be regarded as equal to `"this string"`. To experiment with this, use the above code, but replace the call of `equals` by a call of `equalsIgnoreCase`.

compareTo

Imagine that we have a number of strings (perhaps holding people's names) which we need to place in alphabetical order. The `compareTo` method allows us to do this. Behind the scenes, the internal integer codes for the characters are used. The only point to be wary of is that lower-case letters have higher codes than upper-case letters. Here are some examples:

ant is before **bee**
and is before **ant**
an is before **and**
ANT is before **BEE**
INSECT is before **ant**
Insect is before **ant**
INSECT is before **insect**

`compareTo` returns an integer result, with the following meaning:

■ 0 if the strings are equal;
■ a negative value if the string object precedes the parameter;
■ a positive value if the string object follows the parameter.

If we put:

```
n = "ant".compareTo("bee");
```

then **n** will be set to a negative value. You can check this with the following code:

```
//String example - compareTo
int n = string1.compareTo(string2);
if (n == 0)
    result = "they are equal";
else if (n < 0)
    result = "string1 precedes string2";
else
    result = "string2 precedes string1";
// end of example
```

Amending strings

Here we look at methods which change a string. Behind the scenes, these methods create a new string rather than changing the original string.

replace

This method replaces one character by another, throughout the string. For example:

```
string1 = "Mississippi".replace('i', 'a');
```

would place **"Massassappa"** in **string1**. You can experiment with the following code. Insert it in the demonstration program.

```
// String example - replace
result = string1.replace('a', 'A'); // replace every 'a' by 'A'
// end of example
```

toLowerCase

The **toLowerCase** method converts any upper-case letters in a string into lower-case letters, as in:

```
string1 = "Version 1.1";
result = string1.toLowerCase();
```

which puts **"version 1.1"** in **result**. You can experiment with this by using the following lines of code:

```
// String example - toLowerCase
result = string1.toLowerCase();
// end of example
```

toUpperCase

The **toUpperCase** method does a similar operation as **toLowerCase**, but changes any lower-case letters into upper-case equivalents. For example:

```
string1 = "Java";
result = string1.toUpperCase();
```

trim

The **trim** method removes white space from both ends of a string. 'White space' means not only space characters, but also newlines and tabs. If we put:

```
string1 = "    Centre    ";
result = string1.trim();
```

then **string1** becomes **"Centre"**. Here is some code to exercise **trim**:

```
// String example - trim
result = string1.trim();
// end of example
```

● Examining strings

These methods allow us to examine a string – for example, to extract a section of it. A section of a string is often called a substring.

length

The **length** method returns the current number of characters in a string, as in:

```
int n = "Java Programming".length();
```

Here, **n** is set to 16. The following code placed within the program will display the length of a string that you input:

```
// String example - length
result = "length is " + string1.length();
// end of example
```

Obtaining the length of an array is done differently. For example, the length of an array named **table** is given by **table.length**.

substring

The **substring** method extracts a specified part of a string. The call provides the starting position, and the position **1** greater than the last character to be extracted. Take care with this second parameter! In this extract:

```
string1 = "position";
result = string1.substring(2,5);
```

`result` is set to the string `"sit"`. The first position in a string is numbered `0`, and the last character is always at `length()-1`, as you can see from the following diagram:

Index	0	1	2	3	4	5	6	7
Character	p	o	s	i	t	i	o	n

(Length is 8)

Here is the code for the example program, which displays its input with the first and last characters removed.

```
// String example - substring
result = string1.substring(1, string1.length()-1);
```

SELF-TEST QUESTION

15.1   Explain the effect of the following code:

```
String word = "position";
String s = word.substring(2, word.length() );
```

charAt

The `charAt` method returns the character at a specified position. Note that the result is of type `char`, not a string of length 1. In some situations, this will be faster than the use of `substring`. Here is an example:

```
char c1,c2;
string1 = "position";
c1 = string1.charAt(1);     // c1 becomes 'o'
c2 = string1.charAt(4);     // c2 becomes 't'
```

indexOf

This method determines whether a substring is contained within a string. We can provide an offset, specifying where the search is to start. For example:

```
int n = "mississippi".indexOf("is",4);
```

sets `n` to `4`, showing the position of the second `"is"`. (Recall that the first position of a string is numbered `0`.)

However, if we put:

```
int n = "mississippi".indexOf("is",5);
```

then **n** becomes **-1**, indicating that the string has not been found. (The value **5** indicates a search from the third **"s"**.) Here is some code for the example program, which reports on whether a string contains a substring:

```
//string example - indexOf
if (string1.indexOf(string2,0  0)
    result = string2 + " exists in "+string1;
else
    result = string2 + " does not exist in "+string1;
//end of example
```

lastIndexOf

This method is similar in concept to **indexOf**, but returns the position of the rightmost occurrence of a substring. The value **-1** is returned if no match is found. Here is an example:

```
int place = "//a.b.c/directory/file".lastIndexOf("/");
```

The value **17** is returned.

endsWith

This method is used to find out if a string ends with a particular substring. Yes, you could use a combination of other methods to accomplish this, but the provided method is less error prone. The method returns a **boolean** value. For example:

```
boolean r = "http://path/".endsWith("/");
```

would set **r** to **true**.

Here is some code for the example program, which determines whether a substring is present at the end of another string:

```
// string example - endsWith
if (string1.endsWith(string2))
    result = "string1 ends with " + string2;
else
    result = "string1 does not end with " + string2;
// end of example
```

The StringTokenizer class

We have seen that strings can be searched for a substring and, based on the result, can be split into parts. However, when our data contains repeated substrings separated by special characters, the splitting up can be more easily done using the **StringTokenizer** class. Here are some typical strings that we might want to take apart:

```
January 21 5
4,6     ,7,10,10,12,13,    15, 21,20,19, 8
```

In both of these strings, there is the concept of a delimiter, which breaks up the separate items (or tokens). In the first example, representing the hours of sunshine on **21 January**, the delimiter is a space, or a series of spaces. In the second example, the delimiter is a comma, but there are also spaces present. The above strings are typical of the kind of data that exists in files. Sometimes such files are created by other Java programs, or they could have been produced by exporting data from a spreadsheet. (For details of file processing, see Chapter 17.)

Here is how we can view the strings token by token:

```
String example1 = "January 21 5";
String month, day, hours;
StringTokenizer sunData = new StringTokenizer(example1, " ");
month = sunData.nextToken();
day = sunData.nextToken();
hours = sunData.nextToken();
```

What we have done is to create a new instance of the **StringTokenizer** class, called **sunData**. In the constructor, we supply the string to be taken apart and a string which contains the delimiter (or delimiters). To deal with the first string, we used **" "**, with the result that any spaces will be treated as delimiters rather than as data. We then make use of the **nextToken** method to fetch each item in turn. Depending on the problem, we could choose to convert the strings of digits into an **int**.

For the second string, let us assume that we don't know in advance how many tokens it contains. We can make use of the **hasMoreTokens** method, which returns true if there is more data for **nextToken** to fetch. We also supply a delimiter string of **" ,"**, indicating that spaces and/or commas are delimiters. We might put:

```
String example2 = "4,6 ,7,10,10,12,13, 15, 21,20,19, 8";
String item;
StringTokenizer numberList = new StringTokenizer(example2," ,");
while (numberList.hasMoreTokens()) {
    item = numberList.nextToken();
    // .... process item
}
```

To summarize, the main methods of the class **StringTokenizer** are:

```
nextToken()
hasMoreTokens()
```

The `StringTokenizer` class is in the `util` library, so place:

```
import java.util.*;
```

at the head of your program.

● String conversions

Data that we display on the screen or input from the keyboard is in the form of strings – but the internal form that we use may be different. For example, we may need to input a series of digits as a string, and then convert them to an `int` type. Java has a range of 'parse' methods, which convert strings into a variety of types, and many classes in the Java library provide a `toString` method, which produces a string representation of an instance.

Recall that `int` and `double` are primitive 'built-in' types, and do not have any methods associated with them. To compensate for this, Java has classes which provide facilities for the primitive types, wrapping them up so that they look like instances of classes. The relevant ones are:

```
Integer
Double
Boolean
Character
```

Note carefully that the names follow the Java convention of using a capital letter to start the class name. Thus, `double` is the built-in type, and `Double` is its wrapper class. We need to know about the above classes because they provide 'parse' and `toString` methods for use in conversion. Here are some examples.

To convert an `int` to a `String`:

```
int n = 123;
String s = Integer.toString(n);    // s becomes "123"
```

Note the use of the class name `Integer` before the static method name.

To convert a `double` to a `String`:

```
double d = 12.34;
String s = Double.toString(d);    // s becomes "12.34"
```

Again, note the use of the class name `Double` (with a capital `D`) before the static method name.

To convert a `String` to an `int`:

```
String s = "1234";
int n = Integer.parseInt(s);
```

The `parseInt` method returns an `int` type. A common use of this is when a string of digits is obtained from a text field, as in:

```
n = Integer.parseInt(someTextField.getText());
```

To convert a `String` to a `double`, we can use `parseDouble` as follows:

```
String s = "12.34";
double d = Double.parseDouble(s);
```

When converting user input into numbers, there is always the problem of errors. The user might type:

```
123XY3
```

Here we have assumed that an input error is not dangerous, and in fact our programs which use the above conversion approach will simply not deal with errors. This is not acceptable for serious software, and in Chapter 16 we will see how to detect and handle such errors.

● String parameters

As we have seen in our review of available methods, strings can be passed as parameters and returned as results; their use is reasonably intuitive.

Here is an example. We will create a method which doubles a string; thus `"hello"` becomes `"hellohello"`.

```
private String doubleIt(String any) {
    return any + any;
}
```

Here is how we might call the method:

```
String s1 = "hello";
s1 = doubleIt(s1);
```

We pass the string to the method as a parameter. A new string is created and passed back as the return value. Finally, this new value is assigned to `s1`.

● An example of string processing

Here we will look at the creation of a string-processing method which performs a commonly required function – to examine a string, replacing every occurrence of a given substring by another substring (of potentially different length). Note that the `String` class has a `replace` method, but it can only handle single characters. We will create a method which works with substrings. Here is an example. If we have the string:

```
"to be or not to be"
```

and we replace every occurrence of 'be' by 'eat', we will create:

```
"to eat or not to eat"
```

The basic process is to use **indexOf** to determine the position of a substring **"be"** here. We then form a new string made up of the left part of the string, the right part and the replacement string in the centre. We have:

```
"to " + "eat" + " or not to be"
```

The process must then be repeated until there are no more occurrences of 'be'. There are two problem cases:

- The user of **replace** asks us to replace a value of **""**. We could regard any string as being preceded by an infinite number of such empty strings! Our approach here is to simply return the unchanged original string.

- The replacement string contains the string to be replaced. For example, we might try to change **"be"** to **"beat"**. To prevent an infinite number of replacements taking place, we ensure that we only consider substrings in the right-hand part of the string. We use the variable **startSearch** to keep track of the start of the right-hand part of the string.

The full code is:

```java
private String replace(String original, String from,
                        String to) {
    String leftBit, rightBit;
    int startSearch = 0;
    int place = original.indexOf(from);
    if (from.length() != 0) {
        while (place = startSearch) {
            leftBit = original.substring(0, place);
            rightBit = original.substring(place +
                        from.length(), original.length());
            original = leftBit + to + rightBit;
            startSearch = leftBit.length() + to.length();
            place = original.indexOf(from);
        }
    }
    return original;
}
```

Here is how we might call our method:

```java
String original = "to be or not to be";
String changed = replace(original, "be", "eat");
```

Obviously, the above extract will not work in isolation, so now we will incorporate it into a program.

String case study – Frasier

In 1970, Joseph Weizenbaum wrote a program known as ELIZA to simulate a particular style of psychiatrist. It was a simple program, in the sense that it made little attempt to understand the sense of the input that users (patients) typed. For example, if the patient entered:

```
I am feeling sad
```

then ELIZA might respond with:

```
you are feeling sad - why?
```

Similarly, if the patient typed:

```
I am feeling Java
```

then ELIZA might respond with:

```
You are feeling Java - why?
```

Here we present an even more simplified version, which we will call Frasier, after the US TV sitcom character. The approach to the design will be to separate the user interface from the string processing. We shall create a **Psychiatrist** class with two methods – to accept a question, and to produce a reply. Here is the class:

```java
import java.util.*;

public class Psychiatrist {

    private String question;
    private String reply;
    private Random randomValue = new Random();

    public void putQuestion(String q) {
        question = " " + q + " ";
    }

    public String getReply() {
        int variation = randomValue.nextInt(3);
        switch (variation) {
        case 0:
            reply = transformQuestion();
            break;
        case 1:
            reply = "Why do you feel that?";
            break;
        case 2:
```

```
                    reply = "please be frank!";
                    break;
            }
            return reply;
    }

    private String transformQuestion() {
        if (question.indexOf(" I ") >= 0) {
            String tempReply = replace (question,
                                        " I ", " you ");
            tempReply = replace(tempReply,
                                " am ", " are ");
            return replace(tempReply, " my "," your ") +
                            "-why?";
        }
        else
            if (question.indexOf(" no ") >= 0)
                return "no? that is negative! Please explain...";
            else
                return "\"" + question + "\"-Please re-phrase..";
    }

    private String replace(String original, String from,
                            String to) {
        String leftBit, rightBit;
        int startSearch = 0;
        int place = original.indexOf(from);
        if (from.length() != 0) {
            while (place >= startSearch) {
                leftBit = original.substring(0, place);
                rightBit = original.substring(place +
                            from.length(), original.length());
                original = leftBit + to + rightBit;
                startSearch = leftBit.length() + to.length();
                place = original.indexOf(from);
            }
        }
        return original;
    }
}
```

The user interface is straightforward. It takes the form of two text fields, one to accept user input, and another (uneditable) one to show output from the program. Figure 15.2 shows a screenshot, and here is the user-interface class:

```
import java.awt.*;
import java.awt.event.*;
import javax.swing.*;
```

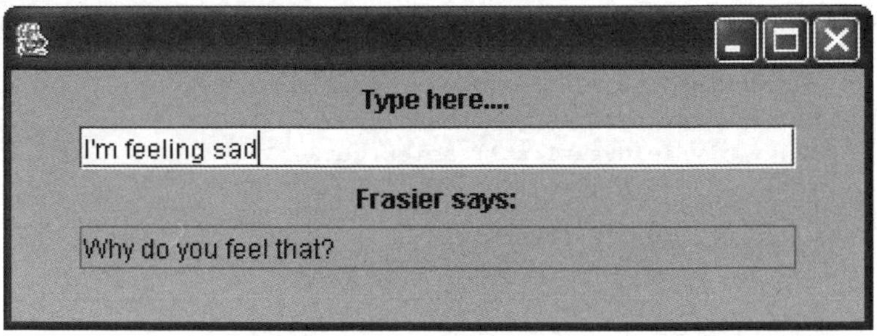

Figure 15.2 The Frasier program.

```java
public class AskFrasier extends JFrame
    implements ActionListener {

    private JTextField questionField, replyField;
    private JLabel psychiatristLabel, questionLabel;
    private Psychiatrist frasier;

    public static void main(String[] args) {
        AskFrasier frame = new AskFrasier();
        frame.setSize(400, 150);
        frame.createGUI();
        frame.show();
    }

    private void createGUI() {
        setDefaultCloseOperation(EXIT_ON_CLOSE);
        Container window = getContentPane();
        window.setLayout(new FlowLayout());

        questionLabel = new JLabel("Type here.... ");
        window.add(questionLabel);

        questionField = new JTextField(30);
        window. add(questionField);
        questionField.addActionListener(this);

        psychiatristLabel = new JLabel("Frasier says: ");
        window.add(psychiatristLabel);

        replyField = new JTextField(
            "Go ahead please... I'm listening.", 30);
        replyField.setEditable(false);
        window.add(replyField);

        frasier = new Psychiatrist();
    }
```

```
        public void actionPerformed(ActionEvent event) {
            if (event.getSource() == questionField) {
                String itsValue = questionField.getText();
                frasier.putQuestion(itsValue);
                replyField.setText(frasier.getReply() );
            }
        }
    }
```

Event handling is straightforward – when the user hits 'enter', the question is put to Frasier, and he is then asked for a reply. This is where the real string work gets performed:

```
if (event.getSource() == questionField) {
    String itsValue = questionField.getText();
    frasier.putQuestion(itsValue);
    replyField.setText(frasier.getReply() );
}
```

To make the responses seem more human, we add an element of randomness to the **Psychiatrist**:

```
int variation = randomValue.nextInt(3);
switch (variation) {
case 0:
    reply = transformQuestion();
    break;
case 1:
    reply = "Why do you feel that?";
    break;
case 2:
    reply = "please be frank!";
    break;
}
```

The random integer provides three cases. In two of them, we produce a standard reply, but in the other case, we transform the question by, for example, replacing every " I " by " you ". We add extra spaces at the start and end of the question to assist in detecting whole words. Note that the program has no knowledge of English meanings or grammar. To add this would involve a major programming effort.

Programming principles

- An instance of the **String** class can hold any number of characters.
- Methods of the **String** class can manipulate strings.

Programming pitfalls

- Strings are objects, and the **String** class provides methods. The correct usage is, for example:

  ```
  int n = string1.length();
  ```

  rather than:

  ```
  int n = length(string1);
  ```

- do not use **==** to compare strings. Instead, use **equals** or **equalsIgnoreCase**, as in:

  ```
  if (reply.equals("go")) {
      // etc...
  ```

- The input of **int** and **double** items uses strings, and is intricate. Follow our examples carefully.

- The final parameter of **substring** needs care. It indicates the position one beyond the item to be extracted.

- A **StringIndexOutOfBoundsException** message will direct you to a line of your program in which one of the index parameters is negative, or attempts to access a character beyond the end of the string.

Grammar spot

The **String** class methods require us to provide a string to be operated on, as in:

```
String s = "demo";
int n = s.length();
```

Note that we can supply a literal string, or a method call which returns a string, as in:

```
n = "another demo".length();
n = s.substring(0, 2).length();
```

New language elements

- The **char** primitive (built-in) type.
- The \ as the escape character.

Summary

- Instances of the class **String** contain a sequence of characters. The first character is at position **0**.

- **String** instances can be declared and created by, for example:

      String name = "a sequence of chars";

- The most useful methods for string manipulation are:

  - **Comparing strings**

        equals
        equalsIgnoreCase
        compareTo

  - **Amending strings**

        replace
        toLowerCase
        toUpperCase
        trim

  - **Examining strings**

        length
        substring
        charAt
        indexOf
        lastIndexOf
        endsWith
        StringTokenizer (class)

  - **Conversion**

        toString
        parseInt
        parseDouble

  (along with the **Double** and **Integer** wrapper classes).

Exercises

15.1   Write a program which inputs two strings from text fields, and which joins them together. Show the resulting string in a text field.

15.2   Write a program which inputs one string and determines whether or not it is a palindrome. A palindrome reads the same backwards and forwards, so **"abba"** is a palindrome.

15.3 Write a program to input a string which can be a **double** or an **int**. Display the type of the number. Assume that a **double** contains a decimal point.

15.4 Modify the Frasier program to make it more human, by adding more variation to the replies.

15.5 Write a program which generates Java code for a **JButton** instance. Provide two text fields, where the user enters the name of the required button and its caption (without quotes). A button-click should initiate the generating process. For output, use two text areas:

■ the first one should display the appropriate **private** declarations;

■ the second one should display the code which creates the buttons, adds it to the window, and registers for action events.

Recall that the user can copy from the text areas, and paste the code into a program they are creating. Ensure that several buttons can be specified, with the created code being appended to the text areas.

15.6 Enhance Exercise 15.5 with a third text area containing the text of an **actionPerformed** method. This should hold a series of **if** statements for identifying which button was clicked.

15.7 Write a program which allows calculations to be entered into a text field, of the form:

```
123 + 45
6783 - 5
```

(i.e. two integers with + or − between them, spaces separating items) and which displays the result of the calculation in a second text field.

15.8 Extend Exercise 15.7 so that input of the form:

```
12 + 345 - 44 - 23 - 57 + 2345
```

can be handled. Assume that the user will make no errors.

   Hint: the pattern of such input is an initial number, followed by any number of operator/number pairs. Use **StringTokenizer**. Your program should handle the initial number, then loop to handle the following pairs.

15.9 Extend Exercise 15.7 so that input can take two forms:

```
setm 2 426
12 + m2
```

The **setm** instruction is followed by two numbers. The first one refers to a memory store numbered from **0** to **9**, and the second one is a number which is to be stored in the memory. Calculations can now be done using integers as earlier, and also memory names. The above calculation results in **438**. (Hint: use an **int** array to represent the memory.) Extend your program so that the following forms are processed:

```
m3 = 12 + m5 - 328 - m7
display m3
```

15.10 Write a program which stores integers as strings, up to a digit length of 50. It should allow the input of two such strings, and provide buttons to select addition or subtraction. (Hint: recall how you were taught to add numbers by hand.) Provide multiply and divide buttons, and implement these features by repeated addition or subtraction.

Answer to self-test question

15.1 The value of **s** is `sition`.

CHAPTER
16

Exceptions

This chapter explains:

- what an exception is;
- why exceptions are useful;
- the Java exception facilities.

Introduction

The term 'exception' is used in Java to convey the idea that something has gone wrong – in other words, an error has occurred. It is an 'exceptional circumstance'. Note that we mean exception in the sense of unusual, rather than wonderful! As you will be aware from your use of computers, there are a variety of circumstances in which software can go wrong, but good-quality software should cope with predictable problems in a satisfactory way. For example, here are some awkward situations involving a typical word processor, with possible (sometimes unsatisfactory) outcomes:

- The system invites you to type a font size as a number, and you type a name. The system could quit and return you to the operating system, it could ignore your input and leave the font size as it was, or it could display a helpful message and invite you to try again.

- You attempt to load a file which cannot be found on disk. The responses could be similar to the previous case.

- You attempt to print a file, but your printer is out of paper. Again, this can be predicted, and software can be written to take sensible actions. However, this depends on the printer making its current state available to the software. In actual printers, the software can examine various status bits which indicate out of paper, on/offline, paper misfeed, etc.

16.1 In the above cases, decide on the best course of action the word processor should take.

Let us look at why we need some form of error notification, and how it might be provided.

When we build software and hardware systems, much of them comes as pre-packaged items, e.g. circuit boards, Java classes and methods. To simplify the design process it is essential to regard these items as encapsulated – we don't want to be bothered with how they work internally, but it is vital that the components which we use can inform our software about error situations. The software can then be set up to detect such notification and to take alternative action. But what action to take? This is the difficult bit! Complex systems consist of a hierarchy of methods – some exceptions can be handled locally in the method in which they occur, but some more serious cases may need to be passed upstairs to higher-level methods. It depends on the nature of the error. In short, there are different categories of error, which may need to be handled in different places.

Here is an analogy which illustrates this. Imagine an organization. The managing director starts things happening by giving the managers some instructions. In turn, they might instruct programmers and technicians. But things can go wrong. Here are two cases:

■ A printer runs out of paper. Normally, the technician handles it. In the case that the organization is out of paper, a manager might need to be informed.

■ A technician trips over a cable and breaks a leg. Exceptions in this category (which might result in legal action etc.) should be handled by the managing director.

The analogy is that each person doing a job is a method. The job was initiated by someone superior to them. When errors occur, there really needs to be a plan in place stating who handles a particular type of error. The exception facilities of Java allow us to set this up.

As we said, things go wrong. But do we need a special facility for errors? Surely our `if` statement will do? We could imagine code of this form:

```
if (something wrong)
    handle the problem;
else
    handle the normal situation;
```

Here we have used a mixture of English and Java to convey the main point. However, if we have a series of method calls, any of which could go wrong, the logic becomes complex and can swamp the normal case. The initially simple flow of:

```
doA();
doB();
doC();
```

would become:

```
doA();
if (doA went wrong)
    handle the doA problem;
else
    doB();
    if (doB went wrong)
        handle the doB problem;
    else
        doC();
        if (doC went wrong)
            handle the doC problem;
    else
etc...
```

The error cases (which we hope won't happen very often) dominate the logic, and this complexity can make programmers shy away from taking them on. In fact, we will see that the Java exception facilities allow us to stick to the coding for the normal case, and to handle exceptions in a separate area of the program.

The above **if**-based scheme has a further drawback in Java. Recall that methods can have input parameters and can return a single result. What if a method already returns a result as part of its job? It cannot return an additional error indication value easily. We would be forced into returning special values, such as **-1** or a zero-length string. Such an approach is not general.

● Exceptions and objects

What kind of item allows the programmer to indicate that an error has happened and allows the error to be detected in another region of the program? For the beginner, it is tempting (but wrong) to assume that this might be done by using **boolean** variables, in the form of:

```
boolean errorHappened = false;

...code which affects errorCase

if(errorHappened == true) {
    handle problem...
```

However, this is not how errors are indicated in Java. Instead of using variables, we use an object approach. When we want to indicate an exception, we use **new** to create an instance of an appropriate exception class. Another region of the program can then check for its existence. To summarize, an instance of an exception class is created to indicate that an error has happened.

When to use exceptions

Exceptions provide a kind of control structure – so when should we use them instead of `if` or `while`?

Obviously, if we are using provided classes which have been written to produce exceptions, then we need to handle them. But consider this situation: we have to write a program to add up a series of positive numbers, to be typed in by the user. To indicate the end of the sequence, `-1` will be entered. Is the `-1` an exception? No – it is expected as part of the normal input. A similar situation occurs when encountering the end of the file when reading a file. This should not be regarded as an exception. To return to our number problem, the correct solution (in informal English/Java) takes the form:

```
get number;
while (number >= 0) {
    sum = sum + number;
    get number;
}
```

In short, we use the exception-handling facilities for errors rather than predictable normal cases.

The jargon of exceptions

Java has its own terminology for exceptions. Exceptions are indicated by being thrown, and are detected elsewhere by being caught. Java has **throws**, **throw**, **try** and **catch** keywords to carry out these tasks. Initially, we will look at the simplest case of catching an exception thrown by a library class.

A `try-catch` example

Here we present a simple number-doubling program which invites the user to enter an integer into a text field, and then either displays the doubled value in another text field, or displays a message dialog if a non-integer has been entered. If the input string contains a non-digit, the **parseInt** method will not be able to process it, and will indicate this situation by throwing an exception. We will look at the new features introduced in this particular program, then move on to general cases.

```
import java.awt.*;
import java.awt.event.*;
import javax.swing.*;
```

```java
class ExceptionDemo1 extends JFrame implements ActionListener {

    private JTextField inputField;
    private JTextField resultField;
    private JLabel resultLabel, inputLabel;
    private JButton doubleButton;

    public static void main(String[] args) {
        ExceptionDemo1 frame = new ExceptionDemo1();
        frame.setSize(300, 150);
        frame.createGUI();
        frame.show();
    }

    private void createGUI() {
        setDefaultCloseOperation(EXIT_ON_CLOSE);
        Container window = getContentPane();
        window.setLayout(new FlowLayout());

        inputLabel = new JLabel("Integer: ");
        window.add(inputLabel);

        inputField = new JTextField(10);
        window.add(inputField);

        doubleButton = new JButton("Double it !");
        window.add(doubleButton);
        doubleButton.addActionListener(this);

        resultLabel = new JLabel("Doubled value is: ");
        window.add(resultLabel);

        resultField = new JTextField(10);
        window.add(resultField);
    }

    public void actionPerformed(ActionEvent event) {
        if (event.getSource() == doubleButton) {
            resultField.setText("");
            try{
                int number = Integer.parseInt
                    (inputField.getText());
                resultField.setText(Integer.toString(2*number));
            }
            catch (NumberFormatException errorObject) {
                JOptionPane.showMessageDialog(null,
                    "Error in number: retype");
            }
        }
    }
}
```

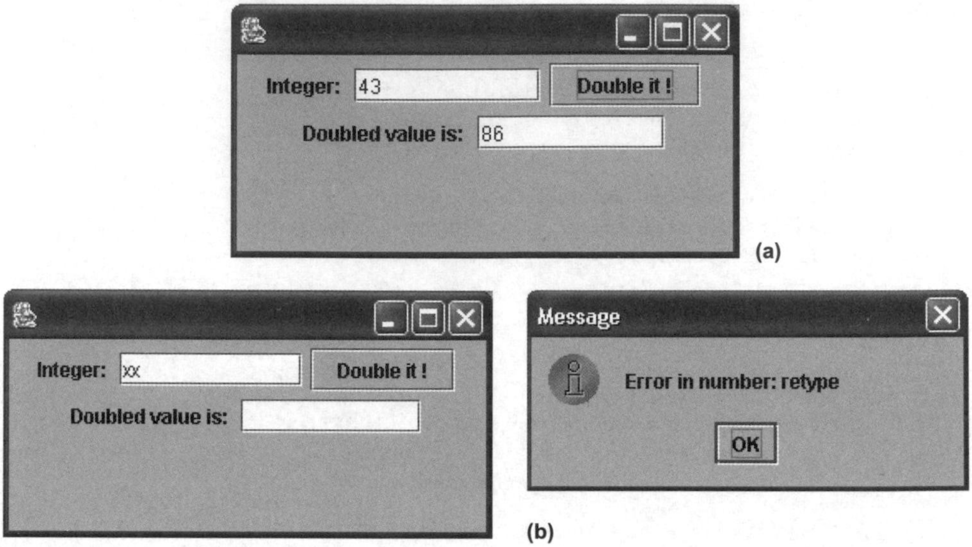

Figure 16.1 (a) Screenshot of `ExceptionDemo1` (no error); (b) Screenshot of `ExceptionDemo1` (with a message).

Figures 16.1(a) and (b) show a run with correct input and a run with the exception handling in use.

The key part of this program is:

```
try{
    int number = Integer.parseInt
        (inputField.getText());
    resultField.setText(Integer.toString(2*number));
}
catch (NumberFormatException errorObject) {
    JOptionPane.showMessageDialog(null,
        "Error in number: retype");
}
```

This is where we say 'if something has gone wrong inside **parseInt**, handle it!'

There is a new statement here, which is basically a control structure. It takes the form:

```
try {
    a series of statements;
}
catch (SomeException errorObject) {
    handle the exception;
}
```

In Java, a group of statements enclosed in { } is known as a 'block'. We talk about the 'try block' and the 'catch block'.

The concept is that we instruct Java to try to execute a block of statements. If it executes without producing an exception, the `catch` block is ignored, and execution continues beneath the `catch` block. However, if an exception is produced, we can specify that the `catch` block executes by stating the class of exception that we wish to catch. In our example, we consulted the library documentation for `parseInt`, and found that an exception of class `NumberFormatException` can be produced, i.e. thrown. If another class of exception occurs, our catch will not be executed, and Java will attempt to find a catch which specifies this exception type. We will describe this process in more detail below. In our example, we have:

```
catch (NumberFormatException errorObject) {
```

which is rather like the declaration of a method. Java deposits an object of type `NumberFormatException` in the parameter, which we chose to name as `errorObject`. We could make use of it if required, by using `toString`, as in:

```
catch (NumberFormatException errorObject) {
    JOptionPane.showMessageDialog(null,
        "Error: " + errorObject.toString());
}
```

The `toString` method returns the name of the exception together with a possible additional message clarifying the exception. The above statements produce the message:

```
Error: java.lang.NumberFormatException
```

After the `catch` block executes, execution continues beneath the `catch` block. In many cases, because methods deal with one particular task which cannot sensibly continue after an exception related to that task, it is common to return from the method, as in:

```
private void aMethod() {
    try {
    // some code
    }
    catch(Exception errorObject) {
        // handle it
    }
}           // return
```

In our example program, this is just what is required – the exception handler displays an error message and then continues, returning from the method. The user can then enter a new number into the text field.

● try and scopes

As we stated above, when a `try` block produces an exception, its execution terminates – it is abandoned. A consequence of this is that any variables declared within it become inaccessible and, in particular, they cannot be used in the `catch` block, even when it is in the same method. This can be a problem if we want to use those variables to produce a specific error message. For example, we might want to display an offending string if it could not be converted to an integer. Fortunately, the solution is simple: any variables that are required in both the **try** block and the **catch** block must be declared outside the **try** block. We put:

```
String s;           // available in both the try and the catch
try {
    // code involving s
}
catch (Exception errorObject) {
    JOptionPane.showMessageDialog(null, "Error: s is "+ s);
}
```

The alternative is the following, which will not compile. The variable **s** is local to the **try** block only, not the **catch** block as well.

```
try {
    String s;
    // code involving s
}
catch (Exception errorObject) {
    JOptionPane.showMessageDialog(null, "Error: s is "+ s); // No
}
```

SELF-TEST QUESTION

16.2   Investigate the names of any exceptions that the methods of the **Integer** class might throw.

● The search for a catcher

What if the program doesn't catch a thrown exception? The precise rules for this depend on the class of exception, as we will see later. The basic principle is based on the fact that all programs above a handful of lines are made up of methods. Thus, at run-time, an initial method is called, which itself calls other methods, which in their turn. . . . The run-time method usage is hierarchical (a top-level method calls lower-level methods, etc.) and this pattern of calls is unpredictable before run-time – because the decision on whether a method is to be called or not might be part of an **if**, based on input data.

Imagine that **methodA** calls **methodB** which calls **methodC**. If an exception occurs in **methodC**, the search for an appropriate catch begins in **methodC**. If one is not found, the search moves to **methodB**. If **methodB** does not provide a catch, then the search moves up to **methodA**, and if the top-level method does not provide a catch, an exception message is displayed on the screen.

The failure to catch an exception does not always mean that the program will terminate after the display of an exception message. It depends on the nature of the program. Here are the cases:

- If the program is a console application with no GUI (as we discuss in Chapter 17), then the program does in fact terminate.

- If the program has a GUI and the exception happens when the GUI is being created (e.g. when components are being added to the screen) the program also terminates. A typical cause of this is the omission of the instantiation of a component with **new**. Once the GUI program is up and running, exceptions do **not** terminate the program. It continues, but its operation cannot be relied on. For example, incorrect return values may have been passed back from methods.

Throwing – an introduction

Most of the methods you write will not need to create and throw exceptions. Rather, you will mainly be concerned with catching exceptions thrown from library methods. However, for completeness, we will illustrate the way that many exceptions are thrown. Recall our use of **parseInt** in the first example. You don't need to examine the source code of the libraries – the documentation will suffice – but here is part of its code, from the class **Integer**:

```
public static int parseInt(String s)
                        throws NumberFormatException {

    ...code for the method...

    // error is detected:
    throw new NumberFormatException();
    ...etc
}
```

Note the use of **throws** in the header of the method, and the use of **throw** in the body of the method. The **throw** statement is often executed as the result of an **if**: it causes the current method to be abandoned, and starts a search for a matching **catch**. When you set about using provided methods (and you should always search for existing code before writing your own) you will examine a Java library reference manual, whether in book form, in your development environment or on a web site. The information that such documentation will provide is:

- a short description of the purpose of the method;
- its name, parameter types and return type;
- the classes of any exceptions that it may throw.

Our next step in preparing to use a method is to consider in more detail any exceptions it may throw.

Exception classes

Here we will explore the varieties of exception classes that are provided in the Java library. Basically, the library provides us with a list of exception class names, but if there is no suitably named exception we can also create our own. We will not cover the process of inventing new exceptions, trusting that you will be able to find a suitably named existing one.

Inheritance is used to classify errors into different types – for example, there are exceptions that are classified as 'big trouble' (such as **OutOfMemoryError**), and exceptions that are less serious (such as **NumberFormatException**). There are many pre-declared exception classes, but the main ones are shown in Figure 16.2, which shows their inheritance structure, i.e. class hierarchy.

The library documentation tells you the type of exceptions that a method may throw. To fit it into the above hierarchy you may have to work up the tree, by looking up the parent (i.e. the class that the exception extends) and the parent of the parent. For example, our familiar **parseInt** method, of the **Integer** class, is specified as throwing a **NumberFormatException**. From Figure 16.2, we see that this is derived from **IllegalArgumentException**, which is within the unchecked class **RuntimeException**.

From the position of an exception in the class hierarchy, it is possible to figure out how it can be processed. Basically, all exceptions are under the class **Throwable**. There are two main subclasses: **Error** and **Exception**. The **Error** class has exceptions which are serious but difficult to fix up – you will not be concerned with their catching. The class **Exception** is more significant. Most of the exceptions within this class are *checked*, meaning that you have to deal with them – your program will not compile if you ignore them. We have put these in the box of Figure 16.2 to show their importance. The odd one out is the class **RuntimeException**, which is unchecked – your program will compile even if you ignore this. We will examine these concepts in more detail below.

Compilation and checked exceptions

The compiler makes stringent checks on the matching of **throw** and **try–catch** statements. There are three cases:

- A method states that it can throw a class of exception that must be acknowledged by the caller of the method – either by catching it, or stating that it can be thrown – i.e.

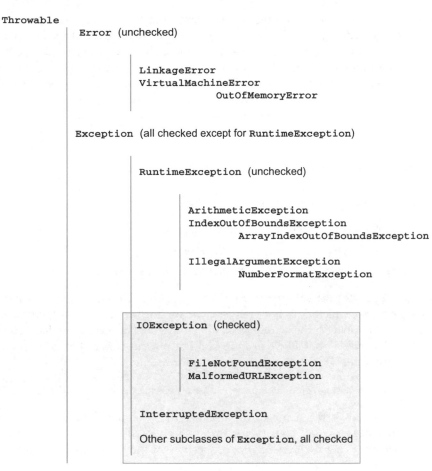

Figure 16.2 Inheritance structure of the main exceptions. The major checked exceptions have been enclosed in a box.

propagated upwards. If this is omitted, a compilation error will result. In other words, some methods which you use can force you to use **try–catch**.

- A method states that it can throw a class of exception that need not be handled. It is your choice whether you use **try–catch** or not. If you don't handle such an exception, the exception is not ignored – it gets passed upward to the method which called your method (and then to the method which called that method, etc.), in an attempt to find the first matching **catch**. A match occurs if a **catch** specifies the particular exception, or any class superior to the exception. If no appropriate **catch** exists, an exception message will be displayed by the Java system.

- The final case involves the throwing of exceptions which are not stated in a method's header. Here is the reasoning: the use of (for example) integer arithmetic and arrays is widespread throughout the Java library and the code that you will write. Such code can produce errors (e.g. `ArithmeticException` in the case of integer divide by zero, and `ArrayIndexOutOfBoundsException` in the class `IndexOutOfBoundsException`, when an array index value is outside the declared range of an array). Both of these are in the `RuntimeException` class. Because many methods can produce these situations, they are not declared, and it is the programmer's decision on whether to use `try–catch` or not.

● Catching – the common cases

We will look at the possible alternatives with three common cases:

■ the checked exception `FileNotFoundException`;

■ the unchecked exception `NumberFormatException`;

■ the unchecked exception `ArrayIndexOutOfBoundsException`.

A `FileNotFoundException` (in the class `IOException`) is produced when a program tries to access a file which does not exist – maybe we got the name wrong, or are in the wrong folder, or maybe the wrong disk was inserted. The details of file access are covered in Chapter 17, but all we need to know at present is that, before reading data from a file, we 'open' it with a statement of the form:

```
inFile = new BufferedReader(new FileReader("c:\\myfile.txt"));
```

where `myfile.txt` is the name of the file that the program expects to be present. However, the `FileReader` constructor throws a checked exception which we must deal with: we can either use `try–catch`, or specify that the method which contains the above statement can throw the exception.

In programs where the file name is entered by a user, the first approach is best – we deal with the exception immediately by asking the user to make another choice, rather than complicating things for other methods. The approach is basically like our `NumberFormatException` number-doubling example. We put:

```
try {
    inFile = new BufferedReader(new
        FileReader("c:\\myfile.txt"));
}
catch (FileNotFoundException errorObject) {
    JOptionPane.showMessageDialog(null,
        "Error: missing file-try again!");
}
```

The second approach is to pass the exception up to the calling method. We create a method:

```
private void openFile() throws IOException {
    inFile = new BufferedReader(new
        FileReader("c:\\myfile.txt"));
}
```

With this approach, the caller of `openFile` must either catch or pass it upwards.

Our second example, involving `NumberFormatException` thrown by `parseInt`, is basically similar; we either catch, or can pass the exception up. The difference from the previous `FileNotFoundException` case is that the compiler does not force us to handle the exception, because `NumberFormatException` (in the class `RuntimeException`) is unchecked.

What options do we have? The simplest option is to ignore the exception intentionally. The compiler will not force us to check it. However, the only time it would be sensible to do this is when we know that the string to be converted to an integer is error free. (Maybe it has been input from a correct file, or generated internally.) For interactive GUI-based software, though, it is essential that we catch potential input errors, as we did in the number-doubling program.

As with our file exception we could specify that the method which calls `parseInt` could throw `NumberFormatException`, hence forcing any calling methods to catch or explicitly pass it upwards. There is no advantage in doing this, and this approach is not illustrated.

Our final `ArrayIndexOutOfBoundsException` example is not so straightforward. Catching it is fine, but then what? The above examples involved user input, and could be fixed by inviting another attempt from the user. Here is a program fragment with an exception:

```
int a[] = new int[10];        // 0 to 9 inclusive
for(int n = 0; n <= 10; n++) {
    a[n] = 0;
}
```

The `n <= 10` produces a loop from `0` to `10` inclusive, and thus attempts to access `a[10]` – we should have put `n<10`. As with all exceptions in the `RuntimeException` class, it involves a programming mistake, which needs fixing by debugging and recompiling.

So what do we do with a `RuntimeException`? In the vast majority of cases, we want the origin of the exception to be indicated, so it can be tracked down and fixed. This is easily done by ignoring the exceptions, which the compiler allows us to do with the `RuntimeException` class, because it is unchecked. The exception is passed upwards and a message will be displayed, showing the name of the exception followed by a trace of the method calls, with line numbers relating to the Java source code.

We have now covered exceptions in sufficient detail for the beginner, who could sensibly stop here. The following is for the more experienced programmer.

● Using the exception class structure

Figure 16.2 shows the inheritance structure of exceptions. By referring to a parent class, we can catch any exception of that class. For example, we might put:

```
try {
    // some code
}
catch (Exception errorObject) {
    // handle it...
}
```

which would catch **RuntimeException**, **IOException**, etc., because **Exception** is their superclass. If we wanted to treat individual exceptions specially, but still catch all of a particular class, we can put:

```
try {
    // some code
}
catch (IOException errorObject) {
    // handle IO problem
}
catch (Exception errorObject) {
    // handle any others
}
```

The Java compiler requires that you put the more general class at the end. Reversing the order of the above two catches would produce a compilation error.

Programming principles

■ When writing general-purpose methods (where their future use might be unknown) you should throw exceptions rather than terminating the program, concealing errors or producing wrong results.

■ An exception changes the order in which statements are obeyed; hence it is a form of control structure. Exceptions should not be used where conventional control structures can conveniently deal with the problem.

Programming pitfalls

- Failing to acknowledge a checked exception produces a compilation error. You must either catch an exception locally, or specify that your method throws it.

- Allowing an exception to be thrown from a method, when it can sensibly be handled locally.

- Declaring an item in a **try** block and attempting to refer to it in a **catch** block. Such items must be declared above (outside) the **try** block.

- Attempting to catch and process the **RuntimeException** class. In most cases, there is little that can be done. Catching such errors can conceal them, when instead the programmer needs to know about them.

Grammar spot

The basic **try–catch** form is:

```
try {
    a series of statements;
}
catch (SomeException errorObject) {
    handle the exception;
}
```

New language elements

- **try**
- **catch**
- the exception class hierarchy.

Summary

- An exception is an unusual situation.

- Exceptions are instances of classes, created by **new**.

- When an exceptional situation is detected, an exception is thrown.

- **try–catch** blocks are used. We surround code which could throw an exception by **try { }** and supply a matching **catch** block.

- A checked exception is one which must be acknowledged.

- The inheritance tree of the class **Throwable** (Figure 16.2) is crucial. It shows you the main exceptions you will have to deal with and which class they are in.

- Exceptions within the **RuntimeException** class are difficult to fix up, and in many cases can be intentionally ignored. Any other exceptions underneath the **Exception** class are checked, and must be dealt with.

Exercises

16.1 Write a program which provides two text fields for integer inputs **a** and **b**. Display the result of **a / b**. Now incorporate exception handling for the text fields: display a message if non-integer input is used.

16.2 Alter Exercise 16.1 so it handles **double** values instead.

16.3 Write a program which calculates one year's interest on an initial amount. The user inputs the initial amount and the interest per year as a percentage value (**double** values). Provide exception handling for non-numeric input.

16.4 Refer to Exercise 16.3. Accomplish the same task, but write a method:

```
private double interest(double initial,
                        double perYear)
```

which returns the interest. Add exception handling to the method to check that all the values are positive. The method header should use **throws** with a **NumberFormatException**, and the body should incorporate a **throw** statement.

16.5 If you know the length of the three sides of a triangle, the area can be calculated by:

```
area = Math.sqrt(s * (s - a) * (s - b) * (s - c));
```

where

```
s = (a + b + c) / 2;
```

Write a method for calculating and returning the area. Make it throw an exception when the three lengths cannot form a triangle.

Write a calling method for your area method, which catches your exception.

16.6 Write a program which inputs a string from a text field, representing a date in the form MM/DD/YY (e.g. 03/02/01). Use **StringTokenizer** to split it up, and produce an error message if an item is non-numeric, missing completely or specifies an impossible date. Ignore leap years.

Answers to self-test questions

16.1 In the first two cases, quitting the program would be a poor course of action. A more useful response is to display some sort of error indication, and allow the user either to have another go or to abandon the selection of the item.

In the third case, the complication is that the printer may run out of paper part-way through a print. The user needs to be informed of this, and may be provided with options to abandon the print request or, assuming that paper has been loaded, continue printing from a particular page.

16.2 A search of the documentation reveals that **NumberFormatException** is the only exception.

Files and console applications

This chapter explains:

- what a text file is;
- how to read and write data to files;
- how to manipulate folder paths and file names;
- how to write console applications.

● Introduction

You already know a considerable amount about files, in the sense of having used an editor to create Java source files, and an operating system to view a hierarchical structure of directories (folders). Here we will look at the nature of the information you may choose to store in files, and how you can write programs to manipulate files. Initially, let us clarify the difference between RAM and file storage devices (e.g. disks, hard-disk drives and CD-ROMs). Storage capacity is measured in bytes in all these cases. There are several major differences between RAM and file storage:

- The time to access an item in RAM is much faster. The cost of RAM is higher (megabyte for megabyte).
- Data in RAM is temporary – it is erased when power is switched off. File storage devices can hold data permanently.
- RAM is used to store programs as they execute. They are copied from a file storage device immediately before execution.

The capacity of file storage devices is higher. CD-ROMs have a capacity of around 650 Mbyte (megabytes), and DVDs (Digital Versatile Disks) have a capacity of 4.7 Gbyte (gigabytes, 1024 Mbyte). Both CD-ROMs and DVDs have writable versions.

Typical hard drives hold 100 Gbyte, and the lowly floppy disk holds 1.44 Mbyte – though this is still useful for Java source and class files. However, technology is evolving rapidly – the race is to create cheap, fast storage devices that modern computer software requires, especially in the area of high-quality still images, moving images and sound.

● File access: stream or random?

Java has over 20 classes for file access, each with its own particular set of methods. But with such a wide choice, which classes should we choose? A major decision involves the choice between stream access and random access. When we use stream access on a file, we must treat the file as a sequence of items which must be processed one after another, starting with the first one. For many tasks, this is completely appropriate. If we use random access, we can skip immediately to a particular byte position in a file. In certain applications (such as databases), this can speed up processing, but is also more intricate to program. In reality, you will be more likely to use a database class library rather than code your own low-level disk access. For this reason, we will focus on streams.

● The essentials of streams

First, let us introduce the jargon, which is similar in most programming languages. If we wish to process the data in an existing file, we must:

1. Open the file.
2. Read or input the data item by item into variables.
3. Close the file when we have finished with it.

To transfer some data from variables into a file, we must:

1. Open the file.
2. Output (or write) our items in the required sequence.
3. Close the file when we have finished with it.

Note that, when reading from a file, all we can do is read the next item in the file. If, for example, we want to examine the last item, we would have to code a loop to read each preceding item in turn, until the required item is reached. For many tasks, it is convenient to visualize a file as a series of lines of text, each made up of a number of characters. Each line is terminated by an end-of-line character. We shall make use of the Java classes that allow us to access a file line by line. A benefit of this approach is that it is simple to transfer files between applications. For example, you could create a file by running a Java program, and then load the file into a word processor, text editor or email package.

● The Java I/O classes

Predictably, the stream classes are organized hierarchically. Here are the most useful input classes:

```
Reader
    BufferedReader
    InputStreamReader
        FileReader
Writer
    PrintWriter
        FileWriter
```

The **Reader** and **Writer** classes are at the top of an inheritance tree, and are extended by a number of character-based classes. For files, we will make use of the **BufferedReader** and **PrintWriter** classes to read and write lines of text, and for non-file input (from keyboard and web pages) we will also use **InputStreamReader**. As you will see in our examples, programs which use files should import **java.io.***.

Incidentally, the use of the term 'buffer' means that behind the scenes the software reads a large chunk of data from the slow file storage device (e.g. CD-ROM or hard drive), storing it in high-speed RAM. Successive calls of methods which need to read a small amount of data from the file storage device can swiftly obtain the data from RAM. Thus, a buffer acts as a cushion between the storage device and the program.

● The BufferedReader and PrintWriter classes

To read and write lines of text, we will use:

- The **readLine** method of **BufferedReader**. This reads a whole line of text into a string. If we need to split the line into separate parts, we can use the **StringTokenizer** class, described in Chapter 15.

- The **PrintWriter** class. This has two main methods: **print** and **println**. Note the lower-case **l**. These methods write a string to a file, and **println** adds the end-of-line character after the string. If we need to build a line from separate parts, we can use the string operator **+** to join substrings.

● File output

Here, we will present a program which allows you to type in a file name, type some text, and then save the text in a file. The basic elements of the user interface are:

- a text field to accept the file name;
- a scrollable text area to accept your text (and remember that a text area allows cut, copy and paste);
- a 'save' button to initiate the transfer of text from the text area to the file.

Here is the complete application. Figure 17.1 shows it running.

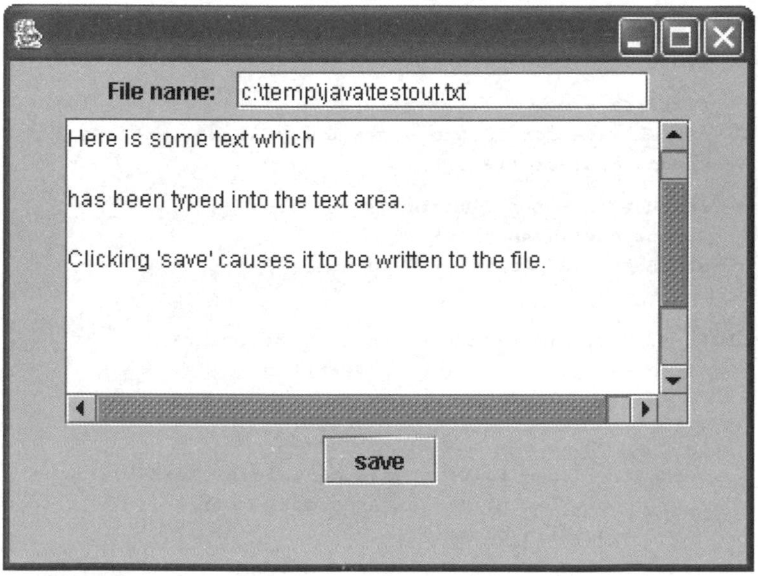

Figure 17.1 Screenshot of the `FileOutputDemo` program.

```
import java.awt.*;
import java.awt.event.*;
import javax.swing.*;
import java.util.*;
import java.io.*;

class FileOutputDemo extends JFrame
implements ActionListener {
    private JTextArea textArea;
    private JButton saveButton;
    private JTextField nameField;
    private JLabel nameLabel;
    private PrintWriter outFile;
```

```
    public static void main(String [] args) {
        FileOutputDemo frame = new FileOutputDemo();
        frame.setSize(400, 300);
        frame.createGUI();
        frame.show();
    }

    private void createGUI() {
        setDefaultCloseOperation(EXIT_ON_CLOSE);
        Container window = getContentPane();
        window.setLayout(new FlowLayout());

        nameLabel = new JLabel("File name: ");
        window.add(nameLabel);

        nameField = new JTextField(20);
        window.add(nameField);

        textArea = new JTextArea(10,30);
        JScrollPane scrollPane = new JScrollPane(textArea);
        window.add(scrollPane);

        saveButton = new JButton("save");
        window.add(saveButton);
        saveButton.addActionListener(this);
    }

    public void actionPerformed(ActionEvent event) {
        if (event.getSource() == saveButton) {
            try{

                outFile = new PrintWriter(
                    new FileWriter(nameField.getText()), true);
                outFile.print(textArea.getText());
                outFile.close();
            }
            catch (IOException e) {
                JOptionPane.showMessageDialog(null,
                    "File Error: "+ e.toString());
            }
        }
    }
}
```

Firstly, we declare:

```
    private PrintWriter outFile;
```

We could have made this local to **actionPerformed**, but, in larger programs, several methods might need file access. Next, we create an instance:

```
    outFile = new PrintWriter(
        new FileWriter(nameField.getText()), true);
```

This seems rather longwinded. Basically, it opens the file whose name was entered. As you will see from Figure 17.1, we chose the file named `testout.txt`, in the `temp` directory on the `c:` drive. The \ is used to separate directories and file names. On Unix and GNU/Linux operating systems, this separator is /. If the file does not exist, it will be created; if it does exist, it will be overwritten and replaced with its new contents. The detail is that we first construct an instance of `FileWriter`, whose constructor allows us to specify a file name as a string. (The `PrintWriter` class has no such constructor.) Then we create an instance of `PrintWriter`, whose constructor can accept two parameters:

- an instance of `FileWriter`;
- a `boolean` value. If we provide a `true` value, the internal buffer will automatically be written ('flushed') to the file whenever a `println` is called. We have chosen this so-called 'autoflush' option so that the contents of the file are kept relatively up to date. This can assist during debugging. (If we didn't specify this option and the program crashed part-way through, the buffered characters might never reach the file.)

The new instance of `PrintWriter` is then assigned to `outFile`. There are two items, which can be confused initially: one is the name of the file that your operating system uses, and the other is the name of a stream variable within the program – you have free choice of this stream name.

Actually, to write to the stream, we use `print`, as in:

```
outFile.print(textArea.getText());
```

Recall that `getText` fetches the entire string from the text area (which may consist of several lines). We then print it to the file. Finally, we close the file:

```
outFile.close();
```

Creating the output stream with `new` might produce a checked exception, so we have to surround the code with a `try–catch` block, detecting an `IOException` (or a more specific exception which extends it). In addition, many of the I/O classes can throw exceptions when reading or writing, so we have extended the range of the `try` block to cover the calls of `print` and `close`.

Unfortunately, we are guilty of ignoring a special case here: `PrintWriter` is highly unusual because its potential `print` errors can only be detected by calling a method known as `checkError`, rather than by catching an exception. We should really put:

```
outFile.print(inputTextArea.getText());
if (outFile.checkError())      // true if error
    JOptionPane.showMessageDialog(null,
        "Error during writing to file.");
```

However, because very few exceptions can occur when writing strings to a file (filling the disk is a possibility) we shall intentionally ignore the `PrintWriter/checkError` special case, and emphasize a pattern which fits the overwhelming majority of the I/O classes.

In summary, when the user clicks on the 'save' button, the program:

1. Opens the selected file.
2. Obtains a string from the text area, which may contain several lines.
3. Outputs (writes) the string to the file.
4. Closes the file.

To verify that the text has been transferred, use a text editor to view the file.

SELF-TEST QUESTION

17.1 Correct the error in this code:

```
private PrintWriter outFile;
outFile = new PrintWriter(nameField.getText()):
```

● File input

Here we will present a program which displays the contents of a file on the screen. The user interface has:

- A scrollable text area to display the text that will be input from the file.
- A text field to accept your file name. Later we will use a file chooser, which allows a user to select a file by browsing and clicking.
- An 'open' button to initiate the transfer of text from the file to the text area.

Here is the complete application. Figure 17.2 shows a run. We entered the same file name as in **FileOutputDemo**, so the text is the same.

```
import java.awt.*;
import java.awt.event.*;
import javax.swing.*;
import java.util.*;
import java.io.*;

class FileInputDemo extends JFrame
    implements ActionListener {

    private JTextArea textArea;
    private JButton openButton;
    private BufferedReader inFile;
    private JTextField nameField;
    private JLabel nameLabel;

    public static void main (String [] args) {
        FileInputDemo frame = new FileInputDemo();
```

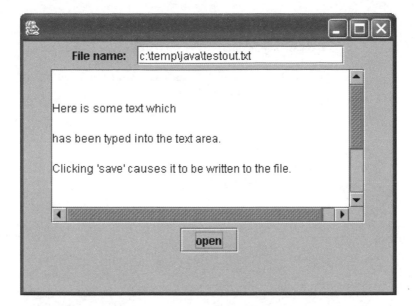

Figure 17.2 Screenshot of the `FileInputDemo` program.

```
        frame.setSize(400, 300);
        frame.createGUI();
        frame.show();
    }

    private void createGUI() {
        setDefaultCloseOperation(EXIT_ON_CLOSE);
        Container window = getContentPane();
        window.setLayout(new FlowLayout());

        nameLabel = new JLabel("File name: ");
        window.add(nameLabel);

        nameField = new JTextField(20);
        window.add(nameField);
        nameField.addActionListener(this);

        textArea = new JTextArea("",10,30);
        JScrollPane scrollPane = new JScrollPane(textArea);
        window.add(scrollPane);

        openButton = new JButton("open");
        window.add(openButton);
        openButton.addActionListener(this);
    }

    public void actionPerformed(ActionEvent event) {
        if (event.getSource() == openButton) {
            try {
```

```
            inFile = new BufferedReader(
                new FileReader(nameField.getText()));
            textArea.setText( ""); // clear the input area
            String line;
            while ( ( line = inFile.readLine()) != null) {
                textArea.append(line+"\n");
            }
            inFile.close();
        }
        catch (IOException e) {
            JOptionPane.showMessageDialog(null,
                "File Error: "+ e.toString());
        }
    }
}
```

We will focus on the use made of files. Firstly, we declare:

```
private BufferedReader inFile;
```

Next, we create an instance:

```
inFile = new BufferedReader(
    new FileReader(nameField.getText()));
```

Then we use **readLine** to input the series of lines in the file, appending each one to our text area. There is one crucial point here: we don't know how many lines are in the file, so we set up a loop which terminates when there is nothing more to read:

```
while ( ( line = inFile.readLine()) != null) {
    textArea.append(line + "\n");
}
inFile.close();
```

The **while** condition is rather unusual, but is commonly used. When **readLine** can't find any more data, it returns **null**, and this is assigned to **line**. However, in Java it is possible to make use of the value assigned to a variable directly, and we do this here. The brackets are essential, to ensure that the assignment is performed before the comparison. We could have put:

```
line = inFile.readLine();
while(line != null) {
    inputTextArea.append(line + "\n");
    line = inFile.readLine();
}
inFile.close();
```

but the condensed version (with its roots in the C language) is the idiom which you will see in most published programs.

In summary, when the user clicks on the 'open' button, the program:

1. inputs a file name from the text field;
2. opens a file with this name;
3. inputs lines from the file and appends them to the text area, as long as the end of the file is not reached;
4. closes the file.

SELF-TEST QUESTIONS

17.2 Explain what would happen in the **FileInputDemo** program if we replaced the line:

```
textArea.append(line + "\n");
```

by:

```
textArea.append(line);
```

17.3 Explain the problem with this code, intended to read every line in a file. Assume that all the variables have been declared:

```
line = inFile.readLine();
while (line != null) {
    textarea.append(line + "\n");
}
```

● File searching

Searching a file for an item that meets some specified criteria is a classic requirement. Here we will construct a program which searches a file of exam marks, which takes the form:

```
J.Doe,   43, 67
D.Bell, 87, 99
K.Bush, 54, 32
etc...
```

We can create this file by writing and running a Java program, or with a text editor. Each line is split into three areas, separated by commas. However, there may be extra spaces. In database terms, such areas are known as fields. The program will allow us to enter a file name, and to enter a student name, which we assume is unique. If the names are not unique, we would have to introduce an extra field to hold a unique identification number for each person. The program will search the file, and display the marks for our chosen student. The code we need to add to our previous file input example is a **while** which terminates when the end of the file is encountered or when the required name is found. We will use a **StringTokenizer** object to allow access to each field in turn from the complete line.

Because there are two ways that the loop can terminate, we introduce an additional variable, **found**, to indicate whether the item was found or not. The informal English/ Java structure of the search is:

```
boolean found = false;
while ((more lines) && (not found)) {
    get first field;
    if (first field matches name) {
        found = true;
        put rest of fields in text fields;
    }
}
```

We have provided a 'search' button, which causes the file to be opened and searched. The user can select any file for searching. We have made the exception handling more specific: a missing file name is indicated, and an error during reading is indicated. Here is the program, which produces the screen of Figure 17.3.

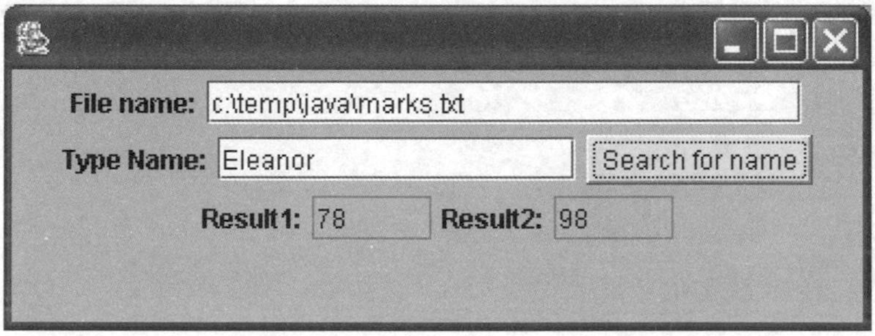

Figure 17.3 Screenshot of the **FileSearch** program.

```
import java.awt.*;
import java.awt.event.*;
import javax.swing.*;
import java.util.*; //StringTokenizer
import java.io.*;

public class FileSearch extends JFrame
    implements ActionListener {

    private BufferedReader inFile;
    private Button searchButton;
    private JTextField result1Field;
```

```
        private JTextField result2Field;
        private JTextField personField;
        private JTextField fileNameField;
        private String fileName;
        private JLabel result1Label, result2Label;
        private JLabel personNameLabel;
        private JLabel fileLabel;

        public static void main (String [ ] args) {
            FileSearch frame = new FileSearch();
            frame.setSize(400, 150);
            frame.createGUI();
            frame.show();
        }

        private void createGUI() {
            setDefaultCloseOperation(EXIT_ON_CLOSE);
            Container window = getContentPane();
            window.setLayout(new FlowLayout());

            fileLabel = new JLabel("File name:");
            window.add(fileLabel);

            fileNameField = new JTextField(25);
            fileNameField.setText("");
            window.add(fileNameField);

            personNameLabel = new JLabel("Type Name:");
            window.add(personNameLabel);

            personField = new JTextField(15);
            personField.setText("");
            window.add(personField);

            searchButton = new Button("Search for name");
            window.add(searchButton);
            searchButton.addActionListener(this);

            result1Label = new JLabel("Result1:");
            window.add(result1Label);

            result1Field = new JTextField(5);
            result1Field.setEditable(false);
            window.add(result1Field);

            result2Label = new JLabel("Result2:");
            window.add(result2Label);

            result2Field= new JTextField(5);
            result2Field.setEditable(false);
            window.add(result2Field);
        }

        public void actionPerformed(ActionEvent evt) {
            if (evt.getSource() == searchButton) {
```

```
        result1Field.setText("");
        result2Field.setText("");
        fileName = fileNameField.getText();
        try {
            inFile = new BufferedReader(
                new FileReader(fileName));
        }
        catch (IOException e) {
            JOptionPane.showMessageDialog(null,
            "Can't find file: " + fileNameField.getText());
            return;
        }

        // now read the file
        try {
            String line;
            boolean found = false;
            while ((( line = inFile.readLine() ) != null)
                && (! found)) {
                // tokens split on commas, spaces
                StringTokenizer tokens = new
                    StringTokenizer(line, ",");
                String nameInFile = tokens.nextToken();
                if (personField.getText().equals(nameInFile)) {
                    found = true;
                    result1Field.setText(tokens.nextToken());
                    result2Field.setText(tokens.nextToken());
                }
            }
            inFile.close();
        }
        catch (IOException e) {
            JOptionPane.showMessageDialog(null,
                "Error reading file "+ fileName +
                ": "+ e.toString());
        }
    }
  }
 }
```

SELF-TEST QUESTION

17.4 Modify the **FileSearch** program so that it allows the user to type a name in upper or lower case (i.e. so that **john** matches **John** or **JOHN**). Use **equalsIgnoreCase** from the **String** class.

The `File` class

This class provides facilities to manipulate file paths and directories (folders) as a whole. It is not concerned with accessing the data within files. You can make use of the `File` class without making use of stream I/O, and vice versa. In each case, though, you need to import `java.io.*`.

Firstly, we will make a brief detour into directory structures. As you know, operating systems provide a hierarchical structure, with a path through such a structure of the form:

```
c:\temp\java\demo.txt
```

This is a Windows-style path, on the `c:` drive, with `\` used as a separator. On a Unix or GNU/Linux system, the separator is `/`.

The above path is absolute – it starts from the very top of the directory structure and leads you to the file.

Now we will examine a program (named **`FileClassDemo`**) which uses various methods of the `File` class. We will make use of the above directory structure. To obtain the same results as the code we show, use your file manager (e.g. Windows Explorer on a Windows system) and create a new directory named **`java`** within the `c:\temp` directory. Then, use a text editor and key in a few lines of text. Save the file as **`demo.txt`** in the **`java`** directory.

The **`FileClassDemo`** program only needs a single 'start' button, so a screenshot is not given. Here is the event-handling code:

```
if (event.getSource() == startButton) {
    File myFile = new File("c:\\temp\\java\\demo.txt");
    String parent = myFile.getParent();
    JOptionPane.showMessageDialog(null,
                            "Parent is: " + parent);

    String absolute = myFile.getAbsolutePath();
    JOptionPane.showMessageDialog(null,
                    "Absolute path is: " + absolute);
    boolean isThere = myFile.exists();

    String name = myFile.getName();
    JOptionPane.showMessageDialog(null,
                            "Name is: "+ name);

    boolean checkDirectory = myFile.isDirectory();
    long myLength = myFile.length();
    String [] allFiles = myFile.list();
}
```

and here is an explanation of the methods of the `File` class which were used.

Initially, we can construct an instance of the class `File` by supplying a string. Once this instance has been created, we can use it. Here is the instance:

```
File myFile = new File("c:\\temp\\java\\demo.txt");
```

Alternatively, we might use a text field as before, or a file chooser which allows the user to browse directories and click on a file. The file chooser returns a **File** instance to the program. This facility is covered later.

Note that the Java escape character \ is coincidentally the same as the Windows file separator. Here, we need to say that the backslash is merely a normal character of the string rather than a special one, so we escape it. Effectively, when we use a quoted file name in a program \\ represents an ordinary \.

getAbsolutePath

To find the absolute path of a **File** instance, we put:

```
String absolute = myFile.getAbsolutePath();
```

which returns:

```
c:\temp\java\demo.txt
```

getName

We can extract the file name using:

```
String name = myFile.getName();
```

The value returned is **demo.txt**.

getParent

To find the parent directory (the one containing the **File** instance in question) we put:

```
String parent = myFile.getParent();
```

which returns the result:

```
c:\temp\java
```

exists

To check that the file exists, we can put:

```
boolean isThere = myFile.exists();
```

which returns **true** in this case.

isDirectory

The file might be a directory. We can check this by:

```
boolean checkDirectory = myFile.isDirectory();
```

which returns **true** if the file is a directory, and **false** otherwise.

length

We can find the size of the file in bytes. Note that we cast the returned value to an `int`.

```
int myLength = (int)myFile.length();
```

list

We can fill a string array with a list of file names within a directory:

```
String[] allFiles = myFile.list();
```

In the current example, our **File** object (referring to **"demo.txt"**) is not a directory, and **null** would be returned by the method **list**.

● The JFileChooser class

When you open a file using a word processor or editor, you will typically be provided with a dialog which allows you to browse through folders and select a file. This component is provided in Swing via the **JFileChooser** class. It has two variations, for opening files and for saving files.

Here is a program which shows the file chooser's main features. The user interface merely consists of an 'open' button and a 'save' button, together with a text field to display the name of the selected file. Figure 17.4(a) shows the **FileChooserDemo** interface, and Figure 17.4(b) shows the file chooser in action when the 'open' button is clicked.

```
import java.awt.*;
import java.awt.event.*;
import javax.swing.*;
import java.io.*;

class FileChooserDemo extends JFrame
implements ActionListener {
```

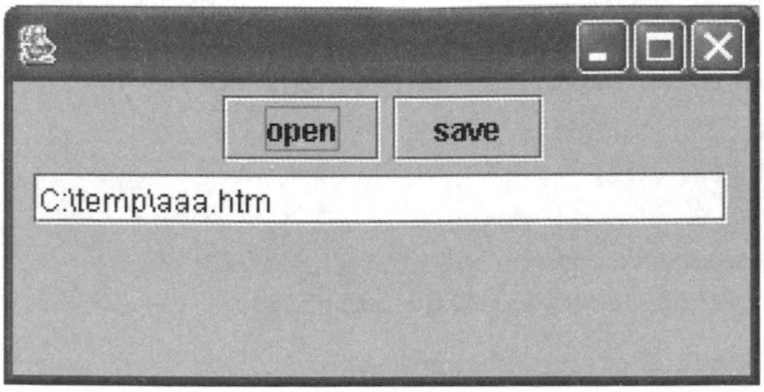

Figure 17.4 (a) Screenshot of the **FileChooserDemo** program.

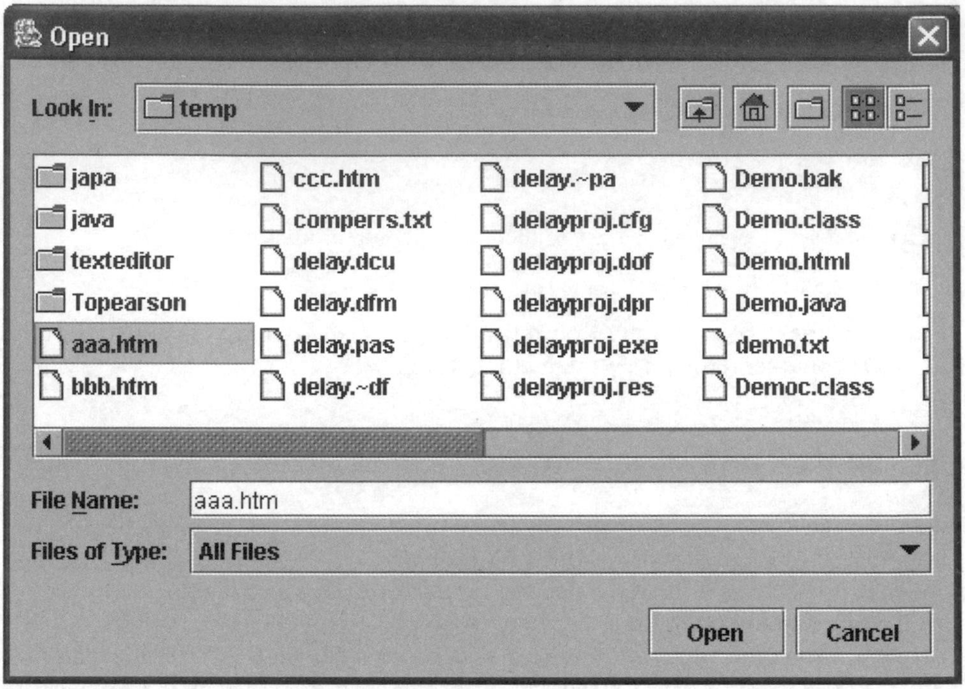

Figure 17.4 (b) File chooser shown when `Open` in `FileChooserDemo` in clicked.

```
private JButton openButton, saveButton;
private JFileChooser fileChooser;
private JTextField nameField;

public static void main(String[] args) {
    FileChooserDemo frame = new FileChooserDemo();
    frame.setSize(300, 150);
    frame.createGUI();
    frame.show();
}

private void createGUI() {
    setDefaultCloseOperation(EXIT_ON_CLOSE);
    Container window = getContentPane();
    window.setLayout(new FlowLayout());

    openButton = new JButton("open");
    window.add(openButton);
    openButton.addActionListener(this);

    saveButton = new JButton("save");
    window.add(saveButton);
    saveButton.addActionListener(this);
```

```
        nameField = new JTextField(25);
        window.add(nameField);
    }

    public void actionPerformed(ActionEvent event) {
        File selectedFile;
        int reply;
        if (event.getSource() == saveButton) {
            fileChooser = new JFileChooser();
            reply = fileChooser.showSaveDialog(this);
            if(reply == JFileChooser.APPROVE_OPTION) {
                selectedFile = fileChooser.getSelectedFile();
                nameField.setText(selectedFile.getAbsolutePath());
            }
        }
        if (event.getSource() == openButton) {
            fileChooser = new JFileChooser();
            reply = fileChooser.showOpenDialog(this);
            if (reply == JFileChooser.APPROVE_OPTION) {
                selectedFile = fileChooser.getSelectedFile();
                nameField.setText(selectedFile.getAbsolutePath());
            }
        }
    }
}
```

It is important to note that the file chooser component does not actually transfer any data into files. This has to be coded by the programmer, as we saw in the previous examples. All it does is provide the program with details about the file that the user selected. This is far superior to our use of text fields because it reduces possible user errors, such as selecting a non-existent file.

Here are the main features of a file chooser.

- We create an instance of the **JFileChooser** class.

- We display the file chooser by using either the **showOpenDialog** or the **showSaveDialog** method. Normally we display it centred over the current frame, by providing the parameter **this**.

- The file chooser returns a numeric code which indicates whether the user cancelled the dialog or not. We can compare this code to the **JFileChooser.APPROVE_OPTION** constant to find out if a file was selected.

- The **getSelectedFile** method returns an instance of the **File** class. To obtain the file path as a string we use the **getAbsolutePath** method of the **File** class.

- The same instance of **JFileChooser** can be used as a 'save' or an 'open' dialog.

Here is the code fragment which creates a dialog for saving:

```
fileChooser = new JFileChooser();
reply = fileChooser.showSaveDialog(this);
if (reply == JFileChooser.APPROVE_OPTION) {
    selectedFile = fileChooser.getSelectedFile();
    nameField.setText(selectedFile.getAbsolutePath());
}
```

SELF-TEST QUESTION

17.5   Run the **FileChooserDemo** program. What is the difference between the 'save' version and the 'open' version?

● Console I/O

In the history of computing, three styles of user interface have evolved. Initially, the command-line approach was used, in which a prompt was displayed on the screen, console or 'terminal' (at the end of a cable) and the user typed data or a command after the prompt, on the command line. The screen then 'scrolled up', and the next prompt appeared. Input and output was purely textual, and there was just one place that input could occur. The next advance was the use of menus, where users could move a cursor over a menu and use key presses to enter data or select options. More recently, windowing systems added a mouse as a pointing device, and made it possible to have several applications on screen at once.

In fact, the Java language can be used to write any of these styles of program, and here we will look at the facilities for command-line software. But why might we want to create such software? Well, the Unix and GNU/Linux operating systems are based on this approach, and they have a large collection of utility programs – software tools. The power comes in part from the capability of building new programs by joining together the existing tools. Typically, each tool is a free-standing application which accepts some textual input, processes it in some way, and passes the modified text on to another tool. Such software need not use the Swing classes at all. We only need to be able to display messages on the screen and input data or commands. This can be done most simply by a combination of streams and the **System** class.

● The **System** class

This class provides three ready-made streams:

```
System.out
System.in
System.err
```

These streams can be used with a scrolling window known as a 'terminal' or 'console' I/O screen.

The **System.out** stream provides either **print**, which prints a string, or **println**, which prints a string followed by the end-of-line code **\n**. Recall that we can also use **+** to join strings prior to printing. The term 'print' is a legacy from the days of paper print-out. Here is a complete program which outputs some text:

```
public class ConsoleDemo{
    public static void main(String[] args){
        System.out.println("Hello World");
    }
}
```

The **System** class is imported automatically, and no exception handling is needed for output. Note that the string to be printed might also contain several lines of text. This stream is the direct equivalent of **System.in**, in that its output can be redirected or piped at operating system level. We don't need to create this stream with **new** – it exists already.

The **System.in** stream can be used for direct keyboard input, and can also receive text that is piped or redirected into it via an operating system command. However, the methods that are provided with it are so low level as to be unusable to the Java programmer who is used to the convenience of strings. We recommend the following approach to console I/O, which provides us with a **BufferedReader** and the ability to use our familiar **readLine**. To create the stream we can use:

```
private BufferedReader keyboard;
keyboard = new BufferedReader(
    new InputStreamReader(System.in));
```

We used **BufferedReader** to read from files in our earlier examples. Here, we use it with an **InputStreamReader** working on **System.in**.

Once the stream is created, we read from it by:

```
String line = keyboard.readLine();
```

In the **Finder** and **TinyBrowser** classes below, you will see a method **prompt**, which makes use of keyboard input and output. The main points are:

- It is used by supplying a message to be displayed, and it returns the string that the user typed. For example:

    ```
    String reply = prompt("type your name:");
    ```

- The buffering method for console output is slightly different from that of files. We put:

    ```
    System.out.flush();
    ```

    which ensures that any text sent with **print** will be displayed immediately, rather than when the next **println** occurs.

- The use of the input stream involves a checked exception. This is very unlikely to happen, so we handle it locally, rather than complicating matters for the caller of **prompt**.

The **System.err** stream can similarly be used with **print** and **println**, but its output cannot be redirected or piped – it won't interfere with the real output of the program. Here is an example:

```
System.err.println("Error...program terminating.");
```

The **System** class also provides a method to terminate applications immediately, known as **System.exit**. We must also supply an integer code, which can be used by the operating system to determine the cause of termination. The convention is that zero means OK, whereas non-zero means something went wrong. You can choose which non-zero error codes to use, and these should be noted in your documentation for the application. Here are some examples:

```
if (age >= 0 ){
    System.exit(0);              // normal exit
}
else {
    System.err.println("Error in program");
    System.exit(3);              // error exit
}
```

Using JOptionPane

As an alternative to the **System** input and output streams, we can make use of the **JOptionPane** facilities from the Swing library. This does not require the creation of a graphical window, as we did with full Swing applications. Here is an example:

```
import javax.swing.*;
public class ConsoleJOptionDemo{
    public static void main(String[] args){
        JOptionPane.showMessageDialog(null, "Hello World");
    }
}
```

Note that we need to import the Swing libraries.

A console example: Finder

Let us make use of the **System** streams. We will write a program which requests a file name and a substring. It then displays each line of the file which contains the substring.

Because files can contain many similar lines, we will provide a context by also displaying the preceding line and the following line.

So, our program has two console inputs – the file to search and the required substring. We display prompts for both of these and read them from **System.in**. Later we look at the 'command-line arguments' approach to getting data into console programs. When the file has been opened, we use the **indexOf** method to search for a substring – it returns **-1** if the substring is not present. The **prompt** method illustrates keyboard I/O. Here is the program:

```java
import java.io.*;
class Finder {
    private String line1, line2, line3;
    private BufferedReader keyboard;
    private BufferedReader inStream;

    public static void main (String [] args) {
        Finder aFind = new Finder();
        aFind.doSearch();
    }

    private void doSearch() {
        keyboard = new BufferedReader(
            new InputStreamReader(System.in));
        String fileName = prompt("Type file to search: ");
        String wanted = prompt("Type string to find: ");
        line1 = "";
        line2 = "";
        try {
            inStream = new BufferedReader(new
                FileReader(fileName));
            while ((line3 = inStream.readLine()) != null) {
                if (line2.indexOf(wanted) >= 0) {
                    displayLine();
                }
                // advance to the next group of 3
                line1 = line2;
                line2 = line3;
                // and get new line3 from file...
            }
            // check the last line
            line3 = "";                    //remove null eof value
            if (line2.indexOf(wanted) >= 0) {
                displayLine();
            }
            inStream.close();
        }
        catch (IOException e) {
            System.err.println("Error in Finder: "+ e.toString());
            System.exit(1);
        }
    }
}
```

```
    private void displayLine() {
        System.out.println("[=== context:");
        System.out.println(line1);
        System.out.println(line2);
        System.out.println(line3);
        System.out.println("===]");
        System.out.println("");
    }

    private String prompt(String message) {
        String reply = "";
        try {
            System.out.print(message);
            System.out.flush();
            reply = keyboard.readLine();
        }
        catch (IOException e) {
            System.err.println("Keyboard "+ e.toString());
            System.exit(2);
        }
        return reply;
    }
}
```

Figure 17.5 shows what you see if you search the file **Finder.java** for the string **if**.

```
Type file to search: c:\temp\java\Finder.java
Type string to find: if
[=== context:
        while ((line3 = inStream.readLine()) != null) {
            if ( line2.indexOf(wanted) >= 0) {
                displayLine();
===]

[=== context:
        line3 = ""                      //remove null eof value
        if (line2.indexOf(wanted) >= 0) {
            displayLine();
===]
```

Figure 17.5 Screenshot of the **Finder** program.

● Reading from a remote site

Surprisingly, reading a web page from a remote server is no more difficult in Java than reading a local file – this is because of the power of the Java library. Rather than a file name, we need to supply the web address (URL – Uniform Resource Locator) of the

```
Type a URL (e.g. http://java.sun.com): http://java.sun.com

<!DOCTYPE HTML PUBLIC "-//W3C//DTD HTML 4.01 Transitional//EN">
<html>
<head>
<title>Java Technology</title>
<meta name="keywords" content="Java, platform" />
<meta name="description" content="Java technology is a portfolio
of products that are based on the power of networks and the idea
that the same software should run on many different kinds of
systems and devices." />
```

Figure 17.6 Screenshot of the **TinyBrowser** program.

file. Below we illustrate a console application, which prompts the user to enter a URL, and which displays the content of the file on the screen. The program can only display text, as you can see from the console view in Figure 17.6.

```java
import java.io.*;
import java.net.*;
class TinyBrowser {
    private BufferedReader inStream, keyboard;
    public static void main (String [] args) {
        TinyBrowser aBrowser = new TinyBrowser();
        aBrowser.fetch();
    }

    private void fetch() {
        String urlString = "";
        String line;
        keyboard = new BufferedReader(new
            InputStreamReader(System.in));
        try {
            urlString = prompt("Type a URL " +
                            "(e.g. http://java.sun.com/): ");
            // create a connection to a URL
            URL urlAddress = new URL(urlString);
            URLConnection connection =
                            urlAddress.openConnection();
            inStream = new BufferedReader(new
                InputStreamReader(connection.getInputStream()));
            while ((line = inStream.readLine()) != null) {
                System.out.print(line);
            }
        }
        catch (MalformedURLException e) {
            System.err.println(urlString + e.toString());
            System.exit(2);
```

```
        }
        catch (IOException e) {
            System.err.println("Error in accessing URL: "+
                                 e.toString());
            System.exit(1);
        }
    }

    private String prompt(String message) {
        String reply = "";
        try {
            System.out.print(message);
            System.out.flush();
            reply = keyboard.readLine();
        }
        catch (IOException e) {
            System.err.println("Keyboard "+ e.toString());
            System.exit(2);
        }
        return reply;
    }
}
```

Most of the program is concerned with exception handling and console I/O. The essential URL code is:

```
import java.net.*;
// create a connection to a URL
URL urlAddress = new URL(urlString);
URLConnection connection =
                 urlAddress.openConnection();
inStream = new BufferedReader(new
    InputStreamReader(connection.getInputStream()));
```

Firstly, we supply a string to the **URL** class, which performs checks on the syntax – such as correct use of **/** and **.** characters. If they are wrong, a **MalformedURLException** is thrown.

Next, we actually create a connection with the **URLConnection** class.

As you can see from Figure 17.6, this is a rather primitive browser – it cannot interpret HTML tags (enclosed in angle brackets). All we see is the 'raw' HTML.

● Command-line arguments

Command-line arguments provide another way of inputting initial values (such as file names) into console programs. To use them, you need to run the program from the command line, as described in Appendix I. Recall our **Finder** program. We will rewrite it so that the file to use and the string to find are passed in from the command line. Here is part of the code. The omitted part is identical to **Finder**.

```java
import java.io.*;
public class FinderWithArgs {
    public static void main(String[] args){
        if (args.length != 2) {
            System.err.println("Error: 2 arguments are required.");
            System.exit(2);
        }
        else {
            FinderWithArgs aFind = new FinderWithArgs();
            aFind.doSearch(args[0], args[1]);
        }
    }

    private void doSearch(String fileName, String wanted) {

        // search the file as before...
    }
}
```

Here is an example of how we execute the program.

```
java FinderWithArguments "c:\temp\myfile.txt" "my interests"
```

Here are the main points:

- The phrase 'command-line arguments' is traditional. In Java terms, an argument is a parameter, so we will stick to 'parameter' below.

- The **main** method of the program has an array of strings as its parameter. In previous examples, we have not made use of the parameter.

- The parameter array is named **args**. We could choose our own name, but there is a tradition of using **args**.

- When the program starts running, **main** is called as usual. In addition, any items following the program name on the command line are transferred into the **args** array. The first item goes into **args[0]**, the second into **args[1]**, etc.

- On the command line, items are separated by a space or spaces. If an item itself contains a space, the item can be enclosed in double-quote marks. In the above command line, we chose to enclose both items in quotes. The quotes are stripped off before the items are placed in the **args** array.

- We can find out the number of parameters by using **length**. It is good practice to check for the correct number of parameters, as shown in the above code.

The use of command-line arguments can simplify the use of a program, but it is not suitable for interactive programs, where we wish to check a user's input and request correct input in the case of errors.

Programming principles

- Programs use streams to read and write data to files.

- Files are used to preserve data after a program terminates, or for passing data to other programs.

Programming pitfalls

- File access requires us either to use **try-catch** for an **IOException** (which is preferable) or to state that a method which uses streams throws an **IOException**.

- It is not possible to put:

```
myFile = new PrintWriter("c:\\temp\\demo.txt");
```

Instead we must put:

```
myFile = new PrintWriter(
    new FileWriter("c:\\temp\\demo.txt"), true);
```

or, for input:

```
myFile = new BufferedReader(
    new FileReader("c:\\temp\\demo.txt"));
```

- To produce a \ between quotes, we must use \\.

- The **System.exit** method requires an integer parameter.

Grammar spot

We have seen no new statements or language features, because file facilities are provided by classes rather than being built into the language.

New language elements

We have introduced these classes:

```
PrintWriter
BufferedReader
URL
URLConnection
File
JFileChooser
```

Summary

- Files are opened, then written to (or read from), and finally closed.

- We declare and create file streams by, for example:

```
private PrintWriter outStream;
outStream = new PrintWriter(
    new FileWriter("c:\\temp\\demo.txt"), true);

private FileReader inStream;
inStream = new BufferedReader(
    new FileReader("c:\\temp\\any.txt"));
```

- The programmer has free choice of the stream variable names. These names become associated with actual operating system file names.

- The `readLine` method is a convenient method to access input streams.

- The `print` and `println` methods are convenient for output streams.

- The popular idiom to read a file line by line is:

```
String line;
while((line = inStream.readLine()) != null) {
    // process line
}
```

- We close streams by, for example:

```
inStream.close();
```

- The `JFileChooser` class provides dialogs which allow the user to browse and click to select a file name.

- The `System` class provides ready-created streams:

```
System.in
System.out
System.err
```

- The `System.exit(n)` method can be used to abandon an application immediately.

- Command-line arguments (parameters) are transferred from the command line into the `String` array parameter of the `main` method.

● **Exercises**

The first set of questions involves Swing applications.

17.1   Write a Swing program which, when a button is clicked, outputs your name and address to a specified file. Use an editor to check that the file has the expected contents.

17.2   Write a Swing program which counts the number of lines in a specified file. Ensure it works on an empty file, producing a value of 0.

17.3   Write a Swing program which can read a file containing lines with three items – a name (with no spaces) and two integers. The items are separated by commas. The application should allow the file name to be selected via a text field, and should provide a 'next' button which causes the next line of the file to be input and displayed in three text fields. Provide the user with an indication of when the end of the file has been reached.

17.4   (a)   Write a Swing program which is a simple text editor. Initially, use a text field for file names. It should have:
- a text field to accept the file name;
- a text area for editing;
- an 'open' button to input the text from the selected file;
- a 'save' button to save the contents of the text area in the selected file;
- an 'exit' button.

(b)   Modify your editor to use a file chooser instead of a text field.

(c)   Instead of buttons, incorporate menus, as described in Appendix A.

17.5   Write a Swing program which reads two files line by line, and compares the files for equality. It should display a message stating that the files are equal or not equal. Use file choosers to obtain the file names.

17.6   Write a Swing program which replaces one string by another throughout a file, writing the new version to another file. Use file choosers to obtain the file names, and use two text fields to accept the 'from' and 'to' strings. Make use of the `replace` method from Chapter 15.

The following questions involve console applications.

17.7   Write a console program which compares two files line by line. It should print a message stating that the files are either equal or not equal. Use input dialogs to obtain the file names from the user.

17.8   Write a console program which replaces one substring by another in a file, writing the new version to another file. The application should use command-line arguments for the old and new file names and the two substrings.

17.9   Write a console 'directory lister' program, which prompts the user for an absolute path and then displays every file name in the directory. If any files are directories, the word 'dir' should be printed after their name.

17.10 Modify the **TinyBrowser** program so that it repeats its prompt if a **MalformedURLException** is produced. Use a **try-catch** inside a **while**.

17.11 Modify the **TinyBrowser** program so that instead of printing the HTML on the screen, it sends it to a file. The file name should be requested from the user. To ensure that the file is being written properly, view it with a web browser.

Answers to self-test questions

17.1 **PrintWriter** does not have a constructor with a string containing a file name as its parameter. Instead, we must put:

```
private PrintWriter outFile;

...

outFile = new PrintWriter(
    new FileWriter(nameField.getText()), true);
```

17.2 The text area would end up containing one long line. When a string is input from a file, the end-of-line marker is removed, so we need to insert one when we append the line.

17.3 There is no **readLine** in the loop, so the loop will not advance through the file. The first value of **line** will be appended to the text area again and again.

17.4 Modify the following code:

```
if (personField.getText().equals(nameInFile)) {
    found = true;
```

so that it becomes:

```
if (nameInFile.equalsIgnoreCase(personField.getText())) {
    found = true;
}
```

17.5 The 'open' version has a title bar and a button labelled 'Open', whereas the 'save' version uses 'Save'. Their functionality is similar.

Object-oriented design

This chapter explains:

- how to identify the classes that are needed in a program;
- how to distinguish between composition and inheritance;
- some guidelines for class design.

● Introduction

You probably wouldn't start to design a bridge by thinking about the size of the rivets. You would first make major decisions – like whether the bridge is cantilever or suspension. You wouldn't begin to design a building by thinking about the colour of the carpets. You would make major decisions first – like how many floors there are to be and where the elevators should be.

With a small program, design is not really needed – you can simply create the user interface and then go on to write the Java statements. But with a large program, it is widely recognized that the programmer should start with the major decisions rather than the detail. This means thinking about what classes are needed. The programmer should do design, do it first and do it well. Decisions about detail – like the exact format of a number, or the position of a button – should be postponed. All the stages of programming are crucial, of course, but some are more crucial than others.

When you start out to write programs, you usually spend a lot of time in trial and error. This is often great fun and very creative. Sometimes you spend some time wrestling with the programming language. It takes some time to learn good practice and to recognize bad practice. It takes even longer to adopt an effective design approach to programming. The fun remains, the creativity remains, but the nuisance parts of programming are reduced.

The design process takes as its input the specification of what the program is to do. The end product of the design process is a description of the classes and methods that the program will employ.

This chapter explains how to use one mainstream approach to designing OO programs. We shall use the simple example of the balloon program to illustrate how to do design. We will also introduce a more complex design example.

● The design problem

We have seen that an OO program consists of a collection of objects. The problem when starting to develop a new program is to identify suitable objects. We know that once we have identified the objects, we will reap all the benefits of OOP. But the fundamental problem of OOP is how to identify the objects. This is what a design method offers: an approach, a series of steps to identifying the objects. It is just like any other kind of design – you need a method. Knowing the principles of OOP is not enough. By analogy, knowing the laws of physics doesn't mean you can design a space shuttle; you also have to carry out some design.

One of the principles used in the design of OO programs is to simulate real-world situations as objects. You build a software model of things in the real world. Here are some examples:

- If we are developing an office automation system, we set out to simulate users, mail, shared documents and files.
- In a factory automation system, we set out to simulate the different machines, queues of work, orders and deliveries.

The approach is to identify the objects in the problem to be addressed and to model them as objects in the program.

Abstraction plays a role in this process. We only need to model relevant parts for the problem to be solved, and we can ignore any irrelevant detail. If we model a balloon, we need to represent its position, its size and its colour. But we need not model the material from which it is made. If we are creating an employee records system, we would probably model names, addresses and job descriptions but not hobbies and preferred music styles.

● Identifying objects and methods

An effective way to carry out OO design is to examine the software specification in order to extract information about the objects and methods. The approach to identifying objects and methods is:

1. Look for nouns (things) in the specification – these are the objects.
2. Look for verbs (doing words) in the specification – these are the methods.

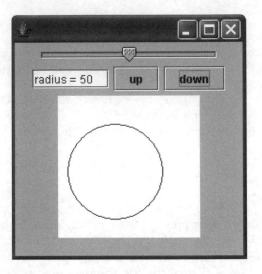

Figure 18.1 The balloon program.

Here, for example, is the specification for the simple balloon program:

> Write a program to represent a balloon and manipulate the balloon via a GUI. The balloon is displayed as a circle in a panel. Using buttons, the position of the balloon can be changed by moving it a fixed distance up or down. Using a slider, the radius of the balloon can be altered. The radius is displayed in a text field.

The window is shown in Figure 18.1.

We look for verbs and nouns in the specification. In the above specification, we can see the following nouns:

```
GUI, panel, button, slider, text field, balloon, position, distance,
radius
```

The GUI provides the user interface to the program. It consists of buttons, a slider, a text field and a panel. The GUI is represented by an object that is an instance of the class `JFrame`. The button, slider, text field and panel objects are available as classes in the Java library.

The GUI object:

1. Creates the buttons, slider, text field and panel on the screen.
2. Handles the events from mouse-clicks on the buttons and slider.
3. Creates any other objects that are needed, such as the `balloon` object.
4. Calls the methods of the `balloon` object.

The next major object is the balloon. It makes use of information to represent its position (*x* and *y* coordinates), the distance it moves and its radius. One option would be to create completely distinct full-blown objects to represent these items. But it is simpler to represent them simply as `int` variables.

Figure 18.2 Class diagram showing the two main classes in the balloon program.

This completes the identification of the objects within the program. We now generalize the objects and design classes corresponding to each object. Thus we need classes `GUI`, `JTextField`, `Balloon`, etc.

We now extract the verbs from the specification. They are effectively:

> `changeRadius, moveUp, moveDown, displayBalloon, displayRadius`

We must create corresponding methods within the program we are designing. But we need to decide which object they apply to – the `GUI` object or the `balloon` object. It seems reasonable that the verbs `moveUp`, `moveDown` and `displayBalloon` are methods associated with the `balloon` object.

Now we turn our attention to the verbs `changeRadius` and `displayRadius`. We have already decided that the value of the radius is implemented as an `int` variable within the `Balloon` object. However, the `GUI` object needs access to this value to display it in the text field. It also needs to change the value in response to changes in the value of the slider. Thus the class `Balloon` needs to provide access to the value of the radius, and this can be accomplished using methods (named `getRadius` and `setRadius`).

To sum up, our design for this program consists of two non-library classes, `GUI` and `Balloon`, shown in the UML class diagram (Figure 18.2). This diagram shows the major classes in the program and their interrelationships. Class `GUI` uses class `Balloon` by making calls on its methods.

We can document each class by means of more detailed class diagrams. In these diagrams, each box describes a single class. It has three compartments, providing information on:

1. the class name;
2. a list of instance variables;
3. a list of methods.

Firstly, here is the description of the class `GUI`:

```
class GUI

Instance variables

upButton
downButton
slider
textField
panel

Methods

upButtonClick
downButtonClick
sliderChange
```

Next, here is the class diagram for the `Balloon` class:

class Balloon
Instance variables
x
y
radius
yStep
Methods
moveUp
moveDown
display
getRadius
setRadius

The design of this program is now complete. Design ends at the stage where all the classes, objects and methods are specified. Design is not concerned with writing (coding) the Java statements that make up these classes and methods. However, it is natural for the reader to be curious about the code, so here is the code for the class `GUI`.

At the head of the class is the instance variable:

```
private Balloon balloon ;
```

When we create new objects, we need to create a `Balloon` object:

```
balloon = new Balloon();
```

Then we have the methods to respond to the events:

```
private void downButtonClick() {
    balloon.moveDown();
    draw();
}

private void upButtonClick() {
    balloon.moveUp();
    draw();
}

private void sliderChange() {
    int radius = slider.getValue();
    textField.setText("radius = " + radius);
    balloon.setRadius(radius);
    draw();
}
```

And a shared method:

```
private void draw() {
    balloon.display(panel);
}
```

Next, here is the code for the class **Balloon**:

```
public class Balloon {

    private int x = 50;
    private int y = 50;
    private int radius = 20;
    private int yStep = 20;

    public void moveUp() {
        y = y - yStep;
    }

    public void moveDown() {
        y = y + yStep;
    }

    public void display(JPanel panel) {
        Graphics paper = panel.getGraphics();
        paper.setColor(Color.black);
        paper.drawOval(x, y, radius * 2, radius * 2);
    }

    public int getRadius() {
        return radius;
    }

    public void setRadius(int newRadius) {
        radius = newRadius;
    }

}
```

This program is a simple one, with just two non-library objects. Nonetheless, it illustrates how to extract objects and methods from a specification. We will look at a more complex example in a moment.

To summarize, the design method for identifying objects and methods is:

1. Look for nouns in the specification – these are objects (or sometimes simple variables).

2. Look for verbs in the specification – these are methods.

Once the objects have been identified, it is a simple step to generalize them by converting them into classes.

Note that although this program has been designed as two classes, it could alternatively be designed as a single class. However, the design we have shown makes much more explicit use of the objects present in the specification of the program. The design also separates the GUI part of the program from the balloon itself. This is a widely recommended program structure in which the presentation code (GUI) and the model (sometimes termed the domain logic) are separated from each other. This structure is sometimes referred to (for historical reasons) as the model–view–controller architecture. It means a program is easier to modify because it allows the GUI to be changed independently of the internal logic. Suppose, for example, that we wanted to add another slider to the GUI so as to control the position of the balloon. We would obviously need to make a small change to class **GUI**, but no changes would be needed to the class **Balloon**.

● Case study in design

Here is the specification for a rather larger program:

Cyberspace invader
The panel (Figure 18.3) displays the defender and an alien. The alien moves sideways. When it hits a wall, it reverses its direction. The alien launches a bomb that moves vertically downwards, but there is only one bomb in existence at a given time. If the bomb hits the defender, the user loses. The defender moves left or right according to mouse movements. When the mouse is clicked, the defender launches a laser that moves upwards, but there is only one laser in existence at a given time. If the laser hits the alien, the user wins.

Figure 18.3 The cyberspace invader program.

Remember that the major steps in design are:

1. Identify objects by searching for nouns in the specification.
2. Identify methods by searching for verbs in the specification.

Scanning through the specification, we find the following nouns. As we might expect, some of these nouns are mentioned more than once.

`panel, defender, alien, wall, bomb, mouse, laser`

These nouns correspond to potential objects, and therefore classes within the program. So we translate these nouns into the names of classes in the model. The noun `panel` translates into the `JPanel` class, available in the library. The nouns `defender` and `alien` translate into the classes `Defender` and `Alien` respectively. The noun `wall` need not be implemented as a class because it can be simply accommodated as a detail within the class `Alien`. The noun `bomb` translates into class `Bomb`. The noun `mouse` need not be a class because mouse-click events can be simply handled by the `JFrame` class or the `Defender` class. Finally we need a class `Laser`. Thus we arrive at the following list of non-library classes:

`Game, Defender, Alien, Laser, Bomb`

These are shown in the class diagram (Figure 18.4). This states that the class `Game` uses the classes `Defender`, `Alien`, `Laser` and `Bomb`.

We have not yet quite completed our search for objects in the program. In order that collisions can be detected, objects need to know where other objects are and how big they are. Therefore, implicit in the specification are the ideas of the position and size of each object. These are the *x* and *y* coordinates, height and width of each object. Although these are potentially objects, they can instead be simply implemented as `int` variables within classes `Defender`, `Alien`, `Laser` and `Bomb`. These can be accessed via methods named `getX`, `getY`, `getHeight` and `getWidth`.

One object that we have so far ignored in the design is a timer from the Java library that is set to click at small, regular time intervals, in order to implement the animation. Whenever the timer ticks, the objects are moved, the panel is cleared and all the objects

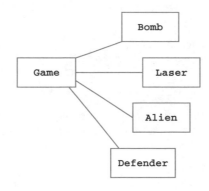

Figure 18.4 The non-library classes involved in the game program.

are displayed. Another object is a random number generator, created from the library class **Random**, to control when the alien launches bombs.

We have now identified the classes that make up the game program.

We scan the specification again, this time looking for verbs that we can attach to the above list of objects. We see:

```
display, move, hit, launch, click, win, lose
```

Again, some of these words are mentioned more than once. For example, both the aliens and the defender move. Also all the objects in the game need to be displayed.

We now allocate methods to classes, and the specification helps us to do this.

We can document each class as a UML class diagram that shows for each class its instance variables and its methods. We start with class **Game**:

class Game
Instance variables
panel timer
Methods
mouseMoved mouseClicked actionPerformed

Here is the code for this class. It begins with the instance variable declarations of the major game objects:

```
private Graphics paper;
private Defender defender;
private Laser laser;
private Bomb bomb;
```

When a new game is about to start, we create new objects and start the timer:

```
private void newGame() {
    defender = new Defender();
    alien = new Alien();
    timer.start();
}
```

Then the methods that handle the events:

```
private void timer_Tick() {
    if (bomb == null) {
        bomb = new Bomb(alien.getX(), alien.getY());
    }
```

```
        moveAll();
        drawAll();
        checkHits();
    }

    public void mouseClicked(MouseEvent event) {
        int initialX = defender.getX();
        int initialY = defender.getY();
        if (laser == null) {
            laser = new Laser(initialX, initialY);
        }
    }

    public void mouseMoved(MouseEvent event) {
        defender.move(event.getX());
    }
```

Then the subsidiary methods:

```
    private void moveAll() {
        alien.move();
        if (bomb != null) {
            bomb.move();
        }
        if (laser != null) {
            laser.move();
        }
    }

    private void drawAll() {
        Graphics paper = panel.getGraphics();
        paper.setColor(Color.white);
        paper.fillRect(0, 0, panel.getWidth(), panel.getHeight());
        paper.setColor(Color.black);
        defender.draw(panel);
        alien.draw(panel);
        if (laser != null) {
            laser.draw(panel);
        }
        if (bomb != null) {
            bomb.draw(panel);
        }
    }

    private void checkHits() {
        if (collides(laser, alien)) {
            endGame("user");
        }
```

```
        else {
            if (collides(bomb, defender)) {
                endGame("alien");
            }
        }
        if (bomb != null) {
            if (bomb.getY() > panel.getHeight()) {
                bomb = null;
            }
        }
        if (laser != null) {
            if (laser.getY() < 0) {
                laser = null;
            }
        }
    }

    private boolean collides(Sprite one, Sprite two) {
        if (one == null || two == null) {
            return false;
        }
        if (    one.getX() > two.getX()
            &&  one.getY() < (two.getY() + two.getHeight())
            && (one.getX() + one.getWidth()) <
                            (two.getX() + two.getWidth())
            && (one.getY() + one.getWidth()) > (two.getY())) {
            return true;
        }
        else {
            return false;
        }
    }
```

And finally:

```
    private void endGame(String winner) {
        laser = null;
        bomb = null;
        timer.stop();
        JOptionPane.showMessageDialog(null,
            "game over - " + winner + " wins");
    }
```

In this design, the class `Game` carries out a large portion of the work of the program. For example, it launches a laser and a bomb. Also it checks whether the alien or the defender has been hit with something. These are verbs that we identified in the analysis of the specification above.

Next we consider the defender object. It has a position within the panel and a size. In response to a mouse movement, it moves. It can be displayed. Therefore its class has the specification:

class Defender
Instance variables
x y height width
Methods
move display getX getY getHeight getWidth

Then we design the **Alien** class. The alien has a position and a size. Whenever the clock ticks, it moves. Its direction and speed are controlled by the step size that is used when it moves. It can be created and displayed.

class Alien
Instance variables
x y height width xStep
Methods
Alien move display getX getY getHeight getWidth

Next we consider a laser object. A laser has a position and a size. It is created, moves and is displayed. We must also check whether it hits an alien.

class Laser
Instance variables x y height width yStep
Methods Laser move display getX getY getHeight getWidth

Finally, a bomb is very similar to a laser. One difference is that a bomb moves downwards, whereas a laser moves upwards.

SELF-TEST QUESTION

18.1 Write the class diagram for the **Bomb** class.

We now have the full list of classes, and the methods and instance variables associated with each class. We have modelled the game and designed a structure for the program.

● Looking for reuse

The next act of design is to check to make sure that we are not reinventing the wheel. One of the main aims of OOP is to promote reuse of software components. At this stage we should check whether:

■ what we need might be in one of the libraries;

■ we may have written a class last month that is what we need;

■ we may be able to generalize some of the classes we have designed for our program into a more general class that we can inherit from.

We see in the cyberspace invader program that we can make good use of GUI components such as the panel, available in the Java library. Other library components that are useful are a timer and a random number generator.

If you find an existing class that is similar to what you need, think about using inheritance to customize it in order to do what you want. We looked at how to write the code to achieve inheritance in Chapter 10. We next examine an approach to exploring the relationships between classes using the 'is-a' and 'has-a' tests.

● Composition or inheritance?

Once we have identified the classes within a program, the next step is to review the relationships between the classes. The classes that make up a program collaborate with each other to achieve the required behaviour, but they use each other in different ways. There are two ways in which classes relate to each other:

1. **Composition** One object creates another object from a class using **new**. An example is a frame that creates a button. Another example is the relationships between the classes in the game program shown in Figure 18.4.

2. **Inheritance** One class inherits from another. An example is a class that extends the library **JFrame** class. (All of the programs in this book do this.)

The important task of design is to distinguish these two cases, so that inheritance can be successfully applied or avoided. One way of checking that we have correctly identified the appropriate relationships between classes is to use the 'is-a' or 'has-a' test:

■ The use of the phrase 'is-a' in the description of an object (or class) signifies that it is probably an inheritance relationship.

■ The use of the phrase 'has-a' indicates that there is no inheritance relationship. Instead the relationship is composition. (An alternative phrase that has the same meaning is 'consists-of'.)

Let us look at an example to see how inheritance is identified. In the specification for a program to support the transactions in a bank, we find the following information:

> A bank account consists of a person's name, address, account number and current balance. There are two types of account – current and deposit. Borrowers have to give one week's notice to withdraw from a deposit account, but the account accrues interest.

Paraphrasing this specification, we could say 'a current account is a bank account' and 'a deposit account is a bank account'. We see the crucial words 'is a' and so recognize that bank account is the superclass of both deposit account and current account. Deposit account and current account are each subclasses of account. They inherit the methods from the superclass; for example, a method to get the address and a method to update the balance.

A class diagram, Figure 18.5, is useful in describing the inheritance relationships between classes.

As another example, consider the description of a window: 'the window has a button and a text field'. This is a 'has-a' relationship, which is composition, not inheritance.

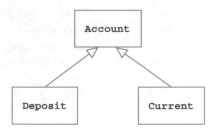

Figure 18.5 Class diagram for bank accounts.

The class representing the window simply declares and creates **JButton** and **JTextField** objects and then uses them.

We now return to the game program, seeking to find any inheritance relationships. If we can find any such relationships, we can simplify and shorten the program, benefiting from reuse. In the game program, several of the classes – **Defender**, **Alien**, **Laser** and **Bomb** – incorporate the same methods. These methods are **getX**, **getY**, **getHeight** and **getWidth** that obtain the position and size of the graphical objects. We will remove these ingredients from each class and place them in a superclass. We will name this class **Sprite**, since the word sprite is a commonly used term for a moving graphical object in games programming. The UML diagram for the **Sprite** class is:

class Sprite
Instance variables
x y height width
Methods
getX getY getHeight getWidth

This design is clarified when we look at the code. The Java code for the class **Sprite** is as follows:

```java
public class Sprite {

    protected int x, y, width, height;

    public int getX() {
        return x;
    }
```

```
    public int getY() {
        return y;
    }

    public int getWidth() {
        return width;
    }

    public int getHeight() {
        return height;
    }
}
```

The classes **Defender**, **Alien**, **Laser** and **Bomb** now inherit these methods from this superclass **Sprite**. Checking the validity of this design, we say 'each of the classes **Defender**, **Alien**, **Laser** and **Bomb** is a **Sprite**'. Figure 18.6 shows these relationships in a class diagram. Remember that an arrow points from a subclass to a superclass.

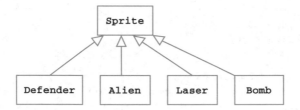

Figure 18.6 Class diagram for inherited components in the game.

We have now successfully identified inheritance relationships between classes in the game program.

We now delve again into the detail of the program. The code for class **Alien** is:

```
class Alien extends Sprite {

    private int stepSize;

    public Alien() {
        x = 0;
        y = 25;
        width = 20;
        height = 10;
        stepSize = 10;
    }

    public void draw(JPanel panel) {
        Graphics paper = panel.getGraphics();
        paper.fillOval(x, y, width, height);
    }
```

```
    public void move() {
        if (x > 200 || x < 0) {
            stepSize = -stepSize;
        }
        x = x + stepSize;
    }
}
```

The code for class **Bomb** is:

```
class Bomb extends Sprite {

    private int stepSize;

    public Bomb(int initialX, int initialY) {
        x = initialX;
        y = initialY;
        width = 5;
        height = 10;
        stepSize = 10;
    }

    public void draw(JPanel panel) {
        Graphics paper = panel.getGraphics();
        paper.fillOval(x, y, width, height);
    }

    public void move() {
        y = y + stepSize;
    }
}
```

SELF-TEST QUESTION

18.2 Write the code for class **Laser**.

To sum up, the two kinds of relationship between classes are as follows.

Relationship between classes	Test	Java code involves
inheritance	is-a	extends
composition	has-a or consists-of	new

SELF-TEST QUESTION

18.3 Analyze the relationships between the following groups of classes (are they 'is-a' or 'has-a'?):

1. house, door, roof, dwelling
2. person, man, woman
3. car, piston, gearbox, engine
4. vehicle, car, bus

Guidelines for class design

Use of the design approach that we have described is not guaranteed to lead to the perfect design. It is always worthwhile checking the design of each class against the following guidelines.

Keep data private

Variables should always be declared as **private** (or sometimes **protected**), but never as **public**. This maintains data hiding, one of the central principles of OOP. If data needs to be accessed or changed, do it via methods provided as part of the class.

Initialize the data

Although Java automatically initializes instance variables (but not local variables) to particular values, it is good practice to initialize them explicitly, either within the data declaration itself or by means of a constructor method.

Avoid large classes

If a class is more than two pages of text, it is a candidate for consideration for division into two or smaller classes. But this should only be done if there are clearly obvious classes to be formed from the large one. It is counter-productive to split an elegant cohesive class into contrived and ugly classes.

Make the class and method names meaningful

This will make them easy to use and more appealing for reuse.

Do not contrive inheritance

In the game program discussed above, we might create a superclass **MovesHorizontally** and make **Defender** and **Alien** subclasses. Similarly, a class **MovesVertically** might be a superclass of **Laser** and **Bomb**. But if we consider the individual requirements of these classes, we find that they are quite distinct and nothing is to be gained.

Using inheritance when it is not really appropriate can lead to contrived classes, which are more complex and perhaps longer than they need be.

When using inheritance, put shared items in the superclass

In the example of the bank account discussed above, all those variables and methods that are common to all bank accounts should be written as part of the superclass so that they can be shared by all the subclasses without duplication. Examples are the methods to update the address and to update the balance.

We also saw in the game program that we could identify identical methods in several of the classes, and thus create a superclass named `Sprite`.

Use refactoring

After an initial design has been created, or when some coding has been carried out, a study of the design may reveal that some simplification is possible. This may mean moving some methods to another class. It may mean creating new classes or amalgamating existing classes. This process is termed *refactoring*. We have already met a guideline for refactoring – place shared methods in the superclass.

For example, in the game program, there is an obvious need to test repeatedly whether objects are colliding. But there are several alternative places in the program where this collision detection can be carried out. As implemented above, there is a method named `collides`, part of class `Game` that carries out the collision detection. But an alternative would be to create a distinct class, named `CollisionDetection`, that provides a static method `collides` to carry out collision detection. Furthermore, initiating the collision detection could be dispersed throughout the program, into the classless `Laser` and `Bomb`.

Refactoring recognizes that it is often not possible to create an initial design that is ideal. Instead the design sometimes evolves towards an optimal structure. This may involve changing the design after coding is under way. Thus development is not carried out in distinct stages.

Summary

The OO design task consists of identifying appropriate objects and classes. The steps in the approach to OO design advocated in this chapter are:

1. Study the specification and clarify it if necessary.
2. Derive objects and methods from the specification, so that the design acts as a model of the application. The verbs are methods and the nouns are objects.
3. Generalize the objects into classes.
4. Check for reuse of library classes and other existing classes, using composition and inheritance as appropriate. 'Is-a' and 'has-a' analyses help check out whether inheritance or composition is appropriate.
5. Use guidelines to refine a design.

Exercises

18.1 Complete the development of the cyberspace invader program.

18.2 Enhance the cyberspace invader program so that the alien can drop multiple bombs and the defender can fire multiple lasers at the same time.

18.3 A good design can be judged on how well it copes with modifications or enhancements. Consider the following enhancements to the cyberspace invader program. Assess what changes are needed to the design and coding:
(a) a row of aliens;
(b) a line of bunkers that protects the defender from bombs;
(c) the player's performance is displayed.

18.4 An alternative design for the cyberspace invader program uses a class named **ScreenManager** that:
 ▪ maintains information about all the objects displayed on the screen;
 ▪ calls all the objects to display themselves;
 ▪ detects collisions between any pairs of objects on the screen.

 Redesign the program so as to use this class.

18.5 Design the classes for a program with the following specification.
 The program acts as a simple desk calculator (Figure 18.7) that acts on integer numbers. A text field acts as a display. The calculator has one button for each of the 10 digits, 0 to 9. It has a button to add and a button to subtract. It has a 'clear' button, to clear the display, and an equals (=) button to get the answer.
 When the 'clear' button is pressed the display is set to 0 and the (hidden) total is set to 0.
 When a digit button is pressed, the digit is added to the right of those already in the display (if any).
 When the + button is pressed, the number in the display is added to the total (and similar for the – button).
 When the equals button is pressed, the value of the total is displayed.

Figure 18.7 The desk calculator.

Answers to self-test questions

18.1

class Bomb
Instance variables
x y height width yStep
Methods
Bomb move display getX getY getHeight getWidth

18.2
```
class Laser extends Sprite {

    private int stepSize;

    public Laser(int newX, int newY) {
        x = newX;
        y = newY;
        width = 5;
        height = 5;
        stepSize = 10;
    }

    public void draw(JPanel panel) {
        Graphics paper = panel.getGraphics();
        paper.fillOval(x, y, width, height);
    }

    public void move() {
        y = y - stepSize;
    }
}
```

18.3
1. has-a
2. is-a
3. has-a
4. is-a

CHAPTER 19

Program style

This chapter suggests style guidelines for:

- program layout;
- names;
- classes;
- comments;
- constants;
- methods;
- nested **if**s;
- nested loops;
- complex conditions;
- documentation.

● Introduction

Programming is a highly creative and exciting activity. Programmers often get very absorbed in their work and regard the programs that they produce as being very much their personal creations. Stereotypical programmers (men or women) wear jeans and a T-shirt. They drink 20 cups of coffee in a day and stay up all night just for the fun of programming.

The facts of programming life are often rather different. Most programming is done within commercial organizations. Most programs are worked on by several different people. Many organizations have standards manuals that detail what programs should look like.

Most programs are read by several people – and certainly not just their author. The others are: the people who take on your work when you get promoted or move to another project, the people who will test your program, and the generations of programmers who will look after your program, fixing bugs and making improvements long after you have got another job. So, making your program easy to read is a vital ingredient of programming.

Another aspect of good style is reusability. A program that exhibits style will have classes that can be reused later in another program, written by the same person or someone else.

Unless you are a hobbyist, it's important in practice to know how to produce programs that have good style.

● Program layout

The Java programmer has enormous scope in deciding how to lay out a program. The language is free format – blank lines, spaces and new pages can be used almost anywhere. Comments can be placed on a line by themselves or on the end of a line of code. There's certainly plenty of scope for creativity and individuality.

However, as we have seen, most programs are read by several people other than the original author, so good appearance is vital. We will now look at a set of layout guidelines for Java programs. There is always controversy about guidelines like this. No doubt you, the reader, will disagree with some of them.

Indentation

Indentation emphasizes program structure. There are various styles for indentation, of which just one has been used throughout this book. People also disagree about how many spaces should be used for indentation – four are used in this book.

Blank lines

Blank lines are usually used to separate methods visually. They are also often used within a class to separate the variable declarations from the methods and one method from another.

If there are a lot of variable declarations, different blocks of data can also be separated by blank lines.

New pages

A class is something in itself, distinct from any others. If you can, start each new class at the start of a new page. If you only ever look at a screen, restrict your methods to one screen.

Perhaps one of the worst crimes in laying out a program is when a method starts on one page of hard copy but then spills over onto another. The reader's concentration is broken between the end of one page and the start of the new.

● Names

In Java, the programmer gives names to variables, classes and methods. There's plenty of scope for imagination because:

■ names can consist of letters and digits,

■ names can be as long as you like,

provided that the name starts with a letter and provided that you avoid Java keywords.

The usual advice on names is to make them as meaningful as possible. This rules out cryptic names like i, j, x, y which usually signify that the programmer has some background in maths (but not much imagination for creating meaningful names).

The convention for variables and methods is that they start with a lower-case letter and use an upper-case (capital) letter when the name has two or more words glued together. Examples are **myBalloon**, **theLargestSalary**.

The convention for class names is that they start with an upper-case letter. Examples are **String**, **Balloon**. This allows the reader easily to distinguish class names from other names in a program without having to search for their declarations.

Package names conventionally begin with a lower-case letter.

● Classes

Classes are an important building block of OO programs. They are also the unit that facilitates reusability of software components – by instantiation or inheritance. So it is important that classes have good style. Here are some style guidelines.

Modularity

A Java program is constructed as a collection of objects created from classes. Good design of classes helps to ensure that the program is clear and comprehensible because the program consists of distinct modules. The chapter on object-oriented design (OOD) explained an approach to good design.

Complexity

OOD attempts to design classes that correspond to classes in the problem being solved. These classes are usually present in the specification for the program. A good design will be such that the classes are recognizable as being a model of the specification. The design will reflect the complexity of the problem and no more.

Hiding data

The idea of OOD is to hide or encapsulate data, so that all the interactions between classes take place via the methods rather than by direct access to data. A good class design has a minimum of public variables.

Class size

If a class is longer than, say, two pages it suggests that it may be too long and complex. Consider dividing it (tenderly) into two or more classes, in such a way as to create viable new classes. It is damaging, however, to divide a coherent class into clumsy incoherent classes. Restructuring a class is termed refactoring.

Field order

Remembering that fields are the variables and methods within a class, what order should they appear in? There are both public and private fields to consider. The convention adopted in the Java libraries and in the definitive books on Java is to present them in the following order:

1. variables (public and private);
2. public methods;
3. private methods.

● Comments

There are three ways of putting comments into Java programs:

// this is a comment to the end of the line

/* with this kind of comment
you can use as many lines
as you like */

/** this style of comment
is for use in conjunction with a software tool to
produce automatic documentation
*/

There is a software tool called javadoc (the Java Documentation Generator) that scans the text of a program and produces an HTML (HyperText Markup Language) document. This shows for each class: the class inheritance hierarchy and the public variables and methods within the class. It also detects and incorporates the above kinds of comments (when they are associated with a class, a method or a variable) and uses them in the report. This report can be viewed by a web browser.

There is always great controversy about comments in programs. Some people argue that the 'more the better'. However, sometimes you see code like this:

```
// display the hello message
textField.setText("hello");
```

in which the comment merely repeats the code, and is therefore superfluous.

Sometimes code is overwhelmed by suffocating comments which add little to the understanding of the code. It's like a Christmas tree that is overwhelmed with tinsel, baubles and lights – you can't see the tree for the decorations. There is another problem: some studies have shown that, where there are a lot of comments, the reader reads the comments and ignores the code. Thus, if the code is wrong, it will remain so.

Some people argue that comments are needed when the code is complex or difficult to understand in some way. This seems reasonable until you wonder why the code needs to be complex in the first place. Sometimes, perhaps, the code can be simplified so that it is easy to understand without comments. We give examples of such situations below.

Some programmers like to place a comment at the start of every class and, perhaps, the start of a method in order to describe the overall purpose of the class (or method). The Java library classes are documented in this way. Class and method names should, of course, try to describe what they do, so a comment can be redundant.

Our view is that perhaps comments should be used sparingly and judiciously.

● Constants

Many programs have values that do not change while the program is running – and don't change very often anyway. Examples are a sales tax, the age for voting, the threshold for paying tax, mathematical constants. Java provides the facility to declare data items as constants and give them a value. So, for these examples, we can write:

```
final double taxRate = 17.5;
final int votingAge = 18;
final int taxThreshold = 5000;
final double pi = 3.142;
```

Variables like this with constant values can only be declared at the top of a class and not as local variables within a method.

Strings and arrays can also be given constant values:

```
final String ourPlanet = "Earth";
final int [] prices = {12, 18, 24};
```

One benefit of using **final** values is that the compiler will detect any attempt (no doubt by mistake!) to change the value of a constant. Thus, for example, given the declaration above, the statement:

```
votingAge = 17;
```

will provoke a compiler error message.

Another, more powerful, benefit is that a program that otherwise might be peppered with rather meaningless numbers contains variables (which are constant) with clear, meaningful names. This enhances program clarity, with all its consequent benefits.

Suppose, for example, we need to alter a tax program to reflect a change in regulations. We have a nightmare task if the tax thresholds and tax rates are built into the program as numbers that appear as and when throughout the program. Suppose that the old tax threshold is 5000. We could use a text editor to search for all occurrences of 5000. The editor will dutifully tell us where all the occurrences are, but we are left unsure that this number has the same meaning everywhere. What if the number 4999 appears in the program? Is it the tax threshold − 1? Or does it have some other completely unrelated meaning? The answer, of course, is to use constants, with good names, and to distinguish carefully between different data items.

Another common use for **final** values is to specify the sizes of any arrays used in a program, as in:

```
final int arraySize = 10;
```

and thereafter:

```
int [] myArray = new int[arraySize];
```

It is the convention to use upper-case letters for the names of constants that are provided in the libraries. Thus, for example: **PI**, **E**, **HORIZONTAL**. Using upper case distinguishes these values from others in the program and makes it evident that they are indeed constants. Most programmers use this same convention for the names of their own constants.

● Methods

Method names

We have already emphasized the importance of meaningful names. Method names are almost always verbs. When a method has the simple role of obtaining the value of some data item (called, say, **salary**) it is conventional to call it **getSalary**. Similarly, if a method is to be provided to change the value of this same variable, then the conventional name is **setSalary**.

Method size

It is possible to get into long and enjoyable arguments about how long a method should be.

One view is that a method should not be longer than the screen or a single page of listing (say 40 lines of text). That way, you do not have to scroll or turn a page to study it as a whole. You can thoroughly study the method in its entirety. It is not so long that you lose track of some parts of it.

Any method that is longer than half a page is a serious candidate for restructuring into smaller methods. However, it depends on what the method does – it may do a single cohesive task, and an attempt to split it up may introduce complications involving parameters and scope. Do not apply any length recommendation blindly.

If you look at programs on the screen, restricting the length of methods to what is visible on one screen can help.

● Nested ifs

Nesting is the term given to the situation in a program when there is a statement within another statement: for example, a **while** loop within a **for** loop, or an **if** statement within an **if** statement. Sometimes a nested program is simple and clear. But generally, a high degree of nesting is considered to be bad, and best avoided. It is always avoidable by rewriting the program.

Let us look at nested **if**s. Consider the problem of finding the largest of three numbers:

```
int a, b, c;
int largest;

if (a > b) {
    if (a > c) {
        largest = a;
    }
    else {
        largest = c;
    }
}
else {
    if (b > c) {
        largest = b;
    }
    else {
        largest = c;
    }
}
```

This is certainly a complicated-looking piece of program, and some people may have a little trouble understanding it. People are not always convinced that it works correctly. So, on the evidence, it is difficult to read and understand. Arguably the complexity arises from the nesting of the **if**s.

An alternative piece of program that avoids the nesting is:

```
int a, b, c;
int largest;

if (a > b && a > c) {
    largest = a;
}
if (b > a && b > c) {
    largest = b;
}
if (c > a && c > b) {
    largest = c;
}
```

which may be clearer to some people. The trouble with this un-nested solution is that the three **if** statements are **always** executed, whereas in the first program only **two** tests are performed. So the second program will run slightly slower. This is true in general – programs with nested **if**s run faster.

Here's another example of nesting. In a program to play a card game, the suit of a card is encoded as an integer (1 to 4). In this part of the program the integer is converted to the string name of the suit. This code makes use of a number of nested **if** statements. Remember that where there is only a single statement within the **if**, the curly brackets (braces) are not necessary. So we can write the code more concisely with the following style:

```
int s;
String suit;

if (s == 1)
    suit = "hearts";
else if (s == 2)
        suit = "clubs";
    else if (s == 3)
            suit = "spades";
        else if (s == 4)
                suit = "diamonds";
```

where there is an **if** within an **if**, within an **if**, etc. This piece of program uses consistent indentation, but maybe it is not too easy to understand. So some people recommend laying out this code in this alternative manner:

```
int s;
String suit;

if (s == 1)
    suit = "hearts";
else if (s == 2)
        suit = "clubs";
else if (s == 3)
        suit = "spades";
else if (s == 4)
        suit = "diamonds";
```

which is more compact, but does not show the nesting as clearly.

An alternative is to write the code without nesting, as follows:

```
int s;
String suit;

if (s == 1) {
    suit = "hearts";
}
if (s == 2) {
    suit = "clubs";
}
if (s == 3) {
    suit = "spades";
}
if (s == 4) {
    suit = "diamonds";
}
```

which is arguably much clearer. Again, the penalty is that the clearer program is slower – because all the **ifs** are always executed.

No doubt you, the reader, have seen that there is perhaps a resolution to this dilemma. We could recode this piece of program using the **switch** statement as:

```
int s;
String suit;

switch(s) {
    case 1 : suit = "hearts"; break;
    case 2 : suit = "clubs"; break;
    case 3 : suit = "spades"; break;
    case 4 : suit = "diamonds"; break;
}
```

which is both clear and fast. The problem is, however, that the **switch** statement is restricted; you can only use it to switch on the value of an integer or a single character. So, for example, it cannot be used in the program above to find the largest of three numbers. Use of **switch** is not a general solution to the problem of nested **ifs**.

The conclusion is this: if you avoid nested **ifs** you may suffer a performance penalty. In practice, reduced performance will only matter if the test is carried out inside a loop repeated many times within a program that is time critical.

Finally, nested **if** statements are not always bad, and there are occasions where nesting simply and clearly describes what needs to be done.

● Nested loops

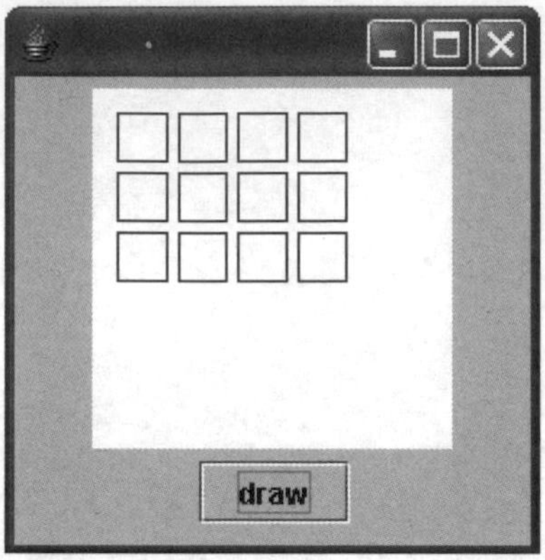

Figure 19.1 Nested loops.

Let us now look at nesting within loops. Suppose we are writing a program that displays a pattern such as the screen shown in Figure 19.1, which is a crude graphic of a block of flats (apartments). The piece of program could look like this:

```
private void drawApartments(int floors, int apartments) {
    int xCoord, yCoord;
    yCoord = 10;
    for (int floor = 0; floor < floors; floor++) {
        xCoord = 10;
        for (int count = 0; count < apartments; count++) {
            paper.drawRect(xCoord, yCoord, 20, 20);
            xCoord = xCoord + 25;
        }
    yCoord = yCoord + 25;
    }
}
```

in which one loop is nested within the other. This is not a particularly complex piece of code, but we can simplify it using another method:

```
private void drawApartments(int floors, int apartments) {
    int yCoord = 10;
    for (int count = 0; count < floors; count++) {
        drawFloor(yCoord, apartments);
        yCoord = yCoord + 25;
    }
}
```

```
private void drawFloor(int yCoord, int apartments) {
    int xCoord = 10;
    for (int count = 0; count < apartments; count++) {
        paper.drawRect(xCoord, yCoord, 20, 20);
        xCoord = xCoord + 25;
    }
}
```

By using an additional method we have eliminated the nesting. We have also expressed explicitly in the coding the fact that the apartment block consists of a number of floors. We have clarified the requirement that there is a change in the *y* coordinate for each floor of the block. It is always possible to eliminate nested loops in this manner, and sometimes this achieves a simplification of the program.

Research studies have shown that we humans find it difficult to understand programs that use nesting. One researcher has summed this up by saying, 'Nesting is for the birds.' But nesting is not **always** bad. Take, for example, the coding to initialize a two-dimensional array:

```
int[][] table = new int[10][10];

for (int row = 0; row < 10; row++) {
    for (int col = 0; col < 10; col++) {
        table[row][col] = 0;
    }
}
```

which is clear even with nesting.

Complex conditions

Complexity in an **if**, **for** or **while** statement can arise when the condition being tested involves one or more ands and ors. A complex condition can make a program very difficult to understand, debug and get right. As an example, we will look at a program that searches an array of numbers to find a desired number:

```
final int length = 100;
int[] table = new int[length];

int wanted;
int index;

index = 0;
while (index < length && table[index] != wanted) {
    index++;
}
```

```
    if (index == length) {
        status.setText("not found");
    }
    else {
        status.setText("found");
    }
```

The problem with this program is that the condition in the **for** is complex. Even for an experienced programmer it can be difficult to check what has been written and to convince yourself that it is correct. There is an alternative: we will use a flag. It is simply an integer variable, but its value at any time records the status of the search. There are three possible states that the search can be in:

■ The program is still searching; the item is not yet found. This is also the initial state of the search. The flag has the value 0.

■ The item has been found. The flag value is 1.

■ The search has been completed but without finding the item. The flag value is 2.

Using this flag, called **state**, the program becomes:

```
    final int length = 100;
    int[] table = new int[length];

    int wanted;
    int state;
    final int stillSearching = 0;
    final int found = 1;
    final int notFound = 2;

    state = stillSearching;
    for (int index = 0; state == stillSearching; index++) {
        if (wanted == table[index]) {
            state = found;
        }
        else {
            if (index == length - 1) {
                state = notFound;
            }
        }
    }

    if (state == notFound) {
        status.setText("not found");
    }
    else {
        status.setText("found");
    }
```

What has been accomplished is that the various tests have been disentangled. The condition in the `for` loop is clearer and simpler. The other tests are separate and simple. The program overall is arguably simpler.

The moral is that it is often possible to write a piece of program in different ways. Some solutions are simpler and clearer than others. Sometimes it is possible to avoid complexity in a condition by rewriting the program fragment with the use of a flag.

Documentation

Documentation is the bugbear of the programmer – until, of course, the programmer has to sort out someone else's program! Commercial organizations usually try to encourage programmers to document their programs well. They tell the old and probably fictitious story about the programmer who had a program 95% complete, did no documentation and then went out and got run over by a bus. The colleagues who remained allegedly had a terrible job trying to continue work on the program.

Program documentation typically consists of the following ingredients:

- the program specification;
- the source code, including appropriate comments;
- design information, e.g. class diagrams;
- the test schedule;
- the test results;
- the modification history;
- the user manual (if needed).

If you ever get asked to take over someone's program, this is what you will need – but don't expect to get it!

Programmers generally find creating documentation a boring chore and tend to skimp on it. They generally leave it to the end of the project, when there's little time available. No wonder it is often not done or done poorly.

The only way to ease the pain is to do the documentation as you go along, mixing it in with the more interesting tasks of programming.

Consistency

Though people's views on programming style often differ, one thing that they always agree on is that a style should be applied consistently throughout a program. If the style is inconsistent it makes the program hard to read (not to say annoying). It also creates a worry that the original programmer didn't really care about the program and that there is something wrong with it. Throughout this book we have used one consistent style for the layout of programs. It is the style used in the Java libraries and used in the definitive books on Java, by James Gosling (the principal designer of Java) and his colleagues.

Programming pitfalls

Don't spend hours and hours making your program beautiful only then to find that there is a useful tool available. A pretty-printer, prettyfier, beautifier or indenter program will do what its name suggests. Check what prettyfiers are available **before** you start to code. Also check whether there are any house standards in your organization before you start to code. You might have to follow them. If you do want to stick to a plan for laying out the program, it's often better to do it from the start, rather than type it in roughly and change it later.

Summary

- Program style is important to promote readability for debugging and maintenance.

- Guidelines for good program layout embrace good names, indentation, blank lines, new pages and comments.

- The Java **final** description makes a data item constant.

- Methods should not be too long.

- Nested **if**s, loops and complex conditions should be used judiciously.

- Good documentation is always worthy.

Exercises

19.1 Look at as many programs as you can (including your own) and review their styles. Are they good or bad? Why?

19.2 Discuss the issue of guidelines with colleagues or friends. Does style matter? If so, what constitutes good style?

19.3 Investigate what beautifier (pretty-printer) programs are available to you.

19.4 Devise a set of style guidelines for Java programs.

19.5 (Optional) Use your style guidelines for evermore.

CHAPTER
20

Testing

This chapter explains:

- why exhaustive testing is not feasible;
- how to carry out functional testing;
- how to carry out structural testing;
- how to perform walkthroughs;
- how to carry out testing using single stepping;
- the role of formal verification;
- incremental development.

● Introduction

Programs are complex and it is difficult to make them work correctly. Testing is the set of techniques used to attempt to verify that a program does work correctly. Put another way, testing attempts to reveal the existence of bugs. Once you realize that there is a bug, you need to locate it using debugging (see Chapter 21) and then fix it. As we shall see, testing techniques cannot guarantee to expose all the bugs in a program and so most large programs have hidden bugs in them. Nonetheless testing is enormously important. This is evidenced by the fact that it can typically consume up to one-half of the total time spent on developing a program. In some organizations, testing is considered to be so important that there are teams of programmers (who write programs) and separate teams of testers (who test programs). There are usually as many testers as programmers.

Because it needs so much time and effort to test and debug programs thoroughly, a difficult decision has sometimes to be made: whether to continue the testing or whether to deliver the program in its current state to the clients.

In academic circles, the task of trying to ensure that a program does what is expected is called *verification*. The aim is to *verify* that a program meets its specification.

In this chapter we will see how to carry out testing systematically, review different approaches to verification, and see what their deficiencies are.

The techniques we will review are:

■ black box or functional testing;

■ white box or structural testing;

■ reviews or walkthroughs;

■ stepping through code with a debugger;

■ formal methods.

A small program that consists only of a single class can usually be tested all at once. A larger program that involves two or more classes may be of such complexity that it must be tested in pieces. In Java the natural size for these pieces is the class and it is convenient to test a program class by class. This is called *unit testing*. When the complete program is brought together for testing the task is called *integration* or *system testing*.

We will also look at developing a program bit by bit, rather than as a complete program.

● Program specifications

The starting point for any testing is the specification. It is never a waste of time to study and clarify the specification. This may well necessitate going back to the client or the future user of the program. Take the following specification, for example:

> Write a program that inputs a series of numbers via a text box. The program calculates and displays the sum of the numbers.

On first reading, this specification may look simple and clear. But, even though it is so short, it contains pitfalls:

■ Are the numbers integers or floating point?

■ What is the permissible range and precision of the numbers?

■ Are negative numbers to be included in the sum?

These questions should be clarified before the programmer starts any programming. Indeed it is part of the job of programming to study the specification, discover any omissions or confusions, and gain agreement to a clear specification. After all, it is no use writing a brilliant program if it doesn't do what the client wanted.

Here now is a clearer version of the specification, which we will use as a case study in looking at testing methods:

Write a program that inputs a series of integers via a text box. The integers are in the range 0 to 10000. The program calculates and displays the sum of the numbers.

You can see that this specification is more precise – for example, it stipulates the permissible range of input values.

Exhaustive testing

One approach to testing would be to test a program with all possible data values as input. But consider the simplest of programs: a program that inputs a pair of integer numbers and displays their product. Exhaustive testing would mean that we select all possible values of the first number and all possible values for the second. And then we use all possible combinations of numbers. In Java, an `int` number has a huge range of possible values. All in all, the number of possible combinations of numbers is enormous. All the different values would have to be keyed in and the program run. The human time taken to assemble the test data would be years. Even the time that the computer needs would be days, fast as computers are. Finally, checking that the computer had got the answers correct would drive someone mad with tedium.

Thus exhaustive testing – even for a small and simple program – is not feasible. It is important to recognize that complete testing, for all but the smallest program, is impossible. Therefore we have to adopt some other approach.

Black box (functional) testing

Knowing that exhaustive testing is infeasible, the *black box* approach to testing is to devise sample data that is representative of all possible data. Then we run the program, input the data and see what happens. This type of testing is termed black box testing because no knowledge of the workings of the program is used as part of the testing – we only consider inputs and outputs. The program is thought of as being invisibly enclosed within a black box. Black box testing is also known as functional testing because it uses only knowledge of the function of the program (not how it works).

Ideally, testing proceeds by writing down the test data and the expected outcome of the test, before testing takes place. This is called a test specification or schedule. Then you run the program, input the data and examine the outputs for discrepancies between the predicted outcome and the actual outcome. Test data should also check whether exceptions are handled by the program in accordance with its specification.

Consider a program that decides whether a person can vote, depending on their age (Figure 20.1). The minimum voting age is 18.

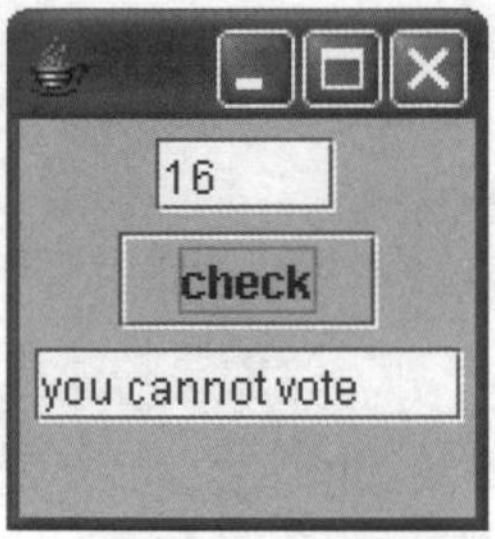

Figure 20.1 The voting checker program.

We know that we cannot realistically test this program with all possible values, but instead we need some typical values. The approach to devising test data for black box testing is to use *equivalence partitioning*. This means looking at the nature of the input data to identify common features. Such a common feature is called a partition. In the voting program, we recognize that the input data falls into two partitions:

■ the numbers less than 18;

■ the numbers greater than or equal to 18.

This can be diagrammed as follows:

0	17	18	infinity

There are two partitions, one including the age range 0 to 17 and the other partition with numbers 18 to infinity. We then take the step of asserting that every number within a partition is equivalent to any other, for the purpose of testing this program. (Hence the term equivalence partitioning.) So we argue that the number 12 is equivalent to any other in the first partition and the number 21 is equivalent to any number in the second. So we devise two tests:

Test number	Data	Outcome
1	12	cannot vote
2	21	can vote

We have reasoned that we need two sets of test data to test this program. These two sets, together with a statement of the expected outcomes from testing, constitute a test specification. We run the program with the two sets of data and note any discrepancies between predicted and actual outcome.

Unfortunately, we can see that these tests have not investigated the important distinction between someone aged 17 and someone aged 18. Anyone who has ever written a program knows that using `if` statements is error prone. So it is advisable to investigate this particular region of the data. This is the same as recognizing that data values at the edges of the partitions are worthy of inclusion in the testing. Therefore we create two additional tests:

Test number	Data	Outcome
3	17	cannot vote
4	18	can vote

In summary, the rules for selecting test data for black box testing using equivalence partitioning are:

1. Partition the input data values.
2. Select representative data from each partition (equivalent data).
3. Select data at the boundaries of partitions.

In the last program, there is a single input; there are four data values and therefore four tests. However, most programs process a number of inputs. Suppose we wish to test a program that displays the larger of two numbers, each in the range 0 to 10000, entered into a pair of text boxes. If the values are equal, the program displays either value.

Each input is within a partition that runs from 0 to 10000. We choose values at each end of the partitions and sample values somewhere in the middle:

first number:	0	54	10000
second number:	0	142	10000

Now that we have selected representative values, we need to consider what combinations of values we should use. Exhaustive testing would mean using every possible combination of every possible data value – but this is, of course, infeasible. Instead, we use every combination of the representative values. So the tests are:

Test number	First number	Second number	Outcome
1	0	0	0
2	0	142	142
3	0	10000	10000
4	54	0	54
5	54	142	142
6	54	10000	10000
7	10000	0	10000
8	10000	142	10000
9	10000	10000	10000

Thus the additional step in testing is to use every combination of the (limited) representative data values.

SELF-TEST QUESTION

20.2 In a program to play the game of chess, the player specifies the destination for a move as a pair of indices, the row and column number. The program checks that the destination square is valid; that is, not outside the board. Devise black box test data to check that this part of the program is working correctly.

● White box (structural) testing

White box testing makes use of knowledge of how the program works – the structure of the program – as the basis for devising test data. In white box testing every statement in the program is executed at some time during the testing. This is equivalent to ensuring that every path (every sequence of instructions) through the program is executed at some time during testing. This includes null paths, so an `if` statement without an `else` has two paths and every loop has two paths. Testing should also include any exception handling carried out by the program.

Here is the code for the voting checker program we are using as a case study:

```java
public void actionPerformed(ActionEvent event) {
    int age;
    age = Integer.parseInt(textField.getText());
    if (age >= 18) {
        result.setText("you can vote");
    }
    else {
        result.setText("you cannot vote");
    }
}
```

In this program, there are two paths (because the `if` has two branches) and therefore two sets of data will serve to ensure that all statements are executed at some time during the testing:

Test number	Data	Expected outcome
1	12	cannot vote
2	21	can vote

If we are cautious, we realize that errors in programming are often made within the conditions of `if` and `while` statements. So we add a further two tests to ensure that the `if` statement is working correctly:

Test number	Data	Expected outcome
3	17	cannot vote
4	18	can vote

Thus we need four sets of data to test this program in a white box fashion. This happens to be the same data that we devised for black box testing. But the reasoning that led to the two sets of data is different. Had the program been written differently, the white box test data would be different. Suppose, for example, the program used an array, named **table**, with one element for each age specifying whether someone of that age can vote. Then the program is simply the following statement to lookup eligibility:

```
result.setText(table[age]);
```

and the white box testing data is different.

SELF-TEST QUESTIONS

20.3 A program's function is to find the largest of three numbers. Devise white box test data for this section of program.
The code is:

```
int a, b, c;
int largest;
if (a >= b) {
    if (a >= c) {
        largest = a;
    }
    else {
        largest = c;
    }
}
else {
    if (b >= c) {
        largest = b;
    }
    else {
        largest = c;
    }
}
```

20.4 In a program to play the game of chess, the player specifies the destination for a move as a pair of integer indices, the row and column number. The program checks that the destination square is valid; that is, not outside the board. Devise white box test data to check that this part of the program is working correctly.

The code for this part of the program is:

```
if ((row > 8) || (row < 1)) {
    JOptionPane.showMessageDialog(null, "error");
}
if ((col > 8) || (col < 1)) {
    JOptionPane.showMessageDialog(null, "error");
}
```

● Inspections and walkthroughs

There is an approach that doesn't make use of a computer at all in trying to eradicate faults – it is called inspection or a walkthrough. In an inspection (or walkthrough), someone simply studies the program listing (along with the specification) in order to try to see bugs. It works better if the person doing the inspecting is not the person who wrote the program. This is because people tend to be blind to their own errors. So get a friend or a colleague to inspect your program. It is extraordinary to witness how quickly someone else sees an error that has been defeating you for hours.

To inspect a program you need:

■ the specification;
■ the text of the program on paper.

In carrying out an inspection, one approach is to study the program a method at a time. Some of the checks are fairly mechanical:

■ variables initialized;
■ loops correctly initialized and terminated;
■ method calls have the correct parameters.

Further checking examines the logic of the program. Pretend to execute the method as if you were a computer, avoiding following any method calls into other methods. (This is why a walkthrough is so called.) Check that:

■ the logic of the method achieves its desired purpose.

During inspection, you can check that:

- variable and method names are meaningful;
- the logic is clear and correct.

Although the prime goal of an inspection is not to check for style, a weakness in any of these areas may point to a bug.

The evidence from controlled experiments suggests that inspections are a very effective way of finding errors. In fact, inspections are at least as good a way of identifying bugs as actually running the program (doing testing).

Stepping through code

Some Java development systems provide a debugger with a single-stepping facility. This allows you to step through a program, executing just one instruction at a time. Each time you execute an instruction you can see which path of execution has been taken. The debugger may also allow you to display (or watch) the values of variables. It is rather like an automated structured walkthrough.

In this form of testing you concentrate on:

- Checking that the computer is executing the expected path through the program.
- Checking the values of variables as they are changed by the program, to verify that they have been changed correctly.

Whereas the debugger is usually used for debugging (locating a bug), in this technique it is used for testing (denying or confirming the existence of a bug).

Formal verification

Formal methods employ the precision and power of mathematics in attempting to verify that a program meets its specification. They place emphasis on the precision of the specification, which must first be rewritten in a formal mathematical notation. One such specification language is called Z. Once the formal specification for a program has been written, there are two alternative approaches:

1. Write the program and then verify that it conforms to the specification. This requires considerable time and skill.
2. Derive the program from the specification by means of a series of transformations, each of which preserves the correctness of the product. This is currently the favoured approach.

Formal verification is very appealing because of its potential for rigorously verifying a program's correctness beyond all possible doubt. However, it must be remembered that these methods are carried out by fallible human beings who make mistakes. So they are not a cure-all.

Formal verification is still in its infancy and is not widely used in industry and commerce, except in a few safety-critical applications. Further discussion of this approach is beyond the scope of this book.

● Incremental development

One approach to writing a program is to write the complete program, key it in and try to run it. The salient word here is 'try' – because most programmers find that the friendly compiler will find lots of errors in their program. It can be very disheartening – particularly for novices – to see so many errors displayed by a program that was the result of so much effort. Once the compilation errors have been banished, the program will usually exhibit unwanted behaviours during the (sometimes lengthy) period of debugging and testing. If all the parts of a program are keyed in together for testing, it can be difficult to locate any errors. This is sometimes called *big-bang* development.

An alternative useful technique for helping to avoid these frustrations is to do things bit by bit. Thus an alternative to big-bang development is piece-by-piece programming – usually called *incremental* programming. The steps are:

1. Design and code the user interface.
2. Write a small piece of the program.
3. Key it in, fix the syntax errors, run it and debug it.
4. Add a new small piece of the program.
5. Repeat from step 2 until the program is complete.

The trick is to identify which piece of program to start with and which order to do things in. The best approach is probably to start by writing the simplest of the event-handling methods. Then write any methods that are used by this first method. Then write another event-handling method, and so on.

Incremental testing avoids looking for a needle in a haystack, since a newly discovered error is probably in the newly incorporated code.

Programming principles

There is no foolproof testing method that will ensure that a program is free of errors. The best approach would be to use a combination of testing methods – black box, white box and inspection – because they have been shown to find different errors. To use all three methods is, however, very time consuming. So you need to exercise considerable judgement and skill to decide what sort of testing to do and how much testing to do. A systematic approach is vital.

Testing is a frustrating business – because we know that, however patient and systematic we are, we can never be sure that we have done enough. Testing requires massive patience, attention to detail and organization.

Writing a program is a constructive experience, but testing is destructive. It can be difficult to try to demolish an object of pride that has taken hours to create – knowing that if an error is found, then further hours may be needed in order to rectify the problem. So it is all too easy to behave like an ostrich during testing, trying to avoid the problems.

Summary

- Testing is a technique that tries to establish that a program is free from errors.

- Testing cannot be exhaustive because there are too many cases.

- Black box testing uses only the specification to choose test data.

- White box testing uses a knowledge of how the program works in order to choose test data.

- Inspection simply means studying the program listing in order to find errors.

- Stepping through code using a debugger can be a valuable way of testing a program.

- Incremental development can avoid the complexities of developing large programs.

● Exercises

20.1 Devise black box and white box test data to test the following program. The specification is:

> The program inputs integers using a text field and a button. The program displays the largest of the numbers entered so far.

Try not to look at the text of the program, given below, until you have completed the design of the black box data.

At class level, there is an instance variable declaration:

```
private int largest = 0;
```

The event-handling code is:

```
public void actionPerformed(ActionEvent event) {
    int number;
    number = Integer.parseInt(textField.getText());
    if (number > largest) {
        largest = number;
    }
    result.setText("largest so far is " + Integer.toString(largest));
}
```

20.2 Devise black box and white box test data to test the following program. The specification is given below. Try not to look at the text of the program, also given below, until you have completed the design of the black box data.

The program determines insurance premiums for a holiday, based upon the age and gender (male or female) of the client:

For a female of age >= 18 and <= 30 the premium is $5.
A female aged >= 31 pays $3.50.
A male of age >= 18 and <= 35 pays $6.
A male aged >= 36 pays $5.50.
Any other ages or genders are an error, which is signalled as a premium of 0.

The code for this program is:

```java
public double calcPremium(double age, String gender) {
    double premium;
    if (gender.("female")) {
        if ((age >= 18) && (age <= 30)) {
            premium = 5.0;
        }
        else {
            if (age >= 31) {
                premium = 3.50;
            }
            else {
                premium = 0;
            }
        }
    }
    else {
        if (gender.("male")) {
            if ((age >= 18) && (age <= 35)) {
                premium = 6.0;
            }
            else {
                if (age >= 36) {
                    premium = 5.5;
                }
                else {
                    premium = 0;
                }
            }
        }
        else {
            premium = 0;
        }
    }
    return premium;
}
```

Answers to self-test questions

20.1 The specification does not say what is to happen if an exception arises. There are several possibilities. The first situation is if the user enters data that is not a valid integer – for example, a letter is entered instead of a digit. The next situation is if the user enters a number greater than 10000. The final eventuality that might arise is if the sum of the numbers exceeds the size of number that can be accommodated by the computer. If integers are represented as `int` types in the program, this limit is huge, but it could arise.

20.2 A row number is in three partitions:

1. within the range 1 to 8;
2. less than 1;
3. greater than 8.

If we choose one representative value in each partition (say 3, –3 and 11 respectively) and a similar set of values for the column numbers (say 5, –2 and 34), the test data will be:

Test number	Row	Column	Outcome
1	3	5	OK
2	–3	5	invalid
3	11	5	invalid
4	3	–2	invalid
5	–3	–2	invalid
6	11	–2	invalid
7	3	34	invalid
8	–3	34	invalid
9	11	34	invalid

We now remember that data near the boundary of the partitions is important and therefore add to the test data for each partition so that it becomes:

1. within the range 1 to 8 (say 3);
2. less than 1 (say –3);
3. greater than 8 (say 11);
4. boundary value 1;
5. boundary value 8;
6. boundary value 0;
7. boundary value 9.

which now gives many more combinations to use as test data.

▶

▶ *Answers to self-test questions*

20.3 There are four paths through the program, which can be exercised by the following test data:

Test number				Outcome
1	3	2	1	3
2	3	2	5	5
3	2	3	1	3
4	2	3	5	5

20.4 There are three paths through the program extract, including the path where neither of the conditions in the `if` statements are true. But each of the error messages can be triggered by two conditions. Suitable test data is therefore:

Test number	Row	Column	Outcome
1	5	6	OK
2	0	4	invalid
3	9	4	invalid
4	5	9	invalid
5	5	0	invalid

CHAPTER
21

Debugging

This chapter explains:

- how to debug programs;
- how to use a debugger;
- common errors.

● Introduction

Debugging is the name given to the job of finding out where the bugs are in a program and then fixing the problem. A bug is an error in a program and, because we are all human, all programs tend to have bugs in them when they are first written. There are three things that happen to a program as it is being developed:

1. compilation;
2. linking;
3. running.

We now look at these in turn.

Compilation

After you have keyed in a program, you usually have to spend some time eradicating the compilation errors. A common example is a semicolon missing. The Java compiler carries out comprehensive series of checks on a program, thus exposing many errors that might otherwise persist. Eventually the program compiles 'cleanly'. Once a program is free of compilation errors, it usually does something visible – even though it may not do exactly what you want.

Linking

All programs make use of library methods and some make use of programmer-written methods. A method **is** linked only when it is called, while the program is running. But when the program is compiled, checks are carried out that all the methods that are called do exist and that the parameters match in number and type. So linking errors are detected at compile-time.

Running

A program runs, but it is most unusual for it to work as expected. In fact it is usual for the program to fail in some way or behave in a way other than was intended. Some errors are detected automatically and the programmer is notified – like an attempt to access a part of an array that does not exist (an index error). Others are more subtle and simply give rise to unexpected behaviour. You have a bug in the program – or more likely many bugs! So you have to carry out some debugging.

Later on in this chapter we give examples of common errors that arise in Java programming.

The term 'bug' originated in the days of valve computers, when (the story goes) a large insect became lodged in the circuitry of an early computer, causing it to malfunction. Hence the term 'bug' and the term 'debugging'.

The problem with debugging is that the symptoms of a bug are usually very uninformative. So we have to resort to detective work to find the cause. It's like being a doctor: there is a symptom, you have to find the cause, and then you have to fix the problem.

Once the more obvious faults in a program have been eliminated, it is usual to start carrying out some systematic testing. Testing is the repeated running of a program with a variety of data as input. It is discussed in Chapter 20. The aim of testing is to convince the world that the program works properly. But normally testing reveals the existence of more bugs. Then it's time to do some debugging. So testing and debugging go hand in hand.

SELF-TEST QUESTION

21.1   What is the difference between debugging and testing?

Many programmers like debugging; they see it as exciting – like watching a mystery thriller in which the villain is revealed only at the last moment. Certainly, along with testing, debugging often takes a long time. In fact debugging often takes longer than writing the program in the first place. Do not be worried that debugging takes you some time – this is normal!

● Debugging without a debugger

A program runs but behaves unexpectedly. How do we find the source of the problem? Most programs display something on the screen, but otherwise what they do is invisible. We need something like x-ray specs to gain some insight into how the program is behaving. This is the key to successful debugging – getting additional information about the running program.

One way to obtain additional information is to insert extra output statements in the program so that it displays information as it is running. One convenient way to display information is using option panes.

For example, take the **Balloon** class that was used in Chapter 9. Suppose that the balloon object is not displayed or it is displayed in the wrong place. In order to obtain additional information, we insert a statement to display an option pane that reveals the *x* coordinate, the *y* coordinate and the diameter of the balloon. The code to do this is:

```
JOptionPane.showMessageDialog(null,
            "x = " + x +
            " y = " + y +
            " diameter = " + diameter);
```

and the display is shown in Figure 21.1.

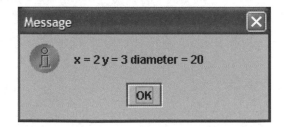

Figure 21.1 Display used for debugging.

We can now see whether this information is correct, or whether it gives us useful information about the bug.

The trick is to choose the best points in the program to put the statements to display option panes. If we insert too many probes into the program, there will be too much irrelevant and annoying information. Generally, good places to choose are:

■ just before a method is called (to check that the parameters are OK) or right at the start of the method;

■ just after a method is called (to check that the method has done its work correctly) or right at the end of the method.

● Using a debugger

This book deliberately avoids reference to any particular development package. The Java system that you are using may have a 'debugger'. A debugger is a program that helps you debug your program. It runs alongside your program, allowing the progress of the program to be inspected. A debugger provides several facilities but unfortunately debuggers are not standardized – they are all different and therefore we can't explain all the different facilities in detail. Some of the debuggers that are available are rather primitive. For example, the jdb (java debugger) is text based and command-line oriented, with Unix ancestry. There are also good debuggers available, which are part of an IDE.

However, we will explain the principles of using a good interactive, integrated debugger. Imagine three windows on the screen, all visible at once:

- the window created by the running program;
- the display of the source code of the Java program;
- a display of the names of selected variables together with their current values.

Breakpoints

Using a debugger, the programmer places a *breakpoint* in the program. A breakpoint is a place in the program where execution stops. A breakpoint is inserted by pointing to a line in the text of the program with the cursor and selecting a menu option. Then the program is set running. When a breakpoint is reached, the program freezes, a pointer highlights the position of the breakpoint in the program text and the debugger displays the values of variables as they are at the moment in the program's execution. Any discrepancy between what they actually are and what they should be provides valuable information for debugging.

Single stepping

A debugger will also let you execute a program one line at a time; this is called *single shotting* or *stepping*. You can follow the progress of the program and check that it behaves as expected. When it doesn't, you know you are close to locating a bug.

It can safely be assumed that library methods are free from errors, so you do not want to waste time single stepping through library methods. Debuggers normally provide an option to execute selected methods at full speed.

It is easy to have a lot of fun with a debugger, but the downside can be using a lot of time. A productive way to use a debugger is as follows:

1. From the symptoms of the bug, make a hypothesis about where the bug lies. You may be able to predict that the error lies within any of two or three methods.

2. Place breakpoints at the entry and exit of the methods under suspicion.

3. Run the program. When the program stops at the entry to a method, inspect the values of the parameters. At the exit, inspect the value of the return value and the

values of significant instance variables. Thus identify the method within which the bug lies.

4. Run the program again, stopping at the entry to the erroneous method. Single step through this method until you see the discrepancy between expectation and reality.

5. You have found the bug.

Certain errors are commonly made by Java programmers. We list some of them below. It's worthwhile checking any suspect program for these errors.

● Common errors – compilation errors

The Java compiler carries out a lot of checking on a program as it compiles it to byte code. This is part of trying to ensure that Java programs are robust. An error caught at compile-time is easily fixed, but if it is left undetected until run-time it may take a lot of debugging. So although compile-time errors can be annoying, they are worthwhile.

Semicolons

This is the most common compilation error: leaving out semicolons. Note that the compiler will usually flag up the statement after the one in error.

`if` statements

It is easy to forget that `if` statements must have brackets surrounding the condition, like this:

```
if (a == b) etc
```

Curly brackets (braces)

A common error is to omit a curly bracket { or } or have one in the wrong place. Good and consistent indentation can help you to see and correct this problem.

Method calling with zero parameters

If a method named **doIt** takes no parameters, it is easy to write a method call with the brackets missing:

```
object.doIt;    rather than    object.doIt();
```

The former is regarded as an attempt to access a variable named **doIt** within the object.

Method calling

A common error is a method name spelled wrongly. Another error is to get the number of parameters wrong or the type of a parameter wrong.

Method calling – `import` missing

An **import** statement is missing or specifies the wrong package. This often happens if you are using Swing components such as sliders.

Method calling – `extends` missing

The class heading omits the word **extends**, followed by the relevant class name. Most programs in this book extend the **JFrame** class.

● Common errors – run-time errors

Run-time errors are errors that occur as the program is running, but are caught by the run-time system. Again this is part of the measures designed to ensure that programs are robust. Without run-time checking a program that has gone wrong may act like a bull in a china shop. When a run-time error is detected, an error message is displayed and the program is stopped.

Array indices

Suppose that an array is declared as:

```
int[] table = new int[10];
```

then the following **for** loop will incorrectly try to use the 10th element of the array:

```
for (int s = 0; s <= 10; s++) {
    table[s]=0;
}
```

When this happens the program is stopped and an **ArrayIndexOutOfBoundsException** is thrown.

Arithmetic exceptions

If a program attempts to divide an integer by 0 the program will stop and an error message describing an **ArithmeticException** is displayed. It is fairly easy to let this happen inadvertently, e.g. in a program that contains this fragment:

```
int a, b, c, d;
a = b/(c-d);
```

Floating-point arithmetic does not give rise to exceptions like this; instead the program continues and the result of dividing by 0 is infinity (see Chapter 11).

Null pointer exception

If you declare an object like this:

```
JButton button;
```

and then use it without creating an instance of the object (using **new**):

```
add(button);
```

you will get a **NullPointerException** to say that you are trying to use an object that has not been created.

Common errors – logic errors

Logic errors are the hardest to find, because they depend on the way that the individual program works. Therefore there cannot be any automatic detection of such errors. Some specific errors are, however, common.

Initialization

It is easy to fail to initialize a variable appropriately. In Java, all variables are automatically initialized to some definite value – for example, integers are initialized to zero automatically – but this may not be the intended value. Some compilers flag variables that are used without being initialized. Arrays are initially full of garbage, unless they are initialized in some way. The best practice is to initialize all data explicitly.

Events

You click on a button but nothing happens. You may have failed to provide handling for an event.

Common errors – misunderstanding the language

If the programmer does not fully understand how to use Java properly, programs that look perfectly healthy will not work as expected. Here are some common cases.

Braces

You can omit braces in **if** statements and in loops – provided that only one statement is involved. This can lead to code such as this:

```
if (a > b)
    x = x + a;
    y = y + b;
z = z + c;
```

The layout suggests that two statements should be executed if the condition is true. But braces are omitted, so only one statement will be executed if the condition is true. The indentation is misleading. To make it work as the indentation suggests, insert brackets as follows:

```
if (a > b) {
    x = x + a;
    y = y + b;
}
z = z + c;
```

Equality part 1

When you use an **if** statement to test whether two things are equal, the following is always wrong:

```
if (a = b) ...
```

Because you are using the assignment operator (=) instead of the comparison operator (==). Unfortunately, the compiler does not flag this error.

Equality part 2

It is tempting to write statements such as:

```
if (s == "abc") ...
```

where **s** is a string. This will compile correctly, but if the programmer wants to test to see whether **s** is equal to **"abc"**, it will not work as intended. To achieve this end, the following test is required:

```
if (s.equals("abc")) ...
```

which uses the method **equals** from the class **String**.

The first **if** statement is meaningful, but tests whether the string **s** and the literal **"abc"** are actually the same object – which they are not. The string **s** is an object which the program has created using **new**:

```
String s = new String();
```

whereas the string **"abc"** is a completely distinct string, created automatically by the compiler. So these two strings are not, and can never be, the same object. (Their values could be the same, but they are not the same object.)

This example uses strings, but the same idea applies when any two objects are being compared for equality – the operator **==** is almost certainly wrong and instead the **equals** method of the object should be used. The only occasion on which it is fine to use **==** is to compare integers and other primitive types.

Infinite loops

It is easy to make a slip and place a semicolon immediately after a **while** statement, such as:

```
int a;
while (a == 0);
```

This error is not detected by the compiler and will cause the program to loop for ever.

Summary

- Debugging is finding errors (bugs) in a program and fixing them.

- Some Java development systems provide a 'debugger' program that can assist.

- A breakpoint is a place where the program temporarily stops to permit inspection of the values of variables.

- Single shotting is watching the execution flow through the program, one instruction at a time.

Answer to self-test question

21.1 Testing is attempting to demonstrate that a program is free of bugs.
Knowing that a bug exists (as a result of testing), debugging is trying to locate the bug.

CHAPTER 22

Threads

This chapter explains:

- the concepts of a thread and multithreading;
- how to create threads;
- how to initiate and kill threads;
- the different states of a thread.

● Introduction

We begin by examining a number of situations, some real and some involving computers.

Our first example is a real, human one – a group of people shopping for a meal. Suppose that three students share a house. They decide to have a meal and to split up the work of shopping:

- one buys the meat (they are not vegetarians);
- one buys the vegetables;
- one buys the beer;

and these things they do concurrently. But notice that at some time they must synchronize their activities in order that the meal gets prepared and that they all sit down to eat it at the same time.

A group of musicians in an orchestra play different instruments simultaneously, reading their different parts from a musical score. The score tells each of them what to do and helps them synchronize their notes.

Next, consider a computer controlling an industrial plant such as a biscuit factory. The plant consists of a variety of equipment such as ovens, weighing machines, valves and pumps. These must be controlled concurrently.

When you use a PC, you can ask it to do several things at once: print a file, edit a different file, display the time, and receive email. In reality, a single computer can do only one thing at a time, but because a computer works so quickly, it can share its time between a number of activities. It does this so fast that it gives the impression that it is doing them all at once.

When a Java program does several things at once it is called multithreading. (Some other terms that are used for multithreading are parallelism and concurrency.) Such a program can do several things seemingly at once: display several animations, play sounds, allow the user to interact. Any one of the activities that it is performing is called a thread. This chapter is about writing threads in Java.

We have seen that a program is a series of instructions to the computer, which the computer normally obeys in sequence. The sequence is diverted by method calls, loops and selection (`if`) statements, but it is still a single path that moves through the program. We can use a pencil to simulate the execution of a program, following the path through the program. In multithreading, two or more paths are set in motion. To follow the paths of execution now requires several pencils, one for each thread. Remembering that a computer is only capable of doing one thing at once, we realize that it is dividing its available time between the different threads so as to give the impression that they are all executing at the same time.

All of the programs we have seen thus far in this book consist of a single thread. The computer follows a single path through the program. Sometimes the program does nothing, awaiting an event. However, when an event arises, there is again a single path of execution through the program until the event handling is complete.

But suppose that the program has to carry out a task that takes some time. Examples are:

- copying a file;
- downloading a web page;
- displaying an animation.

In cases such as these, the single thread is preoccupied with the time-consuming task. The consequence is that the program is unable to respond to user events. Any buttons in the window do not work. Even the icons on the window – to minimize and move the window – do not work. A program such as this needs to be restructured to use multithreading. One thread is the GUI, ready to respond at any time to events. A second thread carries out the time-consuming activity.

● Threads

In this chapter we study a program that makes a ball bounce around a panel and a second ball bounce around a second panel (Figure 22.1) – an animation program. The program provides a button labelled 'go' to start one ball bouncing, and a second button to start the other ball.

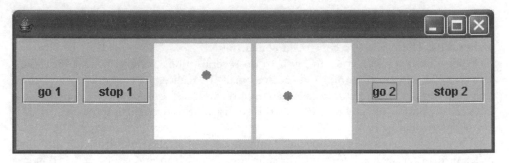

Figure 22.1 Bouncing balls.

The program uses one object to handle the user input and another object to represent a ball object. To ensure that the program is responsive to user events, we create threads running at once. Each thread is a distinct class:

■ One thread is the user-interface object. It has the job of creating other objects and then waiting for any user events, which it will then handle.

■ One thread to draw each bouncing ball.

The first thread creates the other two threads. Thereafter, the three run together, sharing the processor.

This program works very nicely. When you press a 'go' button, a ball is created and bounces around the panel until you press the 'stop' button. The user-interface thread is always responsive to user actions (clicking on a button). The ball threads run independently. Each ball is displayed by its own independent thread.

Animation works by moving an object, drawing its image, waiting a short time, deleting the image and so on repeatedly. The program waits by calling a library method **Thread.sleep**, which has a parameter specifying how long the program waits. The parameter passed to **sleep** is the time in milliseconds that the program wants to sleep. When you use the method **sleep**, Java insists that the programmer must provide an exception handler as shown. (Exceptions are explained in Chapter 16.) When a thread is sleeping, some other thread could attempt to interrupt the sleep. This situation is termed an **InterruptedException**, and in this particular program it can be safely ignored (because there are no other threads around that might do this).

Here is the complete program:

```
import java.awt.*;
import java.awt.event.*;
import javax.swing.*;

class Balls extends JFrame implements ActionListener {

    private JButton go1, go2, stop1, stop2;
    private JPanel panel1, panel2;
```

```
    private Ball ball1, ball2;

    public static void main(String[] args) {
        Balls frame = new Balls();
        frame.setSize(500,150);
        frame.createGUI();
        frame.show();
    }

    private void createGUI() {
        setDefaultCloseOperation(EXIT_ON_CLOSE);
        Container window = getContentPane();
        window.setLayout(new FlowLayout());

        go1 = new JButton("go 1");
        window.add(go1);
        go1.addActionListener(this);

        stop1 = new JButton("stop 1");
        window.add(stop1);
        stop1.addActionListener(this);

        panel1 = new JPanel();
        panel1.setPreferredSize(new Dimension(100, 100));
        panel1.setBackground(Color.white);
        window.add(panel1);

        panel2 = new JPanel();
        panel2.setPreferredSize(new Dimension(100, 100));
        panel2.setBackground(Color.white);
        window.add(panel2);

        go2 = new JButton("go 2");
        window.add(go2);
        go2.addActionListener(this);

        stop2 = new JButton("stop 2");
        window.add(stop2);
        stop2.addActionListener(this);
    }

    public void actionPerformed(ActionEvent event) {
        if (event.getSource() == go1) {
            ball1 = new Ball(panel1);
            ball1.start();
        }
        if (event.getSource() == go2) {
            ball2 = new Ball(panel2);
            ball2.start();
        }
        if (event.getSource() == stop1) {
            ball1.pleaseStop();
```

```
            }
            if (event.getSource() == stop2) {
                ball2.pleaseStop();
            }
        }
    }

class Ball extends Thread {
    private JPanel panel;
    private int x = 7, xChange = 7;
    private int y = 0, yChange = 2;
    private final int diameter = 10;
    private final int width = 100, height = 100;
    boolean keepGoing;
    public Ball(JPanel thePanel) {
        panel = thePanel;
    }

    public void run() {
        keepGoing = true;
        while (keepGoing) {
            move();
            bounce();
            draw();
            delay();
            delete();
        }
    }

    private void move() {
        x = x + xChange;
        y = y + yChange;
    }

    private void bounce() {
        if (x <= 0 || x >= width) {
            xChange = -xChange;
        }
        if (y <= 0 || y >= height) {
            yChange = -yChange;
        }
    }

    private void delay() {
        try {
            Thread.sleep(50);
        }
        catch (InterruptedException e) {
            return;
        }
    }
```

```
private void draw() {
    Graphics paper = panel.getGraphics();
    paper.setColor(Color.red);
    paper.fillOval(x, y, diameter, diameter);
}

private void delete() {
    Graphics paper = panel.getGraphics();
    paper.setColor(Color.white);
    paper.fillOval (x, y, diameter, diameter);
}

public void pleaseStop() {
    keepGoing = false;
}
}
```

Starting a thread

In the bouncing ball program, the user-interface thread is, as usual, an extension of the library **JFrame** class. It creates a new ball object, just as any other object is created, using **new**:

```
Ball ball1 = new Ball(panel1);
```

The user-interface object also asks the Java system to run the thread using the library method **start**:

```
ball1.start();
```

The second class, the class **Ball,** is a distinct thread. A thread must always:

1. Extend (inherit from) the library class **Thread**.
2. Provide a method named **run** which is called by the Java system to set the thread running.

So calling **start** initiates a thread, which in turn causes **run** to be called. As soon as this happens, the original thread (the one that called **start**) continues and the new thread runs. So they run together, in parallel.

SELF-TEST QUESTION

22.1   How many threads:

1. Before you click on a button?
2. After you click on 'go ball 1'?
3. After you click on 'go ball 2'?

● Thread dying

In the bouncing ball program, a ball keeps bouncing until we stop it, by clicking on a button. The way to terminate a bouncing ball thread is to use a `boolean` flag which we will name `keepGoing`. This is initially made `true` when the thread starts, but is set `false` when the user presses the 'stop' button. The loop in the ball object is:

```
while (keepGoing) {
    // body of loop
}
```

which will make a ball bounce while the `boolean` is `true`, and stop when the value is `false`.

In the user-interface thread, we provide a button, labelled 'stop', in the usual way. The part of the event handler needed to handle this 'stop' button is:

```
if (event.getSource() == stop) {
    ball1.pleaseStop();
}
```

and the method in the class `Ball` is:

```
public void pleaseStop() {
    keepGoing = false;
}
```

When the thread `ball1` has finished looping, it exits the method **run** and thereby dies. This is the normal way in which a thread dies.

SELF-TEST QUESTION

22.2   How many threads when you 'go ball 1', 'go ball 2', then 'stop ball 1'?

● join

When using multithreading, you might want to make a thread wait until another has died. This is done with the method `join`. For example, suppose `ball1` does this:

```
ball2.join();
```

Then `ball1` waits until thread `ball2` has died.

● The state of a thread

It can be useful to understand the idea of the states of a thread. A thread can be in any one of these states:

■ **new** It has just been created with the **new** operator, just like any other object, but it has not yet been set runnable by means of the **start** method.

- **running** It is actually running on the computer, executing instructions.
- **runnable** It would like to run, is able to run, but some other thread is currently running.
- **blocked** For some reason the thread cannot proceed until something happens. A typical example would be that the thread has called **sleep** and is suspended for a number of milliseconds.
- **dead** The **run** method has exited normally.

One thread can find out the state of another thread by calling the library method **isAlive**. It returns **true** if the thread is runnable or blocked. It returns **false** if the thread is new or dead. For example:

```
if (ball1.isAlive()) {
    status.setText("ball 1 is alive");
}
```

SELF-TEST QUESTION

22.3 Alter the bouncing ball program so that clicking on a 'go' button does not work when the ball thread is already alive.

Scheduling, thread priorities and `yield`

The Java system has the job of sharing the single (or sometimes multi) processor among the threads in a program. It is often the case that there are several threads that are runnable – they are ready and able to run when the processor becomes available. The scheduler must choose between them. Different schedulers on different machines and Java systems may work differently. There is no guarantee that any particular scheduling is provided. The programmer must be careful not to make any assumptions about when a particular thread will be selected to run.

By default, the Java system gives all the threads that are created the same priority. Thereafter the Java system will share the processor equitably among the active threads. Even so, it is easy for a thread to hog the processor, shutting out other threads. Therefore any thread with a social conscience should call the method **yield** like this:

```
yield();
```

at times when the programmer assesses that the thread may be greedy. If other threads are runnable, they are given a share of processor time. But if no other threads are runnable, the same thread continues.

Programming principles

The main motivation for multithreading is the need to do two or more things at once. In particular, programs need a user interface that is always responsive. So a program is split up into parts that execute concurrently.

Concurrency is very common, both in real life and in computer systems. A parallel activity inside a computer is called a thread, task or sometimes a process. (Java uses the first term.) The code of each individual thread looks like a normal sequential program. The Java system shares out the processor time among the threads in such a way that it seems like they are all executing in parallel. This is sometimes called apparent concurrency. If two people are collaborating over a meal, or if a computer system consists of a number of processors, then there is real concurrency. Some computer scientists call apparent concurrency 'parallelism' and real concurrency simply 'concurrency'. Whatever the terminology we adopt, an essential characteristic of the situation is that the parallelism is explicitly in the hands of the programmer.

We have seen how to create threads that run in parallel, sharing the processor. A key feature of this example is that the threads do not interact or communicate with each other. Once created, they are independent threads. This is a common and very useful scenario in multithreading.

There are more complex multithreading scenarios. One scenario is where the threads communicate with each other in carrying out some task. One needs to tell another that something has happened. Another scenario is where two or more threads need to access some shared data, such as a text field. There is a danger that they will interfere with each other and that the data will become unreliable. These situations introduce complications beyond the scope of this book.

Summary

You now have all you need to write programs that do lots of things simultaneously. You can display a clock, display an animation and play a game – all at the same time. You need to create a thread for each of these parallel activities as shown above.

It is common in Java programs for two or more threads to run in parallel. Each thread behaves like a normal sequential program. The scheduler shares the processor time among the threads that are ready to execute. The **start** method is used to set a new thread running. A thread class must be declared as extending class **Thread**, and must provide a method **run** that is executed when the thread is started.

A thread dies when it exits its **run** method.

Using threads can sometimes be avoided. For example, in an animation program, such as that used in this chapter, an alternative is to use the library **Timer** class. This class can be used to deliver events at preset intervals. These events can be used to move and redraw the image, instead of using the **sleep** method to suspend a thread. However, using a timer is not generally applicable as an alternative to using threads.

● Exercises

22.1 **Bouncing balls** Extend and change the program so that there are three bouncing balls, all bouncing within the same panel.

22.2 **Clock** Write a program to display a digital clock. The clock shows the hours, minutes and seconds, each in its own text field. A 'go' button starts the clock and a 'stop' button stops the clock.

Create a thread for the GUI and a second thread for the clock. The clock thread obtains the time (see below) and then sleeps for 100 milliseconds, which is 1/10 second. (A millisecond is one-thousandth of a second.)

The program obtains the time by using library class **Calendar**, within package **Java.util**. To create an instance of this class, do this:

```
Calendar calendar = Calendar.getInstance();
```

Then to obtain the value for the seconds part of the current time, do this:

```
int seconds = calendar.get(Calendar.SECOND);
```

and similarly for the hours (**HOUR**), minutes (**MINUTE**) and milliseconds (**MILLISECOND**) parts of the current time.

22.3 **Scrolling text field** This is a classic multithreading program. A program displays a text field, containing text that moves from right to left. A button starts the scrolling and another stops it. You will need to use method **substring** for string manipulation (see Chapter 15).

Answers to self-test questions

22.1 1. One, the user-interface thread.
2. Two.
3. Three.

22.2 Two, the user-interface thread and one ball thread.

22.3
```
if ((event.getSource() == go1) && !(ball1.isAlive())) {
    ball1 = new Ball(panel1);
    ball1.start();
}
```

Interfaces

This chapter explains:

- how to use interfaces to describe the structure of a program;
- how to use interfaces to ensure the interoperability of the classes within a program;
- how a class can implement multiple interfaces;
- the differences between interfaces and abstract classes.

● Introduction

Java provides a notation for describing the outward appearance of a class, called an *interface*. An interface is just like the description of a class but with the bodies of the methods omitted. Do not confuse this use of the word interface with the same word in the term graphical user interface (GUI). Two uses for interfaces are:

- in design;
- to promote interoperability.

● Interfaces for design

The importance of design during the initial planning of a large program is often emphasized. This involves designing all the classes for the program. A specification of the class names and their methods, written in English, is one way to document such a design. But it is also possible to write this description in Java. For example, the interface for the class **Balloon**, used often in this book, is:

```
public interface BalloonInterface {
    void changeSize(int newDiameter);
    int getX();
    void setX(int x);
    void display(Graphics paper);
}
```

Notice that the word `class` is omitted in an interface description. Notice also that methods are not declared as `public` (or anything else) because they are implicitly `public`.

Only the method names and their parameters are described in an interface, while the bodies of the methods are omitted. An interface describes a class, but does not say how the methods and the data items are implemented. It thus describes only the services provided by the class – it represents the outward appearance of a class as seen by users of the class (or an object instantiated from it). By implication it also says what the person who implements the class must provide.

SELF-TEST QUESTION

23.1 Add statements to the interface `BalloonInterface` that describe methods to access and change the value of *y*.

An interface can be compiled along with any other classes, but clearly cannot be executed. However, someone who is planning to *use* a class can compile the program along with the interface and thereby check that it is being used correctly. Anyone who has written a Java program knows that the compiler is extremely vigilant in finding errors that otherwise might cause mischievous problems when the program executes. So any checking that can be done at compile-time is most worthwhile.

A person who is implementing an interface can specify in the heading of the class that a particular interface is being implemented. Earlier, as an example, we wrote an interface describing the interface to a class `Balloon`. Now we write the class `Balloon` itself to match the interface:

```
public class Balloon implements BalloonInterface {

    private int diameter, x, y;

    public void changeSize(int newDiameter) {
        diameter = newDiameter;
    }

    public int getX() {
        return x;
    }
```

```
    public void setX(int newX) {
        x = newX;
    }

    public void display(Graphics paper){
        paper.setColor(Color.black);
        paper.fillOval(x, y, diameter, diameter);
    }
}
```

Notice that the class as a whole is described as implementing the `BalloonInterface` interface. The compiler will then check that this class has been written to comply with the interface declaration – that is, it provides the methods `changeSize`, `setX`, `getX` and `display`, together with their appropriate parameters. The rule is that if you implement an interface, you have to implement **every** method described in the interface. Any deviation results in compiler errors.

We can describe the relationship between a class and its interface using a UML class diagram. See for example Figure 23.1. In a UML class diagram, an interface is shown as a rectangle. The interface name is preceded by the word `<<Interface>>`. The `implements` relationship is shown as a dotted arrow.

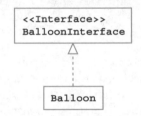

Figure 23.1 A class and its interface.

SELF-TEST QUESTION

23.2 Write methods that implement additional features of interface `BalloonInterface`, to access and change the value of *y*.

Interfaces can also be used to describe an inheritance structure. For example, suppose we wanted to describe an interface for a `ColoredBalloon` that is a subclass of the `Balloon` interface described above. We can write:

```
public interface ColoredBalloonInterface
                extends BalloonInterface {
    void setColor(Color color);
}
```

which inherits the interface `BalloonInterface` and states that the interface `ColoredBalloonInterface` has an additional method to set the colour of an object. We could similarly describe a whole tree structure of classes as interfaces, describing purely their outward appearance and their subclass–superclass relationships.

SELF-TEST QUESTION

23.3   Write the additional code necessary for a class `ColoredBalloon` to implement the `ColoredBalloonInterface` interface.

In summary, interfaces can be used to describe:

- the classes in a program;
- the inheritance structure in a program, the 'is-a' relationships.

What interfaces *cannot* describe are:

- the implementations of methods (this is the whole point of interfaces);
- which classes use which other classes, the 'has-a' relationships (this needs some other notation).

To use interfaces in design, write the interfaces for all the classes in the program before beginning the coding of the classes.

Interfaces become particularly useful in medium-sized and large programs that make use of more than a few classes. In large programs that involve teams of programmers, their use is almost vital as a way of facilitating communication amongst the team members. Interfaces also complement class diagrams as the documentation of a program's design.

● Interfaces and interoperability

Household appliances such as toasters and electric kettles come with a power cord with a plug on the end of it. The design of the plug is standard (throughout a country) and ensures that an appliance can be used anywhere (within the country). Thus the adoption of a common interface ensures interoperability. In Java, interfaces can be used in a similar fashion to ensure that objects exhibit a common interface. When such an object is passed around a program we can be sure that it supports all the methods specified by the interface description.

As an example, we declare an interface named `Displayable`. Any class complying with this interface must include a method named `display` which displays the object. The interface declaration is:

```
public interface Displayable {
    void display(Graphics paper);
}
```

Now we write a new class, named `Square`, which represents square graphical objects. We say in the header of the class that it extends `Displayable`. We include within the body of the class the method `display`:

```
public class Square implements Displayable {

    private int x, y, size;

    public void display(Graphics paper) {
        paper.setColor(Color.black);
        paper.drawRectangle(x, y, size, size);
    }

    // other methods of the class Square

}
```

As the heading states, this class (and any object created from it) conforms to the `Displayable` interface. It means that any object of this class can be passed around a program and we are confident that, when necessary, it can be displayed by calling its method `display`.

SELF-TEST QUESTION

23.4   We wish to write a new class `Circle` that implements the `Displayable` interface. Write the header for the class.

● Interfaces and the Java library

Most of the programs in this book use interfaces to perform event handling. Look at the heading of nearly every program. It says:

```
public class Any extends JFrame implements ActionListener
```

This means that the program conforms to the library interface `ActionListener`. It implies that the program must provide all the methods described in that interface. In this case, there is only one method – the method `actionPerformed`.

A program typically creates a `button` object:

```
JButton button = new JButton("press"):
```

It then calls method `addActionListener` of the `button` object to tell it which object to call when an event occurs:

```
button.addActionListener(this);
```

Finally, when an event occurs, method `actionPerformed` of the program is called.

But suppose that we provide method `actionPerformed` but omit the `implements ActionListener`. What would happen? The answer is that the program would not compile correctly. It is this statement that would be found to be incorrect:

```
button.addActionListener(this);
```

This is a call on method `addActionListener` of the `JButton` class. The header of method `addActionListener` is as follows:

```
public void addActionListener(ActionListener object)
```

which declares its parameter as being of type `ActionListener`. Thus this method expects its parameter to implement the `ActionListener` interface. So if it is not, the compiler complains.

The bottom line is that the programmer is forced both:

1. to declare the class as implementing an interface, and
2. to provide the associated method within the class,

thus ensuring that the program will compile and then run correctly.

● Multiple interfaces

Just as a TV has interfaces both to a power source and to a signal source, so in Java we can specify that a class implements a number of interfaces. So while a class can only inherit from one other class, it can implement any number of interfaces.

Java is a language that provides single inheritance – a class can inherit from (or be the subclass of) only one class. The class structure is a tree, with the root at the top, in which a class can have many subclasses but only one superclass. Figure 23.2 shows illustrative classes **Balloon** and **Game** as subclasses of superclass **JFrame**. Each class appears only within a single tree and each class has only a single superclass.

Sometimes we would like a class to inherit from more than one superclass as described in the following class header and shown in Figure 23.3:

```
public class Game extends JFrame, Thread // error
```

But this heading is wrong because it attempts to extend two classes. This would be called *multiple inheritance*. Some languages, such as C++, permit multiple inheritance

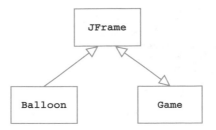

Figure 23.2 Single inheritance.

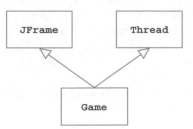

Figure 23.3 Multiple inheritance (not supported in Java).

but Java does not. Multiple inheritance allows a class to inherit sets of methods from a number of classes, and it is therefore potentially very powerful.

If we think about classification systems in science and nature, it is often the case that objects belong to more than one class. We humans, for example, belong to one gender class, but also to a class that likes a particular type of music. So we all belong in one inheritance tree for gender, another for musical taste, another for mother tongue, and so on.

Java was designed to be a simple (but powerful) language and so permits only single inheritance – a class can only inherit from one superclass. This avoids several of the confusions of multiple inheritance which we will not discuss here.

There is, however, a way of emulating a facility similar to multiple inheritance in Java by using interfaces. This is because, while a class can only extend a single class, it can implement any number of interfaces.

Multiple interfaces are illustrated in Figure 23.4. This example is coded as follows:

```
public class Game extends JFrame implements InterfaceA, InterfaceB
```

If `Game` inherited from `InterfaceA` and `InterfaceB`, it would inherit a set of methods from `InterfaceA` and `InterfaceB`. But instead `Game` is implementing interfaces `InterfaceA` and `InterfaceB`, and these interfaces have no methods on offer. What this means is that class `Game` agrees to provide the methods described in `InterfaceA` and `InterfaceB` – that `Game` has agreed to conform to certain behaviour. The code for implementing `InterfaceA` and `InterfaceB` has to be written as part of the class `Game`.

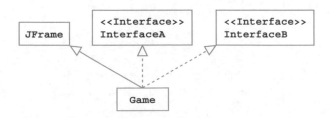

Figure 23.4 Multiple interfaces.

Interfaces versus abstract classes

Interfaces and abstract classes are similar, and the purpose of this section is to clarify their differences. (Abstract classes are described in Chapter 10 on inheritance.) The purpose of an abstract class is to describe, as a superclass, the common features of a group of classes, and is introduced by the keyword `abstract`. The differences between abstract classes and interfaces are as follows:

1. An abstract class often provides an implementation of some of the methods. In contrast, an interface never describes any implementation.

2. A class can implement more than one interface, but only inherit from one abstract class.

3. An interface is used at compile-time to perform checking. By contrast, an abstract class implies inheritance, which involves linking the appropriate method at run-time.

4. An abstract class implies that its `abstract` methods will be fleshed out by classes that extend it. Inheritance is expected. But an interface simply specifies the skeleton for a class, with no implication that it will be used for inheritance.

Programming principles

Interfaces complete the set of facilities provided by Java to describe classes and their interrelationships. Classes describe a collection of actions and data. An interface describes the outward appearance of a class – the methods that are publicly available. Inheritance allows us to create a new class from an old class, with useful additional methods or changed methods. An abstract class describes the common features of a group of classes, and may provide implementation of some of the shared methods.

Programming pitfalls

Remember that:

■ A class can only inherit from one other class, including an abstract class.

■ A class can implement any number of interfaces.

Grammar spot

An interface description has the following structure:

```
public interface Name {
    void methodA(parameters);
    int methodB(parameters);
}
```

The methods are implicitly `public`. The method bodies are omitted.

New language elements

- ■ `interface` – the description of the external interface to a class (which may not yet be written);

- ■ `implements` – used in the header of a class to specify that the class implements a named interface.

Summary

- ■ Interfaces are used to describe the services provided by a class.

- ■ Interfaces are useful for describing the structure of a program. This description can be checked by the Java compiler.

- ■ Interfaces can be used to ensure that a class conforms to a particular interface. This supports interoperability.

- ■ Java supports multiple interfaces, but only supports single inheritance.

● Exercises

Interfaces as design descriptions

23.1 Write an interface to describe selected methods of the `JTextField` class.

23.2 Write an interface to describe a class that represents bank accounts. The class is called `Account`. It has methods `deposit, withdraw` and `getCurrentBalance`. Decide on suitable parameters for the methods.

23.3 Write interfaces to describe the structure of a program that consists of a number of classes, such as the game program described in Chapter 18 on design.

Interfaces for interoperability

23.4 Write a class named **Circle** that describes circle objects and conforms to the **Displayable** interface given above.

Answers to self-test questions

23.1
```
int getY();
void setY(int y);
```

23.2
```
public int getY() {
    return y;
}

public void setY(int newY) {
    y = newY;
}
```

23.3
```
public class ColoredBalloon implements ColoredBalloonInterface {

    private Color color;

    public setColor(Color newColor) {
        color = newColor;
    }
}
```

23.4
```
public class Circle implements Displayable
```

Programming in the large – packages

This chapter explains:

- why packages are used;
- how to use classes from a package by employing the **import** statement;
- how to group classes within a package using the **package** statement;
- the scope rules for packages.

● Introduction

The classes of the Java libraries are grouped into packages. Every Java program uses classes from the library and therefore makes use of packages. Examples of Java library packages are **java.awt** and **javax.swing**.

When you write a large program, with many classes, it is also convenient to create your own packages.

Individual statements and variables are grouped into a method. Then methods and instance variables are grouped into a class. Finally classes are grouped into a package. Packages are the largest structure in Java.

● Using classes and the import statement

The Java libraries provide thousands of useful classes. For convenience, the classes are grouped into packages. Most of the programs in this book start with the following **import** statements:

```
import java.awt.*;
import java.awt.event.*;
import javax.swing.*;
```

`java.awt`, `java.awt.event` and `javax.swing` are packages. Each of these packages contains a number of useful classes. For example, the class `JButton` is in the package `javax.swing`. The `import` statements enable the program conveniently to use the classes in the packages. Because the `import` statement is present, we can simply refer to `JButton` without difficulty. For example:

```
JButton button = new JButton("go");
```

If the `import` statement was omitted, we could still use the class `JButton`, but we would need to refer to it by its full name – `javax.swing.JButton`. This would be inconvenient and cumbersome. Hence we see the value of the `import` statement.

If we only need to import an individual class, say `JButton`, from within a package, we can spell it out:

```
import javax.swing.JButton;
```

Using `*` means that we want to import all the classes within the named package. So if we need several classes from a package, it is simpler to use the `*` notation.

For convenience, Java automatically imports two packages:

- the `java.lang` package;
- the current package.

The `java.lang` package provides a number of commonly used classes, including `String`, `Thread`, `Math`, `Integer` and `Double`.

SELF-TEST QUESTION

24.1 Classes called `Monday`, `Tuesday`, `Wednesday`, `Thursday`, `Friday`, `Saturday` and `Sunday` are grouped in a package called `week`. Write down the `import` statement that will be needed to use the class `Friday`. Write the statement to create an object `friday` of the class `Friday`. Write down the `import` statement that will be needed to use all the classes in the package.

Creating packages using the `package` statement

In this book, the most complex program has only five classes. But a large program may consist of tens or hundreds of classes. With a large program it is often convenient to group the classes into packages and the programmer invents a name for each package. The reasons for using packages are:

- it is a good way of controlling the complexity of a large program;
- classes within the same package have special access rights to each other.

Thus the programmer groups into the same package the classes that are similar or relate strongly to each other.

Suppose a program consists of three groups of classes:

- classes that handle the user interface;
- classes that access the database; and
- classes that handle the central logic of the program.

We create three packages, named **gui**, **database** and **logic**. Note that package names begin with a lower-case letter. Next we need to ensure that individual classes are in the correct package. This is accomplished using the **package** statement, written at the head of the class. So, if we have a class named **Login** that handles the login part of the GUI, we write the following at the head of the class:

```
package gui;
public class Login
```

The programs presented in this book do not have a **package** statement at their head. If you omit a **package** statement, it means that the class is placed, by default, in a package with no name.

SELF-TEST QUESTION

24.2 A class named **Backup** is to be placed in a package named **database**. Write the **package** statement and the class heading.

● Packages, files and folders

We have already seen that it is good practice to:

- put each class in its own file (with extension .**java**);
- give the file name the same name as the class.

When you create a package:

- create a folder with the same name as the package;
- place all the class files for that package in the folder;
- place the package folder in the same folder as the file that holds your code that imports the package.

This ensures that the compiler and the run-time system can find all the files.

SELF-TEST QUESTION

24.3 Classes called **Monday**, **Tuesday**, **Wednesday**, **Thursday**, **Friday**, **Saturday** and **Sunday** are grouped into a package called **week**. Name the files and the directory (folder) that are needed. Write down the **package** statements that are needed.

Scope rules

When you create and use packages, some new scope rules come into play. The essence is that classes within the same package can access each other very easily.

When you write a method, you specify that it is **private**, **public**, **protected** or simply give it no prefix. The prefix determines who can access the method. As we have seen, **public** means that the method is available to all. **private** means that it is accessible only within the class. **protected** means that the method can be used by that class and any subclass of that class.

If you give a method no prefix, it means that the method is accessible from anywhere within the same package, but inaccessible from outside. This is also true of classes, constructors and variables. This means that the programmer can establish a close relationship between methods in the same package. This accords with the idea that classes in the same package are related to each other.

The complete rules for visibility are given in Appendix G.

The Java library packages

Here are some of the Java packages with an outline of their contents:

`java.lang`	Contains the classes that support the main features of the language like **Object**, **String**, number, exception and threads
`java.util`	These are useful utility classes such as **Random** and **ArrayList**
`java.io`	Text input and output streams for characters and numbers
`java.net`	Classes that carry out networking functions, socket programming, interacting with the Internet
`javax.swing`	This includes the classes to provide GUI components such as buttons (**JButton**), labels (**JLabel**) and sliders (**JSlider**)
`java.awt`	awt stands for Abstract Window Toolkit. The graphics methods such as **drawLine** are here
`java.applet`	The classes provide support for Java applets (programs run from a web browser)

● Programming pitfalls

It is very tempting to use an **import** statement to make it easier to use certain class methods and constants from the libraries. For example, rather than say **Math.sqrt** and **Color.white**, it would seem easier to supply **import** statements:

```
import java.lang.Math.*;
import java.awt.Color.*;
```

and then simply refer to **sqrt** and **white**. This, however, does not work. One reason is that Java grammar demands that a class method is always preceded by its class name. The other reason is that the **import** statement allows you to avoid using a package name, not a class name.

New language elements

- **import** – allows the user easy access to classes in a package;

- **package** – specifies that this class is to be placed in the named package.

Summary

Packages are a way of grouping classes together. The many classes of the Java library are grouped into convenient packages.

Classes within a package can be used by giving the full name of the package and class. A more convenient alternative is to use **import** statements.

It is often convenient to group the classes of a large program in different packages. Each package is given a name. The classes can be placed in the appropriate package by employing the **package** statement.

The Java scope rules mean that classes within the same package have special access rights to each other.

Exercise

24.1 You will be unlikely to create your own packages unless you write programs that are larger than those given or suggested as exercises in this book. However, the library classes are grouped into packages. If you have a browser, browse the Java libraries. Start with the package **java.util**. Alternatively, consult Appendix A to see how library classes are arranged into packages.

Answers to self-test questions

24.1 To use class **Friday**, put:

```
import week.Friday;
```

To create an object of the class **Friday**, put:

```
Friday friday = new Friday();
```

To use all the classes in the package put:

```
import week.*;
```

24.2
```
package database;
public class Backup
```

24.3 The files are **Monday.java**, **Tuesday.java**, etc.
The folder should be named **week**.
The first line of each file should be:

```
package week;
```

CHAPTER
25

Polymorphism

This chapter explains:

- how to use polymorphism;
- how to carry out casting;
- when to use polymorphism.

● Introduction

We introduce the idea of polymorphism with a simple example. Suppose we have two classes, named **Sphere** and **Bubble**. We can create an instance of **Sphere** and an instance of **Bubble** in the usual way:

```
Sphere sphere = new Sphere();
Bubble bubble = new Bubble();
```

Suppose that each class has a method named **display**. Then we can display the two objects as follows:

```
sphere.display(paper);
bubble.display(paper);
```

and although these two calls look very similar, in each case the appropriate version of **display** is called. Although there are two methods with the same name (**display**), they are different and the Java system makes sure that the correct one is selected. So when **display** is called for the object **sphere**, it is the method defined within the class

Sphere that is called. When **display** is called for the object **bubble**, it is the method defined within the class **Bubble** that is called. This is the essence of polymorphism.

● Polymorphism in action

In this chapter we use as an example a program that displays graphical shapes on the screen – squares, circles and similar. The program uses an abstract class named **Shape**, which describes all the shared attributes of these shapes, including where they are on the screen. (Abstract classes were explained in Chapter 10 on inheritance.) Class **Shape** is:

```
public abstract class Shape {
    protected int x, y;
    protected int size = 20;
    public abstract void display(Graphics drawArea);
}
```

Each shape is described by its own class, a subclass of class **Shape**. For example, classes **Circle** and **Square** are:

```
public class Circle extends Shape {

    public Circle(int initX, int initY) {
        x = initX;
        y = initY;
    }

    public void display(Graphics drawArea) {
        drawArea.drawOval(x, y, size, size);
    }
}

public class Square extends Shape {

    public Square(int initX, int initY) {
        x = initX;
        y = initY;
    }

    public void display(Graphics drawArea) {
        drawArea.drawRect(x, y, size, size);
    }
}
```

Here is a program that uses these classes to create two shapes, storing them in an array list named **group**, and displaying them. (An array list, discussed in Chapter 12, is a convenient data structure that expands or contracts to accommodate the required data.) The output is shown in Figure 25.1.

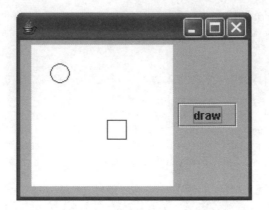

Figure 25.1 Display of the shapes using polymorphism.

```java
public class Shapes extends JFrame implements ActionListener {

    private JButton button;
    private JPanel panel;

    public static void main(String[] args) {
        Shapes demo = new Shapes();
        demo.setSize(250,200);
        demo.createGUI();
        demo.show();
    }

    private void createGUI() {
        setDefaultCloseOperation(EXIT_ON_CLOSE);
        Container window = getContentPane();
        window.setLayout(new FlowLayout());

        panel = new JPanel();
        panel.setPreferredSize(new Dimension(150, 150));
        panel.setBackground(Color.white);
        window.add(panel);

        button = new JButton("draw");
        window.add(button);
        button.addActionListener(this);
    }

    public void actionPerformed(ActionEvent event) {
        Graphics paper = panel.getGraphics();
```

```
            Circle circle = new Circle(20, 20);
            Square square = new Square(80, 80);
            ArrayList group = new ArrayList();
            group.add(circle);
            group.add(square);

            paper.setColor(Color.white);
            paper.fillRect(0, 0, 150, 150);
            paper.setColor(Color.black);
            for (int s = 0; s < group.size(); s++) {
                Object item = group.get(s);
                Shape shape = (Shape) item;
                shape.display(paper);
            }
        }
    }
}
```

Polymorphism is in use here – the method **display** is called on two occasions with different results according to which object is in use. You can see that the two calls of **display** within the **for** loop:

```
    shape.display(paper);
```

give two different outputs. This is not necessarily what you might expect, but it is entirely correct. Two different outputs are displayed because the Java system automatically selects the version of **display** associated with the class of the object. When method **display** is first called, the variable shape contains the object **circle** and so the version of **display** in the class **Circle** is called. Then the corresponding thing happens with **square**.

The class of an object is determined when the object is created using **new**, and stays the same whatever happens to the object. Whatever you do to an object in a program, it always retains the features it had when it was created. An object can be assigned to a variable of another class and passed around the program as a parameter, but it never loses its true identity. In the analogy of a family, you retain your identity and your relationship with your ancestors whether you get married, change your name, or move to another country. This seems common sense, and indeed it is. 'Once a square, always a square' might be an appropriate slogan.

When you call a method, polymorphism makes sure that the appropriate version of the method is automatically selected. Most of the times when you program in Java you are not aware that the Java system is selecting the correct method to call. It is automatic and invisible.

Polymorphism allows us to write a single concise statement such as:

```
    shape.display(paper);
```

instead of a series of `if` statements like this:

```
if (shape instanceof Circle) {
    Circle circle = shape;
    circle.display(paper);
}
if (shape instanceof Square) {
    Square square = shape;
    square.display(paper);
}
```

which is clumsy and longwinded. This uses the keyword **instanceof** to ask if an object is a member of a named class. (Yes, it is spelled like that.) If there were a large number of shapes, there would be a correspondingly large number of `if` statements. Avoiding this demonstrates how powerful and concise polymorphism is.

As we have seen in this small example, polymorphism often makes a segment of program smaller and neater through the elimination of a series of `if` statements. But this achievement is much more significant than it may seem. It means that statements such as:

```
shape.display(paper);
```

know nothing about the possible variety of objects that may be used as the value of **shape**. So information hiding (already present in large measure in an OO program) is extended. We can check this out by assessing how much we would need to change this program to accommodate some new type of shape (some additional subclass of **Shape**), say an ellipse. The answer is that we would not need to modify it at all. This means that the program is enormously flexible. Thus polymorphism enhances modularity, reusability and maintainability.

● Casting

The above program has used a facility that must be addressed – casting. We placed some objects (a circle and a square) in an array list. But an array list always holds objects of the class **Object**. (As we have seen, the class **Object** is the superclass of all classes.) Thus by placing them in the array list they become stored in objects of the class **Object**. But when we need to use the shapes, we need to convert them back into **Shape** objects. We will now do this more explicitly, emphasizing the need for casting.

Firstly, we add the objects to the array list as before:

```
group.add(circle);
group.add(square);
```

Next we extract an object from the array list and we will choose as an example the element with index value 0. The statement:

```
Object item = group.get(0);
```

copies an item from the array list, placing it in the variable named `item`, an instance of the class `Object`. But before we can use this object, it must be copied back into a `Shape` object. This is accomplished using explicit conversion or casting:

```
Shape shape = (Shape) item;
```

The cast operator `(Shape)` converts or casts `item` into a `Shape` object. Now, finally, we use the object copied from the array list:

```
shape.display(paper);
```

In summary we:

1. placed two items in an array list, thereby storing them in `Object` objects;
2. copied an item from the list into an `Object` object and then copied it back into a `Shape` object using casting.

Rules for casting

What happens if you try to assign an object of one class to a variable of another class? It isn't immediately obvious that this is either necessary or legal. Java is, after all, a strongly typed language in which data of different types has to be carefully declared and used. However, as we have seen, there are occasional, but vital, programming situations where it is necessary to assign an object of one class to a variable of another class. For example, using the shapes classes declared above, we can write:

```
Square square = new Square(10, 10);
Shape shape = square;
```

in which an object `square` of the class `Square` is assigned to a variable shape belonging to the class `Shape`. Looking at the class diagram in Figure 25.2 makes it obvious that this assignment moves the object `square` up the hierarchy. As we will see shortly, this is completely valid.

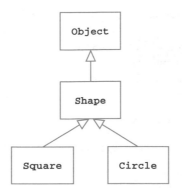

Figure 25.2 Class diagram for the shapes classes.

The rules for assigning objects are:

1. You cannot assign something across the class hierarchy.
2. You can assign something up the tree without problems.
3. You can assign something down the tree, but you must be explicit and use casting.

Here are the respective reasons for these rules.

Across the tree

If you consider the (illegal) act of moving across the tree, then the methods associated with the destination class are almost certainly not valid or may be absent. In the above example you can't assign an object of class **Square** to a variable of class **Circle**. This is prevented because there are fundamental differences between these two classes, and there could easily be methods that are unique to each class. A **Square** is not a **Circle**. This is the spirit of strong typing, which is a feature of Java. Strong typing means that when an object is declared it has a precise type, defined by its class. Subsequently, only the methods defined by that class (or its superclasses) are valid for use with the object.

Up the tree

If you assign something up the tree, the methods provided by the superclass are valid. In the example, every **Square** object (say square) is a **Shape**. So, for example, it is valid to do this:

```
Square square = new Square(10, 20);
Shape shape = square;
```

The object **square** is an instance of the class **Square**, but now it is assigned to a variable of class **Shape** – the superclass. When you assign an object to a variable of a superclass, all the methods of the superclass are guaranteed to work. Nothing can go wrong.

Down the tree

If you assign from a superclass to a subclass, down the tree, you are moving to an arena where there may be additional methods – which might not be valid for the object. In the example, every **Shape** object (say **shape**) is not a **Square** – though some are. So we have to be careful when we do this – and Java forces us to be careful by making us use casting. For example, the following is wrong and is flagged as an error by the compiler:

```
Object object = new Object();
Square square;
square = object;        // not allowed
```

The reason for this restriction is as follows. A subclass usually provides methods additional to those in its superclass. (This is, after all, the purpose of extending a class.) These methods simply are not applicable to an object of the superclass. If such a method in the subclass were to be called, a catastrophic error might occur. For example, suppose class **Square** has an additional method:

```
public int getArea() {
    return size * size;
}
```

Then the sequence:

```
Object object = new Object();
Square square = object;
int area = square.getArea();
```

would probably not be what was intended, because it implies that it is valid for all objects to have a **getArea** method. Luckily, the compiler helps the programmer to avoid this occurrence. And, in fact, the compiler would find fault with the second statement in this sequence. One of the features of Java is that it helps write robust programs. This is one case where the compiler detects that the programmer may be trying to do something that is unsafe.

As we have seen, it is possible to assign objects down the class hierarchy, provided that the programmer does it deliberately and explicitly using casting. For example:

```
Square square = (Square) object;
```

Remember that this operation will only be valid, and allowed by the compiler, provided that object **object** belongs to a class which is the superclass of **Square**. This is another example of how the Java language helps the programmer to avoid making mistakes.

SELF-TEST QUESTION

25.1 Write code to assign the object **shape** of type **Shape** to a variable of type **Circle**.

Programming principles

Polymorphism constitutes the third major element of OOP. Here is the complete set:

1. Encapsulation means that objects can be made highly modular.
2. Inheritance means that desirable features in an existing class can be reused in other classes, without affecting the integrity of the original class.
3. Polymorphism means designing code that can easily manipulate objects of different classes. Differences between similar objects can be processed transparently.

Novice programmers normally start out by using encapsulation, later move on to inheritance and subsequently use polymorphism.

▶ *Programming principles continued*

The case study used above uses a diversity of objects (shapes) that have common factors incorporated into a superclass. Now we know that the facility of inheritance helps describe the similarity of groups of objects in an economical fashion. The other side of the coin is using objects, and this is where polymorphism helps us to use objects in a concise uniform way. The diversity is handled not by a proliferation of `if` statements, but instead by a single method call. So, should you see code that looks like this:

```
if (shape instanceof Circle) {
    shape.displayCircle(paper);
}
if (shape instanceof Square) {
    shape.displaySquare(paper);
}
```

you should instead think of using polymorphism. As **displayCircle** and **displaySquare** represent a similar concept, make this concept a method of a superclass and rewrite this code sequence more simply as:

```
shape.display(paper);
```

so making use of polymorphism to select the appropriate method. When this happens the version of the method **display** that matches the actual object is selected. This can only be decided when the program is running, immediately before the method is called. This is termed late binding, dynamic linking or delayed binding. It is an essential feature of a language that supports polymorphism.

In summary, an object (once created) retains its fundamental identity, whatever is done to it. An analogy: even if you change your name, you remain the same person – your genes do not change. If you place an object in a variable of a different type, the object can only be assigned to a variable whose class is a superclass of the object or a subclass of the object. In other words, things are kept strictly in the family. But to assign something down the tree, you must use explicit casting. Casting of objects is not a common thing to do, but when it is needed, it is vital. Very few of the programs in this book use it.

Polymorphism helps construct programs that are:

■ concise (shorter than they might otherwise be);

■ modular (unrelated parts are kept separate);

■ easy to change and adapt (e.g. introducing new objects).

In general, the approach to exploiting polymorphism within a particular program is as follows:

1. Identify any similarities (common methods and variables) between any objects or classes in the program.

2. Design a superclass that embodies the common features of the classes.

3. Design the subclasses that describe the distinctive features of each of the classes, whilst inheriting the common features from the superclass.

4. Identify any place in the program where the same operation must be applied to any of the similar objects. It may be tempting to use **if** statements at this location. Instead, this is the place to use polymorphism.

5. Make sure that the superclass contains an abstract method corresponding to the method that is to be used polymorphically.

Java is a strongly typed language, which means that checks are carried out at every opportunity to ensure that data is used properly. However, Java is also a strongly statically typed language, which means that many checks are carried out at compile-time. The Java compiler will always detect the following errors:

- assignment across the inheritance tree;
- assignment down the inheritance tree without proper casting;
- calling a method that is not valid for the named class.

At run-time, the following checking is carried out:

- assignment down the inheritance tree, when the object is not an instance of the destination class. This produces an **InvalidCastException** when the program is running.

Programming pitfalls

If you write a casting operation, you must be completely certain that the destination variable belongs to the same class (or a superclass of) as the class of the object. The penalty is a run-time error called an **InvalidCastException**.

If you are exploiting polymorphism, and grouping a number of classes under a single superclass, you must ensure that the superclass describes all the methods that will be used on any instance of the superclass. Sometimes this will require abstract methods in the superclass that serve no purpose other than enabling the program to compile.

New language elements

- The casting operator is the name of the destination class, enclosed in brackets – for example, **(Square)**.

- The keyword **instanceof** allows a program to test an object to see which class it belongs to.

Summary

The principles of polymorphism are:

1. An object always retains the identity of the class from which it was created. (An object can never be converted into an object of another class.)

2. When a method is used on an object, the method associated with the class of the object is always used.

The rules for assigning an object to a variable of another class are:

1. You cannot assign something across the class hierarchy.

2. You can assign something up the tree without problems.

3. You can assign something down the tree, but you must be explicit and use casting.

Polymorphism enhances information hiding and reusability by helping to make pieces of code widely applicable.

● Exercises

25.1 An abstract class **Animal** has a constructor method, methods **setWeight** and **getWeight**, and a function method **says**. The value of **weight** represents the weight of the animal, an **int** value. **says** returns a string, the noise that the animal makes.

Class **Animal** has subclasses **Cow**, **Snake** and **Pig**. These subclasses have different implementations of **says**, returning values 'moo', 'hiss' and 'grunt' respectively. Write the class **Animal** and the three subclasses. Create objects **daisy**, **sid** and **wilbur** respectively from the three classes, add them to an array list and use their methods. Display the sounds that the animals make in a text area.

25.2 In the shapes program, presented in the text, add a new shape – a straight line – to the collection of available shapes. Use the library method **drawLine** actually to draw a line object. Add code to create a line object, add it to the list of objects (in the array list) and display it along with the other shapes.

25.3 Enhance the shapes program into a full-blown drawing package that allows shapes to be selected from a menu and placed at a desired location in a panel. The user specifies the position with a mouse-click. So the user:

1. First clicks somewhere in the panel.

2. Then clicks on the desired menu item.

Provide a 'clear' button.

25.4 A bank offers its customers two kinds of account – a regular account and a gold account. The two types of account provide some shared facilities but they also offer distinctive features. The common facilities are:

- open an account with a name and an initial balance;

- maintain a record of the current balance;

- deposit or withdraw an amount of money.

Whenever a withdrawal is made, a regular account is checked to see if the account is overdrawn. A gold account holder can overdraw indefinitely. A regular account has interest calculated as 5% of the amount. A gold account has interest at 6%, less a fixed charge of $100 per year.

Write a class that describes the common features and individual classes to describe regular and gold accounts.

Construct a program to use these classes by creating two bank accounts – one a regular account, and the other a gold account. Each is created with a person's name and some initial amount of money. Place the objects representing each account in an array list. Display the name, balance and interest of the accounts in a text area when a button is clicked. (Assume for simplicity that amounts of money are held as **int**.)

Answer to self-test question

25.1   `Circle circle = (Circle) shape;`

CHAPTER
26

Java in context

This chapter explains:

- the design principles behind Java;
- Microsoft and Java;
- Java and internationalization;
- Java and databases;
- RMI, beans and servlets;
- Java and JavaScript.

● Introduction

In this chapter we explain how Java relates to the computing and Internet scene. In addition, Java is constantly being updated by new class libraries, tools and technologies. We provide a survey of the current scope. We begin by reviewing the main features of Java as summarized in a paper, called the 'White Paper', from Sun Microsystems that launched the language. The features were identified as:

- simple;
- object oriented;
- network savvy;
- interpreted;
- robust;
- secure;
- architecture neutral;

440

- portable;
- high performance;
- multithreaded;
- dynamic.

● Simple

Java was partly conceived as a reaction to a perceived complexity in other mainstream languages – primarily C++. Some see C++ as a large and unwieldy language, difficult to learn, displaying inconsistent concepts and prone to accidental misuse. Java, by contrast, is small and beautiful. For example, while C++ has multiple inheritance, Java has the simpler single inheritance. In C++ the programmer can directly manipulate pointers to objects in memory, but this highly dangerous practice is unavailable to the Java programmer.

Of course we need to distinguish between the language and its libraries. There are now hundreds of classes and thousands of methods, and it takes time to master such scale. But the language is relatively simple.

Simplicity means ease of learning, mastery of the language by its users and fewer errors. Java was designed as a small language, with the hope that it would be widely and completely understood, implemented and adopted. Most languages, as they have evolved, have got bigger and it may be that the same will happen to Java. As the designers of Java say: 'realizing that the system will only get larger in later releases we have elected to start small'. Let us hope that their original design vision prevails.

● Object oriented

Java is an object-oriented (OO) language. This book has explained that this means that a program is constructed from objects, in turn created from classes. This promotes program modularity. Classes can inherit variables and methods from superclasses. This is enormously powerful in supporting the reuse of software. In consequence, OO programs are generally much smaller than equivalent programs that are not OO. There is also the bonus of increased reliability obtained by using tried-and-tested software, rather than starting from scratch.

The OO paradigm currently dominates computing, not only in programming but in analysis and in design.

● Platform independence (portability)

How much work is involved in moving (porting) a program onto a different platform? In essence, this is the issue of portability. Java was designed as a language that can be ported easily to any computer and operating system. It currently runs on all the major computers and operating systems. Portability is achieved by compiling Java to a machine-independent code named byte code. This is code for a 'pretend' computer – one that can be simulated in software. The simulation software is named the Java Virtual Machine (JVM). A JVM is needed for every type of computer that runs Java and a JVM has been written for nearly all computers. A JVM is in fact a comparatively small program – about 256 kbyte – and is fairly easy to write. The JVM is available to run on a whole number of processors, not just Intel processors. Neither is the JVM locked into any one operating system, like Windows, Unix or GNU/Linux. Thus a Java program can be distributed (as byte code) and run on any of a large range of machines.

When a Java program is compiled, information about which library methods and variables are used is retained in the file of byte code. Traditionally the next phase is linking, combining the byte code of the program with the byte code of the libraries that have been used. In Java the linking to libraries is postponed until the program is actually run. This dynamic linking has several advantages. Firstly, it means that Java byte code can be transmitted more rapidly around the network, free of the encumbrance of library software. This improves speed. Secondly, when the Java code arrives at a site and begins execution, it is linked with the Java library that is specific to that site. This improves portability. Finally, when any of the libraries are updated, the Java program picks up the very latest version automatically. This enormously assists in maintaining and updating software.

Another feature of Java that contributes to portability is the fact that data types are defined to have sizes that are independent of an individual machine. Thus, for example, an integer is always 32 bits, irrespective of the machine. This means that the programmer can be confident about the behaviour of a program, wherever it is executed. This very simple standardization is not the case in other languages, notably C and C++, where the size of data types changes from one machine to another.

● Performance

Transmission of Java programs around the Internet or within an intranet is fast, because Java code is compact. Moreover, the library software is not transmitted with the program, but is linked at the time of execution on the target machine. Any performance problems with Java arise at execution time. Java programs are interpreted by the JVM and therefore they run slower than similar programs that directly use the machine instructions of the computer. For example, programs written in C or C++ are compiled directly to machine code and run about 10 times faster than a similar Java program. (The C or C++ program is not, of course, portable.) For many purposes, the running speed is not important. However, for certain types of application – some embedded systems or real-time systems – performance is crucial. Java is running faster owing to improved JVM construction and faster machines – but choose it with care for certain problem domains.

● Security

If you access (visit) a remote Internet site, retrieve a program and bring (download) it for execution on your own machine, you are taking a risk. An unknown program might:

- crash your machine;
- delete files;
- access and transmit private information to another machine;
- fill up your disk space;
- introduce a virus.

Such damage may be the result of malice or accident – the result is the same. Worries about such damage restrict the use of the Internet and users need to protect themselves. Java provides the necessary mechanisms for users to protect themselves from rogue programs. Indeed, this was one of the major design aims of Java. It does this by means of a whole series of devices which we will now describe.

The Java language itself

Unlike some other languages, Java does not allow the use of pointers. In some languages the programmer is allowed to set up pointers, normally to data structures. But once given the access to a pointer, the programmer can by accident or design then access anything in memory. For example (if it was allowed), a program could access private data within an object. So the banning of pointers in Java is itself a security measure.

Java is strongly typed. This means that if you declare a variable as, say, an integer, the compiler ensures that it is consistently used as an integer and not, for example, as a character. If the programmer wants to convert a piece of data from one type to another, it has to be done explicitly. (This is called casting.) Compile-time checking like this is cheap and effective compared with detecting and eradicating bugs that become evident only when the program is running.

The Java language is completely object oriented, and one major aspect of this is encapsulation. Variables and methods within an object that are declared private cannot be accessed from outside the object. So there is clear and explicit control over access to data and actions.

The Java language prevents a programmer from accessing a variable that has not been initialized. Some other languages allow access to a variable that has not been initialized. This is an error by the programmer in assuming either that they have done it explicitly or that the system does it for them implicitly.

The verifier

When a new piece of Java byte code arrives for execution the verifier checks it to ensure that it is safe. This is to minimize any risk that the code was damaged in transit or that unsafe code has been created using a tool other than the regular Java compiler. The checks ensure that:

- the code does not create dangerous pointers;
- access to private variables and methods is valid;
- methods are called with parameters of the correct type;
- no illegal data conversions are done.

The class loader

One way that a villain could penetrate Java's defences is to supply some classes that pretend to be standard Java classes. If such classes were mistakenly loaded instead of the proper classes, any amount of damage could be done. To prevent this, the class loader carefully distinguishes between different packages and particularly between local built-in classes and any others.

The Java Virtual Machine (JVM)

Once checked, byte code is not directly executed on the machine but is interpreted. This means that the program is prevented from accessing the raw machine instructions – with all the power and danger that that would imply. It is by this mechanism that a whole series of facilities are denied to the program:

- access to areas of memory that contain operating system information;
- access to files and to the Internet by applets.

Thus a Java program runs in a box or a cage (sometimes called a sandbox), and everything it does is constrained.

Arrays

One potential way in which a rogue program could do damage is to declare an array and then access elements of the array that don't actually exist – elements with a subscript that is greater than the size of the array. This is prevented in Java because the JVM checks that a subscript is within the defined bounds.

Garbage collection

When an object in a Java program is no longer used, the system automatically releases the memory that was allocated to it. This is called automatic garbage collection. In languages like C++ it is the responsibility of the programmer explicitly to invoke the operating system informing it that a piece of memory is free. The following errors can and do occur in such languages:

- failing to free memory when it is no longer needed, causing the program to accumulate ever increasing regions of memory;

- freeing the same piece of memory twice, causing subtle memory corruption bugs that can be difficult to find;
- freeing memory but continuing to use it, causing similar problems.

These problems are completely avoided because Java provides automatic garbage collection.

The filing system

The person invoking a Java applet can control that applet's access to files by specifying an option to the browser. The user can assess the reliability of the applet and decide (for example) that it can read from a local file, but not write to a local file. The default settings do not provide access to files.

Summary

Java provides several mechanisms for protection:

- the language and the compiler, e.g. absence of pointers;
- verification of byte code;
- the class loader;
- the filing system and network access.

Java's security measures are comprehensive and wide ranging. There is, however, no cast-iron guarantee that a malicious programmer cannot penetrate the defences.

● Netcentric

Java is a language intimately connected with the Internet and intranets. (An intranet is a network supported within an organization that uses Internet technology.) It is a language that allows many Internet-related activities to be performed easily. We saw in Chapter 17 on files that a program can read data from any file on the Internet (provided that it has appropriate security privileges). This means that the Internet is seen as one huge global filing system. Information anywhere can be accessed by a Java program, just as easily as if it is on a local disk. Textual, graphical, animation and audio information can be retrieved and displayed. Orders for products can be placed by adding information to a remote file (security provisions allowing).

Java is a world language in a different sense. It uses the Unicode standard for representing and manipulating characters. This is a recent international standard that provides 16 bits for the representation of a character, in contrast to earlier standards like ASCII which provide only 8 bits. This means that Java programs can manipulate characters of all the languages of the world, including (for example) Mandarin, Urdu and Japanese. This also means that programmers can use their own language for names of variables, methods and classes.

Last, but certainly not least, parts of a Java program can reside in different places on the Internet, to be retrieved and run as necessary. As we have seen, Java programs are constructed from classes. The Java system uses dynamic linking. This means that a class is only loaded and linked with the object that uses it when it is first referred to. This first reference is usually the creation of an instance of the class using **new** and the constructor method of the class. The different classes from which a program is made can be stored on different computers across the Internet. When a class is needed, it can be retrieved, loaded, linked and finally executed. It is not always that there is a need to use this facility, but it can be very useful.

● Microsoft versus the world

Microsoft Windows operating systems currently account for around 90% of the world market for PC operating systems. This has been seen as a massive near-monopoly. Microsoft operating systems run on Intel processors and this powerful combination is sometimes known as Wintel. The other companies in the computer industry are jealous of this power and would like to break the alleged monopoly. They see Microsoft as dominating the market, weakening their market share and eventually forcing them out of business. Java has become a weapon in this battle. Led by Sun Microsystems, the opponents of Microsoft have promoted Java as a means of creating portable software that will run on any machine and under any operating system.

Java has been the subject of legal skirmishes between Sun and Microsoft, concerned with Microsoft's support for a standard Java system, and other legal cases have involved the alleged monopoly of Microsoft. This is a moving target, and we suggest you check the latest news on the Internet. One thing that is relatively certain is that Microsoft is not strongly behind Java. In fact Microsoft has brought out a major new product, referred to as .NET ('dot-net'). Here are the main features of .NET:

■ It has a vast library of classes.

■ It is strongly Internet oriented.

■ It has several fully OO languages, including a new version of Visual Basic, and a new language called C# ('C sharp'). C# is very similar to Java.

■ It has a standard IDE for all its languages.

■ Programs written for .NET are compiled into byte code, in a similar manner to Java. Though .NET currently only runs on Microsoft operating systems, porting the whole system to other operating systems is not impossible.

■ There is a cut-down version for hand-held systems.

■ At the time of writing, the .NET framework (the libraries and command-line compilers) is free. The IDE is not.

This is a major venture for Microsoft, and Java (C++ based, portable) has been influential. It is too early to assess the impact of .NET on Java.

In 2003, Sun introduced JDS (Java Desktop System), which can be viewed as an alternative to the Microsoft Windows/Microsoft Office combination. JDS includes a version of the GNU/Linux operating system, the StarOffice package (with Microsoft-compatible word processor, spreadsheet and database software), and various tools written in Java. Though Java is not the main point of JDS, this might have an effect in spreading the name of Sun and Java.

The versions of Java

In the beginning there was version 1.0. Significant changes were introduced (especially in event handling) resulting in version 1.1. Version 1.2 quickly progressed to Java 2, the current one and the one we use in this book.

But the situation is not quite so simple! In recognition of the range of devices which might contain processors (e.g. cookers, phones, etc.) Sun has provided three editions:

1. Standard. Probably the version you are using on a PC.

2. Enterprise, for (potentially large) organizations requiring major server software, distributed databases, Internet sales, etc.

3. Micro. This edition is capable of running in a very small amount of memory, and it is aimed at embedding code in such devices as mobile phones, pagers, smart cards and set-top boxes.

As regards the language itself, this seems likely to have small changes incorporated soon. For example, there is likely to be a 'generics' facility. Recall that the `ArrayList` can hold any type of data, and that we need to cast items when accessing them. The generic feature will allow us to specify what type of data an `ArrayList` will hold, thus allowing compile-time checks for misuse. The need for casting will be removed. Note that existing programs will still compile and execute normally.

Java capabilities

Enhancements to Java normally arise through the addition of new libraries (helped by Java's object orientation), and also through software which allows Java to be used in new ways (e.g. Remote Method Invocation). Here we survey the most significant capabilities provided by Sun, in the form of libraries and technologies. However, note that many other companies also create Java software.

Java libraries

Java is a small language and much of the power of Java programs arises from the facilities provided by the large (and sometimes complex) libraries. There has been much effort made to add to these libraries to promote the usage of Java. The following is a selection from the complete list:

- Java Language and Utilities. These provide the facilities (described in this book) for windowing and file I/O. They also support networking – writing programs that communicate with programs on another computer.

- Java Electronic Commerce Framework. The race is on to commercialize the Internet and this library should help. This library consists of facilities to send credit card information or electronic money securely across the Internet.

- Java Security. This provides facilities for digital signatures and authentication.

- Java Media Framework. Comprehensive facilities for media playback.

- Java Collections Framework. Data structures such as sets, linked lists and maps.

- Java 3D. Classes for creating and displaying three-dimensional worlds.

● Internationalization

There are hundreds of human languages in the world and, ideally, software should be able to adapt itself to any one of these. Internationalization is the process of giving software this quality. Let us look at some of the problems:

- Different languages have different character sets. For example, Spanish has accented letters, and uses inverted question marks at the start of questions. And then there are non-European languages, such as Chinese.

- Dates and times. The UK uses day/month/year format, whilst the USA uses month/day/year format. Other countries have other conventions – and of course there are different names for the months and days of the week!

- Currency format. Different countries have different currency symbols: sometimes the symbol comes before the amount, and sometimes after.

The internationalization of a program might involve all these issues, together with the obvious issue of the translation of all the text that the user sees. Captions of buttons, labels, error messages and help screens are all to be changed. Basically, full internationalization is difficult to achieve!

Java doesn't provide for full internationalization automatically. But it has classes which help, and it also works with the Unicode character standard:

1. Classes: there is the concept of a locale – an area with its own language. A Java program can find out its locale, and then make use of classes which do the appropriate formatting of currency, date and time.

2. The use of Unicode: this is a 16-bit agreed coding of the characters used by most of the world's languages, and it is built into Java. In fact, the classes we used for file I/O will work with Unicode files. You could use such files to contain the text to be displayed on (for example) buttons, rather than fix it in the code. It is then possible to supply a new file when a different language is required.

To summarize, you still have to plan how you are going to do your internationalization, but Java provides significant help via its classes and Unicode.

● Databases – JDBC

Databases are big business. Without a database, banks, manufacturing companies, airlines, supermarkets, etc., could not function. Aside from the use of word processors, spreadsheets and email, the database can be regarded as the most vital software component of businesses.

As an example, a shop which sells computers would use a database to hold stock levels, customer and supplier addresses, mailshot and invoice production, and staff salaries.

Currently, most databases are termed 'relational'. The data is held in tables which can be related to each other. Most databases can be accessed locally by either menu commands or typed-in queries, in a standard language known as SQL (Structured Query Language).

In larger organizations, there is often a central database with a large number of people accessing it, often from different countries and using different types of computer. This is where the portability of Java pays off. The JDBC (Java DataBase Connectivity) classes allow a Java program running on (for example) a desktop machine to pass SQL queries to a database on another computer. The results are then passed back.

Of course, other software exists which can do this, but Java proponents stress the portability of the Java approach.

To summarize, JDBC allows access to SQL-compatible databases.

● RMI – Remote Method Invocation

A few years ago, the owner of a home PC was never exposed to the possibility of interaction between several computers. Now, with the tremendous increase in Internet use, the idea of interacting with programs on other machines is mainstream. In the corporate computing area as well, networks are the norm.

In certain application areas, it can be beneficial to distribute the processing power over several computers, which will then interact with each other when required. Let us imagine a multinational corporation. It will certainly have a large database, and could use the JDBC library to access this. However, if the application area is rather non-standard, then a database might not fit. What if the corporation wanted to provide software for a group of participants in different countries to cooperate in building up a design? This might require a window onto which anyone could type or draw. Every participant can see everyone else's work. One possible arrangement is for each participant to have a program on their computer to handle the local drawing, and to have a program on a central server to broadcast any new input. Software such as this can be developed more easily if an individual's computer can invoke methods on a server. In Java, this is known as RMI (Remote Method Invocation).

There is already a standard approach to this kind of distributed software, known as CORBA (Common Object Request Broker Architecture), which is not tied to any single company or programming language, and Microsoft has a similar system known as DCOM (Distributed Component Object Model). At the time of writing, it is uncertain whether one approach will dominate.

So, what does RMI let you do? Basically, you (or someone else) can set up Java software on a server. You can then write Java software on another machine which can call methods on the server. In addition, parameters can be passed as in normal method invocation, and part of the power of RMI comes from the fact that parameters of any type can be passed, not just simple numbers or strings.

RMI has a great deal of potential, as it is simpler than its competitors, but market forces rather than technical issues are likely to determine the winner in the world of distributed computing.

● Java beans

Sun states that a bean is 'a reusable software component that can be manipulated visually in a builder tool'. Before explaining the significance of this, let us examine the consumer electronics industry. There are agreed standards which ensure that, for example, your new CD player will work properly with any amplifier that has CD input facilities. The standard is at the level of plug sizes, and at the level of voltage. The result of this is that it is simple to create a new hi-fi system by plugging together a set of modules.

Back to software. Imagine that you are writing a text editor in Java, and you wanted to build in a spellchecker. What if you could open up your favourite word processor and drag its spellcheck button into your text editor? (You can't actually do this at the moment, but it is a nice idea!)

The beans concept is rather similar. A programmer can write beans, which are Java classes written in a particular style. A bean might provide a sophisticated GUI for the programmer (e.g. a spreadsheet bean) or its significant feature might be in the concealed code and data (e.g. a spellchecker bean). In either case, the bean provides an icon at design time, so that the programmer can visually incorporate and manipulate it.

Here is the bean process in more detail:

■ A bean is either designed and coded, or purchased elsewhere. Coding a bean is similar to the coding of any Java class, but the programmer has to follow particular naming and style conventions.

■ The software into which the bean is to be placed is written in such a way as to allow the bean to be incorporated. In some simple cases, no coding is needed.

■ To incorporate the bean into the application, we use a special beans development environment. This allows beans to be selected graphically, and either dropped into an application, or connected to other beans.

So, beans are Java classes written in a particular way. They can easily be incorporated in beans-ready software. Those of you who have used Microsoft's Visual Basic may be familiar with 'custom controls', which can be used in a similar manner. The .NET framework has a similar facility. The future of beans is potentially huge, but this is based on the assumption that a large number of beans will be produced and will be available for purchase in an 'off-the-shelf' manner. Currently, the clear leader in this form of reuse is Microsoft's Visual Basic.

● Java servlets

Web interaction is enabled by programs on a server computer interacting with software (typically a browser) on a client computer. For example, a user might enter a name into a field in a web page, and this data is passed to a program on the server, which might use this name to access a database. There are a number of ways to create server-side software, the most common one being the use of the HTTP/HTML Common Gateway Interface (CGI) facility, which is typically dealt with by a Perl program on the server, though CGI programs can be written in almost any language, including C, C++ and Java.

An alternative to CGI is to use Java servlets on the server. A servlet is a Java program coded according to certain conventions, with useful utility classes (e.g. for accessing data from the client). Many servers (such as Apache and Microsoft IIS) allow servlets to be executed.

The benefits of servlets are as follows:

- Each time the web page is used, and data is sent to the server, the single servlet creates a new thread. In the CGI approach, it is often the case that a fresh copy of the CGI program is created and executed. This is regarded as inefficient.
- A servlet can be run in a sandbox, providing better security.
- A servlet is platform independent (assuming that the existing server software allows servlets to be incorporated).

● JavaScript

JavaScript is a scripting language for use in web pages. The reason for its name is that Netscape (who produced one of the first web browsers) heard about the creation of Java, and named their scripting language after it. There is not much similarity between the languages and their application area.

Here are the main differences:

- JavaScript code is embedded in HTML web pages; if you download a web page with JavaScript embedded, you can view the JavaScript code.
- It looks superficially like Java in terms of control structures (similar keywords, curly brackets) but does not allow the creation of classes, or inheritance. It is regarded as 'object based', not fully object oriented.
- It is weakly typed. Variable names need not be declared in advance of their use, and even if they are, their type cannot be specified.
- It can only execute within a browser, and can only access elements of the browser such as HTML from controls and mouse movements. Thus it can be used to create visually interesting pages, and for validating entries in HTML text fields. It cannot access files, and cannot be used to write applications or applets.

It may be that you will wish to learn JavaScript after learning Java. This will be relatively straightforward, because you understand variables, control structures, methods and the 'dot' object/method notation. JavaScript has all these, but in a slightly different way.

● Conclusion

Several trends are apparent in the computer industry:

- a tremendous growth of Internet use;
- the importance of web interaction and web services;
- use of intranets (an intranet is a local network, usually within a corporation, that uses Internet technology);
- reduction in the cost of networking;
- the fusion of the computer and telecommunications industries;
- the incorporation (embedding) of computers within consumer products;
- interest in multimedia;
- the realization of the vital need for secure computing across networks;
- a fight against the dominance of Microsoft (Windows operating system) and Intel (PCs);
- the introduction of Microsoft's .NET system.

Java has been born out of the need to create new technologies to deal with these trends. Java is no 'silver bullet' that solves problems as if by magic. There is no 'killer application' that makes it indispensable in the way that the VisiCalc spreadsheet made the Apple II computer a success. Instead, Java combines the best of current technologies in a very elegant synthesis to provide a 'Swiss Army knife' of facilities for computing into the new millennium.

Summary

Many of the above topics could fill a book individually, and there are also the areas of security and networking which we have not covered. New Java products are coming out rapidly, and are often significant. Check out Sun's web site frequently, for new products and downloads. They are at: http://java.sun.com/.

● Exercises

26.1 'Java is just another programming language' (Bill Gates). Discuss.

26.2 The performance overheads of Java programs make it impracticable for many applications. Discuss.

26.3 Examine the difference between C# and Java, in terms of language facilities.

26.4 Microsoft's C# language will kill off Java. Discuss.

26.5 Suggest the future for Java.

APPENDIX

A

Java libraries

This appendix describes selected classes and methods from the Java libraries. It is intended for use as reference and for browsing.

All Java programs use some library classes to accomplish their task. Java itself is a small language and the libraries provide most of the functionality that is needed. Java provides a host of methods that are grouped into classes and in turn organized into several libraries (packages) listed below.

The classes listed here are all the classes used within the book. They are more than sufficient to enable a huge variety of programs to be written.

We list the classes in alphabetical order, except for classes that start with the letter J (where they are listed in alphabetical order without the J).

For each method in the libraries, we give the full heading. For example:

```
public void drawLine(int x1, int y1, int x2, int y2)
```

so that all the information on how to use them is available. Inspection of the full heading allows us to see what parameters are needed (or empty brackets if there are none) and what return value is returned (or **void** if no value is returned).

Here is a commentary on the libraries (remembering that a field is either a variable or a method):

- Nearly all the available fields of the libraries are methods – there are very few variables. This reflects the design principle of data hiding whereby access to variables is usually via method calling.

- All the fields are labelled **public**, because it is only public items that can be used.

- Fields labelled **static** belong to a class as a whole and not to individual objects instantiated from the class. The notation for using them is:

```
ClassName.methodName();
```

For example:

```
Integer.toString(integer);
```

- Constructor methods such as **JTextField** and **JLabel** have no return type.

The **import** statement is a way of allowing the programmer to abbreviate the name of a method, rather than give its full package name. For each class we explain which **import** statement, if any, is required to use the class in a convenient way. The **java.lang** package is automatically imported into every Java program, because it provides vital methods which are used by nearly every Java program.

ArrayList

A data structure that allows items to be added and removed. The structure expands and contracts accordingly.

```
import java.util.ArrayList;
```

`public ArrayList()`	Creates a new array list.
`public void add(int index, Object item)`	Inserts the specified item at the specified position. Shifts the item currently at that position and any subsequent items (adds 1 to their index values).
`public boolean add(Object item)`	Appends the specified item to the end of the array list. Returns **true**.
`public void clear()`	Removes all the items from the array list.
`public boolean contains (Object item)`	Returns **true** if the object is in the array list.
`public Object get(int index)`	Returns the element at the specified position.
`public void remove(int index)`	Removes the element at the specified position.
`public Object set(int index, Object item)`	Replaces the item at the specified position with the specified item. Returns the object previously at this position.
`public int size()`	Returns the number of elements in the array list.

BorderLayout

Most of the programs in this book use flow layout to build up a user interface. In this approach, components are added to the screen in a left to right order. If a row of components is unfilled, components are centred.

However, there are other approaches. Consider a typical word processor or drawing package: there is a large central work area, with components (buttons etc.) across the top and/or down the side. When the user widens the window, the central space expands but the space allocated to the buttons remains fixed. We can create this in Java by using border layout. Here is some code which creates a border layout, with a large drawing area and two buttons. Note that we have set the layout of the window to **BorderLayout**.

```java
private void createGUI() {
    setDefaultCloseOperation(EXIT_ON_CLOSE);
    Container window = getContentPane();
    window.setLayout(new BorderLayout());
    buttonPanel = new JPanel();

    drawingPanel = new JPanel();
    drawingPanel.setBackground(Color.white);

    button1 = new JButton("button1");
    buttonPanel.add(button1);
    button1.addActionListener(this);

    button2 = new JButton("button2");
    buttonPanel.add(button2);
    button2.addActionListener(this);

    window.add("South", buttonPanel);
    window.add("Center", drawingPanel);
}
```

The border layout operates as follows.

The window is regarded as being composed of five areas: a central area and strips at each edge. When we call the **add** method for a border layout, we specify the area with a string: **"North"**, **"South"**, **"East"**, **"West"**, **"Center"**.

Each area can have one item added to it. In order to add the two buttons, we create a panel (named **buttonPanel** here). We add each button to the panel, then we add the panel to an edge of the window (**"South"** here). Then we add the drawing panel to the centre. If required, we can add items at every edge of the window.

If you look carefully at the code, you will see that we have not specified a size for the drawing panel – so how large is it? The answer is that the standard-sized buttons are added at the edge, and then the central area expands to fill up the rest of the space. Moreover, this layout is recalculated if the user resizes the window. Figure A.1 shows two screenshots of the above layout, which have been resized.

The border layout involves more thought, but is good in some situations.

▶ *BorderLayout* continued

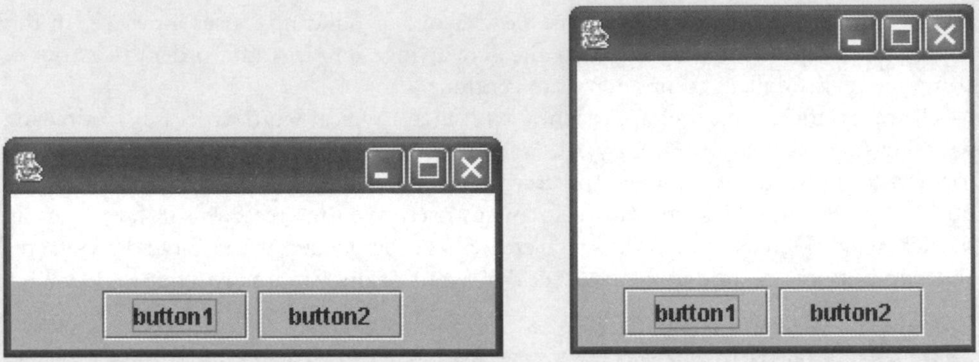

Figure A.1 Border layout (showing two window sizes).

● Button

A GUI button. Clicking on the button creates an event:

```
import javax.swing.JButton; or import javax.swing.*
```

public *JButton*(String label)	Creates a button with the label.
public void *addActionListener* (Object object)	Registers the object to handle the event (usually **this**).
public void *setFont*(Font f)	Sets the font type and size. Example: **button.setFont(new Font(null, Font.BOLD, 60));**. For the **Font** constructor, the second parameter is the style. Options are **Font.BOLD**, **Font.ITALIC**, **Font.PLAIN**. The third parameter is the font size.

Sample program:

```
import java.awt.*;
import java.awt.event.*;
import javax.swing.*;

class ButtonDemo extends JFrame implements ActionListener {

    private JButton button;
    private JTextField textField;

    public static void main(String[] args) {
        ButtonDemo frame = new ButtonDemo();
        frame.setSize(400,300);
        frame.createGUI();
        frame.show();
    }

    private void createGUI() {
        setDefaultCloseOperation(EXIT_ON_CLOSE);
        Container window = getContentPane();
        window.setLayout(new FlowLayout() );

        button = new JButton("Press me");
        window.add(button);
        button.addActionListener(this);

        textField = new JTextField(10);
        window.add(textField);
    }

    public void actionPerformed(ActionEvent event) {
        textField.setText("button clicked");
    }
}
```

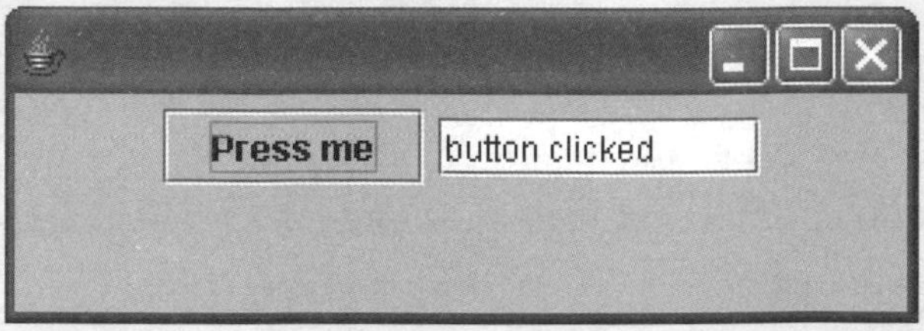

Figure A.2 A button and a text field.

Calendar

```
import java.util.Calendar;
```

`public static Calendar getInstance()`	Returns an instance of class **Calendar**.
`public int get(Calendar.DAY_OF_MONTH)`	Returns the day of the month.
`public int get(Calendar.DAY_OF_WEEK)`	Returns the day of the week. 0 is Sunday.
`public int get(Calendar.DAY_OF_YEAR)`	Returns the day of the year.
`public int get(Calendar.HOUR_OF_DAY)`	Returns the hour of the day, between 0 and 23, in the 24-hour clock system. 0 is midnight.
`public int get(Calendar.MINUTE)`	Returns the number of minutes past the hour.
`public int get(Calendar.MONTH)`	Returns the month. 0 is January.
`public int get(Calendar.SECOND)`	Returns the number of seconds past the minute.
`public int get(Calendar.MILLISECOND)`	Returns the number of milliseconds past the second.
`public int get(Calendar.YEAR)`	Returns the year.

Sample code:

```
Calendar calendar = Calendar.getInstance();
int hour = calendar.get(Calendar.HOUR_OF_DAY);
textField.setText("hour is " + hour);
```

See also **currentTimeMillis** in class **java.lang.System**.

Check box

A check box is a GUI component, added to a frame, just like a button. When the user checks a box, an event is created and handled using the **itemStateChanged** method.

```
import javax.swing.JCheckBox; or import javax.swing.*
```

`public JCheckBox(String s)`	Create a check box with the label **s**.
`public void addItemListener (Object object)`	Register the object to handle events.
`public boolean isSelected()`	Returns true if the box is selected.

Sample program:

```
import java.awt.*;
import java.awt.event.*;
import javax.swing.*;
class CheckBoxDemo extends JFrame implements ItemListener {
    private JCheckBox cola, burger, fries;
    private JTextArea textArea;
    public static void main(String[] args) {
        CheckBoxDemo frame = new CheckBoxDemo();
        frame.setSize(400,300);
        frame.createGUI();
        frame.show();
    }
    private void createGUI() {
        setDefaultCloseOperation(EXIT_ON_CLOSE);
        Container window = getContentPane();
        window.setLayout(new FlowLayout() );
        cola = new JCheckBox("cola");
        window.add(cola);
        cola.addItemListener(this);
        burger = new JCheckBox("burger");
        window.add(burger);
        burger.addItemListener(this);
        fries = new JCheckBox("fries");
        window.add(fries);
        fries.addItemListener(this);
        textArea = new JTextArea(5,3);
        window.add(textArea);
    }
    public void itemStateChanged(ItemEvent event) {
        String newLine = "\n";
        textArea.setText("");
        if (cola.isSelected()) {
            textArea.append("cola selected" + newLine);
        }
        if (burger.isSelected()) {
            textArea.append("burger selected" + newLine);
        }
        if (fries.isSelected()) {
            textArea.append("fries selected" + newLine);
        }
    }
}
```

▶ *Check box continued*

Figure A.3 Check box.

● Combo box

A combo box is a drop-down list of options, rather like a menu. The user can select one item (but only one). When the user clicks on an item an event is created. The event handler can determine the index number or the string that was clicked on. Index values start at 0.

`public JComboBox()`	Create a new combo box.
`public void addItem(Object object)`	Add a new item after the current values to the combo box.
`public void addActionListener(Object object)`	Register the object to handle events.
`public Object getSelectedItem()`	Returns the object selected.
`public int getSelectedIndex()`	Returns the index of the object selected. Returns –1 if there is no selected item.

Sample program:

```
import java.awt.*;
import java.awt.event.*;
import javax.swing.*;
```

```
class ComboDemo extends JFrame implements ActionListener {

    private JComboBox combo;
    private JTextField textField;

    public static void main(String[] args) {
        ComboDemo frame = new ComboDemo();
        frame.setSize(400,300);
        frame.createGUI();
        frame.show();
    }

    private void createGUI() {
        setDefaultCloseOperation(EXIT_ON_CLOSE);
        Container window = getContentPane();
        window.setLayout(new FlowLayout() );

        combo = new JComboBox();

        combo.addItem("red");
        combo.addItem("blue");
        combo.addItem("yellow");

        combo.addActionListener(this);
        window.add(combo);

        textField = new JTextField(15);
        window.add(textField);
    }

    public void actionPerformed(ActionEvent event) {
        int index = combo.getSelectedIndex();
        String item = (String) combo.getSelectedItem();
        textField.setText("item " + Integer.toString(index)
        + ", " + item + " selected");
    }
}
```

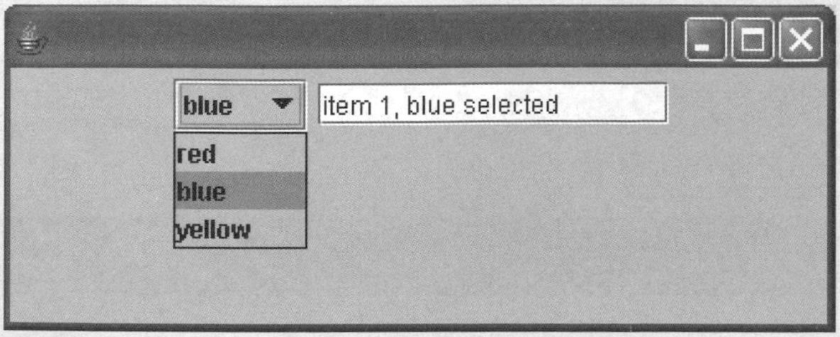

Figure A.4 Combo box.

Container

A container is a component that can contain other GUI components.

```
import java.awt.*;  or  import java.awt.Container;
```

public void *add*(Component c)	Add a component to this container.
public void *setLayout*(LayoutManager m)	Sets the layout manager for this component. See for example **FlowLayout**.

In most of the programs in this book, a container is created from a frame object and used to hold GUI components such as buttons. Most programs in this book do this:

```
Container window = getContentPane();
window.setLayout(new FlowLayout());
window.add(button);
```

DataInputStream

```
import java.io.DataInputStream;  or  import java.io.*;
```

public *DataInputStream*(String name)	Creates a new data input stream.
public final String *readline*()	Reads the next line of text from the data stream.

Date

```
import java.util.Date;
```

public *Date*()	Constructor.
public String *toString*()	Returns a string with the date and time.

DecimalFormat

Provides formatting of numbers for display.

```
import java.text.DecimalFormat;
```

public *DecimalFormat*(String pattern)	Constructor. Creates a **DecimalFormat** object that will use **pattern**.
public String *format*(double d)	Converts the **double** into the equivalent string according to the pattern.
public String *format*(int i)	Converts the **int** into the equivalent string according to the pattern.

The following table summarizes the formatting characters that can be used to make up patterns:

Character	Meaning
#	insert a digit if there is one
0	always insert a digit
,	insert a comma
.	insert a decimal point
E	insert E followed by the power of 10
$	insert a dollar sign

Example:

```
double d = 12.34;
DecimalFormat formatter = new DecimalFormat("###.##");
textField.setText(formatter.format(d));
```

Double

This is in **java.lang**. No **import** required.

public static String *parseDouble*(String s)	Converts a string into a **double**. A **NumberFormatException** is created if the string does not contain valid characters.
public static String *toString*(double d)	Converts the **double** into the equivalent string.

Sample code:

```
double d = Double.parseDouble("0.123");
String s = Double.toString(d);
```

File

```
import java.io.File;
```

public *File*(String name)	Creates an instance of class **File**, with the full file name given as the parameter.
public boolean *exists*()	Returns **true** if the file specified by the object exists, or **false** otherwise.
public String *getAbsolutePath*()	Returns the full path name of the file specified by this object.
public String *getName*()	Returns the full name of the file or directory.
public String *getParent*()	Returns the full path name of this object's parent.
public boolean *isDirectory*()	Returns **true** if this file exists and it is a directory, or **false** otherwise.
public long *length*()	Returns the length of the file in bytes or zero if the file does not exist.
public String[] *list*()	Returns an array of file names in the directory specified by the file object.
public final static String *separator*	This data field holds the value of the path separator character, which is specific to the particular operating system.

FileDialog

```
import java.awt.FileDialog; or import java.awt.*;
```

public *FileDialog*(Frame parent, String title, int mode)	Creates a file dialogue window. The parent is the frame that creates the window. The title is the title of the window. The mode is either **FileDialog.LOAD** or **FileDialog.SAVE**.
public String *getFile*()	Returns the name of the file that has been selected, or **null** if none has been selected.

FileInputStream

```
import java.io.FileInputStream; or import java.io.*;
```

public *FileInputStream*(String name)	Creates an input file stream from a file with the specified name.
public void *close*()	Closes the stream.

See also class **java.io.DataInputStream**.

FileOutputStream

```
import java.io.FileOutputStream; or import java.io.*;
```

public *FileOutputStream* (String name)	Creates an output file stream from a file with the specified name.

See also **java.io.PrintStream**.

FlowLayout

Java offers several ways of positioning components on the screen. The simplest involves using the **FlowLayout** approach, as it appears in the majority of the programs in this book. Here is the familiar code we use. In this example, we add a panel for drawing, and two buttons:

```
private void createGUI() {
    setDefaultCloseOperation(EXIT_ON_CLOSE);
    Container window = getContentPane();
    window.setLayout(new FlowLayout());

    panel = new JPanel();
    panel.setPreferredSize(new Dimension(300, 200));
    panel.setBackground(Color.white);
    window.add(panel);

    button1 = new JButton("button1");
    window.add(button1);
    button1.addActionListener(this);
```

> ▶ *FlowLayout continued*

```
    button2 = new JButton("button2");
    window.add(button2);
    button2.addActionListener(this);
}
```

We create a container named **window**, then set its layout style to flow layout style. From then on, items that we add are placed left to right, until a row is full. Then, a new row is begun underneath. If a row of components is unfilled, the components are centred.

If you experiment with resizing the frame of any of our graphics programs, you will see that the layout is modified, depending on the width of the frame. The flow layout approach is simple to use, but has drawbacks. For example, we might want the graphics panel to increase in size as we increase the size of the frame, but the flow layout does not provide this. Consult the **BorderLayout** section in this appendix for details of an alternative approach.

● Frame

A frame is a top-level window with a title and a border. It is used as the basis for windowing in nearly all the programs presented in this book.

```
    import javax.swing.JFrame; or import javax.swing.*;
```

`public Container getContentPane()`	Returns the container object for this frame, for use as a container for GUI components. See class **Container**.
`public void setSize(int width, int height)`	Resizes the frame so that it has width **width** and height **height**.
`public void show()`	Displays the frame.

● Graphics

```
    import java.awt.Graphics; or import java.awt.*;
```

This group of methods provides facilities for displaying simple graphical objects, normally in a panel.

An object is drawn in the current colour, which can be changed using method **setColor**. The available colours are: **black**, **blue**, **cyan**, **darkGray**, **gray**, **green**, lightGray, magenta, orange, pink, red, white, yellow. For example, to change the colour to red, call:

```
setColor(Color.red);
```

Coordinates of objects are expressed as *x* and *y* pixel coordinates:

x is measured across the screen from the left;
y is measured down the screen, with 0 at the top.

Many of the graphical objects are considered to be drawn inside an invisible (containing) rectangle whose top left pixel coordinates are *x*, *y*. The height and width of the rectangle, measured in pixels, are the two other parameters.

public void *draw3DRect*(int x, int y, int width, int height, boolean raised)	Draws a highlighted 3-D rectangle. If **raised** is **true**, the rectangle appears raised.
public void *drawArc*(int x, int y, int width, int height, int startAngle, int arcAngle)	Draws a circular or elliptical arc. The arc is drawn from **startAngle** to **startAngle** + **arcAngle**. Angles are measured in degrees. An angle of 0 is the 3 o'clock position. A positive **arcAngle** means counter-clockwise.
public void *drawLine*(int x1, int y1, int x2, int y2)	Draws a line from coordinates **x1, y1** to **x2, y2**.
public void *drawOval*(int x, int y, int width, int height)	Draws an ellipse or a circle (if width and height are the same).
public void *drawPolygon*(int xPoints[], int yPoints[], int nPoints)	Draws a closed polygon using the pairs of coordinates in the two arrays. A line is drawn from the first point to the last point.
public void *drawRect*(int x, int y, int width, int height)	Draws a rectangle using the current colour.
public void *drawRoundRect*(int x, int y, int width, int height, int arcWidth, int arcHeight)	Draws a rectangle with rounded corners in the current colour. **arcWidth** is the horizontal diameter of the arc at the four corners, and **arcHeight** is the vertical diameter.
public void *drawString*(String s, int x, int y)	Draws a string. The baseline of the first character is at coordinates *x*, *y*. The characters are in the current font and current colour.
public void *fillArc*(int x, int y, int width, int height, int startAngle, int arcAngle)	Draws a pie shape using the current colour. See **drawArc** for the meanings of the parameters.

▶ *Graphics continued*

`public void fillOval(int x, int y, int width, int height)`	Draws a filled ellipse or circle.
`public void fillPolygon(int xPoints[], int yPoints[], int nPoints)`	Fills a polygon with the current colour. See **drawPolygon** for the meaning of the parameters.
`public void fillRect(int x, int y, int width, int height)`	Fills the rectangle with the current colour.
`public void fillRoundRect(int x, int y, int width, int height, int arcWidth, int arcHeight)`	Fills a rounded rectangle with the current colour. See **drawRoundRect** for the meaning of the parameters.
`public void setColor(Color c)`	Sets the current color. The available colours are listed at the top of this table.

Sample code follows. A complete program is given under the description of the **JPanel** class. Once a panel has been created, the method **getGraphics** must be called to obtain a **Graphics** object. Then the methods can be used.

```
JPanel panel = new JPanel();
Graphics paper = panel.getGraphics();
paper.drawLine(0,0,100,120);
```

● Integer

This is in package **java.lang**. No **import** required.

`public static int parseInt(String s)`	Converts a string of decimal digits into an **int**. The digits may be preceded by a minus sign. A **NumberFormatException** is created if the string does not contain valid characters.
`public static String toString(int i)`	Converts the **int** into the equivalent string.

Sample code:

```
int i = Integer.parseInt(s);
String s = Integer.toString(i);
```

Label

A GUI label, which is displayed with some fixed text.

```
import javax.swing.JLabel; or import javax.swing.*;
```

public *JLabel*(String label)	Creates a new label.
public void *setFont*(Font f)	Sets the font type and size. Example: `label.setFont(new Font(null, Font.BOLD, 60));`. For the **Font** constructor, the second parameter is the style. Options are **Font.BOLD**, **Font.ITALIC**, **Font.PLAIN**. The third parameter is the font size.

Sample code:

```
private JLabel label;
label = new JLabel("something");
```

List

A list is a list of text strings. The user can click on an item to select it and this causes an event. The program can determine the index of the item that was clicked on. (Index values start at 0.) The program can also determine what text was clicked on.

Behind a GUI list is a data structure called a list model, which contains the information to be displayed. The items are added to this structure.

public *JList*(ListModel listmodel)	Creates a new list from a list model.
public void *addListSelectionListener*(Object object)	Registers an event-handler object.
public int *getSelectedIndex*()	Returns the index of the selected item.
public Object *getSelectedValue*()	Returns the object selected.

A sample program is given below. The list is added to a **JScrollPane** object, which means that scrollbars are displayed if the data is too big for the available display area.

▶ *List continued*

```java
import java.awt.*;
import java.awt.event.*;
import javax.swing.*;
import javax.swing.event.*;

class ListDemo extends JFrame implements ListSelectionListener {

    private JList list;
    private DefaultListModel listModel;
    private JTextField textField;

    public static void main(String[] args) {
        ListDemo frame = new ListDemo();
        frame.setSize(400,300);
        frame.createGUI();
        frame.show();
    }

    private void createGUI() {
        setDefaultCloseOperation(EXIT_ON_CLOSE);
        Container window = getContentPane();
        window.setLayout(new FlowLayout());

        listModel = new DefaultListModel();

        listModel.addElement("Mike");
        listModel.addElement("Maggie");
        listModel.addElement("Matthew");
        listModel.addElement("Eleanor");

        list = new JList(listModel);
        list.setSelectionMode(ListSelectionModel.SINGLE_SELECTION);
        list.addListSelectionListener(this);
        window.add(new JScrollPane(list));

        textField = new JTextField(15);
        window.add(textField);
    }

    public void valueChanged(ListSelectionEvent event) {
        int index = list.getSelectedIndex();
        String item = (String) list.getSelectedValue();
        textField.setText("item " + Integer.toString(index)
            + " - " + item + " selected");
    }
}
```

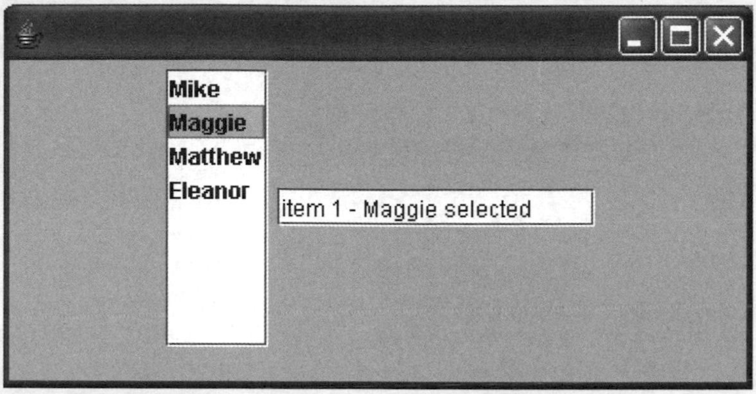

Figure A.5 A list.

Math

This is in package **java.lang**. No **import** is required.
This class provides mathematical methods and two constants.
All angles are expressed in radians.

`public final static double E`	Value of e.
`public final static double PI`	Value of π.
`public static int abs(int a)`	
`public static double abs(double a)`	
`public static double acos(double a)`	
`public static double asin(double a)`	
`public static double atan(double a)`	
`public static double ceil(double a)`	Returns the nearest integer (as a double) that is greater than or equal to **a**.
`public static double cos(double a)`	
`public static double exp(double a)`	e^a.
`public static double floor(double a)`	Returns the nearest integer (as a double) that is less than or equal to **a**.
`public static double log(double a)`	Natural log, to base e.
`public static int max(int a, int b)`	Returns greater value.
`public static double max(double a, double b)`	
`public static int min(int a, int b)`	Returns lesser value.

`public static double min(double a, double b)`	
`public static double pow(double a, double b)`	a^b.
`public static synchronized double random()`	Returns a pseudo-random number in the range 0.0 up to but not including 1.0. See also class `java.util.Random`.
`public static double rint(double a)`	Returns the **double** value that is closest in value to **a** and is equal to an integer.
`public static double sin(double a)`	Sine of **a**.
`public static double sqrt(double a)`	Square root of **a**.
`public static double tan(double a)`	Tangent of **a**.

Math continued

Sample code:

```
y = Math.sqrt(x);
```

Menu

This class supports menus.

A sample program follows. A **JMenuBar** is created. To this are added two **JMenu** objects. In turn **JMenuItem** items are added to these menus. The complete set of menus is added to the panel using **setJMenuBar**.

```
import javax.swing.*;
import java.awt.event.*;
import java.awt.*;

public class MenuDemo extends JFrame implements ActionListener {

    JMenuBar wholeMenuBar;
    JMenu fileMenu, editMenu;
    JMenuItem openItem, saveItem, copyItem, pasteItem;
    JButton quitButton;
    JTextField textField;

    public static void main(String args[]) {
        MenuDemo frame = new MenuDemo();
        frame.setSize(250, 200);
        frame.createGUI();
        frame.show();
    }
```

```java
public void createGUI() {

    setDefaultCloseOperation(EXIT_ON_CLOSE);
    Container window = getContentPane();
    window.setLayout(new FlowLayout());

    wholeMenuBar = new JMenuBar();
    setJMenuBar(wholeMenuBar);

    // file menu, with open, save
    fileMenu = new JMenu("File");

    openItem = new JMenuItem("Open");
    fileMenu.add(openItem);
    openItem.addActionListener(this);

    saveItem = new JMenuItem("Save");
    fileMenu.add(saveItem);
    saveItem.addActionListener(this);

    wholeMenuBar.add(fileMenu);

    // edit menu, with copy, paste
    editMenu = new JMenu("Edit");

    copyItem = new JMenuItem("Copy");
    editMenu.add(copyItem);
    copyItem.addActionListener(this);

    pasteItem = new JMenuItem("Paste");
    editMenu.add(pasteItem);
    pasteItem.addActionListener(this);
    wholeMenuBar.add(editMenu);

    quitButton = new JButton("Quit");
    window.add(quitButton);
    quitButton.addActionListener(this);

    textField = new JTextField(10);
    window.add(textField);
}

public void actionPerformed(ActionEvent e) {
    if (e.getSource() == openItem) {
        textField.setText("Open chosen");
    }
    if (e.getSource() == saveItem) {
        textField.setText("Save chosen");
    }
    if (e.getSource() == copyItem) {
        textField.setText("Copy chosen");
    }
```

Menu *continued*

```java
        if (e.getSource() == pasteItem) {
            textField.setText("Paste chosen");
        }
        if(e.getSource() == quitButton) {
            System.exit(0);
        }
    }
}
```

Figure A.6 A menu.

● Option pane

An option pane is a box that a program can display with a message. An import is needed as follows:

```java
    import javax.swing.JOptionPane;
```

A useful call looks like this:

```java
    JOptionPane.showMessageDialog(null, "your message here");
```

which creates the display shown in Figure A.7.

Figure A.7 An option pane used to ask the user to confirm an action.

The program waits until the **OK** button is clicked. This is a call on a static method of class **JOptionPane**.

This component can also be used to obtain information from the user, as shown in this example:

```
String name = JOptionPane.showInputDialog("enter your name");
```

which creates the display shown in Figure A.8, inviting the user to type some input.

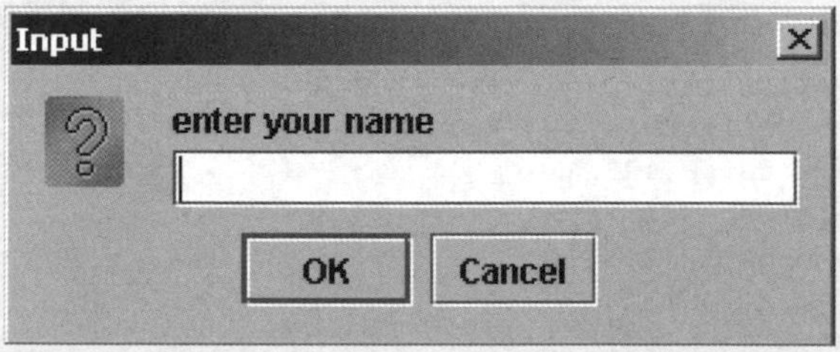

Figure A.8 An option pane used to obtain data from the user.

Panel

A drawing area. Simple graphical objects can be drawn in a panel using the methods within class **Graphics**.

```
import javax.swing.JPanel; or import javax.swing.*;
```

public *JPanel*()	Creates a new panel.
public Graphics *getGraphics*()	Returns the graphics context.
public int *getHeight*()	Returns the height of the panel in pixels.
public int *getWidth*()	Returns the width of the panel in pixels.
public void *setBackground*(Color color)	Sets the background colour.
public void *setPreferredSize*(Dimension preferredSize)	Sets the preferred size. For example: `panel.setPreferredSize(new Dimension(300, 200));`.

Panel continued

Sample program:

```java
import java.awt.*;
import java.awt.event.*;
import javax.swing.*;

class PanelDemo extends JFrame implements ActionListener {
    private JButton button;
    private JPanel panel;

    public static void main(String[] args) {
        PanelDemo frame = new PanelDemo();
        frame.setSize(400,300);
        frame.createGUI();
        frame.show();
    }

    private void createGUI() {
        setDefaultCloseOperation(EXIT_ON_CLOSE);
        Container window = getContentPane();
        window.setLayout(new FlowLayout() );

        panel = new JPanel();
        panel.setPreferredSize(new Dimension(100, 100));
        panel.setBackground(Color.white);
        window.add(panel);

        button = new JButton("Press me");
        window.add(button);
        button.addActionListener(this);
    }
    public void actionPerformed(ActionEvent event) {
        Graphics paper = panel.getGraphics();
        paper.drawLine(0,0,100,120);
    }
}
```

Figure A.9 A line drawn in a panel.

Mouse-clicks

A program can handle mouse-click events within a panel. Here is an example program that detects a mouse-click, draws a small circle at the click, and displays the *x* and *y* coordinates of the click. You must provide all the mouse event-handling methods, even where you do not use them.

```java
import java.awt.*;
import java.awt.event.*;
import javax.swing.*;

class PanelWithMouseDemo extends JFrame implements MouseListener {

    private JPanel panel;
    private JTextField textField;

    public static void main(String[] args) {
        PanelWithMouseDemo frame = new PanelWithMouseDemo();
        frame.setSize(400,300);
        frame.createGUI();
        frame.show();
    }

    private void createGUI() {

        setDefaultCloseOperation(EXIT_ON_CLOSE);
        Container window = getContentPane();
        window.setLayout(new FlowLayout() );

        panel = new JPanel();
        panel.setPreferredSize(new Dimension(100, 100));
        panel.setBackground(Color.white);
        window.add(panel);
        panel.addMouseListener(this);

        textField = new JTextField(10);
        window.add(textField);
    }

    public void mouseClicked(MouseEvent event) {
        int x = event.getX();
        int y = event.getY();
        Graphics paper = panel.getGraphics();
        paper.drawOval(x, y, 5, 5);
        textField.setText(" x = " + Integer.toString(x)
            + "     y = " + Integer.toString(y));
    }

    public void mouseReleased(MouseEvent event) {
    }
```

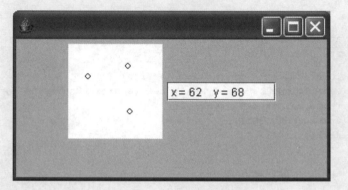

▶ *Panel continued*

```
    public void mousePressed(MouseEvent event) {
    }

    public void mouseExited(MouseEvent event) {
    }

    public void mouseEntered(MouseEvent event) {
    }
}
```

Figure A.10 Handling mouse-clicks in a panel.

Mouse moves

A program can handle mouse move events. Here is an example program that detects a mouse move, draws a line from the old position to the new position, and displays the *x* and *y* coordinates of the mouse. You must provide both the mouse move event-handling methods, even where you do not use them.

```
import java.awt.*;
import java.awt.event.*;
import javax.swing.*;

class Scribbler extends JFrame implements MouseMotionListener {

    private JTextField textField;
    private JPanel panel;

    int oldX = 50, oldY = 50;

    public static void main(String[] args) {
        Scribbler frame = new Scribbler();
        frame.setSize(400,300);
        frame.createGUI();
        frame.show();
    }
```

```
private void createGUI() {
    setDefaultCloseOperation(EXIT_ON_CLOSE);
    Container window = getContentPane();
    window.setLayout(new FlowLayout() );

    panel = new JPanel();
    panel.setPreferredSize(new Dimension(100, 100));
    panel.setBackground(Color.white);
    window.add(panel);
    panel.addMouseMotionListener(this);

    textField = new JTextField(8);
    window.add(textField);
}

public void mouseDragged(MouseEvent event) {
    int newX = event.getX();
    int newY = event.getY();
    Graphics paper = panel.getGraphics();
    paper.drawLine(oldX, oldY, newX, newY);

    oldX = newX;
    oldY = newY;

    textField.setText("x = " + Integer.toString(event.getX())
        + " y = " + Integer.toString(event.getY()));
}

public void mouseMoved(MouseEvent event) {
    int newX = event.getX();
    int newY = event.getY();
    oldX = newX;
    oldY = newY;
}
}
```

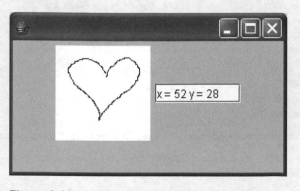

Figure A.11 Handling mouse move events in a panel.

● PrintStream

```
import java.io.PrintStream; or import java,io*;
```

public *PrintStream*(OutputStream out)	Creates an instance of a print stream that sends its output to the output stream **out**.
public void *close*()	Closes the print stream.
public void *flush*()	Flushes this print stream. Any buffered output is written to the stream.
public void *print*(item)	Print the item. The item can be a **char**, **double**, **float**, **int**, **long** or **String**.
public void *println*(item)	Print the item, followed by a newline character.

● Radio button

A group of radio buttons allows the user to select one (but only one) option from alternatives. This is similar to the pre-select buttons on early cars – you could only select one radio station.

When you create a radio button you give the caption as a parameter. The second parameter says whether it is initially selected, or not.

The radio buttons must be added to a **ButtonGroup** object (not a **JButtonGroup** object) to ensure that only one is selected at any one time.

Changing a selection creates an event.

public *JRadioButton*(String s, boolean selected)	Create a radio button with the label **s**. The **boolean** determines whether or not the button is initially selected.
public boolean is Selected()	Returns true if the button is selected.

Example program:

```
import java.awt.*;
import java.awt.event.*;
import javax.swing.*;

class JRadioButtonsDemo extends JFrame implements ItemListener {

    private JRadioButton red, yellow, blue;
    private ButtonGroup buttonGroup; // note: no J

    private JTextField textField;
```

```
    public static void main(String[] args) {
        JRadioButtonsDemo frame = new JRadioButtonsDemo();
        frame.setSize(400,300);
        frame.createGUI();
        frame.show();
    }

    private void createGUI() {
        setDefaultCloseOperation(EXIT_ON_CLOSE);
        Container window = getContentPane();
        window.setLayout(new FlowLayout() );

        buttonGroup = new ButtonGroup();

        red = new JRadioButton("red", true);
        buttonGroup.add(red);
        window.add(red);
        red.addItemListener(this);

        yellow = new JRadioButton("yellow", false);
        buttonGroup.add(yellow);
        window.add(yellow);
        yellow.addItemListener(this);
        blue = new JRadioButton("blue", false);
        buttonGroup.add(blue);
        window.add(blue);
        blue.addItemListener(this);

        textField = new JTextField(8);
        window.add(textField);
    }

    public void itemStateChanged(ItemEvent event) {
        if (event.getSource() == red) {
            textField.setText("red selected");
        }
        if (event.getSource() == yellow) {
            textField.setText("yellow selected");
        }
        if (event.getSource() == blue) {
            textField.setText("blue selected");
        }
    }
}
```

If you want to check the state of a radio button, without handling the event, you can:

```
if (red.isSelected())  etc.
```

> *Radio button continued*

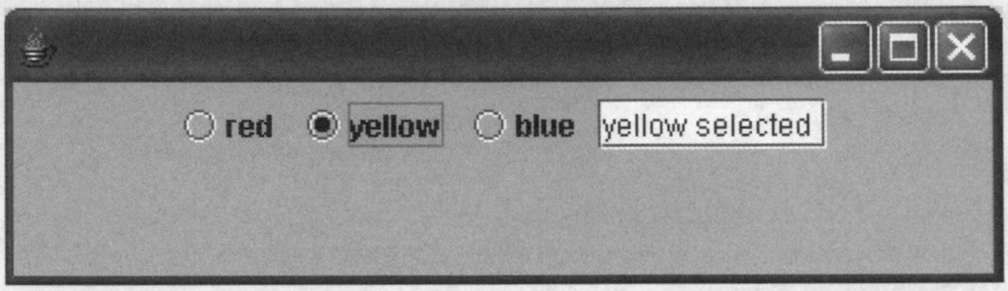

Figure A.12 Radio buttons.

This is useful if, for example, you have a group of radio buttons and another (ordinary) button to initiate some action.

Random

```
import java.util.Random;
```

These methods return what is apparently random numbers. In fact they are only pseudo-random, because one is calculated from the next. To ensure that they appear random, the first value is derived from a seed, which is normally based on the current time. (The milliseconds part of the current time always appears to be random.) To explicitly give the seed a value (when testing, for example) use **setSeed**.

See also method **random** in **Java.lang.Math**.

`Random ()`	Creates a random number generator object
`public nextDouble()`	Returns the next pseudo-random number, uniformly distributed from 0.0 to 0.999. . . .
`public nextInt()`	Returns the next pseudo-random number, uniformly distributed in the range of `int`.
`public nextInt(int n)`	Returns a random integer in the range 0 to $n - 1$.
`public void setSeed(long seed)`	Sets the seed of the random number generator.

Sample code:

```
Random random = new Random();
double d = random.nextDouble();
textField.setText("random is "+ Double.toString(d));
```

Slider

A slider GUI object that can be used to change values in a crude manner.

```
import javax.swing.JSlider; or import javax.swing.*;
```

JSlider()	Creates a horizontal slider in the range 0 to 100 and with an initial value of 50.
JSlider(int min, int max, int value)	Creates a horizontal slider using the specified **min**, **max** and **value**.
JSlider(int orientation, int min, int max, int value)	Creates a slider with the specified orientation and the specified minimum, maximum and initial values. The orientation is either **JSlider.VERTICAL** or **JSlider.HORIZONTAL**.
public void addChangeListener(Object object)	Registers the object to handle events.
public int *getValue*()	Returns the **int** value.

Sample program, with slider that goes from 0 to 10:

```java
import java.awt.*;
import java.awt.event.*;
import javax.swing.*;
import javax.swing.event.*;

class SliderDemo extends JFrame implements ChangeListener{

    private JSlider slider;

    private JTextField textField;

    public static void main(String[] args) {
        SliderDemo frame = new SliderDemo();
        frame.setSize(400,300);
        frame.createGUI();
        frame.show();
    }

    private void createGUI() {
        setDefaultCloseOperation(EXIT_ON_CLOSE);
        Container window = getContentPane();
        window.setLayout(new FlowLayout() );

        slider = new JSlider(JSlider.HORIZONTAL, 0, 10, 5);
        slider.addChangeListener(this);
        window.add(slider);
```

▶

> *Slider continued*

```
        textField = new JTextField(10);
        window.add(textField);
    }

    public void stateChanged(ChangeEvent e) {
        if (e.getSource() == slider) {
            textField.setText("slider moved to " +
                slider.getValue());
        }
    }
}
```

Figure A.13 A slider and a text field.

String

This is in package **java.lang**. No **import** is required because this package is automatically imported.

Note that the + operator can be used to concatenate (join) strings.

`public char charAt(int index)`	Returns the character at the specified position.
`public int compareTo(String string)`	Returns 0 if the strings are equal. Returns a negative value if the string object precedes the parameter. Returns a positive value if the string object follows the parameter.
`public boolean endsWith(String substring)`	Returns **true** if a string ends with a particular substring.
`public boolean equals(Object object)`	Returns **true** if the string has the same value as the parameter.
`public boolean equalsIgnoreCase(String string)`	Returns **true** if the string is the same as the parameter, ignoring cases.

`public int indexOf(String string, int index)`	Returns the index of the first location of the substring in the string, starting from the position of the second parameter. Returns –1 if the substring is not present.
`public int lastIndexOf(String string)`	Returns the index of the rightmost location of the substring in the string. Returns –1 if the substring is not present.
`public int length()`	Returns the length of the string.
`public String replace(char oldChar, char newChar)`	Returns the string with all occurrences of `oldChar` replaced by `newChar`
`public String substring(int startIndex, int endIndex)`	Returns a specified part of a string. The first parameter is the starting position. The second parameter is the position 1 greater than the last character to be extracted. (Note the spelling.)
`public String toLowerCase()`	Returns the string converted to lower case.
`public String toUpperCase()`	Returns the string converted to upper case.
`public String trim()`	Returns the string, but with white space removed from both ends. White space means space characters, newlines and tabs.
`public static String valueOf(param)`	Converts the parameter to a string. The parameter can be of type `Object`, `char[]`, `boolean`, `char`, `int`, `long`, `float`, `double`.

See also class **java.util.StringTokenizer**.
  The tab string is **"\t"**.
  The new line string is **"\n"**.

StringTokenizer

```
import java.util.StringTokenizer;
```

`public StringTokenizer(String s, String delim)`	Constructs a string tokenizer for the string **s**. The characters in the parameter **delim** are the delimiters for separating tokens.
`public boolean hasMoreTokens()`	Returns **true** if there are more tokens in the string, or **false** otherwise.
`public String nextToken()`	Returns the next token from this string tokenizer.

System

This is in package **java.lang**. No **import** is required because this package is automatically imported.

This contains some miscellaneous, but useful, methods and also three convenient streams.

public static long *currentTimeMillis*()	Gets the current time in milliseconds. A millisecond is 1/1000 second. The time is measured from midnight 1 January 1970 UTC.
public static PrintStream *err*	The standard error stream. This stream is already open and ready to accept output data. By convention, this stream is used to display error messages that should come to the immediate attention of the user.
public static InputStream *in*	The standard input stream. This stream is already open and ready to supply input data. Typically this is keyboard input.
public static PrintStream *out*	The standard output stream. This stream is already open and ready to accept output data.
public static void *exit*(int status)	Terminates the application and closes the window. The status should be 0 for a normal exit.

TextArea

A GUI component that holds lines of text – usually for display.

```
import javax.swing.JTextArea;  or  import javax.swing.*;
```

public *JTextArea*(int height, int width)	Creates a new text area of size **height** and **width**, measures in characters. **Note that these are the opposite way round to the parameters in all other calls in the library that use width and height.**
public void *append*(String s)	Appends the string **s** to the end of the current text.
public String *getText*()	Returns the complete text in the text area.
public void *insert*(String s, int pos)	Inserts the string **s** at the position **pos**.

public void *replaceRange*(String s, int start, int end)	Replaces the text from start to (end – 1) with the string **s**.
public void *setTabSize*(int size)	Sets the tab size to **size**.
public void *setText*(String s)	Places the string **s** in the text area.

Sample program to display some text with tabs and newlines:

```java
import java.awt.*;
import java.awt.event.*;
import javax.swing.*;

class TextAreaDemo extends JFrame implements ActionListener {

    private JButton button;
    private JTextArea textArea;

    public static void main(String[] args) {
        TextAreaDemo frame = new TextAreaDemo();
        frame.setSize(400,300);
        frame.createGUI();
        frame.show();
    }

    private void createGUI() {
        setDefaultCloseOperation(EXIT_ON_CLOSE);
        Container window = getContentPane();
        window.setLayout(new FlowLayout() );

        button = new JButton("Press me");
        window.add(button);
        button.addActionListener(this);

        textArea = new JTextArea(10, 10);
        window.add(textArea);
    }

    public void actionPerformed(ActionEvent event) {
        String newLine = "\n";
        String tab = "\t";
        textArea.setTabSize(4);

        textArea.setText(tab + "hello" + newLine);
        textArea.append(tab + "java");
    }
}
```

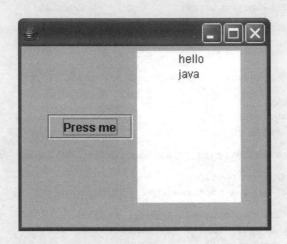

TextArea continued

Figure A.14 A text area.

Scrollbars

If you know how much space you need, you can create a text area of an appropriate size. If you have a lot of information to display or if you do not know how much information there will be, it is a good idea to use scrollbars alongside the text area.

The code to do this is:

```java
import java.awt.*;
import java.awt.event.*;
import javax.swing.*;

class ScrollingTextArea extends JFrame implements ActionListener {

    private JButton button;
    private JTextArea textArea;

    public static void main(String[] args) {
        ScrollingTextArea frame = new ScrollingTextArea();
        frame.setSize(400,300);
        frame.createGUI();
        frame.show();
    }
```

```
private void createGUI() {
    setDefaultCloseOperation(EXIT_ON_CLOSE);
    Container window = getContentPane();
    window.setLayout(new FlowLayout() );

    button = new JButton("display");
    window.add(button);
    button.addActionListener(this);

    textArea = new JTextArea(10, 10);
    JScrollPane scrollPane = new JScrollPane(textArea);
    window.add(scrollPane);
}

public void actionPerformed(ActionEvent event) {
    String newLine = "\n";
    textArea.setText("");
    for (int count = 0; count < 100; count++) {
        textArea.append("line " + count + newLine);
    }
}
}
```

Scrollbars appear on the right and at the bottom of the text area, as necessary. In this example, a scrollbar is only needed to scroll up and down.

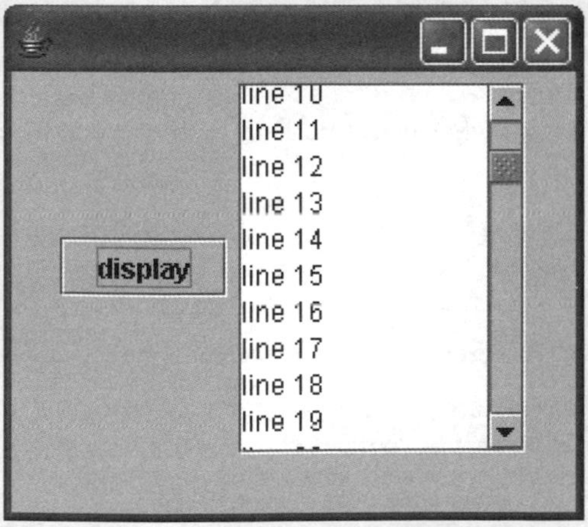

Figure A.15 A text area with a scrollbar.

TextField

A GUI component that holds a line of text – either for display or input.

```
import javax.swing.JTextField; or import javax.swing.*;
```

public *JTextField*(int width)	Creates a new text field, **width** characters wide.
public *JTextField*(String s, int width)	Creates a new text field with initial text.
public String *getText*()	Returns the text that is in the field.
public void *setEditable*(boolean b)	If **b** is **true**, the field is editable – the user can change the value in the text field. This is the default setting. If **b** is **false**, the user cannot change the value in the text field. This can be useful for displaying data.
public void *setFont*(Font f)	Sets the font type and size. Example: **textField.setFont(new Font(null, Font.BOLD, 60));**. For the **Font** constructor, the second parameter is the style. Options are **Font.BOLD**, **Font.ITALIC**, **Font.PLAIN**. The third parameter is the font size.
public void *setText*(String s)	Places the string **s** in the text field.

Sample program, which copies what is in one field to the other when you click on the button:

```
import java.awt.*;
import java.awt.event.*;
import javax.swing.*;

class TextFieldDemo extends JFrame implements ActionListener {

    private JButton button;
    private JTextField input, output;

    public static void main(String[] args) {
        TextFieldDemo frame = new TextFieldDemo();
        frame.setSize(400,300);
        frame.createGUI();
        frame.show();
    }
```

```
private void createGUI() {
    setDefaultCloseOperation(EXIT_ON_CLOSE);
    Container window = getContentPane();
    window.setLayout(new FlowLayout() );

    input = new JTextField(8);
    window.add(input);
    button = new JButton("press");
    window.add(button);
    button.addActionListener(this);

    output = new JTextField(8);
    window.add(output);
}

public void actionPerformed(ActionEvent event) {
    String text;
    text = input.getText();
    output.setText(text);
}
}
```

Figure A.16 Text fields.

Thread

This is in package **java.lang**. No **import** is required.
This class provides the methods for multithreading.

public boolean *isAlive*()	Returns **true** if the thread is running or blocked, **false** if the thread is new or dead.
public final *join*()	Wait until the named thread has terminated.
public void *run*()	Overridden by a thread. This method constitutes the code of a thread that is initiated by the **start** method.
public static void *sleep*(int m)	The thread is suspended for **m** milliseconds. There is no guarantee that the thread will be woken up after exactly the required number of milliseconds. This method must provide an exception handler for an **InterruptedException**.
public void *start*()	Initiates the running of a thread. An object can only be started once. It needs to be recreated using **new** if it needs to be started again.
public void *yield*()	Suspends this thread temporarily and allows some other thread some processor time.

Timer

A timer is an object that delivers events regularly at preset intervals. It can be used to control animations.

public *Timer*(int delay, ActionListener listener)	Creates a timer that will notify its listener every **delay** milliseconds. A millisecond is 1/1000 second.
public void *setDelay*(int delay)	Sets the timer's delay, in milliseconds.
public void *start*()	Starts the timer. It will start to create events.
public void *stop*()	Stops the timer. It will no longer create events.

A sample program follows. It displays an option pane at 10 second intervals. This class is within the **javax.swing** package. Do **not** include the **import**:

```
import java.util.*;
```

because you will gain access to another **Timer** class and there will be a clash.

```
import java.awt.*;
import java.awt.event.*;
import javax.swing.*;

class TimerDemo extends JFrame implements ActionListener {

    Timer timer;

    public static void main(String[] args) {
        TimerDemo frame = new TimerDemo();
        frame.setSize(400,300);
        frame.createGUI();
        frame.show();
    }

    private void createGUI() {
        setDefaultCloseOperation(EXIT_ON_CLOSE);
        Container window = getContentPane();
        window.setLayout(new FlowLayout() );

        timer = new Timer(10000, this);
        timer.start();
    }

    public void actionPerformed(ActionEvent event) {
        JOptionPane.showMessageDialog(null, "tick");
    }
}
```

APPENDIX B

The Abstract Window Toolkit

Introduction

The Abstract Window Toolkit (AWT) is a set of GUI classes, and provides similar facilities to the Swing toolkit. Here is the background.

Swing and AWT

When Java was first released in the early 1990s, the approach taken by the designers of its GUI classes was to use parts of the native GUI components. Thus, a Java button on Microsoft Windows looked like a Microsoft Windows button, and a Java button on an Apple Mac looked like an Apple Mac button. Though this worked, and was impressive at the time, it had drawbacks:

- when a Java program was moved to another platform, its look and feel changed;
- because not all platforms provided the same set of GUI components, the AWT had to be the lowest common denominator. It did not have a large range of components.

To overcome these problems, Sun decided to write the Swing component set. This uses none of the native operating system's components, and is written entirely in Java. The benefits are:

- The components looked the same on any platform. In fact, Swing allows you to specify that the components either have a native look and feel, or have a Swing look and feel. The latter is what we have used in this book.
- The designers of the components could go beyond the lowest common denominator, and create a full set of components. For example, Swing has components which

provide a clickable tree-view (the style used in Windows Explorer) and a table component, which looks like a spreadsheet. Because they are complex, we have not used them here.

Here are the main AWT classes. Note that their name does not begin with a 'J'.

- **Label**, **TextField** and a **TextArea** with built-in scrollbars.
- **Checkbox** and **CheckboxGroup** (known as radio buttons in Swing).
- **Panel** for holding components, and **Canvas** for graphics.
- **Choice** boxes (combo box in Swing) and **List**.
- A standalone **Scrollbar** (slider in Swing). **Menu** and **FileDialog** (file chooser in Swing). The AWT does not provide **JOptionPane** dialogs.

The above lists the majority of the AWT components. With Swing, however, there are many more classes. Even in the overlapping classes listed above, Swing provides more facilities via methods.

Converting Swing to AWT

Because you are familiar with Swing applications as presented throughout this book, we will provide guidelines for converting to AWT. Note that because Swing has more components and facilities, easy conversion is not always possible. But if you are using simple components, a one-to-one conversion can often be done. (Coming the other way – updating an AWT application to Swing is also straightforward.)

Figure B.1 shows a conversion of the Swing **SumTextFields** program from Chapter 6. Here is the code:

```
import java.awt.*;
import java.awt.event.*;

public class SumTextFieldsAWT extends Frame //frame
    implements WindowListener, ActionListener {

    private TextField number1Field, number2Field, sumField;
    private Label equalsLabel;
    private Button plusButton;
```

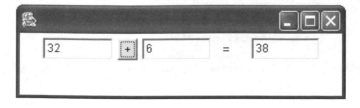

Figure B.1 Screenshot of **SumTextFieldsAWT**.

```java
        public static void main(String[] args) {
            SumTextFieldsAWT frame = new SumTextFieldsAWT();
            frame.setSize(350, 100);
            frame.createGUI();
            frame.show();
        }
        private void createGUI() {
            setLayout(new FlowLayout());

            number1Field = new TextField(7);
            add(number1Field);

            plusButton = new Button("+");
            add(plusButton);
            plusButton.addActionListener(this);

            number2Field = new TextField(7);
            add(number2Field);

            equalsLabel = new Label(" = ");
            add(equalsLabel);

            sumField = new TextField(7);
            add(sumField);

            addWindowListener(this);
        }
        public void actionPerformed(ActionEvent event) {
            int number1 = Integer.parseInt(number1Field.getText());
            int number2 = Integer.parseInt(number2Field.getText());
            sumField.setText(Integer.toString(number1 + number2));
        }
    // standard code for window closing, etc...
        public void windowClosing(WindowEvent e) {
            System.exit(0);
        }
        //empty WindowListener Methods
        public void windowIconified(WindowEvent e) {
        }
        public void windowOpened(WindowEvent e) {
        }
        public void windowClosed(WindowEvent e) {
        }
        public void windowDeiconified(WindowEvent e) {
        }
        public void windowActivated(WindowEvent e) {
        }
        public void windowDeactivated(WindowEvent e) {
        }
    //end of standard window code
    }
```

Here are some steps for the conversion:

1. Remove any Swing **import** instructions from the top of the program. This ensures that the compiler spots any Swing usage, even if you don't.

2. Remove the 'J' from every component. Thus **JFrame** becomes **Frame**, and **JButton** becomes **Button**. Do not mix Swing and AWT in the same program.

3. Find an equivalent AWT component. Thus you may have to use a **Scrollbar** instead of a **JSlider**.

4. State that the program **implements WindowListener**, and add the set of empty window methods shown in the above listing.

5. For basic flow layout user interfaces in which components are added in left to right order, we can add them directly to the frame rather than needing to create a container. Remember that:

   ```
   add(button1);
   ```

   is short for:

   ```
   this.add(button1);
   ```

   where **this** represents the current object. It is an instance of the **Frame** class.

6. Compile the program. It is likely that you have errors. Note that there are variations in method names and event types, so you may need to consult the AWT documentation on the web, in your IDE or on our CD-ROM.

Swing or AWT?

If you are writing an application (as we did throughout this book) use Swing. It provides many more facilities, and is now more widely used than the AWT.

If you are writing applets which are viewed in a web browser (see Appendix C) then the choice is not clear cut. Not all browsers contain the Swing libraries. If your program is to be used by an organization with standard facilities, you may be able to guarantee what is on every computer; therefore Swing may be feasible. But if you want 100% of Internet users to be able to run your applet, use AWT.

APPENDIX C

Applets

Introduction

This book has been about writing 'applications'. They run under the control of your operating system and the Java code and corresponding class files are stored on your computer. Applets are different. The term means a small program. Compiled applet class files are uploaded to a web server computer, in the same folder as you might store your web pages. It is possible to specify that a web page links up to an applet. When a user downloads such a web page, the Java class code comes with it, and the applet runs in an area of the web browser window.

An applet example

Here we will look at the process of creating and running an applet. We will use the `SumTextFields` program of Chapter 6. Note that in Appendix B, we provided an AWT version of this program, and this is the version we will convert to an applet. The reason for this choice is because AWT applets will work with all browsers, but Swing support in browsers is not as widespread. Figure C.1 shows the applet running within a web browser. Here is the code:

```java
import java.awt.*;
import java.applet.Applet;
import java.awt.event.*;

public class SumTextFieldsApplet
    extends Applet implements ActionListener{

    private TextField number1Field, number2Field, sumField;
    private Label equalsLabel;
    private Button plusButton;
```

Figure C.1 The **SumTextFields** applet running in Microsoft's web browser.

```java
public void init() {
    number1Field = new TextField(7);
    add(number1Field);

    plusButton = new Button("+");
    add(plusButton);
    plusButton.addActionListener(this);

    number2Field = new TextField(7);
    add(number2Field);

    equalsLabel = new Label(" = ");
    add(equalsLabel);

    sumField = new TextField(7);
    add(sumField);
}
public void actionPerformed(ActionEvent event) {
    int number1 = Integer.parseInt(number1Field.getText());
    int number2 = Integer.parseInt(number2Field.getText());
    sumField.setText(Integer.toString(number1 + number2));
}
}
```

The program cannot be executed by itself – it has to be called up from a web page. Here is a suitable page containing HTML, which we named as **appletdemo.htm**:

```
<html>
<title>Web page with applet</title>
Here is the applet in a web page.

<applet code = "SumTextFieldsApplet.class"
    width = 300    height = 150>    </applet>
</html>
```

The web page uses a special applet tag, which specifies the name of the class file, and the size of the region of the browser screen it will execute in. If you are using an IDE, it might create the web page for you. If not, type it in yourself, but modify the applet name and the size as appropriate.

Compile the program as normal. Ensure that the class file is in the same folder as the one containing the web page which calls it. To execute the applet on your computer you have two choices:

- Use the Applet Viewer program which comes with your Java system. This is intended for checking out your applet prior to using it within a web page.

- Use a web browser, and surf to the web page you created. You will see the applet execute in the browser window, as in Figure C.1.

If you have web space on a server, upload the HTML file and the compiled class file to your web space. Then your applet will be available for anyone to use. If you wish to upload the Java source code as well so that others can use it, that is fine. But you do not have to.

Note that when your applet is downloaded, it executes using the class libraries stored within the browser. Sun has an agreement that ensures that most of the class libraries are available in browsers; hence the potential massive download of class libraries is avoided.

● Applet coding differences

Here we look at differences between applet and application programming. Here are the main points:

- Import the **Applet** library:

      import java.applet.Applet;

- Specify that your program extends **Applet**, as in:

      public class SumTextFieldsApplet
          extends Applet implements ActionListener{

- Rather than using a `main` method to create a new instance of the program, we use a method named `init`. This method is called up by the browser. We place our GUI initialization code in this method.

- We do not need to add special code to terminate the program. This is done when the user moves to a different web page.

- Applets do not have a menu bar, so menus cannot be used.

- For security reasons, applets cannot read or write files on the computer they are executing on.

In Chapter 26, we discuss security aspects in more detail.

Abstract class – a class that acts as a template for some subclasses. It provides all the features that are common to the subclasses. An abstract class cannot be instantiated. (You cannot create an object from an abstract class.)

Applet – a (usually) small program invoked by a web browser from a web page. Sometimes written in Java, but can be written in other languages. The program typically interacts with the user, displays graphics and animations, plays sounds and video clips. The term applet is derived from the words 'application' and 'let', meaning small.

Application – a full program that runs independently.

Base class – see superclass.

Built-in types – the types `boolean`, `char`, `byte`, `short`, `int`, `long`, `float` and `double` that are provided ready-made as part of the Java language. They are not true objects.

Byte code – the low-level language to which Java programs are compiled. When a Java program is run, byte code is interpreted by the Java Virtual Machine.

Class – a unit of programming in an object-oriented language like Java. Represents the abstraction of a number of similar (or identical) objects. Describes the data (variables) and methods that any object contains.

Class-level variable – see instance variable.

Class method – see static method.

Class variable – see static variable.

Extend – declare a new class that inherits the behaviour of another class.

Inheritance – the way in which a new class can incorporate the features of an existing class.

Instance – an object created from a class.

Instance variable – a variable declared at the head of a class. A copy is made for every object created from the class. Not to be confused with static variable.

Interface – a Java feature which allows the programmer to specify the interface to a class (the way that the class is to be used), without programming the class itself. This separates the specification of what the class will do from how it will do it.

Java – a general-purpose programming language first designed for constructing Internet applications.

Java Virtual Machine (JVM) – a piece of software that allows Java to run on a particular machine. The JVM interprets the byte code produced by the Java compiler.

Keyword – a name such as `if`, `while`, `void` that is part of the Java language and cannot be used as a name by the programmer.

Method – one of the actions associated with an object. A method has a name and may have parameters. (A method is variously termed a *function*, *procedure* or *subroutine* in other programming languages.) The name method derives from the idea of having a method for doing something.

Object – a component of a program in an object-oriented language. An object incorporates some data (variables) and the actions (methods) associated with that data.

Overloading – providing two or more methods (within the same class) with the same name. There must be a different number of parameters, or the types of the parameters may be different, or both. The Java compiler selects the version of the method according to the parameters that are used when the method is called. Not to be confused with overriding.

Overriding – providing a method in a subclass that has the same name and parameters as a method in a superclass. Not to be confused with overloading.

Package – a group of related classes, with a name. Using packages avoids a potential problem of duplicate names which might otherwise arise, particularly in large pieces of software.

Polymorphism – a feature of object-oriented languages in which the appropriate method to act on an object is automatically selected.

Static method – a method that belongs to the class as a whole and not to any object created from the class. A static method is called using the class name as a prefix.

Static variable – a variable declared at the head of a class that belongs to the class as a whole. It is not copied when an object is created from the class.

Subclass – a class which inherits variables and methods from the current class.

Superclass – a class from which the current class inherits variables and methods. Sometimes called the base class.

Widget – a button, scrollbar, text field or similar object in a window that supports user interaction by clicking with the mouse. Derived from the words 'window' and 'gadget'.

Rules for names

In Java the name of a variable, a class or a method is known as an identifier. The programmer chooses identifiers. The rules are:

- An identifier can be as long as you like.
- An identifier consists of letters (upper case and lower case) and digits (0 to 9).
- An identifier must start with a letter.
- An identifier must not be the same as one of the Java keywords listed in Appendix F.

A letter is defined to be A to Z, a to z, dollar ($) or underscore (_). Dollar and under-score are not normally used and are included only for historical reasons. Also included in the category of letters are the letters of many languages of the world.

By convention:

- Class names start with a capital letter and continue in lower case, e.g. `Graphics`.
- Variable and method names start with a lower-case letter, e.g. `add`.
- When a name is a combination of words, the new words start with a capital letter, e.g. `wishYouWereHere`, `drawLine`.

Both upper-case and lower-case letters are valid and distinct, so that `mouse` is distinct from `MOUSE` and `Mouse`.

APPENDIX

F

Keywords

These are the Java keywords. They cannot be used as names by the programmer for variables, methods, classes or packages.

abstract	finally	public
assert	float	return
boolean	for	short
break	goto	static
byte	if	strictfp
case	implements	super
catch	import	switch
char	instanceof	synchronized
class	int	this
const	interface	throw
continue	long	throws
default	native	transient
do	new	try
double	package	void
else	private	volatile
extends	protected	while
final		

The keywords **const** and **goto** are reserved, even though they are not used.

true and **false** appear to be keywords, but they are actually **boolean** literals. Similarly, while **null** might appear to be a keyword, it is technically the null literal. However, none of these words can be used by the programmer (so they might as well be keywords).

APPENDIX G

Scope rules (visibility)

Visibility is the term used to describe what items can be accessed (or referred to) by what other items. In this appendix we present several alternative accounts of the Java rules. We have given a variety because you will probably find some of these easier to comprehend and use than others.

Remember: variables and methods are grouped into classes, and then classes are grouped into packages. A method or variable is described using one of the modifiers in the list below. This modifier describes what type of access is permitted by code in the same or other classes. Access to a method means the permission to call the method. Access to a variable means permission to use the value or change the value of the variable. (But, generally, access to variables is undesirable as it violates the principle of information hiding.)

The rules for accessing methods or variables are:

Method or variable modifier	Meaning
`public`	accessible from anywhere
`protected`	accessible from: 1. this class 2. any subclass 3. any class in same package
default – no modifier	accessible from: 1. this class 2. any class in same package
`private`	accessible only from within this class

This information is displayed in an alternative form in the following table. This, incidentally, illustrates the uniformity of the access scheme:

Method or variable modifier	Accessible from same class?	Accessible from any class in the same package?	Accessible from any subclass?	Accessible from anywhere?
`public`	yes	yes	yes	yes
`protected`	yes	yes	yes	no
default – none	yes	yes	no	no
`private`	yes	no	no	no

The second kind of access to variables and methods is the access provided by inheritance. The following table describes the rules:

Method or variable modifier	Can be inherited by any subclass in the same package?	Can be inherited by any subclass?
`public`	yes	yes
`protected`	yes	yes
default – none	yes	no
`private`	no	no

For a class, there are fewer options. The rules are:

Class modifier	Meaning
`public`	class can be used by any class
default – none	class can only be used by classes in the same package

Constructors follow the same rules as methods. But it is worthwhile spelling them out. The rules are:

Constructor modifier	Meaning
`public`	any class can create an instance of this class by calling this constructor
`protected`	the only classes that can create an instance of this class are: 1. subclasses 2. classes in the same package
default – none	only classes in the same package can create an instance of this class
`private`	no other class can call this constructor. (But a class method within the class can call this constructor to create an object)

Here is a UML diagram showing the Java visibility rules.

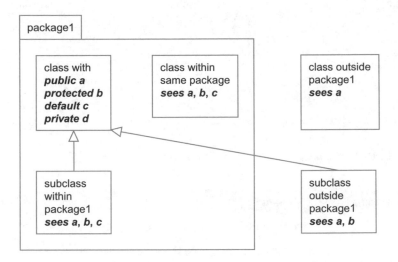

The large rectangle denotes a package. Its name is package1, as shown in the tab at the top left. The other rectangles denote classes. Three are within the package and two are outside. Within the package is a class which declares methods/variables a, b, c and d. The diagram shows what access each of the other classes has to these methods/variables.

APPENDIX H

Bibliography

Java

You really do not need any book, other than the one you are reading. All the necessary information is in here to write a whole variety of programs (and certainly all those in the exercises). Don't forget the appendix on the Java libraries. The books below give other views of Java.

The Java Programming Language, Ken Arnold and James Gosling, Addison-Wesley, various editions.
Written by members of the group at Sun who created Java. A definitive source of information on Java. This book describes the language itself (not the libraries). It is very readable, but not for novices.

The Java Developers Almanac, Patrick Chan, Addison-Wesley, frequent editions.
Once you understand the Java language, you really need to understand what the libraries provide. These two-volume reference books list all the classes and all the class members. A useful reference.

Java How To Program, H.M. Deitel and P.J. Deitel, Prentice Hall, Englewood Cliffs, NJ, frequent editions.
This is very comprehensive, but rather formidable. It is useful for reference.

If you have an Internet connection, perhaps the best way to get information about the libraries is to use your favourite search engine. If you need information on, say, the `JTextField` class, type:

Sun Java 2 JTextField

UML

Here are two short and simple books on UML:

UML Distilled, Martin Fowler, Addison-Wesley, Harlow, 2003.

Using UML, Perdita Stevens and Rob Pooley, Addison-Wesley, Harlow, 1999.

Object-oriented programming languages

Java is one of the latest in a line of object-oriented languages. All share the concepts of encapsulation, classes and inheritance.

Simula Begin, Graham Birtwistle, Ole-Johan Dahl, Bjorn Myrhaug and Kristen Nygaard, Studentliteratur and Auerbach, New York, 1973.
Simula 67 was the first object-oriented language. It was called Simula because it was designed as a language to simulate events. This is the best-known book on Simula.

Smalltalk-80: the language, Adele Goldberg and David Robson, Addison-Wesley, Reading, MA, 1989.
Smalltalk-80 is the Rolls-Royce of object-oriented languages. It is completely object oriented – even control structures like repetition and `if` statements are objects. Like Java it supports single inheritance. Like Java it provides a large and comprehensive library that the programmer uses and inherits from to provide facilities including windowing, graphics and data structures. The definitive book on Smalltalk-80.

Object-Oriented Software Construction, Bertrand Meyer, Prentice Hall, New York, 1988.
The definitive book on the Eiffel language. The first few chapters are a wonderfully clear exposition of the principles of OOP.

Software development

Software Development: Fashioning the Baroque, Darrel Ince, Oxford University Press, Oxford, 1988.
If you would like to know about the problems (and some of the solutions) to developing large-scale software, this gives the big picture.

Debugging the Development Process, Steve Maguire, Microsoft Press, Redmond, WA, 1994.
This book has the subtitle *Practical Strategies for Staying Focused, Hitting Ship Dates and Building Solid Teams*. Life within Microsoft and the lessons that can be learned are well presented in this readable book.

Writing Solid Code: Microsoft's techniques for developing bug-free C programs, Steve Maguire, Microsoft Press, Redmond, WA, 1993.
A book by a Microsoft programmer which describes techniques for debugging software. The many examples are in the C programming language.

Software Engineering, Douglas Bell, Prentice Hall, Harlow, 2005.
Software engineering is the term given to the job of developing large programs. This book describes approaches to this task, taking as the reader's starting point a knowledge of programming.

APPENDIX

I

Using Java on Microsoft Windows

Here we explain how to compile and run Java programs on Microsoft Windows systems. (GNU/Linux installation is straightforward: see the instructions on the CD-ROM.) We do not cover the use of an integrated development environment (IDE), as these vary from product to product. If you have one of these products, do not read this appendix. (Though we do provide a simple IDE below should you wish to use it.)

A note on terminology: a collection of files is stored in a 'folder', but some of the commands below refer to 'directory'. These are the same thing, but we will use 'directory' here.

We assume that you have installed the Java SDK as suggested in Appendix J, from the CD-ROM accompanying this book. You now have a choice:

- You can use our basic IDE, called Japa. This has a GUI with buttons to compile, run and indent your program. It also creates code templates. We describe it in approach 1 below.

- You can use Java from the command line, which requires you to type in commands to compile and run your program. The standard approach requires modifying a Windows system file, but we suggest that you don't do this. Instead, we have provided some shorthand commands which do not require you to change system files. This is described in approach 2 below.

- The standard way as described by Sun is to type the **javac** and **java** commands to compile and run your program. We describe this below. Though this approach is popular, it has the drawback of requiring you to edit a Windows system file to set up what is known as the **PATH** variable. Though this has probably been done where you work or study, we **do not recommend** this unless you are really sure of what you are doing. This is introduced in approach 3 below.

- You can use Sun's NetBeans IDE. The CD-ROM contains it as part of the standard Java installation and explains how to use it.

512

● Approach 1 – Japa

This involves installing a small program, available on the CD-ROM, or as a download from our web site. Read the page `japadownload.htm` for instructions. Note carefully that you must avoid using directory names containing spaces. You do not need to modify any Windows files with this approach.

● Approach 2 – shorthand commands

There is an initial setup stage, which you only need to do once (e.g. at the start of your Java course).

To do the setup, first create a folder named `JavaPrograms`. (The name doesn't matter, but we will use this in our example.)

Next, copy these two files:

```
c.bat
r.bat
```

from the CD-ROM and paste them into the `JavaPrograms` folder. If you do not have the CD-ROM, you can use Notepad to create the files. See note 1 below.

You now have a folder named `JavaPrograms`, containing `c.bat` and `r.bat`. The setup is complete.

To start a Java session

At the start of each Java session, you need to create a new command prompt window, and position it to the `JavaPrograms` folder. Here is how:

- Use the Windows **Start** menu, and choose **Programs**, then **Command Prompt**. You may need to look under **Accessories** on some systems.
- A black text window appears. We must switch it into the `JavaPrograms` folder. Let us assume it is on the `e:` drive, inside the `myWork` folder. There are two steps.
  - Switch to the top level of the required drive, by typing:

    ```
    cd /d e:\
    ```

    Press 'enter' at the end of the line. Here we are using the 'change directory' command. Instead of `e:\`, substitute your appropriate drive.
  - Use the `cd` command to move to the required folder, as in:

    ```
    cd myWork\JavaPrograms
    ```

    Note that the prompt in the command prompt window now shows `JavaPrograms`.

Now you are ready to write programs.

To compile and run programs

■ Run an editor (such as Notepad, available from the **Start** menu, often under **Accessories**). Type in a Java program, and use **Save As . . .** to give it the correct file name (the same as the class it contains, followed by `.java`). Here we will use `Demo.java`. Ensure it is saved in the `JavaPrograms` directory.

■ To compile it, select the window, and type:

```
c Demo.java
```

Compilation errors might appear, of the form:

```
Demo.java:4: ';' Expected.
```

This refers to an error in line 4. To correct it, move into the Notepad window, and attempt to fix the error. In Notepad, you can find a line number by choosing **Edit | Goto . . .** and entering the line number you want to find. When the error is fixed, **Save** the file, and recompile.

■ When there are no more compilation errors, run the program by typing:

```
r Demo
```

If you want to use an additional folder for your code, copy the `c.bat` and `r.bat` files into it.

● Approach 3 – `javac` and `java` commands

If you have modified the Windows system file, open a command prompt window and move into the `JavaPrograms` folder. Open an editor such as Notepad. To compile your program, type:

```
javac Demo.java
```

and to run it, type:

```
java Demo
```

You do not need to bother with the two files as described in approach 2.

● Text editors

Though Notepad is sufficient, there are better editors available, which can also be set up to compile and run code – you don't need to bother with a separate command prompt window. Investigate 'Notetab Light' via Google searching. This version is free-ware, and facilities for running Java 2 can be downloaded separately.

Multiclass programs

You will soon progress to writing programs which are split into several classes. You can open up a text editor window for each class, and compile each class individually. When you compile the top-level program (containing **main**) the compiler also compiles other files that need compiling (e.g. ones that you have edited but not recompiled). It is important that you look at the error messages to see which file they refer to.

Note 1

If you don't have the CD-ROM, you can create the two files here. Each file has two lines in it. Type them in exactly as shown, taking care with spaces.

The first file must be saved as **c.bat** in the **JavaPrograms** folder. It must contain:

```
::compile
"c:\j2sdk1.4.0\bin\javac" %*
```

The second file must be saved as **r.bat** in the **JavaPrograms** folder. It must contain:

```
::run
"c:\j2sdk1.4.0\bin\java" %*
```

The second line of each file refers to the name of the directory where the SDK was installed. If your location is different, modify the files accordingly.

APPENDIX
J

Using the CD-ROM

The supplied CD-ROM contains the following:

- The file **readme.htm**, with more details on how to install the software. Browse the CD-ROM and click on this file to view it.
- Java 1.4.2 for Microsoft Windows.
- Java 1.4.2 for Linux systems.
- Sun's Java documentation.
- The code for the examples from this book.
- The Japa program development system.

● Notes on the software

Version 1.4.2 of Java also contains a Java integrated development environment (IDE) called NetBeans, which you might choose to use instead of Japa or the command line. NetBeans is powerful, but quite involved to use at first. We recommend using it only when you have a bit of familiarity with Java programming.

The version of Japa that we supply has been prepared to work with Java 1.4.2. As you will see when you view the **readme.htm** file, you should accept all the suggested folder names when installing Java and Japa.

Index